# CHOSEN PEOPLE

# CHOSEN PEOPLE

The Rise of American
Black Israelite Religions

Jacob S. Dorman

OXFORD
UNIVERSITY PRESS

# OXFORD
UNIVERSITY PRESS

Oxford University Press is a department of the University of Oxford.
It furthers the University's objective of excellence in research,
scholarship, and education by publishing worldwide.

Oxford   New York
Auckland   Cape Town   Dar es Salaam   Hong Kong   Karachi
Kuala Lumpur   Madrid   Melbourne   Mexico City   Nairobi
New Delhi   Shanghai   Taipei   Toronto

With offices in
Argentina   Austria   Brazil   Chile   Czech Republic   France   Greece
Guatemala   Hungary   Italy   Japan   Poland   Portugal   Singapore
South Korea   Switzerland   Thailand   Turkey   Ukraine   Vietnam

Oxford is a registered trade mark of Oxford University
Press in the UK and certain other countries.

Published in the United States of America by
Oxford University Press
198 Madison Avenue, New York, NY 10016

© Oxford University Press 2013

Library of Congress Cataloging-in-Publication Data
Dorman, Jacob S., 1974–
Chosen people: the rise of American black Israelite religions / Jacob S. Dorman.
p.   cm.
Includes bibliographical references.
ISBN 978-0-19-530140-3 (hardcover : alk. paper)
1. Black Hebrews—United States—History.   I. Title.
BP605.B64D67   2013
299.6'7—dc23       2012010286

1 3 5 7 9 8 6 4 2

Printed in the United States of America
on acid-free paper

For Priscilla, Nathan, Bernhardt, and Stella, z"l

# CONTENTS

# ACKNOWLEDGMENTS

When I began the research for this book, in 1995, Bill Clinton was president, a stamp cost twenty-three cents, and the tech boom gave us both Ebay and *Toy Story*. It seemed as if all of my peers at Stanford were joining Silicon Valley startups. I was studying Black Israelites.

In the fifteen years since, I have accumulated many debts, personal and professional, far more than I could ever acknowledge here. Taking stock, first of all, I have to recognize all members of my family—my brother, sisters, and parents—who loved and sustained me through thick and thin, and who did some copyediting as well! I could not have written this book without their love, nurturing, intellectual engagement, committed friendship, and passionate and undying support. We do not get to choose our families, but I certainly feel chosen to have such a wonderful, well balanced, and committed brood backing me.

Among friends and colleagues, Jeremy Prestholdt is one of the brightest people I know, and his stellar success since I met him a decade ago has been wonderful to witness. Conversations with Jeremy are dense with his brilliant and iconoclastic ideas, matched with a deliciously dry sense of humor and a ready delight in skewering inanities, wherever they are found. The germs of many of my theories, including several in this book, have started in our often-uproarious conversations, which always refresh and recharge my batteries. A whole slew of friends inside and outside of academia have pulled me through: Ogbonna Ogbar, Michael Sokolis, Whitney McKedy, Gregory Williams and Itzel Molina Williams, Chastity Dotson, Juanita Brown, Dominic Hoffman, William Attaway, Jr., Kipchoge Spencer, James Vlahos, Gina Warnick, Yvonne Chireau, Yvette White, and Robert Matsuda all lifted my spirits and saw this book germinate and grow over many years.

My outlook on life and my research interests would not exist without the influence of the Berkeley Public Schools, which I attended from kindergarten to graduation from Berkeley High School, the greatest academic institution

I have ever been a part of as either student or teacher. I thank the Lord for public schools and everything they represent—democracy, antiracism, the public sphere, academic excellence, free thinking, and jazz are at the top of my list. I also spent nearly as many years attending afterschool Hebrew school and Midrasha, the East Bay's Hebrew high school, and I owe the seeds of much of my interest in religion and Jewish American history to their influence. At Stanford University, I was honored to be the student of some amazing professors, including Arnold Eisen, Sylvia Wynter, Clayborne Carson, and the late George Fredrickson. During a few terms in Oxford, I was inspired by tutorials with Anthony Kirk-Greene and, at SOAS, with Tudor Parfitt. This book's many themes very directly began with what I learned before I graduated from college. It was a special pleasure to return to SOAS in 2010 for the first ever conference of the International Society for the Study of African Jewry, organized by Dr. Parfitt and Edith Bruder.

During my Ph.D. at UCLA, the inestimable Donald Cosentino changed my life with the study of Afro-Atlantic religions in general and *vodou* in particular. I was lucky enough to catch the last courses offered by both Joyce Appleby and Gary Nash; I also learned valuable lessons that shaped this text from Henry Yu, Margaret Jacob, Lynn Hunt, David Sabean, Michael Salman, Gabriel Piterberg, and my dissertation advisor, Brenda Stevenson, who deserves special credit for taking an interest in me and my work. Patrick Polk has always been an enthusiastic and helpful colleague, who first introduced me to the most important of the esoteric texts used by black alternative religious practitioners. A brief assistantship on Robert Hill's Rastafarian sacred texts book, part of the Marcus Garvey Paper Project, taught me much that has benefited this book enormously. Chapter 5 began as a seminar paper for Carlo Ginzburg, and a version was published by *Nova Religio: The Journal of Alternative and Emergent Religions.* I am grateful to reviewers for *Nova Religio* and *The Journal of American History* John Kuo Wei Tchen, Jill Watts, James Landing, and anonymous reviewers for comments that greatly improved the chapter and my thinking about the project as a whole. UCLA's David Myers translated crucial Hebrew texts in that chapter and provided important feedback on the project. In their role as editors, eminent scholars of alternative religions Catherine Wessinger, W. Michael Ashcraft, and Eugene V. Gallagher launched my scholarly publishing career.

I have also been the fortunate beneficiary of the largess of numerous funding institutions. Stanford University and Clayborne Carson provided a congenial workplace at the Martin Luther King Research and Education Institute. The Andrew W. Mellon Foundation furnished a most useful year at Wesleyan's

Center for the Humanities, where I found a dedicated group of religionists and others who provided stellar criticism and encouragement. The University of Kansas's generous leave policies and four years of summer research funding have supported this project. KU's Hall Center for the Humanities not only supported me with intellectual communities and timely and useful help with grant proposals, but has also honored me with a Friends of the Hall Center Book Award to support the production of the text. I am also appreciative of a year-long National Endowment for the Humanities Fellowship at the Newberry Library in Chicago, where I finished the text and found an exemplary group of fellow scholars. While in Chicago, I was lucky enough to attend Shabbat services and have a number of long, enjoyable conversations with Rabbi Capers Funnye, a truly remarkable man. Anyone reading this book would greatly enjoy visiting his South Side congregation, Beth Shalom B'Nai Zaken, which builds upon the traditions of Rabbi Matthew's Commandment Keepers Congregation, discussed in Chapter 5.

It seems a cliché, a statement that appears in many acknowledgments, but teaching *did* in fact help my research and writing. For one thing, it both broadened and deepened my interests and expertise. But the exchange of teaching itself, the live discourse of analyzing ideas, makes subjects come alive. Sometimes it even leads to an epiphany that finds its way directly into the text. Among my former students, I would like to recognize Gedney Barclay, who provided research assistance with Chapter 1, and Sean Malone, who did the same for Chapter 3. At the last minute, David Hart, although not my student, did a tremendous job of digging up some rare and exceptional letters in the archives of Tel Aviv University.

I have been extremely fortunate to find such collegial and supportive colleagues in all corners of the University of Kansas, including fellow African American historians Randal Jelks and Shawn Alexander. My colleagues in the Kansas History Department have provided important feedback, and I owe a particular debt to the generous support of Paul Kelton, Jonathan Earle, and Leslie Tuttle. My colleagues in American Studies, especially Cheryl Lester and David Katzman, have been unflagging champions and supporters. Over the years, a number of colleagues have endured my papers in written or oral form and still managed to give cogent advice. My peers in *The New Black Gods* volume provided a collegial forum for my work. Nell Irvin Painter and Natalie Zemon Davis both read chapters and contributed useful feedback, while David Daniels heroically read through the entire text, found many errors, and engaged me in stimulating and detailed conversations about our mutual interests in African American Holiness and Pentecostal churches.

At Oxford University Press, Cynthia Read had the foresight to encourage an unpolished recent college graduate when she first saw an early version of this project in 1997, and has had the patience to bear with me these many years. The reviewers for OUP did yeoman's work in providing the key input that helped turn a disjointed tome into the considerably briefer and more polished book you have in front of you. I would like to thank the anonymous reviewers for their input, as well as reviewer Cheryl Greenberg, who truly rose above and beyond the call of duty, and who gave very useful feedback.

Former archivist Victor Smythe of the Schomburg Center for Research in Black Culture of the New York Public Library and Rabbi Sholomo B. Levy of Beth Elohim collected the Ethiopian Hebrew Commandment Keepers Congregation papers on which much of this book is based. Rabbis Hailu Paris and Curtis Caldwell provided encouragement and assistance. I must thank Diana Lachatanere and her professional staff at the Schomburg, which is one of our nation's cultural treasures. I also gratefully acknowledge librarians and archivists at the National Archives and Records Administration at Bethesda and New York, the Tamiment Library of Labor History at New York University, the New York City Municipal Archives, Department of Old Records, and Dean Lorraine J. Haricombe and the wonderfully helpful librarians of the University of Kansas.

Finally, I would not have asked the questions that led to this book were it not for the inspiration and education provided by a 1994 encounter in Dimona, Israel, with the African Hebrew Israelites. Similarly, the book would not be the same without the cooperation of the Jews of all hues I have met and learned from over the years. Speaking with Black Israelites, Black Jews, and white Jews meant it was always clear that the traditions I studied and wrote about had living stakeholders. I know that I necessarily have gotten things wrong in this text—even the most conscientious author must—but I hope that the book will nonetheless prove useful for those who wish to know more about Black Jews in particular, and our polycultural world in general.

# CHOSEN PEOPLE

# INTRODUCTION

The founder of the largest and one of the earliest African American churches to preach that Black people were descended from the ancient Israelites was Prophet William Saunders Crowdy, who had a revelation while clearing his fields outside an all-Black town in Oklahoma in 1892. The inspiration for one of the first Black Israelite churches is a metaphorically rich example of the search for roots among uprooted people.[1] Imagine, if you will, the metal blade of the plow slicing the fertile soil of the prairie, plowing under the stubble of the prior season's crop as it divides the black clods of dirt to either side and orders the earth into neat furrows. The plow is pulled by a draft animal and guided by the knowing and weathered hands of the farmer. Rarely is culture so directly tied to the literal act of cultivation, or the search for roots so neatly allied with the slicing of them.[2]

Yet understanding Black religion in particular, the Black Atlantic more broadly, and all human culture most generally, requires releasing one's attachment to metaphors of organic cultivation, as rich as they may be, and letting them slip like seeds between the fingers. That act, the sowing of seed, is the literal root of the Greek word *diaspora*, but the term "diaspora" also imbeds reductive assumptions about the direction of cultural transfer from east to west, from Africa to the Americas, and from biological ancestors to cultural actors. In truth, organic metaphors frequently mask human creativity and erase evidentiary traces of the world's invention and social construction. Although past generations of scholars denied any African impact on America, and more recent ones sourced almost all Black American culture to Africa, contemporary scholars are demonstrating that the circum-Atlantic world is a complex system with ideas, peoples, and influences flowing in all directions. This polycultural world is distorted by the ideogram of "roots," which implies a linear and unbroken connection to cultural heritage understood in terms of genetic heritability.

This is a book about narratives and power—both the narratives that groups create to understand themselves and the narratives that scholars use to understand human societies. In particular, it is a book about how English-speaking peoples in general, and more specifically Black West Indians and African Americans, have mobilized the narratives of the Hebrew Bible in a succession of movements that claim descent from the ancient Israelites, beginning in the 1890s. Most of these movements can be called "religious," but they are not simply about beliefs, discourses, rituals, practices, or the divine, as if divinity was ever simple; they are also about history, group belonging, and plans for migration, exodus, and this-worldly liberation. Some of these groups have claimed the titles Hebrew, Israelite, Jewish, Ethiopian, and Falasha; some have worshiped Jesus as Christ, some have practiced Ashkenazi or Sephardic Judaism, and some have created their own paths by mixing a wide variety of religious traditions.

The term "Black Israelite" implies an African American who holds the belief that the ancient Israelites were Black, but in my usage the Blackness of Black Israelites is not denoted by the color of their skin but by the racial identity they ascribe to the ancient Israelites.[3] As Asiel Ben-Israel, a member of the Original Hebrew Israelites of Dimona, Israel, put it in 1975, "it isn't a religion, as such, that I follow. It's the belief that I am a descendant—and that Black people in America are descendants—of the biblical Israelites. We adhere to the laws written in the Bible."[4] Accordingly, the term "Black Judaism" obscures the fact that Judaic religions are only one of several strains of what are more properly thought of as "Black Israelite" religions. These faiths are better thought of as ever-evolving, kinetic polycultural assemblages than as reified, bounded "isms," as Rastafarians would say. It is important to recognize that many "Black Jews" have actually preferred the terms Jews, Hebrews, Israelites, Saints, or Rastafarians. Accordingly, if we broadly define "Black Israelite" religions to be those religions that teach that the ancient Israelites of the Hebrew Bible were Black and that contemporary Black people are their descendants, then most Black Israelites are and always have been believers in the message and messianism of Jesus Christ. Yet some of the groups expounded various versions of Judaism or Christianity, and others developed Rastafarianism. In addition, Black Israelite beliefs became widely accepted among Black Muslims and many African American Christians. This book relates the stories of some of those who adopted the moniker "Jews" as well as their closely related cognate groups who thought of themselves as "Israelites" or "Hebrews." It examines their struggles to claim and defend these discursive identities in the face of skepticism and hostility from many quarters, including African American Christians and white Jews of European descent.

There have been three major periods of Black Israelite religious formation: the earliest decades of developments within Protestant Christian Holiness churches in the 1890s and beyond; a second period of Spiritualist and Judaic groups immediately before and after the First World War; and a third phase of Black nationalist Israelite groups during the civil rights and Black Power eras of the long 1960s. In every case, people, ideas, and organizations moved from one era to the next, clouding any neat theological or temporal schema. Each successive generation of Black Israelite institution building was inspired and populated by the institutional, liturgical, and narrative innovations of earlier ones, and the coming of new movements did not necessarily eclipse prior waves. A good illustration of this is the fact that the largest Israelite group a hundred years ago is the largest Judaic Black Israelite movement today: the Church of God and Saints of Christ, which boasts chapters in the United States, the West Indies, and South Africa, in rival Christian and Jewish denominations.[5]

The history of Black Israelite movements allows us to reconsider how we conceptualize African American cultural formation. "Roots" in African American history has come to mean the perspective that emphasizes the cultural continuities—or "Africanisms"—from Africa to the Americas across the vertical time span. It is worth thinking about how the metaphor of roots functions, and how it can distort our view of the past. A root draws water and nutrients from the soil below ground and funnels them up to feed the plant above ground. Every part of the root, from the tiniest filaments at its tip to the thickest trunk at its top, is connected physically to every other part—there are no gaps, in other words, only natural, material, and bio-mechanical connections. In essence, "roots" is a many-branching family tree, inverted: a genealogical metaphor to explain cultural continuity. As an ideogram, "roots" would appear to be an elegant, organic metaphor for ancestral cultural inheritance.[6]

The metaphor is beset by problems, however. The principal one is a problem of category: culture is not carried in the genes. The disembodied nature of culture means that it can jump the synapses between generations, races, cultures, and continents, necessarily being reinvented and reimagined with every leap. Another limitation of the metaphor of roots is that the soil line of a plant marks a stark division between roots and shoots, darkness and sunshine, past and present, ancestors and individuals, and in this case, Africa and America. Whether intentional or not, the image of roots thus relegates Africa to the timeless darkness of the ancestral past. Although roots imagery is best suited to express material, hereditary connections, the image does not account for the diversity of African Americans' genetic heritages, let alone the cultural ones. Roots theorists use the term to describe African heritage, but few African Diaspora theorists speak of the Welsh roots, the Irish roots, or even the Cherokee roots of Black people or Black culture. Partly this is due to a failure of the metaphor itself: a plant's roots grows in a localized area of soil but almost never out of two pots at once, let alone four pots placed on the continents of Africa, Asia, Europe, and the Americas. The roots theory also grants human culture more permanence than it perhaps possesses. How many of us can speak our ancestors' various languages, inhabit their worldviews, assume their religious beliefs, and know about their life experiences, political commitments, daily customs, overall aesthetics, or psychological profiles?

Facing such problems with roots, others have suggested different metaphors to describe cultural transmission and adaptation. In their 1987 discussion of linguistics and psychology, Gilles Deleuze and Félix Guattari have opposed the treelike model of roots, with its binary choices, hierarchical organization, and its genealogical presumptions. Instead, they have proposed a model of rhizomes and rhizomatic connections. Rhizomatic cultural systems are lateral, nonhierarchical, and multiple. They are modeled on plants such as tubers, grass, or aspen trees, which share complex roots systems. Any point of their underground rhizomes can be connected to any other point. Rhizomes form a subterranean latticework of connections. Instead of the root-tree metaphors which embed notions of causality and false genealogies, grasslike rhizomes endlessly branch and make connections. Rhizomatic systems have "neither beginning nor end, but always a middle…from which it grows and which it overspills." On the level of culture, rhizomes could be said to have "ceaselessly established connections between semiotic chains, organizations of power, and circumstances relative to the arts, sciences, and social struggles."[7]

Even contemporary genetics would support a less materialized conception of cultural inheritance that emphasizes cultural transmission not just between roots and shoots, or ancestors and descendants, but between peers and even between species. Marine biologists studying the simplest life forms on earth are busy documenting that genes don't simply travel vertically, from parents to children, but they can also travel horizontally, from peer to peer. And they can do so not just between individuals but also between different species and even organisms of different genera and phyla, through the mediation of viruses and bacteria. This Horizontal (or Lateral) Gene Transfer (HGT) is now thought to account for a small amount of the genes in the genomes of species such as humans, mice, corn, and wheat.[8] We could likewise speak of "horizontal meme transfer" to describe how people create and pass along culture. Indeed, Deleuze and Guattari mention the transfer of genetic material between species by viruses as a form of rhizomatic connection that destabilizes the branching, phylogenetic treelike logic depicted by conventional theories of evolution. When genes jump species, rhizomatic connections destabilize hierarchical evolutionary assumptions and form a kind of anti-genealogy.[9]

Rhizomatic plants also commonly propagate themselves on the wind, sending out plumes of pollen, spores, or seeds. Culture is similarly dematerialized and airborne, spread by itinerant preachers, by hucksters, by sailors and railroad workers, by advertising, by newspapers, pamphlets, and books, by traveling tented circuses, and by temporary tented revivals. Like seeds carried by little more than the wind, new cultural innovations often spread through means that are more ideational than material, and almost entirely disconnected from ancestry. It is not that people don't pass along cultural memes "vertically" to their children; of course they do. But people also pick up culture more obliquely or "horizontally" from the playground and the street; from books, mass media, and dancehalls; and from that vast primordial soup of the Black Atlantic Dialogue, a source not bounded by heredity.[10]

As Chapter 1 relates, Prophet William Saunders Crowdy, the founder of the Church of God and Saints of Christ, was born into slavery, experienced liberation, participated in the Civil War as a teenager, and moved to Kansas City and then to a Black town in Oklahoma as a middle-aged man. It was there, as the nation endured a horrific era of lynching and the rise of Jim Crow, that Crowdy had the revelation that African Americans were in fact the descendants of the ancient Israelites. Crowdy's extraordinary success in spreading this message, not just among African Americans but also among white Americans and Black South Africans, is a testament to the importance of the idea of the Israelites in American and Christian religious imaginations. The fact that Crowdy's church spread to South Africa in 1903 through the agency of a West Indian missionary demonstrates the transnational reach of Black thinkers and their ideas. The many similarities that Crowdy's teachings bear to white Holiness ideas and to the white Anglo-Israelite movement helps us to see how Black people have reshaped hegemonic discourses around them in a fashion that anthropologists John and Jean Comaroff have termed "recalcitrant," rather than "resistant."[11]

The second chapter breaks chronologically from the others to examine the narratives that circulated ideas of the ancient Israelites in the world that Bishop William S. Crowdy and others inherited. I decided to place this chapter second, although it begins in the seventeenth century, because to do otherwise would effectively suggest that Anglo-Israelite or Masonic narratives "caused" Black Israelite ones, or were their "sources" which then *diffused* to African Americans—no matter how much I protested to the contrary.

Instead, I want to frame Chapter 2 as a rhizomatic repository of ideas and discourses that were available to figures such as Crowdy and Pentecostal theologian Charles Parham, who were both located in Kansas at various times in the 1890s. Chapter 2 also examines the history of interaction between Jews of European descent and people of African descent in the Caribbean and North America from the seventeenth century to the present, and argues that Black-white "contact" did not automatically produce twentieth-century Black Jews. Nor do I find support for the idea that enslaved Africans brought an identification with the ancient Israelites with them as part of an African cultural inheritance that transcended the Middle Passage. Instead, I examine the Methodist, Masonic, and Anglo-Israelite ethnological discourses that developed, on the one hand, to rationalize the subjection of colonized peoples and yet, on the other hand, formed the basis of an early theology of liberation for Britain's marginalized poor. Though we know that Bishops Crowdy and his contemporary William Christian were both dedicated Freemasons, who brought much of their fraternal order into their Black Israelite churches, I have found no "smoking gun" linking Black Jews like Crowdy or Christian to the Israelite discourses that circulated widely in Freemasonry and Anglo-Israelism. However, there is much circumstantial evidence, including the fact that Christian called his teachings "Free Mason religion," suggesting that Crowdy and Christian had access to Masonic legends of the ancient Israelites. Older Masonic-Israelite ideas and African American traditions of Biblical exegesis probably both played a part in the formation of their own identification as Black Israelites.

Chapter 3 effects three major revisions in the narratives that both practitioners and scholars have told about the origins of Black Jews and Judaism. First, rather than narratives of the Israelites being transmitted with enslaved Africans, who were themselves descendants of the ancient Hebrews, this book demonstrates that Crowdy's church introduced Black Israelite theologies to Africa at the start of the twentieth century. His Black Israelite practice developed from the particular history of African American suffering and the historical, spatial, ideological, cultural, and religious contexts of the Western frontier after Reconstruction. This was a time when geographic isolation, religious fervor, and the inability of established churches to police and discipline their members led to a wave of intense sectarianism, scriptural literalism, and theological radicalism. Second, Holiness churches of every racial group adopted Hebraic rituals such as the Passover seder, foot washing, and the seventh day Sabbath, *not* to recreate Judaism but rather to emulate the early Christian church—that is, to be more like Jesus and his Apostles. The Church of God and Saints of Christ only began to think of itself as practicing Judaism after the First World War, long after Bishop Crowdy's death, and the shift led to a major breach among his followers. Finally, whereas various scholars and practitioners have explained the rise of the Pentecostal movement as an American interpretation of essentially African patterns of spirit possession, Chapter 3 contends that the Pentecostal movement itself was inspired by an Anglo-Israelite attempt to recreate the early Christian church on the part of such figures as Frank Sandford in Shiloh, Maine, and Charles Parham in Topeka, Kansas. But the Pentecostal movement only began to flourish with the shift from an Orientalist conception of "mission tongues" to a more egalitarian idea of glossolalia, or tongues with no earthly equivalent, and the simultaneous shift from often dictatorial white male Holiness preachers to member-driven, female-dominated, and interracial worship practices.

Bishop William Saunders Crowdy's story is interesting partly because he ranged widely from Virginia and New York to Denver, Chicago, Kansas, Oklahoma and many points in between. His life illustrates the fact that with the coming of the age of the railroads pounding their way across the vast distances of the country, overland transit became even easier than seafaring. Just as Black sailors knit the African-descended peoples of the Atlantic together, transmitting news of far-off lands, the railroads allowed people like Crowdy to span the continent in a matter of days. The western character of his travels also illustrates the fact that African American migration did not begin with the "Great Migration" of the First World War, but that there were nearly continuous migrations—of Southern whites and Blacks alike—from the end of slavery until the floodgates opened with the cessation of European migration and the need for labor in northern industries during the "Great War."

The final years of the nineteenth century were also the time when the newly consolidated country of Ethiopia defeated the similarly young-but-ancient country of Italy at the climactic Battle of Adwa (Adowa) in 1896. This victory of an African nation over a European one, the only time an African country conclusively repulsed a European invasion during the age of the European colonial "scramble for Africa," reinvigorated traditions of Black political internationalism at least as old as the Haitian Revolution of 1791, inspiring later twentieth-century pan-African political organizing. In Adwa's wake there arose a movement of Black churches preaching that the ancient Israelites originated in Ethiopia. These Ethiopianist preachers led to a second wave of Black Israelite churches during the first Great Migration of the war years in northern cities like Detroit, Chicago, New York, and Philadelphia. In addition, thousands of Black West Indian troops served in the African and

Islamic "Oriental" theaters of the war, exposing these men to "the mystic East" firsthand, while radicalizing and redistributing the Black American population.

With the large-scale population transfer of the "Great Migration" from the American South, and to a lesser extent from the West Indies, due to the availability of northern jobs during the First World War, a diverse group of Black religious and political practitioners in interwar America arose, calling themselves "professors of Oriental and African mystic science" and using Orientalist tropes to valorize Eastern civilization and to criticize Euro-American racism and materialism. Practitioners of new alternative religions, many of whom were West Indian First World War veterans and followers of Marcus Mosiah Garvey, collaborated with each other and created new religious movements such as Black Judaism and Black Islam, building on the foundation established by Holiness Christianity–based Israelite movements. Black Orientalism used imperialist ideology subversively and had inspirations as diverse as conjuring, the Hebrew Bible, Freemasonry, the Shriners, and popular entertainments such as minstrel shows, circuses, and the Chicago International Exposition of 1893.[12]

It was the interwar era, bringing into proximity large numbers of Blacks and Jews, that produced some forms of Black Israelite religion that incorporated rituals that can be called Judaic, in that they were modeled on contemporary Judaism, and not simply Hebraic, in the mold of the Hebrew Bible. Two prominent proponents of these Judaic forms of Black Israelite faiths in New York were Rabbi Arnold Josiah Ford and Rabbi Wentworth Arthur Matthew. As Chapter 4 describes, Ford was a Barbadian musician who became the choirmaster at the Universal Negro Improvement Association's headquarters in New York City and an intimate of its leader, Marcus Garvey, before founding a synagogue in New York and leading a group of Black pioneers to establish a "colony" in Ethiopia. There he ended up playing music in nightclubs and in the palace of Emperor Haile Selassie I. His colony failed, and he perished during the Italo-Ethiopian War of 1935, but his ideas and his example helped inspire future Black Jewish congregations in the United States and played an indirect role in the rise of the Black Israelite religion of Rastafarianism in Jamaica. As an exemplar of "Black Zionism," Rabbi Ford demonstrates the longstanding transnationalism of the African diaspora, and the way ideas, like goods and bodies, have transcribed multidirectional circuits across the globe.

There is no better example of the transnational and polycultural nature of African American religions than the faith formulated by one of Rabbi Ford's associates, Wentworth Arthur Matthew. Chapter 5 illustrates that Matthew, who was born in Nevis-St. Kitt's and immigrated to New York as a young man, composed his version of Black Judaism from a bricolage of Christian, Jewish, Afro-Caribbean, Masonic, and esoteric sources, as part of a wide community of ministers, Freemasons, conjurers, occultists, healers, and "Professors of Mystic Science." Yet although he incorporated such diverse sources, his movement arose at a brief historical moment when white Jews and Blacks of many nationalities and religions lived together in close proximity in New York's Harlem. Partly in order to gain the financial and institutional support of white Jews, Matthew gradually adopted many of the liturgical standards of Ashkenazi and Sephardic Jews, even as he kept his own polycultural faith going behind closed doors in what ethnographer James Scott refers to as the "hidden transcript." It is important to recognize that the public transcript, the partial transcript, and the hidden transcript of religious communities seldom completely coincide.

Like most histories, this work has more to say about the "leaders" than the "followers" of these movements. Yet in this case the leaders are in the main working class, Black, and until now perhaps, relatively anonymous. Moreover, this book strives to show how these people did not act alone but were part of broad social networks of ideas and actors that stretched from the South to the West, from the West Indies to the northern cities, from England to the United States, and from North America to West Africa. I am also aware of a certain slippage that occurs at times in this text between the religious views of the "leaders" of movements and the "religions" that their members followed. One of my operating assumptions is that there are indeed leaders and followers in religious movements; that every individual does not create religious beliefs, ethics, discourses, and rituals as actively as do many leaders. Whether this is true or not is a question for debate, but in the case of Black Israelites, where the relatively few records we have almost invariably focus on the leaders of movements, this slippage between leaders and their movements is an inelegant, if necessary, form of shorthand.

The problem of sources is an impediment in this study as in so many others—most Black Israelite churches and synagogues of the early twentieth century no longer survive, and gaining access to records is often problematic. In the mid-1990s, Sholomo B. Levy, a scholar and rabbi from the New York Ethiopian Hebrew community, and Howard Smythe, an archivist at the Schomburg Library, a branch of the New York Public Library, collected the papers of Rabbi Matthew and the congregations he inspired. Those papers have proven to be an invaluable source for the present study. Yet even when we have lists of members, as is the case for some of the Black Israelite congregations of 1920s Harlem, few of the members turn up in the

United States census, making rigorous demographic analysis of these movements impossible. There are remarkably few records of Black Israelite ritual practice, and the experience of women within these groups has gone largely unrecorded. In other words, there are a host of questions that are unasked in this text, not because the author was incurious but because the necessary sources do not exist. Faced with such problems, this book employs micro-historical and cultural techniques, using close examination of a limited amount of documentary evidence set in an expansive historical context.

While not ignoring the possibility and sometimes the presence of avarice or other vices in alternative religious sects, this study differs sharply from the first wave of studies of Black Israelite, Rastafarian, and Black Muslim faiths, which almost uniformly depicted them as being primarily swindles conducted by con artists and confidence men.[13] Any creation story is preceded or followed by a seemingly infinite series of begetting; contemplating where we come from is the starting point of the search for ultimate truth, and it is this search for meaning, not criminal conspiracy, that is at the heart of the cultural activity that this book chronicles. Although it is true that William Saunders Crowdy's vision while working a dusty Oklahoma field begat a whole chain of other religious practitioners and entire new religions, it is important not to get so lost in the begetting that we lose sight of the fact that at every stage individuals understood themselves to be uncovering historical truths and encountering the numinous presence of the divine. In 1892, when Crowdy fell to his knees in an Oklahoma field and fled in terror into the woods, he was experiencing a mode of human being in the world that has textual analogues as ancient as the Hebrew Bible and as current as this morning's cup of coffee.[14]

I did most of the research for this book at the Schomburg Library, at the historic intersection of 135th and Malcolm X Boulevard, the street that Malcolm X himself used to call "Lenox." As I pursued the stories of the Black Israelites and other self-proclaimed "Professors of Oriental and African Mystic Science" back into the 1920s, I could look out of the window and see the very street corner where the great Hubert Harrison used to educate the masses in his very own open air university—perhaps the very spot where Harrison once tendered his stepladder to a young Jamaican upstart named Marcus Mosiah Garvey. It was there, among the milling crowds, that Wentworth Arthur Matthew used to preach to the passersby that they were not "Negroes" but were in fact Israelites, descendants of West African people who were themselves the direct descendants of God's Chosen People.

During the Harlem Renaissance, Rabbi Matthew was not the only one interested in African history. Indeed, Arturo Schomburg himself acquired the world's largest collection of African history, and his donation to the 135th Street branch of the New York Public Library had created the research library in which I sat, above that famous street corner. But Schomburg, Hubert Harrison, W.E.B. Du Bois, Willis Nathaniel Huggins, Sr., Wentworth Arthur Matthew, and the many other Black intellectuals (organic and otherwise) who opened up the study of African history in the 1920s did not get the lion's share of the credit for doing so. As so often happens, the spoils would go to another man, in this case a white Jewish man, a young professor named Melville Jean Herskovits.[15]

As I sat there in Harlem trying to recreate what I was calling the "everyday" Harlem of the 1920s, my daydream of the real, the everyday, and the ordinary was rudely interrupted by the persistent, and to my mind, the slightly annoying, presence of academicians who had come before me, social scientists who had taken the measure of Harlem on the very same street corners where Harrison and his fellow speakers had exhorted the crowds from their stepladder rostrums. There was an odd couple of anthropologists, the young professor Melville Herskovits, and his graduate student research assistant, the inimitable Zora Neale Hurston, elbowing their way awkwardly into the narrative frame, and threatening to become as interesting as the material they were documenting (figs 0.1 and 0.2). Turning to the microfilm files in the Schomburg's basement, I discovered a decade's worth of Melville J. Herskovits' physical anthropology of the 1920s, including those few years of collaboration between the future founder of the first African Studies Department in the United States and the young woman who would posthumously become the most beloved woman writer of the Harlem Renaissance. In those years, however, neither of them had yet found their true calling, and instead they were engaged in laboriously and meticulously collecting hundreds of thousands of measurements of skin tone, nostril shape, lip thickness, head shape and other indexes of more than 5,000 people and cadavers then labeled "Negro." Even as I was struck by the unappetizing and almost grotesque nature of what contemporary anthropologist John L. Jackson would call a "Warlockian" anthropological enterprise, I could not help but be impressed by the tenacity, work ethic, and prolific publication record of the young Herskovits, then little older than myself, who would soon apply the same admirable work ethic in the more fruitful vineyard of cultural anthropology. Nor could I help but feel an uncomfortable sense of kinship with Herskovits, not only because of my interest in Black history, but because of my Jewish and partially Hungarian Jewish ancestry.[16]

**FIGURE 0.1** Melville and Frances Herskovits, 1920s. Frances not only conducted field-work with her husband, she also prepared the extensive bibliography that undergirded his major work, *The Myth of the Negro Past*. Photograph courtesy of Northwestern University, with permission from Jean Herskovits.

**FIGURE 0.2** A young Zora Neale Hurston, photographed by the writer and Harlem habitué, Carl Van Vechten. Reproduced with the permission of the Carl Van Vechten Trust.

To their credit, Herskovits and his mentor Franz Boas were working to disprove nineteenth-century craniologists who had used flawed evidence to assert that racial hierarchies correlated to physical differences between various peoples from all corners of the globe. Herskovits's careful measurements of Black skulls were critical in disproving the claims that people of African descent were physically inferior to others, and the German-Jewish-born Boas waged a courageous fight against the racist theories of American eugenicists which inspired sterilization laws in twenty-seven states and provided a model for similar programs in Nazi Germany.[17] As a fighter for cultural understanding engaged in real political struggles inside and outside the academy, and as a teacher to generations of anthropologists, including Hurston, Margaret Mead, and Ruth Benedict, "Papa Franz" is deservedly a hero to many. His pupil Herskovits is legendary in his own right, as the person who did more than any other to forward the theory that Africans had retained and transmitted their cultural aesthetics to their American-born descendants, and as the founder in 1948 of the first African Studies program in the United States, at Northwestern University. In later decades, Herskovits turned his attention toward the cultures of African-descended peoples in Africa and the Americas, as part of a larger scholarly and political project to demonstrate that culture was learned, not genetic, and to debunk the Hegelian idea that Africans and their descendants were people without culture or history—the "myth of the Negro past."[18]

Yet Herskovits spent the first decade of his career and formed his theories of culture while studying human physiognomy, not human behavior. "Although the work which took me among them was primarily that connected with a study of the physical anthropology of these people," Herskovits wrote in 1927, "a study of the effects of racial crossing, for which they furnish as near laboratory conditions as may be found in a human population, it was not long before the opportunity to watch at the same time this phenomenon of the manner in which these American negroes had become essentially a part of the general American culture impressed itself upon me."[19] The field of African Diaspora Studies has largely forgotten this anthropometric phase in its scholarly development, and Herskovits himself was the primary author of its erasure: the opening essay of his landmark 1941 study *The Myth of the Negro Past* referenced his 1930 essay calling for a study of African culture, but omitted the portions calling for the study of African nostril widths, lip thicknesses, and cranial measurements with the prim comment that his original expertise "lay outside the relevant sociological field."[20] Herskovits's original "African baseline" morphed seamlessly and silently from physical to cultural anthropology.

But the more I read of Herskovits and the more I attempted to systematize my own ideas of cultural formation in the African diaspora, the more I came to realize that the intellectual genealogy of Herskovits's ideas could not be so summarily erased. Rather, the conservative, biological, organic, and essentialist metaphors of roots theory were deeply embedded in the forgotten decade of their germination in the nursery of Harlem street corner anthropology. As I began to investigate the systems of knowledge that Harlem created, my work took a more reflexive and theoretical turn as it began to engage with the foundational myths embedded within Melville Herskovits's famous *Myth of the Negro Past*. In so doing I hope to help to articulate an emerging consensus concerning the formation of African American culture. This re-vision pays respect to its predecessors but departs from them in key ways, sailing the open waters of world history and navigating by the stars and the newer poles of the humanities rather than depending on the worn charts of the anthropological ancient mariners who kept the old continent of physical anthropology in sight, even while trying to discover new lands. I set off in search of Melville, the great white whale of the Black Atlantic, and hoped to survive the voyage.

Call me Ishmael.

Black Israelite and what we might call Black *Ishmaelite* religions illustrate that Herskovits's foundational concept of syncretism, while intended to provide a sophisticated model of cultural formation, is essentialist and deeply flawed. Here I am in agreement with the many anthropologists and historians of religion who have concluded that the term "syncretism" should not be used "without a lot of definitional labor," in the words of Bruce Lincoln, or, in more extreme cases, that it should not be used at all.[21] Herskovits posited "syncretism" as the allegedly scientific mechanism by which the various strains of culture in Black America might be disentangled along a spectrum of "acculturation." Yet syncretism perhaps obscures more than it explains through its reductive view of culture and its lack of individual agency. Although Herskovits and Boas argued for the importance of nurture over nature and culture over biology, Herskovits remained wedded to the idea of culture as a set of rigid, predictable patterns. His own words in 1926 were that the chief patterns of society were "mechanistic and materialistic." Exhibiting a tendency toward tautological thinking that would also characterize his later work on African retentions, he claimed that patterns "govern our lives with a rigidity which, it is believed, will come to be recognized more and more as studies of society, with the fact of the existence of pattern in mind, are made."[22] As one might expect of someone who spent the better part of the twenties measuring the nostril widths and head shapes of "Negro" children, adults, and even cadavers, Herskovits was inclined to think of culture using physiological metaphors: "For the sociologist," he wrote in 1929, "the application of the notion of pattern to the problems in which he is interested has the effect of laying them open much in the manner in which the student of physiology lays open the muscles of the body which he is dissecting. It gives an ability to see the problem in hand with a clarity which is nothing less than startling in the detachment which the student gains."[23] The young Herskovits thus depicted cultural patterns as physiological systems: materialistic, mechanistic, and knowable according to positivistic scientific principles.

Herskovits argued that American Negroes had no remaining African cultural traits in an article for Alaine Locke's 1925 *The New Negro,* which announced the Harlem Renaissance to the world, and he repeated that assertion in 1927. Yet in 1930 he reversed himself and published the idea that "acculturation" occurred along a continuum, according to the mechanism of "syncretism." It is highly significant that Herskovits originally used these concepts in intertwined discussions of both physiological and cultural changes. The original "African baseline" he proposed to study was not a funky bass line but rather the baseline of nostril widths, lip thicknesses, and skin pigmentations of the West African populations who shared ancestors with African Americans.[24] But after a decade of taking thousands of such measurements, Herskovits was beginning to be more interested in the human behaviors than the human bodies that formed in the Americas. In the next decade, as his wife Frances collected a bibliography of almost everything then published on people of African descent in West Africa, Brazil, the Caribbean, South America, and the United States, the Herskovitses together conducted research in Haiti, Brazil, Surinam, Dutch Guiana, Sierra Leone, Liberia, and Dahomey, collecting and transcribing more than a thousand songs with the zeal formerly employed for the measurement of bodies.

Yet despite his assertions of scientific detachment, for Herskovits Africa was very much in the eye of the beholder. Immediately evident in that first decade of writing, in addition to Herskovits's industriousness and idealism, was his naïve sense of scientific positivism, and his seemingly limitless faith in often subjective and simplistic methods. In 1930 he wondered if "the Negro" had "a definite temperament? Is he always happy? What is it that makes him like to sing and to dance?"[25] Herskovits's ambition, open-minded spirit of scientific inquiry, and general naïveté could be breathtaking. His tendency toward essentialist and simplistic methods continued throughout his career, as when he remarked that unconscious bodily movements and facial expressions on the faces of African American young people listening to recordings of African music indicated a deep, cultural familiarity with African ways, preserved, presumably without interruption or augmentation, for four centuries.[26] For Herskovits, Black culture was not rooted in physical differences, but it was analogically hereditary, subject to "deep seated drives in Negro life; drives so strong, indeed, that it is difficult, if not impossible, to account for them satisfactorily except in terms of a tradition which reaches further than merely to the period of slavery."[27]

Herskovits wrote the pathbreaking work *The Myth of the Negro Past* at the behest of the Carnegie Corporation's study of racism and "race-relations" in America. Herskovits, who had hoped to be named director of the study in place of Gunnar Myrdal, prepared his volume in only nine months, marshaling anthropological evidence from West Africa and the Americas to argue that African culture had survived the Middle Passage and could be located as "survivals," "Africanisms," "retentions," or "reinterpretations" in contemporary Negro culture. He judiciously removed the references to physical anthropology from his earlier work but the concept of "acculturative continuum," "syncretism," and the "social laboratory of the Americas" remained. Although he moved away from the measurement of bodies and moved into cultural anthropology, the intellectual frameworks he developed in that decade of measuring heads remained largely intact.[28] Herskovits' intellectual frameworks led him to think of cultural practices as being just as concrete as physiological traits, and thereby under-appreciated Black American creativity, innovation, and cosmopolitanism.

In 1947, Cuban anthropologist Fernando Ortiz introduced the neologism "transculturation" as an improvement on the simple scale of acculturation that Herskovits had proposed. Ortiz hoped that his new term would prove more flexible in describing the tremendous heterogeneity and multiple registers of cultural contact in the Caribbean—whereas the older model proposed a fictively coherent European culture to which other peoples acculturated. Yet Ortiz still thought of human cultures as discrete, bounded, and metaphorically biological—a change "from one culture to another," he wrote, is akin to the mixing inherent in genetic inheritance from parents to offspring.[29] Replacing Ortiz's prefix "trans," meaning across, beyond, or on the opposite side, with the prefix "poly," meaning many, helps to substitute the old, bounded, and genetic notion of culture for a newer, unbounded, and less embodied concept of *cultures*, in the plural.

To date, historians Robin Kelley and Vijay Prashad have used the term "polycultural" to emphasize that we are all inheritors of wisdoms, myths, technologies, and folkways that originate from all parts of the globe. Kelley has critiqued the essentialism of multiculturalism, which, like the Boasian cultural anthropology that preceded it, views cultures as discrete, holistic, and bounded. Rejecting this "zoological approach to culture," Kelley called instead for an understanding of identities as multiple and unbounded. Speaking of not simply "my own family or even my `hood, but all peoples in the Western world," Kelley explains:

> It is not our skin or hair or walk or talk that renders Black people so incredibly diverse. Rather, it is the fact that most Black people in the Americas are products of a variety of different "cultures"—living cultures, not dead ones. These cultures live in and through us everyday, with almost no self-consciousness about hierarchy or meaning.... Blackness, Black culture, and Black life have never been easily identifiable, secure in their boundaries, or clear to all people who live inside or outside our skin. We were multi-ethnic and polycultural from the get-go.[30]

Materialistic, scientific, and genetic understandings of cultural formation repeatedly run aground against the internal diversity among the people variously referred to as negro, Negro, colored, Black, Afro-, or African American. All Americans and by extension all humans, today as in the past, live lives that are similarly diverse.[31] As Vijay Prashad writes, "Polyculturalism, unlike multiculturalism, assumes that people live coherent lives that are made up of a host of lineages."[32] It is important not to gloss over what a radical departure polyculturalism is from its antecedents. Building on insights from James Clifford and the post-purity anthropologists, polyculturalism jettisons the old, evolutionary, and biological metaphors that characterized even the most culturally minded of the older anthropologists, and instead embraces a concept of cultures that are multiple, unheirarchical, unbounded, and "impure."

Scholars in Religious, Cultural, and African American Studies might consider replacing "syncretism" with "polyculturalism" to describe cultural synthesis in a way that is consonant with the social sciences of today rather than those of 1927, based not on syncretism's acculturation, authenticity, or retention, but rather on social networks, imagination, reinterpretation, and invention. Polycultural bricolage offers the possibility of discussing cultural formation, including religious innovation, without the essentialist, holistic, and hostile binaries of syncretic acculturation—or even the holism of transculturation. Rather, polyculturalism suggests that cultures are not bounded systems but fluid, multivalent processes, constructed by many individual bricoleurs who work by recombining old and new, familiar and foreign, in a process that takes advantage of similarities between cultures and is not so much conflictual, inevitable, or mechanical as it is creative, imaginative, and innovative within recognizable "grammatical" patterns.[33] As anthropologist James Clifford has written, "groups negotiating their identity in contexts of domination and exchange...patch themselves together."[34] The bricoleur is created by the culture he or she creates, and in this sense functions more like a spider on a web than a heroic individual weaver standing apart from her creation on a loom. Just as a spider creates webs out of substances extruded from her own body, the religious bricoleur is suspended in webs of personal and societal signification anchored by the physical and cultural structures of daily life. Some of the anchor points of the bricoleur's web are the anchor lines of the webs of other bricoleurs, not just the material infrastructure of the environment itself. Likewise, the spider is fed by the insects she catches in her web, and so in a very real sense is constituted by the very web that she herself secretes.[35]

Of course, bricoleurs, like spiders, are dependent in some ways on the material and economic conditions of their environments. The bricoleur builds his or her web in the interstitial spaces of the material world, frequently as a tactic of resistance to the power structures and disciplines that would seek to limit and control narratives of identity. Theorist Michel de Certeau wrote about such resistant "tactics" as the contrary, clandestine forms taken by the "dispersed, tactile, and make-shift creativity of groups or individuals already caught in the nets of 'discipline.'"[36] In similar fashion, the new Black religions of the early twentieth century were religions of "subversive bricolage," the creations of remarkably sophisticated, not savage, minds.[37] As Robin Kelley notes, "folk culture is actually *bricolage*, a cutting, pasting, and incorporating of various cultural forms that then become categorized in a racially or ethnically coded aesthetic hierarchy."[38]

Although oppressive hierarchical power, what de Certeau is referring to as "discipline," always plays a part in cultural formation, the outcome of such situations is difficult to predict. Theorist Antonio Gramsci was clear that cultural hegemony, that is, the societal dominance of a particular class's values, is not just struggled for "from above," that is, by the owning classes, but it is struggled for from every direction by *every* class.[39] Cultural prestige can emanate from the working classes as well as the owning classes, from poor as well as rich, and from people of all races and sexes, as George Lipsitz reminds us in his writings on "prestige from below" in U.S. popular cultures.[40] Lower classes, as well as oppressed and marginalized groups, wield their own cultural power. Marginalized groups develop a multitude of tactics for mitigating the oppressive ideological conditions they face on a daily basis.[41] Polycultural Black Israelite religions, which responded to racism and the erasure of African peoples from historical narratives by staking a claim for Black centrality in Western narratives of sacred history, can be understood in related terms: as resourceful and patched-together responses to oppressive ideologies, and as tactics that acquired their own centers of gravity and never merely mimicked the religions practiced by Jews of European descent—even as members of both communities found themselves both attracted and repelled by the other.

Finally, a note on terminology and focus: this book does not always explicitly highlight the power relations between Black and white Jews or the cultural formation of Ashkenazi and Sephardi forms of Judaism.[42] The relations between New York's Black and white Jewish communities deserve a book on its own, which I plan to write as a sequel to the present work. The focus of this text on the religious narratives, histories, choices, and tactics of Black Jews and Black Israelites arises from my belief that these phenomena deserve attention not in isolation but on their own terms. Unfortunately, works that emphasize the fraught relationships between white and Black Jews have often neglected the true polycultural complexity of Black Israelism and one of its variants, Black Judaism.[43] I have taught and even written works in the mold of the whiteness studies scholars who seek to write the story of Ashkenazi Jewish "racial formation" into the framework established by Matthew Frye Jacobson and others. Yet I find myself, with Thomas Guglielmo, something of a skeptic about this narrative of white racial metamorphosis: although I accept that European-descended Jews' *race* changed from "Hebrew" to "Caucasian" sometime after the Second World War, European Jews, like Italians, were "white on arrival" in America in terms of their *color*, and hence their societal status—especially when compared to the subordinate position of people considered "colored."[44] Although it is true that Jews, Irish, Italians, Slavs, and even Germans at certain times faced discrimination based on their race, their *color* status as whites of European descent earned them the wages of whiteness and protected them from the systematic, quotidian, and severe injustices perpetrated against people who could not claim whiteness. Hence, in American contexts, I use the terms "white Jew" and "white Ashkenazi or Sephardic Jews" unapologetically from the moment when Jews of European descent began to benefit from the American racial caste system that placed Africans and their descendants in subordinate positions. I capitalize "Black" and "Blackness" as proper nouns not because they are essential or natural, but because they are recognizable, if constructed, identities, chosen by Black Americans for themselves—much as "Jews" and "Jewishness" are capitalized as proper nouns. I use "African American" and "Black American" relatively interchangeably, not to indicate any particular position on "retention" or "polycultural" theories, which cannot be distilled so simply, but again because those are names adopted by overlapping communities themselves. Finally, I do not capitalize "white" because, as historian Martha Biondi aptly puts it, "historically it has been deployed as a signifier of social domination and privilege, rather than as an indicator of ethnic or national origin."[45]

# 1

## "THIS IS OUR RED SEA"

### EXODUSTERS, PROPHET WILLIAM SAUNDERS CROWDY, AND THE BEGINNINGS OF BLACK ISRAELISM

One of the first people to teach that Black Americans had Israelite ancestry had himself lived the Exodus narrative in at least four different promised lands. William Saunders Crowdy was born into slavery on the southern peninsula of Maryland in 1847, and his first promised land was that of the spirituals and of African American religion during slavery: the longed-for respite for those who suffered the Egypt of slavery in the antebellum South. The second was the promised land of the Union lines, where sixteen-year-old Crowdy escaped slavery and found greater freedom. The third refuge was the promised land of the Great Plains, where Crowdy joined thousands of other African Americans looking for opportunity, including some who came in the wave of "Exodusters" of 1879. Crowdy's fourth and final promised land was in Belleville, Virginia, in the Tidewater region not far from where he had been born, where he returned at the end of his life and where his followers bought land, settled, and established the headquarters of a unique and pioneering Black Israelite faith. In the late nineteenth and early twentieth centuries, the Exodus narrative was not simply a sacred text, a parable, or a religious metaphor for African American deliverance from slavery. Exodus was a sign of God's deliverance, a central organizing principle for the rise of Black national consciousness, and a concrete process of migration. William Saunders Crowdy and his followers had themselves internalized, imagined, and lived the experience of Exodus on the way from figurative to literal identification with the ancient Israelites.

Crowdy was born *Wilson* Saunders Crowdy to Basil and Sarah Ann Crowdy in Virginia in 1847, and grew up an enslaved house-boy on the Chisley Hill plantation in Charlotte Hall, Saint Mary's County, Maryland, where his mother was a cook.[1] His owner was a particularly cruel master, a Southern sympathizer who was a spy for the Confederacy during the Civil War. St. Mary's County is in the southern part of the state, thirty miles south of Washington, D.C. on the trapezoidal promontory, fifteen miles east of the Potomac River and ten miles west of the Chesapeake Bay. Relatively far by road or ferry from the more cosmopolitan ports of Washington, Baltimore, and Annapolis at the northern end of the state, during the Civil War St. Mary's County was a rural area of widespread pro-Confederate, secessionist sympathy, not far removed in either geography or political beliefs from neighboring Virginia, just across the Potomac estuary.[2] Enslaved persons did their best to hasten slavery's demise wherever it was found, flooding across Union lines, driving off overseers, and after 1862, joining the Union Army. When a Union officer and a detachment of Black soldiers came to Chisley Hill to recruit enslaved men to join the Union army, the master tied up some of his men to prevent them from joining the Union forces. After an angry altercation with the Federal officer, the master and his son, a furloughed Confederate soldier, killed the officer, stuffed the body underneath a building on the property, and fled across the Potomac to Virginia. News of the shocking event in nominally pro-Union Maryland, only seventy miles from the nation's capital, came to the attention of President Abraham Lincoln and even made the front page of the *New York Times*.[3] The Union Army took over the administration of the plantation.

During 1863, support for slavery waned in Maryland, and in September of the following year white men in Maryland—the only ones who were enfranchised—became the first citizens of a slave state to adopt a new constitution abolishing slavery, by a slender margin of only 375 votes out of a total of almost 73,000. As the slave system crumbled and the Civil War raged, sixteen-year-old Crowdy, as best as can be determined, gathered what he could carry, bid his loved ones goodbye, and left home to join the Federal forces as a cook in the Quartermaster Corps.[4] He changed his name from Wilson to William, perhaps to assert his self-fashioned personhood and his independence from his enslaved past. Like many other African American camp followers, he served the Union cause without directly bearing arms.

It is no coincidence that two of the twentieth century's important religious movements emerged from the Great Plains in general, and northeastern Kansas in particular, at the turn of the century. Kansas was an unusually dynamic place in the last twenty years of the nineteenth century, and provided the nursery for both William Saunders Crowdy's early Black Israelite movement, as described in this chapter, and for the rise of the theology of Pentecostalism, as told in the following chapter. On the one hand, Kansas became a haven and a symbol for African Americans who longed for self-determination. It was in Kansas, and the neighboring Oklahoma Territory, that Black political and social independence and Black-controlled towns enabled Crowdy to imagine that the ancient Israelites were also Black. On the other hand, African Americans were not the only ones attracted to the fertile lands and rich mines of Kansas in the final decades of the nineteenth century. People poured in from all over the world, and this babble of tongues, following sixty years of prayer for personal and societal perfectionism in the Holiness movement, provided a crucial spark that led to the Pentecostal revival of 1906. Since this one place, northeastern Kansas, played such an important role in both movements, it is worthwhile to spend some time discovering what made it unique.

For African Americans, Kansas was a kind of a promised land, before and after the Civil War. In the decades after the Civil War, African Americans in search of a better life moved not north but south and west. Most, to be sure, remained where they were, or close by, and fought as best they could to secure a better life for themselves in the South. But with the failure of any meaningful land reform during Reconstruction, Blacks still sweltered in the sun, tilling land that they did not own, often as sharecroppers who commonly found themselves in a continual cycle of peonage, owing more to the landlord at harvest time than they had owed at planting time. Cementing this race-based serfdom was a new and virulent strain of racist terror that saw organized gangs of white vigilantes beat, shoot, torture, burn, and lynch Black victims.

As bad as the South became, the North offered little haven to Blacks in the last decades of the nineteenth century. New York was still recovering from the draft riots of 1863, when irate white mobs beat and lynched any Black person they could find, killing more than a hundred African Americans and driving many more out of the city. The northern industrial machine's thirst for manual labor was slaked by the tides of immigrants from central, eastern, and southern Europe who poured into northeastern ports with the end of the American Civil War and the continuation of political turmoil in Europe.

On the other hand, the midwestern and western states offered hope, access to land ownership, greater economic freedom, and more physical safety to Black freed people and their children. Republican veterans of the abolitionist movement ruled Kansas, and contributed to the sense that Blacks could get fair treatment there.[5] John Brown, the white militant who had sacrificed himself to end slavery, had lived and fought in Lawrence, Kansas, in the turbulent 1850s. Black troops from Kansas were the first African Americans to fight in the Union Army when they marched into Missouri in 1861.[6] The prominence of Kansas in the struggle for Black freedom thus helped make it an attractive site for Black settlement.

The Homesteading Act of 1862 provided the legal basis for the founding of new Black settlements in Kansas and elsewhere. The act granted 160 acres of free land in the western states to anyone, regardless of race or sex, who paid a modest filing fee and lived on and improved the land for five years, or, alternatively, purchased the land for $1.25 an acre after living on it for six months.[7] The growth of small Black colonies in the western prairies or in Kansas's eastern towns was gradual but included more people than the better publicized migration of 1879.[8] By the end of the war in 1865, there were 12,527 African Americans in Kansas, concentrated in Leavenworth, Douglas, and Wyandotte counties. Most of the "colored" population were field hands, but there were also 2,400 urban Blacks in Leavenworth and 1,000 in Lawrence.[9] African Americans, chiefly from the Border South states of Kentucky, Missouri, and Tennessee, began making their way into Kansas, establishing businesses, buying land, moving into existing towns, and carefully planning new Black towns. Far from being the paradise that boosters depicted, with a mild climate, verdant valleys, and fertile bottomlands, Kansas was a difficult place to homestead. Despite the challenges of a harsh climate, however, small Black communities clung on and slowly sank roots on the Kansas prairies, laying out streets, building more permanent structures, and farming the fertile land.[10] In 1870 there were 16,250 Blacks in Kansas, and by 1880 there were 43,110.[11] The continuous migration of Blacks from border states such as Tennessee and Kentucky throughout the decade was actually larger than the arrival of refugees from Mississippi and Louisiana during the so-called "Kansas Fever Exodus" of 1879.[12] Kansas also attracted whites from Ohio, Indiana, and Illinois in the 1870s, and the state's population exploded in the period of Reconstruction.

The events of the Civil War and the sacrifices made in the name of freedom had transmogrified Kansas into an almost holy land in the minds of many African Americans. "I am anxious to reach your state, not because of the great race now made for it but because of the sacredness of her soil washed by the blood of humanitarians for the cause of Black freedom," wrote one formerly enslaved person to the Kansas governor.[13] With the help of many Quakers, Presbyterians, and Congregationalists who moved to the state after the Civil War with a religious mission to help freed people, and without the South's history of occupation during Reconstruction, Kansas became a refuge for freed people, much as the United States served as a refuge for European immigrants.[14]

The Kansas Exodus began when the Compromise of 1877 ended Reconstruction and allowed Democratic "Redeemers" to wrest back control of Louisiana, Mississippi, and South Carolina in the violence-filled election of 1878. The Democrats used "bull dozers," or terrorists, to intimidate, murder, and wreck havoc, killing African Americans and destroying their homes and businesses throughout the Gulf Coast.[15] Some estimate that the number of Black men, women, and children killed in this period was as high as 5,000.[16] Black interest in immigration increased as cities like New Orleans and Shreveport filled up with Black refugees from white violence in the countryside.[17] The situation in the South in general, and Louisiana in particular, looked increasingly dire as it became clear that African Americans could expect a future of racist terrorism and poverty as long as they attempted to assert their political rights.

Some of those who determined to try to escape the South set their sights on the distant shores of Africa, but greater numbers set off up the Mississippi for Missouri and Kansas, turning St. Louis into a metaphoric "Red Sea," the gateway to the "promised land" of the West. Kansas at the time was experiencing plentiful rainfall and rich harvests, and bore a special place in Black memory as the land of Free Soil, abolitionism, and John Brown. Estimates of the numbers of Black refugees in St. Louis in 1879–1880 ranged from a low of 6,206 to as high as 20,000.[18] Unlike the previous decade's worth of Black migration to Kansas, which had been more gradual and better planned, many migrants fled in 1879 without adequate funds, desperate to escape Southern terror. The leading historian of the Kansas Exodus, Nell Irvin Painter, has argued that those who fled without the resources to complete their journey or establish themselves as farmers in Kansas were motivated by a millenarian belief that God would deliver them from the South as God had delivered the Hebrew Israelites from ancient Egypt. However, there is reason to doubt that the Kansas migrants of 1879 were either consumed by a "Kansas Fever," or that they were driven by a religious belief in Providential deliverance.[19] Most of the descriptions of the Exodus as irrational, and many of the descriptions of it as a religious belief, came from unsympathetic and racist observers, such as the writers for the *St Louis Globe-Democrat*, one of whom said that the migrants' ignorance was "as dark as their skins."[20] To be sure, there were a couple of accounts attributed to elderly travelers who used the imagery of the Exodus to explain their own experiences. The *St. Louis Globe-Democrat* quoted an old woman as saying, "this is our Red Sea. Right here in St. Louis, a'tween home and Kansas, and out of bondage for sure. We's been set free by Master Lincoln, but it was just such another set free as Pharaoh give the children of Israel. You hear me, child, them as is a'wavering and is afraid is going to sink in this here Red Sea."[21] Yet Southern Blacks frequently disobeyed their ministers to head north, and no scholar has found calls for migration as a precursor to a total, perfect, millennial future. It is more likely that many observers and a few participants used biblical similes not to catalyze the migration but to explain the movement after it had already begun; they compared the promising land of Kansas to the promised land after they arrived. One former slave and Federal soldier, John Solomon Lewis, had just such an experience:

> When we got in sight of Kansas I thought of the land of Canaan, only I was sorry all my family were not there too. When I landed on the soil I looked on the ground and I says this is free ground. Then I looked on the heavens, and I says them is free and beautiful heavens. Then I looked within my heart, and I says to myself I wonder why I never was free before?[22]

Those who fled to the banks of the Mississippi without the funds to homestead in Kansas were not wild-eyed millennialists but cold-eyed refugees from terroristic violence who knew that their life chances were better outside the Deep South, even if they had empty pockets and few possessions.

Determined to prevent the mass exodus of Blacks from the South, Southern whites did their best to prevent it, using violence and economic means. In some cases, Blacks were arrested for breach of contract or attacked on the banks of the river, where they waited in groups to catch passing northbound riverboats. Even more effective at preventing Blacks from leaving the South, however, was the recalcitrance of steamboat captains on the Mississippi River, who increasingly refused to pick up the growing crowds of hundreds and then thousands of poor Blacks who crowded the river's banks with all their possessions in April and May of 1879, vainly trying to flag down passing vessels. There were scenes of terrible suffering on the banks of the river, where hundreds gathered with few provisions in as many as twenty-four separate camps from Greenville to Natchez.[23] Without adequate transportation, only a fraction of the Exodusters who set out for Kansas actually made it there, and without proper planning, many of the ones who made it found conditions difficult at best. Still, few migrants returned to the South, despite the fact that Southern newspapers attempted to stifle the migration with propagandistic letters from migrants complaining about conditions in Kansas.

Yet even if few if any Kansas migrants were millenarians, the destruction of slavery meant that African American identification with the Israelites became a prominent feature not only of Black religion but also of the Black political imagination and Black national identity in the nineteenth century.[24] Kansas, and later the Oklahoma Territory and Liberia, became new promised lands for a generation of African Americans after Reconstruction and before the Great Migration.

Like thousands of other African Americans who had grown up enslaved, William Saunders Crowdy's life after the Civil War was defined by movement. He would surface in Kansas a few decades later, but the first place Crowdy turns up after the Civil War was just west of Kansas, in the Colorado Territory. He moved to Denver, where he married Eveline, or Artie, Allen on September 8, 1874.[25] Both the U.S. census and two city directories report that William S. Crowdy worked as a cook in Denver until 1881.[26] He then remarried in Samuel Clemens's hometown of Hannibal, Missouri, to twenty-five-year-old Lovey J. Higgins on April 3, 1882.[27] Higgins had been born in Missouri to parents from Kentucky, and she was widowed by 1880, when she was running a boarding house in Kansas City.[28] Crowdy and his bride relocated to Des Moines in 1882 and Sioux City, Iowa, in 1884, with Crowdy always making a living as a cook.[29] The couple had three children: Mattie Leah, Isaac, and August, but they suffered a tragedy of biblical proportions when they lost their firstborn as a child.[30] They moved again, to Kansas City in 1886, where they lived first at 1412 Walnut, and then remained at 1825 Grove, in the heart of Kansas City's Black community, from 1887 until 1891.[31]

Kansas City, which straddles the Kansas/Missouri border at the confluence of the Kansas and Missouri Rivers, was an unpolished frontier town in the decade after the Civil War. With the passage of time it acquired railroads, stockyards, and packinghouses, which attracted Black job seekers, and also served as a launching point for the prairie schooners setting off for homesteads in the Great Plains and the Southwest.[32] Kansas City grew rapidly after the Civil War, as it became the meatpacking center of the Southwest and as its railroads expanded to carry western wheat to eastern markets. Its population exploded, and its 32,254 residents in 1870 represented an eightfold increase in only a decade. By 1880, there were 55,785 residents of Kansas City, including 8,000 African Americans scattered in every neighborhood of the city but concentrated in the downtown around Charlotte and Tenth Street, or "Church Hill," where the Allen Chapel A.M.E. and Second Baptist Church faced each other across the intersection.[33] By 1890, the city had tripled in size in a decade, with more than 170,000 people in the greater Kansas City area.[34]

Like the Israelites of yore, Crowdy and his family were soon on the move once again. Perhaps attracted by the dream of creating a Black-majority state, Crowdy soon joined thousands of other African Americans in settling what had been Indian Territory and what would become the Oklahoma Territory on its way to statehood in 1907. Whereas the United States government never forced land reform on the former Confederate states, they were not so lenient with the Five Civilized Tribes of the Western Indian Territory, the lands that today constitute the state of Oklahoma. There, vanquished tribes, who were both former Confederate allies and former slave societies, were forced to accept new railroad construction through their lands, which opened the territory up to new settlers. They also had to give up land for the settlement of freedmen, of other Indians, and, after 1889, of non-Indians.[35] On the recommendation of Brevet Major General John Sanborn, who received a Congressional mandate to assess the condition of formerly enslaved residents of Indian territory in 1865, Congress had voided all past treaties with the Five Tribes in 1866, banned slavery, and forced the tribes to cede the western portion of their lands to the U.S. government. Sanborn urged that the Congress set aside a tract of the most fertile land in the region and settle four freed people for each square mile.[36] Black former slaves of the Five Civilized Tribes received plots of forty to one hundred acres in Indian Territory, a rare attempt to pay reparations for the disgrace of slavery—albeit at the expense of Indian landowners.[37] In the mid-1880s, six companies of Black cavalrymen were deployed to intercept and drive out the more than 2,000 "boomers" illegally infiltrating and settling in Indian Territory from neighboring Kansas and Texas.[38]

In sum, the territory that became Oklahoma was unique in its pattern of settlement and in the balance of power between the races: not only were Native Americans in the majority, but Blacks had substantial land holdings and served as agents of the Federal government, keeping the peace and evicting illegal settlers of all races. There was even some discussion of reserving settlement in the western portion of the Oklahoma territory for Black pioneers. The 1890 census revealed that almost 3,000 Blacks lived in the Oklahoma Territory and another 18,000 lived in Indian Territory to the immediate east.[39] The Black population continued to grow, so that by the turn of the twentieth century there were 19,000 Black residents of the Oklahoma Territory and almost 38,000 in Indian Territory.[40]

William Saunders Crowdy was one of the Black settlers who moved to Oklahoma, thanks in part to the advocacy of Edward P. McCabe, a prominent Republican Party politician and state auditor in Kansas who became one of the most active promoters of Black settlement in Oklahoma. McCabe billed Oklahoma as a "promised land" where Blacks could escape racial discrimination, exercise their citizenship rights, and claim cheap land. McCabe thought that if he could attract enough Black settlers they could form an all-Black state or at least dominate state elections.[41] In 1889, he purchased 320 acres of land near the new town of Guthrie, located along the Santa Fe Railroad, which would become the territorial capital from 1890 to 1910.[42] Guthrie was located on the banks of the Cimarron River, which follows its wide, sandy riverbed southeast from the high plains descending from the Rocky Mountains to the west, passing southeast through the Glass Mountains to a red sandstone region of massive moss-covered boulders.[43] In 1886 and 1887, the Atchison, Topeka, and Santa Fe Railroad laid its tracks across Indian Territory and built a stop just south of a mighty bend in the Cimarron at the site of Guthrie on what were formerly Creek and Seminole lands.[44] On April 22, 1889, the date of the first run on the "Unassigned Lands" of Indian Territory, tens of thousands of settlers massed on the borders. At the stroke of noon, or a little sooner, they raced on horseback, in horse-drawn wagons, and crowded railroad cars to stake their claims to 160-acre homesteads. Known as "the Birthplace of Oklahoma," Guthrie attracted fifteen thousand people on the day of the opening of the Indian Territory, springing to life seemingly overnight. Oklahoma officially became a U.S. territory on May 2, 1889, with Guthrie as its capital. Within three weeks, the new city had become a "prairie metropolis" with a chamber of commerce and three newspapers, the trading center for a large agricultural area. Running water came on line by July, and electrical street fixtures illuminated the streets by September. Columned banks and stately buildings soon rose to fill well-ordered streets. Guthrie boasted broad streets, wide sidewalks, an aesthetically pleasing downtown, and pleasant residential neighborhoods. Yet by 1910 Guthrie was surpassed by its larger and wealthier rival, Oklahoma City, about twenty-five miles to the south. Like a meandering river that jumps its bed and carves a new path to the ocean, the course of commerce bypassed Guthrie, but left some of the nation's finest collection of Victorian public buildings in its wake.

Importantly for the rise of Crowdy's Black Israelite faith, Guthrie was a major center of Masonic activity as well as a launching point for African American settlers determined to create their own towns free of white interference or control. Guthrie claimed the title of "Fraternal Capital of the Southwest" and became the center of Freemasonry in Oklahoma, with the Grand Lodge Temple, Masonic homes for the aged and for needy children, and one of the largest Masonic structures in the world, the Scottish Rite Temple.[45] Moreover, in the 1880s and 1890s, Guthrie was not only a bustling territorial capital but also the embarkation point for the settlement of all-Black towns established by formerly enslaved people who had carved out a modicum of independence for themselves on the Great Plains. Entrepreneur McCabe

subdivided the 320 acres he had bought twelve miles from Guthrie and promoted the settlement of the majority-Black town of Langston there, perched
on a hill overlooking the Cimarron River on the border of Iowa County and
the Sac and Fox Indian reservations. The Langston tract was subdivided into
town lots and McCabe sold seventeen hundred of them within two years, at
prices ranging from ten to fifty dollars.[46]

McCabe founded and ran the *Langston City Herald* from his office on
Oklahoma Street in downtown Guthrie, and used the newspaper both to
attract more Black settlers to Oklahoma and to forward his own political
career, using strident language and colorful descriptions of the freedom available to Black men and women in the new land.[47] The newspaper's circulation
soon reached 600 subscribers, and McCabe's agents solicited pioneers
throughout the South and West.[48] McCabe appealed to African Americans to
better their condition by escaping the terror and lawlessness of the South and
by settling on the fertile plains of Oklahoma. "How long, oh! How long will
the thrifty people of our race put up with the treatment they receive in many,
and, in fact, most parts of the South?" the *Langston City Herald* asked in
1891. "Why not come to Oklahoma, where are peace, happiness, and prosperity, coupled with the best of all blessings, absolute political liberty?"[49]

Langston, Oklahoma, embodied the spirit of Black racial solidarity and
uplift that inspired both William S. Crowdy and, in another generation, the
poet Langston Hughes. McCabe named the new township after John Mercer
Langston, a Black Congressman from Virginia and Howard University professor whose brother had been a prominent member of the Black community
of Lawrence, Kansas, in the 1870s. Congressman Langston's niece Carrie
Mercer Langston grew up in Lawrence, but moved to Guthrie sometime
between 1895 and 1899, where she taught school. It was there that she met
James Nathaniel Hughes, a storekeeper in nearby Langston. They named their
first and only child after her famously high-achieving family—as well as after
the exciting, militant new all-Black town where they met.[50]

Like Langston Hughes and William S. Crowdy, McCabe and his newspaper
dedicated themselves to the betterment of the race. In the 1890s, Langston,
Oklahoma, received national attention as the center of McCabe's ambitions to
create a majority-Black state and as a magnet for the ire of white residents who
feared a flood of Black immigrants. McCabe located his Afro-American Colonization Company in Guthrie, and became the state's only Black elected official
when he became treasurer of Guthrie County.[51] McCabe set about trying to
settle large numbers of Black settlers throughout the state in support of his personal ambition to be elected governor of a majority-Black state (fig.1.1). He

even traveled to Washington, D.C. in order to try and convince President Benjamin Harrison of the merits of settling Blacks in the Unassigned Lands of Indian Territory, arguing that such an arrangement would provide them the chance to prove their capability for self-governance as well as social and economic advancement.[52] Meanwhile, white residents panicked as the coaches of the Santa Fe railroad disgorged new Black settlers with all their possessions at the Guthrie station. Whites spread rumors that they were about to be inundated by thousands of poor Southern Blacks, and whites threatened McCabe with assassination should he be named governor.[53]

FIGURE 1.1 Edwin P. McCabe, promoter of Black settlement in Kansas and Oklahoma. Kansas State Historical Society.

Nevertheless, McCabe was nothing if not persistent, and he used scriptural references and providential promises to sell his new "Promised Land." Under the heading of "NEVER! We cannot ignore the needs of our race," the *Herald* wrote: "The Negro must go forward or backward; he cannot stand still." The purpose of the Langston settlement was to help African Americans "shake off the fetters that bind them. To help them to be free men and women in reality instead of in name only. . . . We know that it will be of untold value to the race if those who are prepared to do so can be induced to come here and secure these lands." Oklahoma promised "more freedom, more money, a better education for your children and a better and more comfortable home for your beloved wife." It was a land where "your future will be just what you make it; a land where you can 'sit under your own vine and fig tree,' and where white caps, kuklux and night raiders are unknown; a land where you can better yourself socially, intellectually, and financially."[54]

Black railroad employees carried McCabe's paper and promotional circulars along the route of the Santa Fe, where they would have come to the attention of William Saunders Crowdy, who worked in a Santa Fe Railroad employee hotel in Kansas City. Around 1891 Crowdy joined McCabe at

Langston, where he purchased 100 acres of farmland. Despite the fact that McCabe's *Langston City Herald* featured fanciful pictures of tall buildings and broad avenues, most residents lived in small wooden shacks or tents surrounding one general store.[55] McCabe's paper, meanwhile, proclaimed in 1892 that the land in Langston's red soil was "as fertile as ever was moistened by nature's falling tears, or kissed by heaven's sunshine." Farmers planted corn, castor beans, oats, wheat, cotton, fruits, vegetables, and tobacco around Langston, but cotton soon gained preeminence.[56] As early as 1895, *Langston Herald* editor R. Emmett Stewart billed the town as "the cotton belt center of Oklahoma," and others predicted that Langston was destined to become "one of the garden spots of Oklahoma."[57] The same year the paper trumpeted a farmer whose corn stalks were "almost large enough for house logs."[58]

In reality, the environment of the Great Plains was capricious and the cotton economy fickle.[59] With little capital and too much riding on a single cash crop, the fortunes of the Black towns rose, but then mostly fell with the price of cotton on global commodity markets as the entry of cotton from new producers in India and Egypt depressed prices. Life in Langston was difficult and bore little resemblance to the images painted by McCabe and his boosters. In 1891, the year Langston's population peaked, there were 200 people living there and a total of 2,000 in the surrounding countryside, some with inadequate means of support and few possessions. Yet Oklahoma's Black pioneers brought with them prior experiences of homesteading in Kansas, and the community sustained itself with cooperative economic practices. Many of Langston settlers brought some assets with them. "We did not come here as paupers," one proudly told a white reporter. Those who did not have a means of supporting themselves were housed in a communal storeroom.[60] The community also plowed eighty-three acres as a communal garden for those who did not have plots of their own, and it was common for multiple Black families to share the same plots while they waited for additional lands to be opened up to non-Indian settlement. In particular, the townspeople hoped to claim the lands of the Iowa Indians, to the east.

By 1900, Langston's population had fallen to 300, where it stayed until the end of the Great Depression. Although its Black town peers like Boley and Clearwater did not survive the impact of the cotton depression of 1913 and 1914, Langston avoided extinction thanks to its Colored Agricultural and Normal University, a segregated public institution founded in 1897 with support from Oklahoma, the Federal government, and Julius Rosenwald, the Jewish department store magnate whose funds supported Black educational institutions throughout the nation. In the mold of Booker T. Washington's

Tuskegee Institute, the Langston university's mission was to train teachers and to give instruction in industrial arts and agricultural occupations.[61]

Despite their difficulties, the Black towns of Oklahoma provided a unique haven for African Americans in an era when racial discrimination and racial violence were increasing. Oklahoma boasted twenty-eight Black towns when it became a state in 1907, more than all of the other western states combined. These places commonly featured bustling downtowns catering to residents of the town and its environs, with many Black-owned businesses, solid bank buildings, and dozens of churches, fraternal, and benevolent societies. Although Blacks had no control over county politics and spending priorities, all-Black town councils ran the towns themselves, and the justices of the peace were likewise African American. All-Black towns frequently included a few white merchants and some Native Americans, but the town elders, bankers, lawyers, doctors, ministers, farmers, and laborers, and almost all of its residents, were commonly African American.

The composition of Black towns and the independence of their residents gave Black town residents a tremendous psychological boost. In its first year as a settlement, Langston boasted 200 residents, "and not a white face is to be found in the place," according to the *New York Times*. Black carpenters and masons built Langston's buildings, and the town had a Black doctor, a Black preacher, and a Black schoolteacher.[62] "Each day the community blanketed individuals with a sense of well-being," writes historian Norman L. Crockett, "and some who were born and grew up there became addicted to the environment."[63] The air of liberty must have felt especially sweet in the lungs of the many middle-aged men and women, like William S. Crowdy, who had grown up in servitude in the South and spent their lives in domestic service. One Southerner remarked that whereas in the South he had to even call small poor white boys "Mister," in Langston "no matter how little you be here, you can still be a man."[64] In 1894, Langston billed itself as "the negro's refuge from lynching, burning at the stake and other lawlessness."[65] Black towns like Langston were sanctuaries and parallel universes where Blacks owned land, ran governments, farmed, steered businesses, and taught in the schools in an era better known for the erosion of Black civil liberties and the escalation of lynching.

Even though it was evident by the turn of the century that white resistance and Black reticence meant that there would not be enough Black settlers to make the vision of a Black majority state a reality, the tumultuous and conflict-ridden years of the early 1890s provided a stirring backdrop for what many hoped would be a new epoch in Black history. Booker T. Washington visited Black towns in Oklahoma in the first years of the twentieth century and wrote: "The Negro towns that have sprung up represent a dawning of race consciousness, a wholesome desire to do something to make the race respected: something which shall demonstrate the right of the Negro, not merely as an individual but as a race, to have a worth and permanent place in the civilization that the American people are creating."[66] The Oklahoma Territory's Black towns were filled with racially conscious, progressive-minded citizens whose towns were bold social experiments on the American plains. It was certainly appropriate, and perhaps even necessary, for Langston resident William Saunders Crowdy to have the vision that the ancient Hebrew Israelites were Black when he was part of a society in which almost all members of the community, all professionals, and all authority figures were Black. Early settlers of the Black town of Boley sang, "Be courageous brother, and forget the past—the great and mighty problem of race has been solved at last."[67] Rather than forget the past, Crowdy's new church refigured the past, solving "the great and mighty problem of race" by making African Americans into the descendants of the ancient Israelites, and creating an inclusive anti-racialist church that accepted members regardless of race.

Crowdy was an admirer of Booker T. Washington, and he viewed his religious work as part of the progress of the race. Not only would he establish businesses and industrial training centers, in the mold of the Wizard of Tuskegee, but also his followers explicitly understood him to be following in the footsteps of Washington. In the early twentieth century a follower of Crowdy's wrote that it had been declared that "no one man could lead this obstinate race to success and prosperity," and that many had refused to follow the lead of Booker T. Washington. "The general situation was very perplexing and it looked as though the race would go heedlessly onward without no one brave and courageous enough to come forth and point out the true way to its salvation," he declared, before the "All-Wise God" sent Crowdy.[68] As a Civil War veteran who had been born into slavery and sought a better life throughout the Midwest, the middle-aged Crowdy was a respected elder, a husband, father, farmer, Mason, and an exemplar of the best of his race and his generation. Crowdy was a leader of his church and Masonic lodge, and part of a small leadership class of decision makers that would have included a few lawyers, teachers, ministers, physicians, and white-collar workers.[69]

Crowdy was also part of a general religious ferment that accompanied the expansion of Black communities onto the wide-open plains, where established Black churches struggled to minister to these new communities. Black churches played a prominent role in the life of Oklahoma's all-Black towns in the 1890s—Baptists made up roughly two-thirds of Oklahoma's Black churchgoers, with the remaining third divided between the African Methodist Episcopal and Colored Methodist Episcopal churches.[70] Crowdy himself joined a local Baptist church and became a deacon. Other churches that bought lots in Langston included the Church of Christ, a Colored Methodist Episcopal church, a Presbyterian church, the African Methodist Episcopal Church, New Hope Baptist church, the Oklahoma Missionary Baptist Church, and the Baptist Foundation of Oklahoma.[71] Despite its presence in Langston, the venerable African Methodist Episcopal (A.M.E.) church struggled to keep up with new Black settlement on the western frontier in the 1890s, just as it would struggle to keep up with Black migration to the North twenty years later.[72] From his base in Wichita, Kansas, the superintendent of the A.M.E. church's Oklahoma district fretted that his church lacked the resources to tend to this new field:

> I cannot say much for it and yet our heroes have stood their ground and held the fort. But what can we do to build up a church without money to even support those who are preaching the gospel after walking ten or fifteen miles for the privilege? We have lots offered us in new cities just for the consideration that we will build the house. What can we do? My men are without means of support or clothing for their families. I don't know that we will be able to hold them much longer; other people have offered them churches and support if they will only bearing (sic) over their people. This is a problem for us to solve now. We have no means of extending our church in new territories.[73]

There was no lack of religiosity among frontier farmers—if their faith had not been strong before, droughts and fierce winds ensured plenty of opportunities to beseech the heavens—but the financial struggles of professional preachers on the hardscrabble frontier left room for a great number of independent religious voices. Most Black towns in Oklahoma contained a surplus of independent-minded men of faith and aspiring ministers, in addition to those of the established churches. A minister writing in the Philadelphia-based A.M.E. newspaper, the *Christian Recorder*, prayed in 1895: "May the Lord help some more live and active men to come to Oklahoma and wheel in line with us. We do not want any more broken down, unacceptable preachers. We have had enough of them, but good workers, filled with the Holy Ghost. This class of preachers are in demand. God help them to come."[74] There was such a glut of religious-minded men in Langston in 1893 that the town's newspaper editor,

Lee J. Merriweather, called "the preaching plague" one of the major impediments to racial progress, adding that many turned to it "to avoid hard work." He urged young men to consider becoming businessmen rather than schoolteachers and preachers, "for the world is getting full of them."[75] Perhaps Merriweather was thinking of Crowdy, who took up preaching in Langston the prior year, but Crowdy came by his religious inspiration honestly, not by shirking work but by actively engaging in manual labor.

Crowdy was tormented by voices in his head for a number of years, voices that frightened him, commanded him to follow their instructions, and threatened him if he disobeyed. According to his granddaughter, "it was many years before he learned that the voice was not of his imagination but actually the voice of God speaking to him."[76] In 1892, almost three decades after the end of the Civil War, the forty-six-year-old Crowdy began to "act strangely." In that year the voices and visions became more coherent and more compelling. His behavior became distant and erratic. He often didn't know when people were talking to him, but would sit staring into space for long periods of time. Sometimes his lips moved but no sounds came out, causing his wife to accuse him of drinking while she was not home and to forbid him from attending his Masonic meetings.[77]

Crowdy was not inebriated, however, and had not attended his lodge meetings for some time; rather, he understood himself to be hearing a voice of God telling him to establish "the true church." Like many residents of western all-Black towns, Crowdy probably lived in town but farmed land in the surrounding countryside.[78] Crowdy's divine communications peaked when he was in his fields clearing ground for a new crop on September 13, 1892, and heard a voice telling him to run for his life. He fled into the forest, marking the trees with his mattock as he fled so that others could find his body, convinced he would not survive the experience. In the woods he fell into a deep sleep and dreamt he was in a large room with several dirty tables descending from above, each inscribed with the name of an established church and covered in filth and vomit. The largest of these was labeled "Baptist." Then, a small, clean table came down with the words: "Church of God and Saints of Christ." Later in the vision, Crowdy received a set of rules, which became known as the Seven Keys and formed the foundation of a new church based on both the Old and New Testaments. In the final part of the vision, Crowdy was given a book, which he ate, in reference to Revelation 10:10.[79] The book contained the "Seven Keys," or revelations of the Holy Bible, which included a ban on wine, ritual foot washing, and a version of the Eucharist (or Lord's Supper), a "holy kiss" greeting, and strict adherence to the Ten

Commandments.[80] At its start, the Church of God and Saints of Christ adopted practices that had gained favor among Holiness churches of the Great Plains.[81] Adopting Hebraic practices did not mean rejecting the language of Christianity, at least initially. The Seven Keys were the plan of salvation, "and if they searched the scriptures according to its direction they would not go astray and their blinding eyes would be opened to the marvelous light of the gospel of Jesus Christ," Crowdy taught.[82]

Crowdy began preaching in the streets of Guthrie and surrounding towns, and was amazed by his own knowledge and ability to communicate his vision of the true church. He began by baptizing his family and other individuals, but there is truth in the saying that no man is a prophet in his hometown. With the new gift of prophecy, Crowdy felt compelled to leave Langston to spread the news. His wife Lovey was not pleased, and made him take along his young son, Isaac, to make sure that he was not running away with another woman, according to family lore. Lovey felt that Crowdy "ought to be working and taking care of his family," in Isaac's recollection.[83] Crowdy, however, heard a higher calling, and like the biblical patriarch Abraham, he set off with his son Isaac, traveling the dusty towns of the Southwest on horseback, spreading his religious vision. He would travel all over the United States, but never return to his home in Oklahoma.[84]

If it is true that no man is a prophet in his hometown, it is equally true that a man is not necessarily a prophet away from home, either. In the account left by Crowdy's granddaughter, the would-be prophet was arrested or held for examination of sanity twenty-two times in western cities and towns. Cowboys made a sport of abusing the eccentric itinerant preacher. In one town, Crowdy related, his harassers beat him, bound him, and wrapped him in the fresh hide of a recently killed buffalo, abandoning him in the wilderness for the buzzards to finish off. Initially he was able to shoo them away, but as he grew dehydrated in the hot sun, his tongue stuck to the roof of his mouth and he grew so hoarse that he could barely speak. The buzzards, sensing his feebleness and proximity to death, edged ever closer, appraising him with their red heads, viciously curved beaks, and cold-blooded eyes, filled with avian cunning as old as the dinosaurs. When it looked as if the prophet was done for, his son Isaac arrived with others to rescue his father, saving him from gruesome vivisection by buzzard.[85] In Crowdy's case, it was the erstwhile Abraham, and not his son Isaac, who found himself bound in the wilderness while attempting to fulfill his Lord's will.

In another town, cowboys made him stand on a box and forced him to "dance" by shooting at his feet. The box he was standing probably was the pulpit from which he preached. In a different town, the locals promised to kill him if he returned. He came back the next night anyway, stood outside a Jewish-owned dry goods store, and asked the owner for a dry-goods box to stand on. The man refused, not wanting a murder to occur outside his store, but Prophet Crowdy insisted on preaching anyway, entering a trance-like state: "the Lord touched him and he started preaching and had forgotten about everything."[86] Fortunately for Crowdy, his ability to reach his audience had improved through the adversity he suffered. Awakening from his reverie, he looked up and found his tormentors assembled, but their guns pointing at the ground. The leader walked up to him, shook his hand, and said that nobody had better fire a shot. Then the leader of the posse passed the hat and made his comrades contribute to the cause. Crowdy's preaching gifts sprang him from jail in another instance, when he had been held for insanity. "The Spirit came upon him" and he began to preach. Finishing, he asked, "Do I talk like an insane man?" and his captors answered "No, sir!" and quickly released him. These stories of frontier preaching exploits are uncorroborated, and perhaps exaggerated, but informative nonetheless.

It is interesting to note how these stories of Crowdy's tribulations and humbling, preserved by his family and followers, functioned to establish his religious authority. Crowdy's sufferings were like those of Daniel in the lion's den or the ancient Christian martyrs killed for sport by cruel pagans. Following the Lord's commandment to found the "true church," Crowdy risked his life time and again by facing down his tormentors and preaching interpretations of scripture that he knew could get him killed. The stories that Crowdy preserved and passed on to his followers show that biblical narratives informed his actions. For example, as others have noted, his original vision of vomit-covered tables refers to Isaiah 28:8, "For all tables are full of vomit and filthiness, so that there is no place clean."[87] The story of the buzzards echoes the binding of Isaac. Like various passages of the New Testament that say that Mosaic law was completed and surpassed by Jesus' life and revelation, the story about Crowdy preaching outside the Jew's dry-goods store could be read to suggest that Crowdy had supplanted contemporary Jews.[88] German Jews and some central and eastern European Jews had a small but visible presence as peddlers, traders, and merchants in many of the towns of the South, West, and Southwest in the nineteenth century. Among residents of Oklahoma's Black towns they had a reputation as perceptive, sinister, and untrustworthy, and it was commonly assumed that they controlled the country's money supply. Yet, because Jews lacked a permanent home and were persecuted wherever they went, Blacks frequently pointed to parallels between their respective experiences. According to historian Norman Crockett, "although disliked, Jews had to be respected, and residents were told that Blacks might do well to follow their economic example."[89] Newspaper editors in the Black towns of Langston, Boley, and Clearview scolded their readers for fretting about the plight of their race when they should follow the Jewish example and increase their wealth, character, and prestige.

Through western trials, Crowdy developed into a rousing preacher and an expert evangelist. He stirred his listeners especially with the teaching that Jesus Christ was Black. Yet Crowdy's message was at heart anti-racialist, and the great majority of his earliest converts were white. Crowdy always kept moving, baptizing a crowd of converts or washing the feet of those who had been previously baptized and appointing one of them as elder in charge of the congregation.[90] The anti-racism of the Church of God and Saints of Christ is remarkable, given the rise of Jim Crow segregation and racist terror in the same era. Not only were Black and white people washing each other's feet, violating taboos against intimate contact between the races, but they also were together worshiping a Black Christ. After three years, twenty-two arrests, and untold beatings in the wilderness of Texas and the Southwest, the prophet continued on north to Kansas, while his son returned to Oklahoma.

Crowdy now called himself the "World's Evangelist," and he kept up a frantic pace, staying just long enough in each place to set up a new tabernacle and designate a leader. Crowdy organized and incorporated the Church of God and Saints of Christ and established his first three tabernacles in Lawrence, Emporia, and Topeka, Kansas, in 1896. The work spread quickly thanks to Crowdy's evangelical gifts, the mobility afforded him by the railroad, and the eagerness of religiously inclined people to hear his message—as well as his message's consonance with the Baptist and Holiness movements. Crowdy's message also transcended racial categories. His first bishop, consecrated in 1897, was a white grocer from Topeka named J. M. Groves, who was attracted to the evangelist's meetings in the streets of Topeka, where he would preach, sing, and calls souls to repentance. Groves, perhaps like others who were attracted to Crowdy's message, was already a sabbatarian—he closed his shop on Saturdays and opened on Sundays, despite his wife's objection. Attracted by Crowdy's message, Groves went to witness Crowdy baptize his new followers, and sat on a hillside overlooking the water. Before he began, the prophet spied Groves, beckoned to him, and told him to put on a robe. Groves became the first to be baptized, and hence was the first member of the Topeka church.[91] Prophet Crowdy left Topeka by train, heading to Lawrence, Kansas, fifty miles east, and Groves gave him a few dollars for his journey. Amazed by the fact that the train made an unscheduled stop to pick up the evangelist on a Sunday, Groves was convinced that the itinerant preacher was truly a prophet of God.[92]

Kansas in the 1890s was a far cry from the battlefield of thirty and forty years before, but it boasted the only five northern cities in the nineteenth century that were more than 10 percent African American—Atchison, Leavenworth, Lawrence, Topeka, and Kansas City. In fact, at 26 percent, Topeka's Black population in 1880 was only one percentage point less than that of New Orleans.[93] In nearby Lawrence, thirty years after the first Black settlement, the "colored" population had increased to 2,155 at the start of the 1890s, more than a fifth of the total population of 9,997.[94] Topeka had a higher percentage of Black residents than did contemporary St. Louis, Baltimore, or Biloxi, Mississippi.[95] In religious terms, there were 4,920 religious bodies in the state in 1890, with the preponderance of these being mainline Protestant churches, primarily Methodists and secondarily Baptists.[96]

In Lawrence, Crowdy began preaching on a street corner, as was his custom, speaking from the corner of Eighth Street and Massachusetts Avenue, Lawrence's main thoroughfare, named in honor of the birthplace of many of the town's abolitionist founders. He soon converted and baptized a growing crowd of followers, and he founded his first congregation, which he called a "tabernacle," in Lawrence on November 5, 1896.[97] Crowdy took his Texas-tested, Kansas-approved message to Chicago later the same year. He preached to motley assemblages of passersby on the streets, most often without any prepared text but through divine inspiration alone, as God had told the Prophet Ezekiel to "open his mouth" and let God supply the words.[98] The denizens of the burgeoning industrial city of Chicago were no more receptive to his theological unorthodoxy and message of racial justice than were the cowpokes of Texas. Sometimes he found an appreciative audience, but more often his jeremiads burned "like vitriolic acid," in his own words.[99] The hostile crowds would sometimes drop stones in his hat when he took up a collection, leaving him without funds to pay for food or shelter. Although he was not physically harmed in Chicago, as he had been in Texas, his suffering was even greater. Unable to pay for food, he once fasted for four days and nights, sickening himself to the point that he had to be hospitalized for six weeks. The prophet understood his illness as the Lord's punishment for not preaching His Word correctly, and he promised to mend his ways so that he would not invite such hostility from the masses. During his time in the hospital, his hair turned snow white, which only added to his imposing prophetic gravitas.[100] Returning to his preaching duties on Chicago's State Street, the prophet met an Irishman whom he reported as being so drunk that he could barely stand straight. The man listened to Crowdy's sermon, observed how he was harassed, and then told him "Old man, there is no mistake that you have the gospel, and if you were organized they wouldn't arrest you so much." This got Crowdy's attention. "Go back and get some of your people to ordain you as Bishop," the man advised.[101]

Taking the spectator's advice, Crowdy returned to Kansas in 1897 and held a large convention in Lawrence. He baptized many people and preached from Luke 6:46—"And why call ye me, Lord, Lord, and do not the things which I say?" The success of this meeting in Lawrence catalyzed the spread of the church in twenty-seven nearby towns—Emporia, Topeka, Strong City, Lawrence, Florence, Peabody, Newton, Wichita, Enterprise, Abilene, Salina, Ottawa, Chanute, Valley Falls, Osage City, Atchinson, Leavenworth, Garden City, Wamego, Coffeyville, Arkansas City, Junction City, Larned, Manhattan, Dodge City, Girard, and Lyons. Crowdy achieved some success in creating a biracial church among the children of the abolitionists and "free-soilers" who had fought the spread of slavery in the West.[102]

After another brief sojourn in Chicago, Crowdy returned to Topeka, laid hands on Groves, and consecrated him his first assistant bishop. The following day, Crowdy selected twelve elders, including Assistant Bishop Groves, to anoint Crowdy with oil and consecrate him as bishop, and then he made Groves a bishop, as well (see fig. 1.2).[103] The rapidly growing organization held its first annual general assembly in Emporia, Kansas, on June 24, 1898, and celebrated its first Passover in Lawrence on October 10, 1899, by which time there were twenty-three tabernacles in the state of Kansas alone, overseen by eight bishops, all of whom were Black men, with the exception of Groves.[104] Black newspapers reported that the church insisted upon complete racial integration and attracted intelligent and respected members of both white and Black communities. In so doing, "they are a conglomeration such as probably was never before amalgamated in any one religious body, at least in America," the press reported. "The color line is totally obliterated." The members of different races "fraternize and meet in a perfect equality and sociability."[105] Contemporaries viewed it as especially remarkable that the church mandated personal contact between whites and Blacks in such ritual actions as the washing of feet and the transmission of the Holy Spirit through a kiss. Crowdy's followers took great pride in their integration, and even claimed to be doing more to achieve integration in the United States than any other organization.[106] Yet they were practicing racial integration in a manner common to many other Holiness churches, as we will

FIGURE 1.2 Bishop Crowdy, seated, second from left, with his Presbytery Board in 1899. Bishop J. M. Groves is seated at the far right. Kansas State Historical Society.

see in subsequent chapters, during a decade that saw interracial Christian fellowship as well as horrific racial violence.

It was there in Lawrence in 1899 that Crowdy presented the church with a formal constitution, whose preamble contained a slightly modified version of the Seven Keys that he had received in his original vision in 1892. It is worth considering the changes Crowdy had made in the intervening years. Whereas the First Key had been the name of the church itself, found in First Corinthians 1:12, the first one later became "repentance of sin." The second key, which had been total abstention from alcohol, later became baptism "by burial in water." The other keys remained the same, except that the fifth and the seventh were transposed, so that keeping the commandments came before the holy kiss and the disciple's prayer. Temperance and Prohibition were active causes among Christians in Oklahoma's Black towns of the 1890s. The fact that Crowdy's wife had accused him of drinking too much when he first started receiving divine communications and the fact that his second tenet of faith initially was total abstention of wine suggests that Crowdy himself might have struggled with alcohol. Crowdy taught that Christians should abstain from wine and spirits.[107] The church used water instead of wine for the Lord's Supper. "There is no life promised us in drinking wine, but there is a life promised us in drinking water," Crowdy taught, citing a number of verses.[108] Keeping the Ten Commandments became keeping the commandments, of unspecified number, and jumped from number seven to five on the list, which may have reflected the fact that observing the Mosaic laws of the Hebrew Bible had become more important to Crowdy and his followers. It certainly foreshadowed the gradual adoption of Judaic rituals in the Church of God and Saints of Christ.[109] Although the New Testament contains a number of passages that emphasize the "completion" of the laws of the Hebrew Bible, it contains almost as many that stress the need to keep the older commandments. In Jesus' epochal Sermon on the Mount, he says that he has not come to destroy the law or the prophets, but to fulfill them, vowing that "Till heaven and earth pass, one jot or one tittle shall in no wise pass from the law, till all be fulfilled." Therefore, Jesus taught, whoever broke the most minor commandment imperiled his or her place in heaven (Matthew 5:17–19, 1 John 2:4).[110]

Crowdy knew the Bible forward and backward, and his published teachings are packed with references to the Gospels and Hebrew scriptures. He was adamant that God wanted the Sabbath to be observed on Saturday, the seventh day, and used dozens of scriptural references to establish that God commanded a day of rest on Saturday, and that Jesus and his disciples observed the seventh-day Sabbath.[111] He also established that Jesus taught foot-washing as a commandment, and he made it a central part of the baptisms he performed for new members.[112] People who wanted to join also had to receive the "holy kiss" from a minister, and they had to learn the Lord's Prayer, which he called the Disciples' Prayer.[113] "Religion is not to get but it is a duty," the prophet wrote. "It is something to do all the time."[114]

Crowdy was fond of quoting the New Testament on the necessity of keeping the commandments, and indeed, his church acquired more Hebraic practices over the course of the next four decades.[115] As early as 1898, he was harassed in Chicago for teaching that Jesus was Black and for teaching dietary laws regarding meat. Prophet Crowdy believed that African Americans were descended from the ten lost tribes of Israel, and accordingly added Old Testament rites to Christian practices. By 1906, the church was observing the Jewish calendar and feast days, observing the Sabbath on Saturday, and using some Hebrew. They put special emphasis on a week-long observance of Passover, even going so far as to smear their doors with blood in commemoration of the biblical story that the Angel of Death passed over the homes of the Israelites while killing the first-born sons of the Egyptians as the culmination of the plagues that God sent to free the Israelites from Egypt. In Chicago, Crowdy became known as "the Black Elijah," and outsiders called his followers "Black Jews."[116]

Yet, importantly, one did not have to leave Christianity, abandon faith in Jesus, or give up familiar rituals like baptism and foot washing to become a follower of Crowdy, or a "Black Jew." Rather, Black Israelite identity and practice were additive, combining new rituals like the Passover meal and new dietary taboos with familiar Christian practices. Although the Church of God and Saints of Christ (COGASOC) took on the practices of biblical Judaism based on the Old Testament, the ritual was not based on any knowledge of contemporary Jewish ritual, which derives from the centuries of oral law created after the First Temple was destroyed.[117] In addition, the church retained important elements of Christianity: new members had to repent for their sins, be baptized by immersion, confess faith in Jesus, and receive unleavened bread and water as a sacrament. As the decades progressed, the Church of God and Saints of Christ gradually deemphasized the divinity of Jesus, so that today the COGASOC teaches that Jesus was a Hebrew prophet, not the messiah. A contemporary member says, "We believe in his [Jesus'] teachings and his way of life because his religion was of the Patriarchs. . . . There was nothing Christian about Jesus."[118] Over time, some versions of the Church of God and Saints of Christ adopted more and more Judaic rituals, so that today their followers understand themselves as Jews and practitioners of Judaism, and view Jesus as a prophet rather than a savior.[119]

Between 1896 and Crowdy's death in 1908, the church solidified into a formal organization, as Crowdy proselytized and composed a series of sermons that became known as his epistles. The most extraordinary of these is the sermon delivered at Lawrence, Kansas, in 1903, urging his followers never to cease in their battle against all forms of racial discrimination.[120] Of the three eminent personalities connected to Langston, Oklahoma, Crowdy may have been a religious prophet, E. P. McCabe a political and journalistic organizer, and Langston Hughes a poet and playwright, but their stories intertwined in eastern Oklahoma and Kansas, and they all shared a similar passion for ameliorating the condition of the Black race.

The independent African American spirit bred on the Great Plains in the last quarter of the nineteenth century spread to the North and Northeast with the start of the new century as Black westerners like Bishop William Saunders Crowdy and later artists such as Hughes, Aaron Douglas, Gwendolyn Brooks, Oscar Micheaux, Wallace Thurman, and Coleman Hawkins picked up and moved from Kansas and other Western locales to the burgeoning cities of Chicago and Harlem. Not long after his church's first general assembly in Emporia, Kansas, on June 24, 1898, Crowdy headed to Chicago, arriving in the fall and reviving the work that he had begun a few years earlier. The Church of God and Saints of Christ grew in Chicago, and again Crowdy placed a white man, Xavier Schneider, at the head of the local branch. The prophet also attracted the attention of newspaper reporters, who spread the news of this eccentric man who preached racial equality and fidelity to the Old Testament. Around this time, Crowdy had a vision in a dream in which the Lord revealed two women who would help him get to New York. About the same time, George Labiel, an African American resident of Oneida, New York, who was light enough to pass for white, read about Crowdy and discussed the unusual prophet with his neighbor, Mrs. Titus. Oneida was the site of a utopian commune and major center for Seventh Day Adventists, who believed in adhering to the Mosaic laws, as Crowdy advocated. It was also a region of such great religious enthusiasm that it had gained the sobriquet "the Burned Over District" for the intensity of the numerous religious revivals that had burned through the land in the eighteenth and nineteenth centuries. This was the region that had spawned Joseph Smith and the most famous American Israelite religion, Mormonism. Like many devout people, Mrs. Titus considered herself to be a follower of no religious denomination, declaring that she belonged to God, not to any church. Together Titus and Labiel wrote to Crowdy, inviting him to visit Oneida and sending him train fare for the journey. Not one to miss an opportunity to spread the gospel, the prophet took a circuitous route east, stopping and seeding new churches in Detroit, Armhurstburg (Ontario), and Syracuse, arriving in Oneida in March of 1899.[121]

According to the account recorded by Crowdy's family, the prophet's arrival from the West created a buzz among the Adventists and other curious citizens of this upstate New York hamlet. Adventists posted notices with press reports of Crowdy's sermons, and when the day of his sermon finally arrived, it was like "opening day at the fair," in the words of Mrs. Titus's daughter, Flora Walker. People came by foot and on horses, wagons and buggies from miles away, packing the streets around the meetinghouse and filling the building until it was overflowing. Those who could not get inside hung around outside the doors, straining to hear. The meeting attracted common people and prominent citizens alike, including doctors, lawyers, and ministers. The walls of the hall were hung with passages of scripture, and Crowdy sat on the pulpit with several Adventist elders. When they asked him to speak, Crowdy politely declined and said he would rather hear what they had to say. When the Adventists had exhausted their ammunition against him in trying to refute the things that they had read about his teachings, he finally took the podium. Summoning the spiritual strength gained from years of suffering and hard-won preaching expertise, the imposing, white-haired fifty-two-year-old prophet commanded the attention of the expectant crowd with his silence, and then quietly stated the simple first key of his sevenfold path to salvation: "Church of God and Saints of Christ." Immediately, Mrs. Titus jumped up, threw off her shawl and screamed, "That's it! That's my church, Church of God! I believe in God! Praise the Lord!" There was a great stir of excitement among the audience that only grew louder when the prophet looked at Titus and said, "That's the woman. That's the woman I saw [in my dream]." When the murmur died down, Crowdy preached, in his customary manner and in a low tone of voice. He interpreted each passage of scripture on the signs around the walls, one at a time, reading each one as a condemnation of the Seventh Day Adventists and their church. Then he preached a sermon unlike any his dumbfounded listeners had ever heard.

The meeting ended with much confusion and excitement, with some of his listeners allegedly plotting to kill Crowdy and others turning to him for baptism. The contrarian prophet, no doubt spent but elated, came down off the pulpit and sought out Mrs. Titus, telling her that the Lord had shown her to him in a dream. His new acolyte took him home, walking by his side to shield him from those who wanted to shoot him. When they arrived and met Titus's daughter, Flora, he immediately identified her as the other woman in the dream, who would help him spread the church in the East. Flora Walker reported that the whole time Crowdy was talking, she was thinking "You don't mean me because you are really too black for me, old man."[122] Yet Crowdy, like Father Divine thirty years later, had a charisma that knew no racial barriers. Flora Walker knew as time went on that "he was no ordinary man," because she did everything she could do to help and followed him everywhere, "even though he never appealed to her as a man."[123]

In fact, Crowdy had more success gaining white followers than Black ones in upstate New York, and he attracted followers of all races in the West. He baptized over sixty people in Oneida, almost all of whom were white. "Most of the members were white," said Sister Walker. "They accepted the Prophet quicker than colored people who said they couldn't do it."[124] Perhaps at the turn of the century the African Americans of the Northeast and Midwest were so invested in the politics of respectability that they did not look kindly on this frequently jailed religious eccentric, even though he preached racial equality. Perhaps in an era of racial segregation and appeals to racial self-reliance, religious fellowship with white neighbors held little appeal for the upwardly striving "colored" people who had invested so much in their own autonomous churches and institutions. It is also possible that Prophet Crowdy's baptisms offered whites absolution of their troubled consciousnesses for the horrors of slavery and the abandoned promises of Reconstruction, whereas Blacks derived little psychic benefit from following a former slave. "Our white brothers and sisters seemed quicker to acknowledge the right while we ourselves were slow to believe," one follower summarized.[125] The church was never exclusively white, however, and neither were its elders always men. In Utica, New York, Crowdy ordained former enslaved person Sister Elder Lavender and placed her at the head of a large congregation.[126]

Crowdy had more success among African Americans, however, in the big cities of the Northeast such as New York and Philadelphia, which suggests that even before the Great Migration of the 1930s, the experience of migration opened up new religious possibilities for African Americans who had left established churches and familiar places behind. From upstate New York, Crowdy journeyed through the state, baptizing members, ordaining one as elder, and moving on. Arriving in New York City, he collected and baptized more than a thousand members in a matter of months, organizing the largest church he had ever built on May 6, 1899, and placing it in the hands of Elder Mark Marsh. Using New York City as a base, he contacted and established followings in towns in the tri-state area of New York, New Jersey, and Connecticut.

Just as Crowdy had challenged the Adventists in upstate New York, the city offered new spiritual challenges in the form of a spiritualist who invited him to speak at one of her meetings. She made a special gown for the prophet, but when he put it on he felt uncomfortable and was unable to preach. The spirit told him to take off the gown, and when he disrobed in the antechamber, a huge black cat ran out from underneath a bed. Disturbed at the symbol of malicious witchcraft, the prophet returned to the meeting and demanded that the spiritualist shake his hand. She refused, saying that she was wearing gloves, but he demanded that she remove them and shake his hand, which she finally did. He then preached a sermon with great vigor, and it was said that from that day forward the woman lost her spiritual powers. Crowdy lived in an era where both conjuring and spiritualism had followings among African Americans. Although his own disturbance at the sight of the black cat suggests that superstitious beliefs held some purchase on him, he presented his own gifts as an antidote to such practices.[127]

In May 1899 Crowdy moved on to Philadelphia, which was temporarily to become his national headquarters, and then returned to Lawrence, Kansas, for the assembly of the Church of God and Saints of Christ in October 1899. He brought with him some of his eastern ministers to testify to the extraordinary accomplishments in his year in the East. The 1899 Lawrence convention included representatives from twelve states and one Canadian province: Kansas, Illinois, New York, New Jersey, Missouri, Pennsylvania, Maryland, Texas, Colorado, Virginia, Nebraska, Michigan, and Ontario. The organization was truly national in its ambition: in addition to those states represented among the attendees, the conventioneers created four districts covering New England, the Midwest, the upper and lower South, and the states of the Mountain West and Pacific Coast. Article X of the church's constitution honored Crowdy as the "Elder Bishop" of the church and "empowered" him to travel as "Evangelist for the World as well as Prophet." The speed with which the church grew suggests that Crowdy's message was well suited to the spirit of the times. The Church of God and Saints of Christ was a collaborative effort that had to build on the prior religious beliefs, life experiences, and aspirations of its members. It combined bold anti-racism and calls for Black empowerment with elements of Freemasonry and the Holiness movement, foot washing, biblical literalism, an intense interest in keeping the Mosaic laws, and the seventh-day Sabbath. The turn of the century found Crowdy directing the church from his home in Philadelphia, where Federal census takers noted his occupation as "Bishop of Church."[128] It was there in 1900 Philadelphia that Crowdy married for the third time, this time to Estella Crowdy, a twenty-one-year-old Black woman from New Jersey.[129] In the same year, in Philadelphia, the bishop introduced the custom of observing Thanksgiving with a free, all-you-can-eat, feast and introduced the observance of Passover with color-coordinated uniforms for men and women.[130]

By 1903, the church had 2,100 followers in Philadelphia, and had a number of businesses such as grocery, dry goods stores, a photography shop, barbershops, print shop, restaurants, wood, and coal stores.[131] In December of the same year, Crowdy resettled once more, this time in Washington, D.C., though he kept up a busy travel schedule. The future of the church, and of religious movements in Africa, shifted inalterably in 1903, when a thirty-five-year-old West Indian named Albert B. Christian left Port Elizabeth, South Africa, with his wife Eva for Philadelphia.[132] Though the church remembers Christian as a missionary worker, he listed his occupation as "seaman" when he entered the United States in 1903, and only reported himself as a "minister" three years later, when he again entered the country to rejoin his wife in Portsmouth, Virginia, and after his fateful encounter with Prophet Crowdy.[133]

According to the church's official history, Christian had originally jour-
neyed to Philadelphia because he had been troubled by dreams while still in
South Africa that featured Prophet Crowdy calling him and telling him that
God had plans for him. Christian left for Philadelphia, and came across
Prophet Crowdy sitting on a shoeshine stand in front of one of the church's
stores, on Fitzwater Street. In a scene that was reminiscent of Revelation
19:10, Christian ran up to him, fell down on his knees in front of him, and
Crowdy jumped down off the stand, saying, "See thou do it not. I am they
fellow servant and of thy brethren that have the testimony of Jesus. Worship
God for the testimony of Jesus is the Spirit of Prophecy."[134] In other words,
Bishop Crowdy and his followers could cite the Christian scriptures chapter
and verse; moreover, like other Holiness churches of the 1890s that we will
learn about in the next chapter, they saw themselves as reviving Hebraic rituals not to distance themselves from Christianity but to embrace the early
Christian church.

Albert Christian studied with Bishop Crowdy, and accepted his teachings. In the church's official history, he "learned of the true gospel of Jesus
Christ. He was baptized and embraced with the whole armor of God."[135]
Christian was ordained in Philadelphia and joined the Presbytery Board as an
evangelist, with the territory of Cape Colony, South Africa, as his dominion;
returning to South Africa, Christian amassed a congregation of thirty members (fig. 1.3).[136] He established a string of churches throughout the eastern
Cape and as far north as the Transvaal in the northeast of South Africa.[137]
Christian won an invitation to the General Assembly of the A.M.E. church at
Uitenhage, South Africa, in recognition of his accomplishments. When
Christian returned to the United States in 1906, he told stories of his many
harrowing escapes evading the authorities and their ban on travel in the Transvaal.[138] And so it was through the agency of a West Indian seaman and minister that the teachings of an African American prophet became popularized
on the African continent—a good illustration of both the transnationalism of
the Black Atlantic world and the fact that influences between Africa and the
Americas have flowed in all directions, in what anthropologist J. Lorand
Matory calls the "Black Atlantic Dialogue," not simply by way of a unidirec-
tional "diaspora" from African origins.[139]

By 1906, in addition to its small band of followers in South Africa,
Crowdy's Church of God and Saints of Christ had seven congregations in
New York State, with thirteen more in Massachusetts, Connecticut, Rhode
Island, Pennsylvania, and New Jersey.[140] In 1908, Crowdy and many of his
followers left Philadelphia in what they called "the Exodus" because of a

FIGURE 1.3 West Indian-born Albert Christian, who became COGASOC evangelist of Cape Colony, South Africa, in 1903, thereby influencing African-led churches in the twentieth century. James Landing papers, 1847–2001, box 4, folder 32, University of Illinois at Chicago Library, University Archives.

disease outbreak. They headed south, to Belleville in the Tidewater region of Virginia, not far from the Chesapeake Bay region where the prophet had been born, and he purchased a sizeable parcel of land that the church still owns. He died the same year, at the age of seventy.[141] With the prophet's passing, his church fractured between a western half led by Evangelist Abel S. Dickerson, and an eastern half led by his son, Chief Evangelist Joseph Crowdy. At Dickerson's urging, Bishop J. M. Groves brought a case to court in Philadelphia and was rewarded with the western churches. Chief Evangelist Crowdy agreed with the court's decision and recognized Groves as bishop of the West, but Dickerson dissented and split from Groves, taking a number of his churches. Groves remarried a woman who had not been a member of the Church of God and Saints of Christ. When an evangelist of the church found Bishop Groves as an old man in his nineties in the 1930s, the elderly bishop reported that his new wife "has never been able to see why I should be so interested in an organization of people mostly of another color of skin, but the hands of a Prophet had been laid on me and his mouth uttered words that

I must obey."[142] Groves faced much dissension, attempted and failed to reunify his churches under the eastern leadership, and very much regretted his role in splitting the church after Crowdy's death.[143]

At the time of Prophet Crowdy's passing, he had thousands of followers who accepted his teachings that Jesus, Moses, and the ancient Israelites were Black, and thereby opened the way for the Judaic, Islamic, and Rastafarian teachings that emerged among peoples of African descent in the subsequent thirty years. Crowdy's Church of God and Saints of Christ trained hundreds of ministers, some of whom went on to form their own groups, and provided a pool of thousands of followers open to religious ideas outside of established Christian churches. Two of Crowdy's followers deserve special recognition: one was Bishop Jesse B. Thornton, who teamed up with John G. Jones, the most prolific founder of so-called "bogus" or "irregular" Black Masonic lodges. The other, according to the church's own history, was Bishop Charles H. Mason, founder of the first and largest Black Pentecostal denomination, the Church of God in Christ, who carried Black Israelite ideas into that hallowed organization.[144] Not all of Crowdy's followers accepted the increasingly Judaic teachings of his successors in the decades after his death, and such disagreements led to a split in the 1930s between the more Judaic Belleville-based church and another branch based in Cleveland, which maintained more Christian beliefs.[145]

As we shall see in the following chapter, Prophet Crowdy's Church of God and Saints of Christ was part of the Holiness movement. Furthermore, it was one of the American Holiness, and later, Pentecostal churches, that helped to transform African religiosity and inspire the rise of over 6,000 African Initiated Churches (A.I.C.s) in the twentieth century. Frustrated by the gulf between European Christian missionaries' doctrines and their behavior, and perhaps looking for greater economic and political freedom, as well, Black South Africans had begun forming their own local independent churches in the 1880s.[146] In 1892, the formerly Wesleyan Reverend Mangena Mokone formed South Africa's first nationwide "Ethiopian" church in South Africa, the *Ibandla lase Tiyopiya*. The church affiliated itself with the Philadelphia-based African Methodist Episcopal Church in 1896, although schisms in 1900 and 1904 led to new African-headed denominations. By 1904, these African-headed churches claimed 25,000 members.[147] Perhaps the most important of the American influences was John Alexander Dowie's Christian Catholic Church in Zion, founded in Zion City, Illinois, in 1896, which installed its first official in South Africa in 1897 and had 5,000 members by 1905.[148] Dowie's "Zionist" churches practiced adult baptism by immersion in the name of the Trinity, divine healing, and a millennial belief that the return of Christ the messiah was imminent. Many subsequent A.I.C.s took the name "Zionist," and some combined the teachings of the Ethiopian and Zionist churches with Pentecostal speaking in tongues, introduced by American-based groups such as the Church of God, the Full Gospel, and the Apostolic Faith Mission.[149]

Many African Zionist churches identified with the Old Testament and practiced elements of Hebraic rituals.[150] Bishop Crowdy's Black Israelite rituals and beliefs found their way into the A.I.C. movement in general, and a few African Black Israelite churches in particular. Albert Christian's efforts to spread Crowdy's teachings found an ally in John Msikinya, a South African who had become a follower of the C.O.G.A.S.O.C. while attending college at the historically black Lincoln University in Philadelphia. Msikinya's theology was increasingly millenarian and politically radical, drawing the hostility of the Cape Colony government. Enoch Mgijima inherited leadership of the church upon Msikinya's death in 1918 and intensified the group's millennial and anti-colonial rhetoric, combining the Israelite teachings of the C.O.G.A.S.O.C. with spirit possession, Seventh-Day Adventism, and Christian millennialism. His prophecies led to a violent confrontation with the colonial state. Mgijima's followers, armed with clubs and spears, clashed with an 800-man police force armed with rifles and machine guns, resulting in 163 killed, 129 wounded, and 75 arrested in what became known as the Bulhoek Massacre.[151]

John Chilembwe, a Malawian minister from an African Zionist background, led an uprising against the British in 1913. Like Misinkya, he discovered Black Israelism during his time at Lincoln University in Pennsylvania, and converted it into a theology of resistance to British imperialism.[152] In 1935, a village in Rusape, in northeastern Zimbabwe, adopted William Saunders Crowdy's teachings, and today several thousand of their descendants practice what they call "prophetic Judaism" and worship in a Beth El Church of God and Saints of Christ (C.O.G.A.S.O.C).[153]

But Israelite ideas also spread throughout African Initiated Churches, not simply through the agency of Crowdy's Church of God and Saints of Christ. A number of African Initiated Churches have adopted elements of the Israelite creed and sometimes observance of the Passover holiday, such as the African Church of Israel and the African Remnant of Israel Church in Rhodesia, the Lost Israelites of Kenya, the Church of the Canaanites, which started in Durban, South Africa, in 1916, and the African Apostolic Church of John Maranke.[154] In another strand of Black Israelite movements, Semei Kakungulu, the founder of the Bayudaya Jewish community in Uganda, led the Buganda Kingdom in subduing neighboring tribes and cooperated with the British in hopes that they would recognize him as king. When the British refused to recognize Kakungulu, he became more supportive of the radical Zionist Protestant Bamalaki sect. Through meditation on the Old Testament and strict interpretation of its commandments, he declared himself a Jew in 1919, circumcised himself and his sons, and demanded that his followers do the same. In 1926, he learned the Hebrew alphabet and Jewish customs from a trader named Joseph, and renounced the New Testament and the divinity of Jesus.[155]

William Saunders Crowdy, the pioneering bishop who adopted Hebraic practices and assembled an interracial church in a time of unprecedented racist violence, was born a slave and died a prophet, with followers and legacies on two continents. He lived experiences common to his generation—slavery and liberation, migration and western homesteading, domestic work and racial uplift, Baptist worship and Masonic organization—while he and his church seemingly defied conventional wisdom in their teaching and practice. Yet both the identification with the ancient Israelites and the formation of interracial churches were common features of the Holiness movement of his era. The following chapter looks more deeply into the theology of those Americans, Black and white, who identified as Israelites at the turn of the twentieth century, as well as some of the surprising consequences of such beliefs.

# 2 "EQUIVALENT TO ISRAELISM"

## INHERITANCE, FREEMASONRY, AND THE ANCIENT ISRAELITES

The Liberian Black nationalist Edward Wilmot Blyden wrote in 1898 that "there is not, to my knowledge, a single synagogue in West Africa, along three thousand miles of coast, and probably not two dozen representatives of God's chosen people in that whole extent of country—not a Jewish institution of any kind—either for commercial, religious or educational purposes."[1] The famed Liberian minister's account would surprise twentieth-century African American Black Israelites, who told a very different story: that West Africans and their American descendants have common Israelite ancestors. Perhaps, they might suggest, Blyden simply did not recognize the chosen people.[2] Although Blyden's statement might have held true for Jews of Mediterranean descent along the coast of Africa in the nineteenth century, in fact the presence of such Jews in northern Africa had been noted since antiquity. Jews participated in West African trade, and even settled in small numbers on the West African coast in the early modern period.[3] The Roman historian Tacitus, who lived in the first century of the Common Era, suggested various possible origins for the Jewish people in Africa. He reported that some said their ancestors were the tribe of Idaei, from Mount Ida in Crete, and that they settled on the North African coast in ancient times. Another theory was that they spread from Egypt. Others described them as part of the Assyrian horde, while still others said they were part of the Solymi, "a nation celebrated in the poems of Homer." But the most popular theory placed ancient Jewish origins farther south, in Africa. "Many, again, say that they were a race of Æthiopian origin, who in the time of King Cepheus were driven by fear and hatred of their neighbors to seek a new dwelling-place."[4] What was a rumor in Tacitus's day is not much better known in our own.[5] Jews functioned as skilled workers and traders, and the oasis of Tafilalt, an outpost in the Moroccan Sahara along the trade route with western

Africa, became an important Jewish center before the Jews were expelled in 1050.[6] A series of Jewish explorers in the Middle Ages claimed to have found the Lost Tribes of Israel everywhere from India to Arabia to eastern Africa.[7] In the early sixteenth century, Leo Africanus documented similar Moroccan Jewish involvement with the trade with Timbuctu, and the following century found Portuguese Jewish traders living and cohabitating with natives along the coast of Guinea.[8] As Edith Bruder summarizes, "all of this plausibly suggests an uninterrupted chain of Jewish colonies up to the border of the Sahara, scattered from the Atlantic Ocean to the Libyan Desert, whose economic life and longevity depended at least in part on the trans-Saharan trade."[9]

In contrast to this sparse but available evidence of Jews of Mediterranean descent living in northern Africa and participating in the trade with western Africa, there is no reliable historical evidence of Jewish identification among indigenous peoples outside northern Africa before the twentieth century.[10] However, as Europeans began to colonize Africa, they repeatedly identified the indigenous customs they encountered as being in various ways "Jewish." The idea that peoples outside Europe represented a remnant of the Lost Tribes of Israel appears repeatedly in European explorations of India, Arabia, and Africa.[11] This pattern holds true especially in eastern and southern Africa, where Europeans variously proposed that Masai, Xhosa, and Zulu customs revealed Jewish origins, and that the Great Zimbabwe ruins were the former site of King Solomon's gold mines in the biblical land of Ophir.[12]

In the early 1920s, two Christian missionaries wrote books arguing that the ancient Israelites were the ancestors of contemporary West Africans. Their zeal for finding alleged remnants of Hebrew culture was fueled in part by a millennial fervor to identify and ingather the Lost Tribes of Israel, thus speeding the coming of the messianic age.[13] More recently, Dierk Lange has used similar diffusionist logic to argue for the presence of legends of Assyrian and Israelite origins among eighteenth- and nineteenth-century West African nations.[14] Surveying the same territory, Bruder summarizes that there is no reliable historical record of Jewish identification among sub-Saharan Africans, but lots of myths. "The modern Judaizing movements are often linked more to unexpected reactions to colonialism than to the implantation in Africa of Jewish ideas, practices or people, at some remote time."[15]

If the ancient record of the Israelites is dimly understood, the modern history of Jews and those who adopted Israelite beliefs is better known. This chapter surveys the history of Jews and Judaism in Africa and the African diaspora, and contends that the Israelite faiths of the 1890s arose from ideational rather than ancestral genealogies. Twentieth-century Black Israelites did not descend from ancient Israelites or contemporary Jews in either Africa or the Americas. Rather, like most other "imagined communities" of the late nineteenth century, British and American Israelite adherents invented their identities from a host of ideational rhizomes—subterranean, many-branching, hyper-connected networks.[16] Identification with the Exodus narrative, radical Methodist Christianity, esoteric Masonic historical theories, and the movement known as Anglo-Israelism provided the most salient avenues by which people of all races adopted Israelite identities at the end of the nineteenth century.

Although modern Blacks and Jews met and sometimes intermarried in the Americas, a survey of African and African American history does not support the idea that actual physical contact between people of African descent and either ancient Israelites or modern Jews produced Black Israelite religious movements of the nineteenth and twentieth centuries. First, the ancient historical record is extremely murky—for Jews of all hues.[17] Despite numerous mentions of Africa in the Bible, there is no solid evidence that ancient Israelites entered Africa and maintained their group identities over the course of the ensuing millennia, as many Black Israelites claim.

Among the African groups that claim Israelite origins, the most famous are the Beta Israel, "Falashas," or Jews of Ethiopia. Scholars and enthusiasts have advanced three theories to explain their origins. The first is the "Lost Tribe" perspective, which claims that the Falashas are ethnic Jews directly descended from ancient Israelites. The second is the "convert" theory that holds that they are Agaw converts who refused to become Christian when the Ethiopian state adopted the religion in the fourth century CE. The third school of revisionists have advanced the "rebel" perspective, which claims that the Beta Israel were political and religious dissidents who split off from the main body of Judeo-Christian Ethiopian society after the fourth century of the Common Era. These scholars point to the fact that Mosaic laws of *kashrut* (dietary laws), circumcision on the eighth day after birth, and the keeping of the Sabbath are all practiced by Ethiopian Christians, and that the Beta Israel as well as Ethiopian Christians practice some traditions, such as monasticism and female circumcision, that are not found in other Jewish communities.[18]

Outside of Ethiopia, Judaism did not establish a foothold in sub-Saharan Africa until the twentieth century, when American-trained missionaries introduced Black Israelite and Jewish teachings to southern Africa, and when a charismatic leader named Semei Kakungulu converted his followers en masse from a radical form of Protestantism to Ashkenazi Judaism during an anticolonial struggle with the British. Most scholars have agreed with Robert G.

Weisbord and Robert Stein that, despite episodic contact, before the twentieth century "by dint of geography and sheer numbers, encounters between Jews and Africa-derived peoples were limited."[19]

The Americas and not Europe or sub-Saharan Africa have been the primary theater of contact between modern Jews and people of African descent. Some Ashkenazi and Sephardic Jews owned slaves or profited from trading in the subsidiary products of the triangular trade, but they were not greatly involved in the commerce and transport of human beings across the Atlantic. The largest Jewish contribution to the slave trade was in the other legs of the triangular trade—in the transportation and processing of colonial products such as sugar, diamonds, and timber. They had almost no role in the slaving operations of England and France, which together accounted for 40 percent of Africans forcibly shipped to the Americas. Likewise, Jews were not involved in the Spanish slave trade, which before the 1630s was farmed out to Genoan and Flemish merchants. After the late sixteenth century, first the Portuguese and then the Dutch became the principle carriers to the Spanish territories. "New Christians," the descendants of Jews forced to convert during the Spanish Inquisition, played a significant role in the Portuguese slave trade of the sixteenth and early seventeenth century, but Jews and their descendants were not involved in the more extensive Portuguese slave trade of the eighteenth and nineteenth centuries. Only in the case of Dutch vessels did Jews unambiguously participate in the Atlantic slave trade, though they played a limited and subordinate role, both managerially and financially. Despite the myth of Western European Jewish financial preeminence, Jewish investment in the Dutch West India Company accounted for a mere 0.5 percent of the company's capital.[20]

Although Jewish residency and rights in the New World were severely circumscribed in the early days of the colonies, Jews and recent converts to Christianity achieved the greatest prosperity in Dutch-controlled territories, largely due to the Dutch political rivalry with the Spanish.[21] After 1492, when Spain expelled her Jews and forced those who remained to convert to Catholicism, the Netherlands welcomed many of these Sephardic Jews. Despite many restrictions, Jews prospered when Brazil came under Dutch rule from 1624 until the Portuguese retook Recife in 1654.[22] At that point, Dutch Jewish refugees from Brazil returned to the Netherlands or relocated to North America or the Caribbean islands, then in their economic prime. Because of centuries-old European prohibitions on Jewish land ownership, many of which were still operative in the New World, European Jews tended to stay away from planting, instead using their literacy and international kinship networks to survive as merchants.[23] However, in almost every place in the Caribbean where Jews of European origin prospered, some became planters, and many held Black slaves. When the English captured the Spanish island of Jamaica in 1655 and opened it to Jewish settlement, they noted that half the Europeans were "Portugals," some of whom were no doubt descendants of Jewish converts or "New Christians." Most Jamaican and Barbadian Jews held slaves, and a few were planters.[24] Jews composed one-quarter of the small white population of Nevis in 1723;[25] the 400 Jews on St. Thomas in 1837 were half of the island's whites.[26]

Despite the strong Jewish taboo against marrying outside the faith, many white Jews produced racially mixed children with both enslaved and free Africans, as did other Caribbean whites of similar social stations. Historian Jacob R. Marcus reports that in the French West Indies it was not uncommon for wealthy planters, including Jews, to have children with slaves or free Black women, and even to send them to France to be educated.[27] Many white Jews in the British West Indies also had children with Black women. Marcus writes:

> Some Jews, late in getting a good start in life, did not marry until they had made some progress on the ladder of success, and these late marriages very likely help account for Negro concubinage. Many of the Jewish settlers enfranchised Negro and mulatto women who were obviously their mistresses, and occasionally they made some provision for the children as well.[28]

Of course, there are other possible explanations besides material want and deprivation for why white Jews might have chosen Black partners, and why Blacks might have chosen white ones, including both rape and the willing exercise and surrender of power in intimate relationships. There have been legions of studies in the last few decades establishing that sex across the color line during slavery involved men and women of all races, with varied and diverse motivations. And the fact that there are reports of Jews emancipating and educating their wives and children would indicate that these Black-Jewish unions were not always without affection and human connection.[29] To be sure, many of the mixed descendants of Jews assimilated totally, but some may have retained some knowledge of their Jewish ancestry. A rabbi writing in the Cleveland Jewish Independent in 1911 reported that there were many Black Jews in Jamaica, many of whom were proud of their heritage and their Sephardic Jewish names.[30]

However, it was the Spanish and Dutch West Indian territories, not those of the French or British, that were the real centers of American Judaism before the nineteenth century. Settled initially by Sephardic Jewish refugees who had been displaced after the Portuguese conquest of Brazil, Surinam and Curaçao were the centers of Jewry in the Americas until the nineteenth century. The tiny island of Curaçao had 1,500 Jews by 1745, more than the entire Jewish population of North America at that time. Its Mikve Israel synagogue trained numerous founders of other Jewish communities, supplying them with clergymen and financial aid.[31]

Of 133 European Jewish families on Curaçao in 1735, the vast majority, 105 families, were slave owners.[32] Like Christian slaveholders, Jewish ones eventually came to support the conversion of "their" enslaved people to a milquetoast version of Christianity that tried to make slaves as docile and obedient as possible. Jews of Curaçao usually did not attempt to pass along their religion to their slaves and offspring, and sometimes even banned children born out of wedlock from their synagogue. Nonetheless, Jews and enslaved people interacted extensively on these islands. In Curaçao and Surinam, slaves of white Jews developed a distinct Ladino dialect, combining Portuguese, Spanish, French, and Hebrew words into Papiamentu, the Creole language of the island.[33]

By far the greatest intermixing of Blacks and white Jews was in neighboring Surinam, where Jewish influence was even more pronounced than it was on Curaçao. Jewish influence on Surinam was unparalleled in any community in the Americas. Sephardic Jews first settled the island soon after the English established a colony there in 1651, and remained after the Dutch defeated the English in 1667.[34] By 1682, they were the leading planters, and in 1685 they built a synagogue. In 1694, the island's Jews owned 9,000 slaves, and in 1730 Jews owned 115 of Surinam's 401 plantations, which held a total of 80,000 slaves. In 1780, Surinam had 1,500 Jews, including 100 mixed-race Jews, and Jews composed almost half of the white population. Surinam's Jewish community was unique in the New World in that their slaves rested on Saturday, the Jewish Sabbath, and some planters even converted their slaves to Judaism. Blacks enslaved by Jews on Surinam developed a dialect known as Djoe-tongo (Jew tongue), which includes a mixture of Spanish, Hebrew, and indigenous Amerindian words.[35]

As slave owners and people of European descent, Ashkenazi and Sephardi Jews had fraught relationships with people of African descent on Surinam, including their own mixed-race relations. The threat of attack by maroons in 1789 led a Jewish cantor to compose a prayer for deliverance from "our enemies, the cruel and rebellious Blacks."[36] Laws passed between 1686 and 1761 prohibited mixed-race sexual relations and established a fine of 2,000 pounds of sugar for anyone caught in such relationships. Yet the fact that three such laws were passed is testimony to the fact that some European Jews, women as well as men, were sometimes coupling across the color line. In any event, such laws were not enforced by the late eighteenth century and disappeared by 1817. In 1754, the synagogue at the center of Jewish settlement of Joden Savanna admitted mixed-race Jews as second-class members, or *Congreganten*, and limited where they could sit and which honors they could receive. Sephardic and Ashkenazi Jewish synagogues also tried to legislate against their members sleeping with people of color. In 1772, Surinam's Ashkenazi Jews ruled that anyone who married a Portuguese, Spanish, or Black person would be given the lower status of congregant, rather than full member. Likewise, in 1780 and 1787, the colony's Ashkenazi and Sephardic Jews ruled that mixed-race Jews would be given the second-class status of congregant, and would be allowed to perform *mitzvot*, or commandments, only on weekday mornings and on Sabbath and holiday afternoons.[37] Yet despite these racial restrictions within Surinam's Jewish community, paradoxically the children of Jews could sometimes hold offices unavailable to their Jewish fathers because of bans on Jews holding political office.[38]

Nonetheless, mixed-race Jews strove to be included as full members in Jewish synagogues, or to create their own institutions. In 1759, mixed-race Sephardic Portuguese Jews, with the help of white Ashkenazi and Sephardic Jews, formed their own fraternal organization, *Darhe Jesarim*, The Way of the Righteous, which was the earliest Black Jewish institution in the Americas. But a dispute over proper burial procedure for a mixed-race Jew in 1790 led the Jewish governmental authority, the Mahamad, to demand a copy of the group's bylaws, and to rule that the Jews of color could keep their fraternity only if they also paid dues to the Sephardi synagogue and abstained from bestowing certain burial honors on their members. The mixed-race Jews threatened to join the Ashkenazi German Jewish synagogue in response, and appealed to Surinam's governor to decide the matter in 1793. When the Sephardi leadership maintained that the second-class status of the *colourlingen* was lawful, and intimated that granting the mixed-race Jews' petition could lead to anarchy, the secular authorities ruled in favor of the white Sephardic Mahamad, and the mixed-race fraternity was officially banned.[39]

In some cases, mixed-race Jewish Caribbean communities may have survived into the twentieth century. Yisrael Francis, who became a Chassidic Jew in Crown Heights, New York, claimed white Sephardic ancestors from Curaçao.[40] Other mixed-race Jews might have been descended from individuals, rather than communities. New York cantor Eliezer Brooks was born in 1919 in Colon City, Panama, and claimed descent from Jewish grandfathers and great-grandfathers.[41] Such individual relationships were probably much more common than the rare Surinam community of mixed Jewish and African parentage.

But white Jewish ancestry did not always help those mixed-race descendants of Jews who wanted to formally join European-descended Jewish congregations. Although white Jewish women as well as men were known to marry people of African descent on Surinam, Black Israelites in the Americas were frequently Jewish through patrilineal descent, whereas Judaism traditionally has held that the mother must be Jewish for the children to be considered Jews. Furthermore, Jewish ancestry is not necessarily beneficial if one should choose to formally convert, because of the danger of being labeled a "Sufek Israel," a doubtful Jew, meaning that one might be the descendant of an adulterous liaison, which makes that person unable to convert to Judaism or to marry a Jew within orthodox Judaism.[42]

Because there were relatively few Jews in the Caribbean, the scale of Black-Jewish relations—sexual, economic, religious, or otherwise—was necessarily limited. One unsystematic effort to find Black Jews in the Caribbean in 1979 found a grand total of seventeen in Curaçao, Trinidad, Antigua, Nevis, St. Kitts, Barbados, St. Thomas, the Dominican Republic, and Jamaica, some of whom were West Indian returnees from a New York-based Black Israelite synagogue.[43] In sum, Blacks and Jews mixed in a variety of ways on the islands, but white Jews live on in the ancestry and the language of only a small number of African-descended people in the Caribbean.

With the rise of beet sugar, steam power, and the cotton economy in the nineteenth century, the fortunes of the Caribbean sugar islands declined and the focus of New World Jewish communities and Black-Jewish interaction shifted northward to the southeastern portion of the United States. Until the mid-nineteenth century, Jews of Sephardic origin were concentrated in a few Southern cities and sprinkled in rural areas. The price of acceptance of Jews by antebellum Southern white society was Jewish acceptance of Southern mores, including slavery. Bertram Wallace Korn's foundational study, *Jews and Negro Slavery in the Old South, 1789–1865*, estimates that a quarter of all Southern Jews owned slaves, roughly the same percentage as all Southern whites.[44] In general, although he finds that Jews were not over-represented in the slave economy, he notes "the behavior of Jews towards slaves seems to have been indistinguishable from that of their non-Jewish friends."[45] Jews in the antebellum American South achieved a degree of social acceptance and a level of political influence never achieved by their contemporaneous northern coreligionists. They served at all levels of Southern politics, from mayors of small towns and major cities to the highest echelon of national politics.

The paragon of Southern Jewish political prominence was Judah Philip Benjamin, a self-trained New Orleans lawyer born in the same neighborhood as Edward Wilmot Blyden on St. Vincent's in the Danish West Indies, who rose to the highest ranks of his profession and bought a 300-acre sugar plantation with 100 enslaved persons. In 1852, he won a seat in the United States Senate, where he was widely recognized as one of the greatest orators and intellects ever to serve in that august body. In 1853, President Franklin Pierce nominated him to serve on the Supreme Court, an offer he declined. When the Civil War erupted, Benjamin rapidly ascended the ranks of the Confederate States of America, first as attorney general, then secretary of war, and then secretary of state. Both well loved and well hated, the "Dark Prince" of the Confederacy was known for his portly figure, his enigmatic smile, and his forceful and brilliant personality (fig. 2.1). Jefferson Davis, president of the Confederacy, even called Benjamin "my chief reliance among men."[46] Jews were able to make such great inroads into Southern society at a time when they were frozen out of political power and social acceptance in the North in large part because, no matter what their racial designation, as whites, they benefited from the binary color-based caste system that slavery created.[47] Korn concludes that Jews did not have a large impact on the institution of slavery, but slavery had a large impact on Jews, for whom "the road to social and economic advancement and acceptance...was smoothed by the ever-present race distinction which imputed superiority to all whites."[48] Immigrants readily participated in the slavocracy because it provided them with the privilege of being part of the ruling white caste, and considerably greater status than they would have had in the North.[49] In the South, Jews may have been looked down upon but they were unquestionably white on arrival.

One of the most prominent Americans of mixed Black and Jewish parentage was Francis Lewis Cordoza, who was born in 1835 to Lydia Williams and Jacob Nuñez Cordoza, a Sephardic Jewish supporter of the slavocracy whose family had been in the Americas for almost a hundred years. Jacob Cordoza developed the concept of the South as a model economy created by slavery and low tariffs and was the South's most prominent economic theoretician. Contravening Southern convention, Jacob Cordoza sent his mixed-race son Francis to white schools until the age of twelve, and then to the Universities of Glasgow and London. Upon returning to the United States, Francis Cordoza became a Presbyterian minister and lived in New England. When the Union won the

Civil War, Francis Cordoza rose to become one of the most powerful politicians and among the highest-ranking African American officials during Reconstruction, achieving the offices of secretary of state and treasurer of South Carolina between 1868 and 1876. The founding of a public school system and a welfare system were the focus of Cordoza's Reconstruction career. When the Democratic Party retook the South Carolina state house, Cordoza was unjustly convicted of fraud and sentenced to prison, but was later pardoned. Eventually, he left South Carolina to take a post in the Federal treasury, and later served as the principal of a high school in Washington, D.C.[50]

FIGURE 2.1 Judah P. Benjamin, the "Dark Prince" of the Confederate States of America and one of the most prominent Jewish slaveholders in antebellum America. Library of Congress.

In general, however, rates of Jewish intermixing with African Americans were probably low. "Only now and then does a Jew cross the line and marry into another race," observed a writer for *The Voice of the Negro*.[51] Southern Jewish shopkeepers in Black neighborhoods tended to live with their families above their stores, but still maintained their distance from the Black community. Richard Bowling, a Black Baptist minister in Virginia, remarked that "six days out of seven, [the Jewish businessman], his wife, and his children will see more of colored people than...even their fellow Jews. Howbeit, they all remain Jews. Neither does colored blood filter into their family nor does any of the Jewish blood filter into the veins of Negroes. They are in the Negro world but not of it."[52]

Jews maintained the color line partly by excluding African Americans from their synagogues. Charleston's Congregation Kaal Kodesh Beth Elohim wrote into its constitution an edict barring proselytes "until he or she or they produce legal and satisfactory credentials, from some other congregation, where a Chief [Rabbi] or Rabbi and Hebrew Consistory is established; and provided, he, she, or they are not people of color."[53] The one known exception to this segregation of places of worship, and the only record of a Black Jew in antebellum days, was Billy Simons, a man born around 1780 in Madagascar who was sold into slavery and eventually purchased in 1840 by A. S. Willington, owner of the *Charleston Courier*.[54] Simons told how his father frequently recounted their descent from the biblical Rechabites, and in his lifetime "Uncle" Billy was a practicing Jew "universally respected by his coreligionists."[55] Despite Charleston Congregation Ka'al Kodesh Beth Elohim's ban on people of color, the synagogue accepted Simons as a member, and Rabbi Maurice Mayer said he was "the most observant of those who go to the synagogue."[56] Upon his death on December 10, 1859, his former master remembered the newspaper carrier as "in many respects a remarkable representative of his race—unusually intelligent, shrewd, and quick in learning, yet withal active, devoted and faithful."[57]

Given the existence of Billy Simons, there may have been other practicing Black Jews in the Old South. Indeed, three African American women who had come north with their Jewish master were reported to pray with great devotion in a New York city synagogue, and opera singer Marion Anderson has noted in her autobiography that her Black grandfather was a practicing Jew.[58] However, anecdotal accounts of a few African American Jews do not change the overall pattern of exclusion. Bertram Korn has concluded that the "fact that Jewish masters, with this one exception [Billy Simons], did not educate their slaves in the Jewish faith, and that synagogues did not welcome Negro worshippers would seem to negate the contention that present-day Negroes who regard themselves as Jews are descended from slave-converts or Jewish masters."[59] With vanishingly few known exceptions, Blacks in the nineteenth century did not participate in Jewish worship. Antebellum contact between African-Americans and white Jews in the United States was mostly limited to interactions with a few Jewish merchants in Southern urban centers.[60]

The American Jewish population began to change significantly around 1850: in place of the Sephardic Jews who made up the oldest and most assimilated Jewish communities came Ashkenazi Jews from central and eastern Europe. Whereas many Sephardim brought European and Caribbean business contacts with them, central and eastern European Jews usually started from the bottom, often as peddlers.[61] These new waves of Jews were fleeing political instability, military conscription, and, after 1881, pogroms that terrorized and displaced thousands. According to the 1860 census, while there were approximately 488,000 free people of color, centered in urban areas of the South, and four million Black slaves, the population of

Jews in all of America had tripled in the previous decade to about 150,000 on the eve of the Civil War.[62] At that time, roughly two-thirds of America's Jews were in the South, but of these Southern Jews, 30,000 were from central Europe, and had probably arrived in the previous decade. Most new Jewish immigrants settled in the South's two major port cities, Baltimore and New Orleans, which had the institutions and services required to live observant Jewish lives.[63]

In addition to holding a different socioeconomic position, these central European Jews, most of whose identities had been forged outside the South, brought with them substantially different racial attitudes from their more patrician Sephardic predecessors. Prior to 1850, Jewish involvement in the anti-slavery cause was extremely limited. Unlike almost every white Christian denomination, which polarized around the slavery issue in the years before the Civil War, American Jews had taken an overwhelmingly accommodationist position, perhaps fearful of inciting the anti-Semitism to which they had become all too accustomed.[64] The American and Foreign Anti-Slavery Society reported in 1853 that "Jews of the United States have never taken any steps whatever with regard to the Slavery question.... It cannot be said that Jews have formed any denominational opinion on the subject of American slavery."[65] In the 1850s, however, a generation of Jewish abolitionists emerged who, with one exception, were German-speaking Reform Jewish immigrants. The Reform Judaism of the Jewish abolitionists, like the Protestant Revivalism that motivated many of their Garrisonian counterparts, emphasized progressive ethics over the confining strictures of revealed law. However, unlike their Christian counterparts, Jewish abolitionists were motivated by progressive political identities formed in Europe, not America.[66]

As peddlers and petty merchants, this new generation of Jews was more likely than Christian contemporaries or American Jewish predecessors to have contact with African Americans. Like Jewish abolitionists who retained a central European political orientation, Jewish peddlers who retained European political identities as a persecuted people were more inclined to resist the racism indigenous to the American South. Certainly, there were European Jewish radicals who did not take up the cause of anti-slavery, and no doubt there were peddlers who colluded with Southern racism.[67] But Jews who had fled pogroms and persecution in Europe were more likely than the earlier waves of generally more patrician coreligionists to identify with the plight of persecuted African Americans. One Ashkenazi Jewish peddler who came to America in 1884 soon realized that "The *schwartzers* here are like we are in Russia.... They are the *goyim's* Jews."[68] Against the injunctions of his more acculturated relatives, this peddler insisted on treating his Black and white customers equally.[69] Despite such moments of recognition, extensive contact between white Jews and African Americans remained relatively rare before the twentieth century.

Modern Israelite movements were inspired much more by the idea of the ancient Israelites and the model of the early Christian church than they were by contact with either Jews or modern Judaism. It is well known, for example, that the Exodus story inspired African Americans who suffered in slavery and gave hope of divine deliverance from the desert of American racism. While Christianity under slavery often was an oppressive form of social control, the Hebrew Bible could function as a source of inspiration for escape as well as rebellion.[70] Biblical names in African American spirituals encoded the geography of the North and provided a vocabulary for escape and freedom. Identification with the Hebrew Bible during slavery inspired resistance and even rebellion. Biblical place names provided the lexicon for the famous Underground Railroad that smuggled slaves out of the South "beyond the Jordan" to freedom in the North. Gabriel Prosser, a slave who wore his hair long and identified himself with his hero Samson, led a slave revolt in Richmond, Virginia, in 1800, using the Bible to convince the other slaves that they were in fact the Hebrews and that God would help them win their freedom.[71] Likewise, the slave rebellions led by Nat Turner and Denmark Vesey employed biblical verses to bolster the courage of the conspirators.[72] The Exodus narrative and identification with the Children of Israel became critical aspects of African American Christianity.[73]

The story of Black identification with the Hebrew Israelites and their Exodus from Egyptian slavery is the best known of all of the contexts that helped produce Israelite religions. But no vein was richer at transmitting the idea of descent from the ancient Israelites than the seam of Anglo-Israelism produced between the conspiratorial, historical legends of Freemasonry and the fiery brimstone of radical, millenarian, and Methodist Protestantism. Immediately prior to the age of European expansion, the Protestant Reformation and subsequent religious wars that swept Europe sparked interest in all things Hebraic, especially among Protestants. To pious Protestants who imbibed the Old Testament and fought a century of cataclysmic wars with their Catholic enemies, the promises that God made to care for his "chosen people," the Jews, were particularly attractive. Interest in Hebrew and Judaism among the English went back at least as far as the Protestant Reformation of the sixteenth century, which reformed Catholicism in part by rebelling against priestly authority and emphasizing the importance of individual study of the Bible.

Print culture played a significant part in the rise of the idea that the people of the British Isles could trace their heritage to the ancient Israelites. In 1650, a Dutch rabbi published a book proposing that scattered fragments of the Lost Tribes of Israel, dispersed during the ancient Babylonian captivity, could be found among contemporary peoples of Asia, the Middle East, Africa, and America. The book, *The Hope of Israel*, by Rabbi Menasseh ben Israel, attracted an audience in England, and there were numerous attempts to trace fragments of the Lost Tribes to the British Isles.[74] In seventeenth-century England, there were a number of attempts to reenact Jewish history on English soil, such as one suggestion to model the English government on the Jewish Sanhedrin, or another ill-fated attempt to proclaim an English farmer the "King of Israel" in hopes that he would usher in the messianic age by parting the seas like Moses and returning the Jews to Palestine.[75]

The English Protestant identification with the biblical chosen people became even more pronounced during the deposition of the Catholic monarch James II in the Glorious Revolution of 1688–1689.[76] The belief that the coming of the End Times was supposed to be preceded by the ingathering of the Jews to their ancient homeland added extra urgency to the task of identifying the scattered remnants of the tribes of Israel, at least in the minds of zealous pre-millennial Protestants. A century later, in the 1790s, the British Isles gave rise to a number of millennial sects that appealed to the poor in the wake of the social dislocation following the Enclosure Acts, urbanization, and the doubling of England's population in the preceding century, not to mention the loss of the lower thirteen of the American colonies. These "New Jerusalemites," like Joanna Southcott and her successors, Richard Brothers and Ebenezer Aldred, embraced the language, symbolism, and stories of the Children of Israel's escape from Egyptian oppression. Brothers proclaimed himself a descendent of King David and a divine prophet, and predicted he would lead the Jews back to Palestine as their king and ruler in 1798, fulfilling the prophecies of the Book of Daniel (see fig. 2.2). Brothers's movement dissipated when the predicted Jewish ingathering failed to materialize, but he left behind a large body of followers and fifteen volumes of prophesy identifying the English as the descendants of the ancient Israelites.[77]

Identification with the ancient Israelites did not stop at the shores of the British Isles; instead, radical Methodism traveled with the poor as they left the metropole for the margins of the empire and settled in places like India, Australia, and Jamaica. Meanwhile, Jamaicans and other Black West Indians participated in what historian Iain McCalman calls London's subversive radical underworld. This multiracial collection of political revolutionaries,

**FIGURE 2.2** A derisive caricature of Prophet Richard Brothers by James Gillray, 1756–1815. Brothers holds a Bible turned to Book of Revelations, and leads his followers to a burning "Gate of Jerusalem." Note Brother's Africanized hair and facial features, which have yet to be explained. Library of Congress.

pamphleteers, preacher-pimps, petty criminals, pornographers, seamen, and other subalterns met in London's taverns and established radical political movements and radical churches in the fifty years following the French Revolution. Robert Wedderburn, the illegitimate son of a white Jamaican planter and a Black woman, was nearly illiterate but produced a number of religious pamphlets and became a licensed preacher. After converting to Methodism, he advocated a revolutionary and anticlerical form of apocalyptic millenarianism in his writings and in his fiery sermons, which were recorded by spies for the British Home Office.[78] Blasphemous, revolutionary, and contemptuous of the established order of religion and politics, London's radical underworld produced a range of subversive forms of Methodism that spread to the West Indies and helped redraw the religious map of the Black Atlantic. The radical Methodism of the English lower classes carried with it the French Revolution's promise of social change and political reform, answering the desires of freedmen and enslaved West Indians for a revolution in their political, temporal, and spiritual estates.[79]

British Anglo-Israelism had two basic strategies. On the one hand, it attempted to establish linguistic links between the tribes of Israel and European peoples and place names: the Scots were descendents of Isaac, the Danes children of the tribe of Dan, and so on. On the other hand, proponents of the Anglo-Israelite theory selectively read biblical passages to demonstrate that England had fulfilled biblical promises to the Israelites, and so must be the new Israel. Anglo-Israelism often used linguistic arguments that seem implausible at best; for example, England's nickname of John Bull fulfilled Deuteronomy 33:17: "His glory is like the firstlings of his bullock"; or the contemporary English habit of not pronouncing the letter "h" at the start of a word showed that England was of the tribe of Ephraim, whose spy was unable to pronounce the "sh" in the word "shibboleth."[80] Yet Anglo-Israelism made inroads not because of the strength of any single piece of evidence, but because of the sheer volume of biblical verses that its proponents were able to muster for a public that was weaned on the literal truth of Christian scripture. This potent tradition of Anglo-Israelism found its most effective voice in the 1840s in the writings of John Wilson, whose prolific work spawned dozens of other advocates of the theory throughout the remainder of the nineteenth century.[81] Anglo-Israelism was both an elite and a popular discourse; it thoroughly permeated the culture of radical Protestant Christianity that emerged and spread in the English-speaking world in the later part of the nineteenth century, and infiltrated the core of the Holiness and later the Pentecostal movements, as we shall see in Chapter 3. The theory was a prominent feature of radical evangelical Methodism among the working class of the nascent Industrial Age, as the great historian E. P. Thompson noted in his 1963 classic, *The Making of the English Working Class*. "As in all the cults of the poor, there was a direct identification between their plight and the tribulations of the Children of Israel," Thompson writes. "In the Old Testament working people found more than a vengeful authoritarian God; they also found an allegory of their own tribulations."[82]

On the one hand, Anglo-Israelism offered the poor the promise of liberation through its use of the Exodus narrative of the Israelites' escape from Egyptian slavery. But as the British Empire matured, the same story offered succor for imperialists, through the darker half of the story of the Israelites' military conquest of the promised land and their subjugation of the Canaanites. As literary theorist Edward Said noted in answer to political theorist Michael Walzer, the preeminent story of liberation in the Western canon can be read from a "Canaanite perspective" to be a narrative of conquest and colonialism.[83] In the nineteenth century, Anglo-Israelism exhibited both tendencies, combining millennial interest in identifying the Lost Tribes of Israel with theological support for the British Empire—as in one work with chapters claiming that "Israel must be in possession of Colonies" and "Israel must push the Aborigines of her Colonies to the Corners" where "the Aborigines of Israel's Colonies were to die out."[84] The doctrine of Anglo-Israelism had arisen through the English confrontations first with internal enemies, such as Roman Catholicism and class conflict, and then with external foes, such as foreign peoples. As Britannia spread the sails of her empire across the oceans of the globe, the theory of Anglo-Israelism provided a potent mythological and religious justification for Britain's rule over other peoples. The theory provided a rationale for empire in the language of nineteenth-century religion, racism, nationalism, and imperialism. It thus had great appeal to the "Anglo-Saxons" of England and America in an age when the power of religion, nationalism, and racism far outdistanced knowledge of world cultures or histories.

In America as in England, Anglo-Israelism drew strength from the expansion of empire. After the profound spiritual trauma of the Civil War, the nation began to reforge bonds between whites in different sections and consolidate its western empire, subjugating and settling western lands and their Indian inhabitants. This empire-expanding process leapt the oceans in 1898 with the annexation of Hawaii, Puerto Rico, the Philippines, and Guam. Anglo-Israelism found enthusiastic audiences in the United States, where white elites were actively participating in building ties with the mighty British Empire and creating an "Anglo-Saxon" racial identity that spanned the Atlantic and legitimated white rule at home and abroad. The theory found advocates at the very pinnacle of the American social pyramid: the prominent theologian Rev. Edward Beecher, brother of abolitionist siblings Harriet Beecher Stowe and Henry Ward Beecher, was one of the founders of the First Identity Church of Brooklyn, a congregation formed on January 1, 1881, to prove the identity of the Anglo-Saxon race as the Lost Tribes of the Children of Israel. Historian Edward Blum has demonstrated that Henry and Harriet led the effort to forgive white Southerners for the treason that led to the slaughter of the Civil War. Their brother Edward Beecher was in some senses even more extreme—for believers in Anglo-Israelism, whites' very whiteness bound them together in a providential contract as God's chosen people.[85] Edward Beecher's First Identity Church, included many prominent white citizens among its members, and met in a hall that accommodated 1,200 people. Brooklyn's elite white Anglo-Israelites were very much working with history as well as identity. They resolved: "whereas, in accepting the Anglo-Saxons as the House of Israel, we see in their histories a remarkable fulfillment of the prophecies," citing the existence of a literal House of Judah and a House of Israel. The church was "patiently anticipating the time when both the House of Israel and the House of Judah shall return to Palestine—the glorious land which was promised by God to Abraham and his descendents."[86] Fifteen years before the publication of Theodore Herzl's *Der Judenstaat*, which galvanized political Zionism, white American Christians were already praying for the return of Jews (the House of Judah) and the Anglo-Saxons (the House of Israel) to the land of Palestine.[87]

Anglo-Israelism probably found an even wider audience in Masonic lodges and journals than it did in radical millenarian and elite "Identity" churches. That most treatments of Anglo-Israelism take no account of either the imperial context of its development or the strong Masonic component of its ideology is curious, given that these elements are both very prominent in the writings of the movement. Freemasonry and Anglo-Israelism were fraternal twins that shared similar parentage in the years of European wars between Protestants and Catholics following the Reformation.[88]

Freemasonry traces its lineage from medieval masonry guilds in the British Isles. One story has it that, unlike other craftsmen who were bound by medieval custom to the land, stonemasons were free to travel to work on large-scale public works projects, such as cathedrals and castles, hence the name "freemason."[89] In addition, whereas most craftsmen worked in small workshops with few members, the size of stone structures necessitated large groups of masons. Guilds of masons developed as secret societies to pass along the tricks of the trade, which encompassed architecture, mathematics, and engineering, in addition to building with stone. In the late seventeenth century, so-called symbolic Freemasonry emerged from actual Freemasonry and spread to the continent of Europe. No longer working stonemasons, symbolic Freemasons traced the origins of "the Craft" to the grand monuments of ancient days, ultimately to the temple of King Solomon and the pyramids of the ancient Egyptians, the greatest builders of the ancient world. Like the medieval stonemasons whom they emulated, Freemasons dedicated themselves to preserving secret knowledge, much of which was abstruse, numerological, and associated with the geometry of the building trade.[90]

The fraternity's search for truth, reason, and liberty embodied the ideals of the Enlightenment and threatened both monarchs and ministers. Freemasons spread anti-royalist sentiments and questioned the so-called "divine right of kings" and the other irrational pieties that supported the *ancien régime*, earning themselves the enmity of the old conservative, aristocratic order. Yet paradoxically, although potentially subversive, Freemasonry penetrated the highest rungs of the establishment, especially in England, where the Duke of Edinburgh was the titular head of British Masonry. This alluring, secretive, emancipatory, and richly symbolic tradition spread to England's American and Caribbean colonies as well. America's early elites, including many Founding Fathers and presidents, were Masons. The American one-dollar bill has a Mason, George Washington, on the front, and the Masonic symbols of an Egyptian pyramid and an All-Seeing Eye on the back, a symbol that the Founding Fathers held Enlightenment truths to be self-evident, and that all men were created equal, endowed by a deistic creator-god with certain inalienable rights.[91]

When American Masonic lodges broke from the Grand Lodge of England after the War of Independence, they reorganized themselves on a state-by-state basis. These so-called Blue Lodges offered the basic first three Masonic degrees. Candidates who were given the arduous third degree and who passed the test by emulating the legendary builder of King Solomon's Temple became honorary Master Masons, symbolic versions of the artisans to whom the order owed its origins. But beyond this basic structure, American symbolic Freemasonry evolved into two rival versions with national reach: the Ancient Accepted Scottish Rite, founded in 1801, added eight degrees to the twenty-five degrees of the French Rite of Protection. Its rival, the American or York Rite, organized in 1816, has thirteen degrees, with the rank of Knights Templar at its summit.

African Americans created their own parallel Masonic world, which claimed the loyalty of all of the founders of Black Israelite faiths, from Bishops Christian and Crowdy to Rabbis Ford and Matthew. The African American Masonic establishment traces its origins to Prince Hall, a Barbadian soldier who was inducted into a Masonic lodge by a British military regiment in 1775, and then founded the tradition of African American Freemasonry that has come to be named for him.[92] Freemasonry in the Black Atlantic may be, in historian John Thornton's terms, a "co-revelation," a point of overlap between European and African customs, which fills a deep cultural niche established by the long history of African secret societies that maintained traditions, cosmologies, and esoteric knowledge.[93] Surely, secret societies have played an important role in the development of Afro-Caribbean religions such as Vodou and Santeria.[94] Yet Black Masons of the nineteenth century were much more inclined to ascribe the origins of their tradition not to West Africa but to the fertile crescent of the Near East.[95]

Much of Freemasonry's ideology centers around the two counterbalanced mytho-historical tropes of Israel and Egypt. The fraternity, which fancies itself part of a mythologized community of builders that stretches into the mists of history, holds that Hiram, the builder of King Solomon's Temple, was the first Freemason. The myth and mystique of the Holy Land played a major part in the rites and ritual of American Masonry: while every Master Mason had to emulate the same ability to keep secrets of the legendary architect of King Solomon's Temple, Knights Templars modeled themselves after the Crusaders, who were said to have become masons to rebuild the Tomb of the Holy Sepulcher in Jerusalem.[96] Indeed, Christian Orientalist tales and tales of the Crusades against Muslim foes formed the basis of many Masonic legends.[97] But according to Masons, the greatest builders of all time were the ancient Egyptians, who built the pyramids, and much of the Craft's lore centers around Egypt. Thus, inside the very core of Freemasonry's mythology are the two key elements of the biblical story of Exodus: Israel and Egypt. However, while Freemasonry revels in the ancient imagined glories of wise King Solomon, it does not share the emphasis in Exodus on transcending Egypt. Egyptology outweighs philo-Semitism in the Masonic worldview—Freemasons identify primarily with the Egyptians who built the pyramids, not with the Israelite slaves who hauled the stones. French and British conquests of Egypt during the Napoleonic wars of 1799 to 1815 helped spark a mania for all things Egyptian in the century that followed. In America, the racial identity of the ancient Egyptians became a kind of proxy war in the struggle over the "peculiar institution" of slavery and the even more grotesque physical and ideological contortions of racism during Reconstruction and is bloody aftermath.[98]

Despite the predominant Masonic identification with the glories of ancient Egypt, there is a dissident stream of Freemasonry that has emphasized the Israelite side of the Masonic mythic dyad, and we can see this identification in European and Euro-American Freemasonry as well as African-American Freemasonry. Much of Masonry's ideology in fact draws from the Old Testament and Jewish folklore, and Jews have been prominent members of Masonic lodges in the United States. Freemasonry incorporated both members and beliefs of Jewish origin. In America, Jews played important roles in the founding of Scottish Rite Masonry and have served in many high Masonic offices. American Jews have commonly belonged to Masonic lodges and frequently achieved prominence within them—by 1941 there had been twenty-eight Jewish Grand Masters of state Masonic organizations in fourteen different states.[99] Jews have also established their own fraternal and benevolent burial societies along Masonic lines, such as the Independent Order of the Free Sons of Judah, the Independent Order of the Sons of Abraham, and the Independent Order of the Sons of Benjamin, all of which failed after a few decades. Longer lasting was the Independent Order of B'nai B'rith, founded in a New York City café in 1843 and maintained as a secret society until 1920. Although no longer a fraternal society, B'nai B'rith still exists alongside its progeny, the Hillel Foundation for Jewish Campus Life and the Anti-Defamation League.[100]

Freemasonry fit the beliefs and values of contemporary Judaism, especially the Enlightenment-infused progressivism of Reform Judaism. In his study of Jews and Freemasonry in Gilded-Age San Francisco, historian Tony Fels contends that Freemasonry's "theistic rationalism," its monotheistic and deistic God, and its emphases on the Hebrew Bible and the mystical Jewish Kabbalah, fit perfectly with Reform Jewish beliefs.[101] Other similarities between Masonry and Judaism that Fels enumerates are rationalism, universalism, ritualistic spirituality, and exemplary rather than crusading moralism. The similarities between Masonry and Judaism have prompted comment from Jewish Masons on more than one occasion. Writing in the *San Francisco Hebrew* in 1865, one Jewish Mason wrote, "if there be any religious system more closely connected with the institution [of Masonry] than others, *it is Judaism*."[102] No less an authority than Isaac Mayer Wise, the nineteenth-century leader of the American Reform Judaism movement and a Mason himself, declared that "Masonry is a Jewish institution whose history, degrees, charges, passwords, and explanations are Jewish from the beginning to the end, with the exception of only one by-degree and a few words in the obligation."[103]

A wider perspective reveals that it was not only Freemasonry but also numerous other variations of occult traditions that owed much of their ritual magic to Jewish sources. As historian James Webb writes, "the chief debt of the ritual magician is to Jewish mysticism...The Jewish genius for complicated metaphysics and occult speculation has provided occultists with some of their most erudite Traditional sources of inspiration."[104] Two kabbalistic books were especially important in occult traditions: the early, third-to-sixth-century *Sefer Yetsirah*, the Book of Creation, and the late thirteenth-century *Sefer Ha-Zohar*, the Book of Splendor. The first book is a Jewish variety of Gnosticism, the powerful corpus of banned writing from the early Christian era that claimed the world was divided by a Manichean struggle between the forces of good and evil. The second book refined these ideas into a mystical system by which the student could ascend through ten stages, or Sephirot, toward unity with God, by absorbing the elements of creation in sequence.[105] Frances Yates, the late scholar of the European Renaissance, has identified the foundation of Freemasonry's mysticism as part of a "Renaissance Hermetic-Cabalist tradition" that was heavily influenced by Rabbi Isaac Luria's school of Kabbalah of late sixteenth- and early seventeenth-century Prague and fit well with the "strong Hebraic, Old-Testament-inspired type of piety of the Puritans and Calvinists."[106]

Interest in the Holy Land among American Freemasons during the era of Reconstruction found expression in the formation of a "Masonic Holy Land League," founded in 1867, which had a membership of almost 8,000 by 1879. The league sought to sponsor expeditions to the "Orient," promote research and lectures into Masonic history in those lands, and establish Masonic lodges and a Grand Lodge in the Middle East. Robert Morris, who had been both the founder of the Order of the Eastern Star as well as grand master of the Masons of Kentucky, joined the first expedition of the Masonic Holy Land League in 1868 and wrote a book about his experience, *Freemasonry in Holy Lands: A Narrative of Masonic Explorations made in 1868 in the Lands of King Solomon and the Two Hirams*. Other expeditions visited the Middle East in 1870, 1873, and 1876, and the League organized the Royal Solomon Mother Lodge No. 293 in Jerusalem in May of 1873.[107]

Anglo-Israelism and Freemasonry overlapped and supported one another: both emerged from the conflict between Catholics and Protestants in the seventeenth century, and both movements placed the Israelites of the Old Testament in a place of special significance within a dense, mystical, and mythological reconstruction of the past. Indeed, Freemasonry was first codified in its modern form, the Scottish Rite, by the cognoscenti of the Scottish Enlightenment in the early eighteenth century, soon spreading among the elites of the English court and members of the Royal Academy. It was precisely these Protestant elites who would have been influenced by the rising interest in Hebrew in England's universities. The *philosophes* of the Scottish Enlightenment were not only inheritors of a kind of fire-and-brimstone version of Protestantism that paid particular attention to the Hebrew Bible, but as deists and scientists, they were attracted to the awesome and distant creator god of the Old Testament, as opposed to the more accessible and personable Christ of the New Testament. It is no accident that the God of Freemasonry, the God of the Scottish Enlightenment, and the God of Anglo-Israelism are all referred to with the Hebrew Tetragrammaton, יהוה, translated in English as YHVH or "Jehovah."

Accordingly, Masonic beliefs are a prominent part of the Anglo-Israelite literature of the nineteenth century. Books like *The Irish Prince and the Hebrew Prophet: A Masonic Tale of the Captive Jews and the Ark of the Covenant* (1896) melded Anglo-Israelism and Freemasonry to show that the Anglo-Saxons were the true Israelites, and that the British Empire was the fulfillment of biblical prophecy. Perhaps the best example of this overlap between Anglo-Israelites and the larger community of Freemasons is William Carpenter's 1874 treatise, *The Israelites Found in the Anglo-Saxons. The Ten*

*Tribes Supposed to Have Been Lost, Traced from the Land of Their Captivity to Their Occupation of the Isles of the Sea: with An Exhibition of Those Traits of Character and National Characteristics Assigned to Israel in the Books of the Hebrew Prophets.* Carpenter originally published the book serially in *The Freemason*, the official paper of the Masonic Craft in the United Kingdom, which was printed around the English-speaking world, including the United States and Jamaica. According to Carpenter, Judaism, or, more precisely, Israelism, is the very foundation of Freemasonry, which causes one to wonder why "so large a number of professing Christians" around the world "should have adopted a system and united themselves in a body, the foundation of which is obviously and indisputably laid in Judaism—using the word in its widest sense, as equivalent to Israelism." Having established the kinship between Masonry and Judaism, Carpenter asks what the causes of the similarities are:

> How comes it to pass, then, that the foundation and framework of Freemasonry should be of a purely Jewish character? Its traditions, its ceremonies, its ritual, all bear the impress of, and are, in fact, rooted in Judaism. Christianity, as such, is unknown in our lodges; but Judaism is recognized and accepted; and important lessons of faith and morality are deduced from it.

Carpenter considered and discounted the idea that reverence for the Old Testament in itself explains the kinship, because Christians do not hold the Christian scriptures to be less sacred than the Jewish ones. Surely Christians are not using Jewish rites solely out of a spirit of brotherly fraternity, as "the motive and disposition to unite with them must be extraordinary to induce them to put their own religious attachments and usages aside, and to adopt those of the Jews," Carpenter reasons.[108]

Using biblical proof texts, the writer argues that the reason Masonry has incorporated so much of Jewish theology, mysticism, and lore is that the Anglo-Saxons were in fact descendants of Israelites who migrated to the British Isles from the Holy Land. He expected this realization to invigorate the practice of Freemasonry, but more important, to reinforce the work of—capital "P"—Progress that was an imperative of Freemasonry, the Age of Reason, and imperialism:

> Throughout our ceremonies, especially in the Master's degree and in the Royal Arch, we identify ourselves with Abraham, Isaac, and Jacob,

and we claim them as our forefathers. What life would it infuse in our ceremonies, if we realized this as a truth, and with what life should we ourselves be animated, if we knew, indeed, that we formed part of that race which is to be employed by the Almighty in turning men from darkness to light, and transforming a world of ignorance, and vice, and misery, into a world of knowledge, and virtue, and righteousness, and happiness![109]

In the Victorian era, to be an Israelite meant to have a genealogical, or rather a racial, connection to the people whom God "Himself" had chosen to be "a light unto the nations."[110] Carpenter interprets the identification with the Israelites in view of the era's cultural imperatives as the virtuous work of transformation, progress, and civilization, one part of "turning men from darkness to light, and transforming a world of ignorance and vice, and misery, into a world of knowledge, and virtue, and righteousness, and happiness." In other words, the Israelites' civilizing mission became a central element of the European justification for colonization and dominion over the world's peoples. Israelite identity was so potent in "Western" civilization in the era of imperialism because it both justified racial entitlement, as Anglo-Israelism did, and it spoke the language of improvement and progress—what became known as the "civilizing mission." As Anglo-Israelites in both its religious and Masonic contexts, English-speaking peoples could be both conquerors and transformers, destroyers and redeemers, and they could do so in the dominant lexicons of the era, using the vocabularies of Protestantism, science, progress, imperialism, Romantic racialism, and civilization.[111]

Both of the founders of Black Israelite faiths, Bishop William Christian and Bishop William Saunders Crowdy, were devout Masons. It is likely that Masonic texts as well as Masonic interest in the Holy Land and in biblical history helped both men to formulate their Israelite beliefs. Bishop Christian even referred to his Black Israelite-based beliefs as "Free Mason religion." The first sentence of the 1896 version of his *Poor Pilgrim's Work* reads: "Free Mason religion is the true mode of religion. All other modes of religion are not worth one cent." Ten years later, he changed that to: "Free Mason religion is the true mode of religion; always was and always will be."[112] Bishop Christian called himself "Chief," referred to his churches as "temples," both Masonic terms, and tried unsuccessfully to introduce Masonic dress among his impoverished followers.

In sum, thinking of cultural formation in genealogical terms can easily lead us astray. African American Black Israelite faiths of the 1890s were influenced by the idea of the Israelites, but had little to do with descent from ancient Israelites or contact with modern Jews. Instead, it is important to remember that African American cultural formation occurred within a global system that traded in ideas as much as commodities like cotton and cane sugar. When innovators such as Bishops Christian and Crowdy adopted Israelite identities, they were creatively repurposing discourses transmitted through religious societies and Masonic lodges. Europe's expansion, and her contact with and conquest of the peoples of the world, created a need to comprehend, categorize, and control those peoples through various means, including systems of knowledge. For believers in the Bible's literal truth and infallibility, Holy Scripture provided an apt starting point for comprehending and ordering the fantastic human diversity that Europeans encountered in their widening travels across the globe. This "biblical ethnography" led to the rise of academic anthropology, whereas less scholastic endeavors produced a variety of Anglo-Israelite movements that believed the residents of the British Isles were directly descended from the ancient Israelites, and spread these beliefs through Freemasonry and radical Methodist sects.[113]

As we shall see in subsequent chapters, the rise of modern Israelite movements had more to do with the idea of the early Christian church than it did with modern Jewish emulation or descent. Although European Jews and people of African descent met to a limited degree in the Americas during and after slavery, widespread contact between Blacks and Jews would wait until a massive wave of Jewish immigration at the end of the nineteenth century and the Great Migration of the First World War brought the two groups into contact in northern cities.[114] But before that happened, African Americans had already begun to repurpose Israelite ideas, claiming a foundational role in Christianity and world history, and initiating their own Judaizing movements.

# 3 "WE ARE ISRAELITES BUT NOT JEWS"

## ORIENTALISM AND ISRAELISM IN THE HOLINESS-PENTECOSTAL MOVEMENT

The context for the beginning of William Saunders Crowdy's biblical literalism was provided by the radical Holiness movement of the mid-South and West in the post-Reconstruction era. Like leaders of the Holiness movement, Crowdy and other Black Israelites adopted Old Testament dietary laws, practice of the seventh-day Sabbath, foot washing, and the Lord's Sabbath, and they rejected older mainline Christian denominations. Moreover, the combination of Holiness and Israelite ideas in slightly different form led to the religious movement of Pentecostalism ten years after Bishop Crowdy had organized his denomination. Although many authors have claimed, with little evidence, that Pentecostalism got its ecstatic forms of worship from Africa and transmitted them through Black worshipers to white ones, the best evidence suggests rather that "catching the Spirit" and speaking in tongues were not static "retentions" but were doctrinal and performative innovations developed by thousands of American practitioners of all races over the course of the nineteenth century.[1] John Wesley's first followers experienced spirit-filled worship in England before Methodism had spread to America, and, indeed, spirit possession in various forms has been a part of every recorded human society. Thinking of spirit possession as essentially African is a form of the primitivism that has long associated African-descended peoples as especially emotional, given to wild abandon. Moreover, the millennial fulcrum on which the Holiness movement balanced before tipping into Pentecostalism was not the continuum between Africa and Europe but the imagined chasm between the "unredeemed" East and the Christian West. The Holiness and Pentecostal movements were not African retentions but polycultural American assemblages, and the engine that drove early Pentecostals' identification with the ancient Israelites and acquisition of foreign languages was a Christian form of Orientalism. Although it has been all but unnoticed in the extensive literature on the movement, early Pentecostals were participants in an American Orientalist discourse of more than a century, with its own received ideas about linguistic differences between East and West. These preconceived ideas about what the Orient sounded like helped to shape the movement.[2]

This is not to deny the profound influence of African Americans on the Pentecostal movement. The leap from Parham's doctrine of xenoglossia, or speaking foreign languages, to his student William Seymour's practice of glossolalia, or speaking in tongues (discussed below), marked a break from a semi-scholastic, Orientalist perspective to a more transgressive, less rigid view of communication with the Holy Spirit and with foreign peoples. It also marked a more democratic and racially inclusive practice of worship with one's fellow human beings. African Americans transformed Holiness revivals, identification with the Israelites, and speaking in tongues, in the process contributing their own ethics and standards of worship with definite roots in Black America and aesthetic roots in Africa.[3] With Black influence, Methodist revivals gained enthusiasm; identification with the ancient Israelites became not a justification for imperialism but a vindication of the oppressed; and glossolalia became not the attempt to speak a foreign language, but the acquisition of one's own, God-given tongue. Perhaps enthusiastic worship, a personal relationship with God, and the ability to see one's own struggle as part of a Providential epic are particularly African American qualities, but seeing them as such does not require "outsourcing" all that is creatively and distinctively Black back to Africa. The strengths needed to develop family, community, and spiritual kinship in the face of chattel slavery, grinding oppression, and persistent violence were qualities necessarily developed on American soil.

The Holiness movement in American churches began in the 1830s and was spread by its own preachers, newspapers, associations, and revivals throughout the nineteenth century, catching fire after the Civil War. As Vinson Synan argued in his pioneering study *The Holiness-Pentecostal Tradition*, Holiness people sought the transcendence of sin, or "perfectionism," through a "second blessing," which they thought of as a "baptism of the Holy Spirit" following the conventional watery baptism that first brought the faithful into the Christian community.[4] John Wesley, the founder of Methodism, was most responsible for the spread of the doctrine of "sanctification" as a separate stage of faith after the acceptance of Christ. Wesley was a Church of England minister who developed his theology after what he considered to be a failed trip to spread the Gospel to Indians in the colony of Georgia from 1735 to 1738.

On the return voyage, he noticed how calm a group of German Moravian Pietists remained even when the ship hit rough seas, and began to investigate the Moravian faith.[5] A Moravian missionary passing through England told Wesley that "saving faith brought with it both dominion over sin and true peace of mind both holiness and happiness."[6] Fresh from his failures in the colonies, despondent and suffering from "unusually frequent lapse into sin," Wesley experienced a conversion experience on May 24, 1738, feeling a warming sensation in his heart that suggested the Moravian description of holiness and contentment.[7] By 1740, Wesley had formulated and begun to publicize his teachings, which described a two-stage process of conversion or justification, in which the sinner accepted Jesus Christ but retained "a residue of sin within"; as well as Christian perfection, or sanctification, which purified the believer's "inbred sin." Perfection could come instantly as a "second work of grace," or it could come gradually, but in either case the penitent believer was not sin-proof but rather sin-adverse: through discipline, devotion, self-interrogation, and the avoidance of worldly pleasures, the methodical devotee could achieve a victory over most sin in this life and reach "sinless perfection" in heaven.[8]

Wesley's methodical, or "Methodist" teachings began as a revival movement within the Church of England but found the best reception in those parts of Britain and the New World where the Anglican Church was hard pressed to keep up with the demographic growth and social disruption of industrialization and territorial expansion.[9] Methodism spread to the American colonies in the 1760s, and Wesley's teachings spread rapidly in the land that had inspired its invention, through the efforts of a number of devoted missionaries and circuit-riding preachers who spread the new doctrine to people of all races and classes. The American Methodist Church formally organized itself in 1784, and three years later the Rev. Richard Allen, a minister and free person of color, led African Americans out of St. George's United Methodist Church in Philadelphia and formed the first ever African-American church denomination, the African Methodist Episcopal Church (A.M.E.). Allen and the A.M.E. always used Wesley's second blessing teaching, as did the Rev. James Varick of New York, who formed a new Black denomination in 1821, the A.M.E. Zion Church. Thus, the Methodist quest for holiness and sanctification were present at the very start of African American church organizations.[10] The Methodist movement would grow to become one of the largest denominations in the world, with more than thirty-five million members and three to five times as many adherents by 1909. Methodists worshipers in the United States soon came to represent 75 percent of the global communion.[11]

What became known as the Holiness movement began in large part through the efforts of evangelists Sarah A. Lankford and her sister Phoebe Worrall Palmer. Lankford began holding Tuesday evening prayer meetings in her parlor in 1835, and by 1839 the meetings moved to Palmer's New York City home. Palmer and her husband, a doctor, counted several Methodist bishops among the friends who crowded their parlor to hear Mrs. Palmer's Tuesday night lectures on faith. Palmer taught that even novices might achieve perfection, holiness, or "perfect love" instantaneously, not by methodical diligence but by faith and divine grace. She taught that holiness was not a gradual "growing in grace" but an immediate experience of love and sanctity created by a "baptism of the Holy Spirit."[12] In 1839, Mrs. and Mr. Palmer founded the first journal advocating a program of perfectionism, or "Holiness," which quickly attained a circulation of 30,000. Phoebe gained fame as an evangelist at Methodist revivals, and she and her husband traveled widely preaching the Holiness message for the next thirty years. The teachings of Christian perfectionism gained increasing support within American Methodism in the twenty-five years before the Civil War. Holiness people extended Wesley's teachings about sanctification to claim that not only could individuals attain perfection but society could, as well. Wesley had denounced the slavery he witnessed in his American travels, and a belief in social perfectionism fueled the many reform movements of the mid-nineteenth century, including the campaigns for temperance and abolition. This crusading moralism repelled Southern Methodist churches, which deemphasized Holiness in the 1840s and 1850s in order to defend the institution of slavery. Before the Civil War, the quest for Holiness was largely an urban and a northern movement.[13]

The geographical distribution of the Holiness movement would change with the defeat of the South in the bloody slaughter of the Civil War, which initiated a search for meaning among all Americans and a sustained revival in the South from 1865 to 1867. The established denominations tried, but simply were unable to contain the religious enthusiasm of a nation that was recovering from the killing fields of Antietam and Gettysburg. The total number of churches in the United States increased by 130 percent between 1870 and 1890, and Methodists added an average of 800,000 new members each decade between 1870 and 1910.[14] The postwar Holiness movement started in earnest with the first of many National Camp Meetings for the Promotion of Holiness, held in Vineland, New Jersey, in July of 1867. In the next twenty years there would be sixty-seven national Holiness "camp meetings" and eleven urban "Tabernacle" meetings, most of the later in western locales. These revivals, sometimes conducted under large canvas tents, jousted with the tented circuses that crossed the country in the same decades in the battle for American hearts, minds, souls, time, and money. In promoting the careers of passionate preachers whose oratory could move thousands, the camp meeting circuit innovated spirited forms of "old-time religion" and thereby widened the cultural and theological gulfs between the staid and increasingly worldly churches and the festival-like revivals that sprang up seemingly everywhere.[15]

Critics called Holiness people "Holy Rollers" because of the ecstatic disassociative enthusiasms that occurred in these camp meetings, as they had at the Cane Ridge Revival in Tennessee in 1804 and, indeed, at some of the prayer sessions conducted by John Wesley in England in the 1700s, as well. On occasion, moved by the ecstatic cadences of the preacher and the press of thousands of people, devotees would cry or laugh uncontrollably, overwhelmed, as they understood it, by the Holy Spirit. At other times they would drop and literally roll on the ground, or fall and not be able to move at all. Like sparks catching dry summer grass, the Holiness camp meetings of the late nineteenth century set off fires of religious enthusiasm across the country in the years following the Civil War. The movement brought with it both new kinesthetic experiences of devotion and new doctrinal innovations. Radicals condemned the old mainline churches as bastions of modern worldly temptations and ungodly temples of Mammon, filled with abominations such as fashionable dress and social events with no redeeming spiritual function. A potent faction advocating "come-outism" challenged Holiness groups within established denominations to leave the older churches behind, and twenty-three new holiness denominations arose in the last seven years of the nineteenth century, most in the South, Midwest, and Southwest.[16] Most of these new Holiness movements agreed on what became known as the "fourfold Gospel": personal salvation, spiritual baptism in the Holy Ghost, divine healing, and the imminent return of Jesus Christ.[17]

The Holiness movement affected Christians of all races, including African Americans, who were among its earliest adherents and who were prominently represented in many of its camp meetings, where devotees of all races often mixed freely, united in the Spirit. As scholar David D. Daniels III reports, a number of African Americans, including Sojourner Truth, had advocated the Holiness doctrine of sanctification before the Civil War, but it was not until after the war that the movement spread widely among African American churches. The signal event was the Philadelphia Revival of 1877–1879, which started at Bethel A.M.E., the mother church of the first African American denomination. Bethel's new pastor, Rev. George C. Whitefield, began preaching

Holiness sermons and convened a Holiness conference with prominent guest speakers and representatives from a range of African American congregations as well as nationally prominent white Holiness ministers such as John S. Inskip, the head of the National Camp Meeting for the Promotion of Holiness. Bethel began regular Thursday night Holiness meetings, and other Black churches in Philadelphia began to sponsor their own all-day Holiness revivals. A dozen of the most prominent African American ministers in Philadelphia had accepted the Holiness message within several months of the first meeting. But the A.M.E. church soon discovered, as did other denominations, that it could hardly contain or control the religious enthusiasms of the Holiness movement. The movement's unmethodical teachings conflicted with the Calvinist strain of Methodism, which emphasized the importance of work, prayer, and devotion, rather than instantaneous, love-filled perfection. Consequently, Holiness advocates met with resistance within the A.M.E. church, as they did within many denominations, Black and white. With Whitefield's death in 1879, Bethel's board banned Holiness meetings, and the movement waned in the City of Brotherly Love, moving from established churches to private homes. A similar backlash occurred among other denominations, as well: in 1894 the General Conference of Methodist Episcopal Churches for the Southern United States condemned the Holiness movement and launched an effort to kill off the dozens of new holiness denominations that had sprung up in the prior three decades.[18]

Yet despite the backlash from mainline churches, the Holiness movement continued to spread among white churches, Black churches, and some explicitly interracial Holiness communions. Among African Americans, its expansion was largely due to the efforts of laypeople and women evangelists such as Sister Callund and Emma Williams, who brought their testimony of the Philadelphia Revival with them as they traveled in the West and the North, respectively. The Holiness movement among African Americans drew strength first among Black Baptists in the border South and Mississippi, but also reached into Virginia and North Carolina in the early 1880s. Thomas J. Cox founded the Christian Faith Band, the first African American Holiness church, in Kentucky in the late 1870s.[19] Holiness churches were bastions of interracialism and biblical literalism. The Church of God (Anderson, Indiana) started in 1881, and formed a large and influential interracial Holiness church that declared racial discrimination to be ungodly, as its leaders could find no support for the concept of races in the Bible. The church believed in sanctification and condemned denominations as sinful. The church also studied and adopted some of the practices of the Hebrew Bible, while practicing the rites of baptism, foot washing, and the Lord's Supper, which commemorated Jesus' Last (Passover) Supper. The church's adoption of Hebraic rituals started some Holiness churches down the path toward practicing "Israelite" faiths, emphasizing the rites of the Hebrew Bible from a Christian perspective. In the 1880s, the Holiness message spread through the auspices of the Church of God to African Americans in South Carolina, Michigan, and Alabama.

The theological innovations of the Holiness movement occurred in the middle of a period of ecological, agricultural, and financial hardship created by land speculation, fickle weather, and nationwide financial booms and busts. The Western places that produced the theological radicalism of the Holiness movement were the same places that produced the political radicalism of the Populist movement. Settlers had begun moving into unfarmed prairie lands on the Great Plains soon after the end of the Civil War, taking advantage of the expansion of the railroads, the ethnic cleansing or "Indian removal" policies of the U.S. government, and the fertility of those extensive grasslands. After the economic collapse of 1873 and a plague of grasshoppers and severe drought the following year, settlers on the Great Plains experienced record prosperity beginning in 1875. Boosters hailed Kansas as a new paradise, and a land rush began. The African-American "Exodusters" who headed for St. Louis, Kansas City, and the dusty plains of Kansas in the late 1870s were part of a much larger demographic shift west that increased Kansas' population by 173 percent in the 1870s. But with a return of drought in the late 1880s, there once again was trouble in paradise. The land rush of the prior dozen years led to the Crash of 1887 and its collapse of speculative markets in western real estate and cattle, which in turn triggered an even larger collapse several years later in the Panic of 1893.[20] Thus the Holiness movement grew in the midst of ecological and economic upheaval and hardship.[21]

The most extreme doctrinal innovations of the post-Civil War Holiness movement occurred in the South, Midwest, and the southwestern frontier, furthest from ecclesiastic authorities on the East Coast. Texas was an especially fertile place for the growth of new doctrines disturbing even to the leaders of the older National Holiness Association, who regarded some of the new innovations as heresies. In 1890s Texas, itinerant preachers taught that one could live in a state of "sinless perfection," and some advocated "marital purity," or abstinence within marriage. Others claimed that there was not only a second stage of purification but also a third work of sanctification called "the fire." Once sanctified, these hardscrabble farmers, who might have previously put their faith in patent medicines sold by shady traveling salesmen, believed that they no longer needed either doctors or drugs. Not only could the sanctified faithful look forward to perfect health, but some suggested that the "saints" might even be able to conquer death itself. Only intermittently served by trained preachers by dint of their dispersal across great expanses, people of faith on the Western frontier turned increasingly to the Bible and began to suggest closer adherence to its laws, including those of the Hebrew Testament. Some even rejected consumption of coffee and pork, finding no justification for them in either Testament.[22]

The most radical and influential of the new Holiness denominations was Benjamin Irwin's Fire Baptized Holiness Association, which began in Iowa in 1895 and gained strength on the Great Plains of Kansas, Texas, and the Oklahoma Territory, newly opened to non-Indian settlement. Like the early Populist movement, Irwin's association was interracial, and an African-American minister from South Carolina named William E. Fuller brought fifty Black churches into its fold by the turn of the century. Irwin taught that not only was there a third baptism by fire but there were also baptisms of dynamite, lyddite (an explosive), and oxidite. More consequently for the rise of Israelite faiths, Irwin taught strict adherence to the dietary laws of the Hebrew Bible, banning the consumption of pork, catfish, shellfish, and the other animals deemed unclean by the laws of Leviticus. Thus Bishop William Saunders Crowdy's rejection of established churches and his advocacy of customs found in the Hebrew Bible (see Chapter 1) were part of a wider stream of biblical literalism in the Holiness movement on the Western frontier.[23]

Even Bishop Crowdy's most notable teaching—that Christ and the ancient Israelites were Black—was not entirely unique. One of the first to popularize the idea that African Americans were the descendents of the ancient Israelites was a pastor from Wrightsville, Arkansas, named William Christian, who was born into slavery in Mississippi in 1856. Later in life he recounted how he had served as a Baptist minister for thirteen years, until 1888, before "the Lord, through some unknown power, revealed to me the startling fact that we were preaching the doctrine of men and not of Christ."[24] Christian began a period of intense spiritual interrogation, turning to the scriptures as his guide. He advocated the teachings of Alexander Campbell, an English minister who rejected denominationalism and insisted that the faithful should only follow the teachings of Christ.[25] Campbell, like Bishop Christian, advocated a "primitive" form of Christianity that borrowed much from the Hebrew Bible. Everyone "who would accurately understand the Christian institution must approach it through the Mosaic," Campbell wrote.[26] Like Campbell, William Christian critiqued the practice of naming churches by the old denominational names such as Catholic, Methodist, or Episcopal, which had no scriptural basis. He formed his own band in 1889 and christened it the "Christian Friendship Work," but later renamed it the "Church of God," and finally the "Church of the Living God." Bishop Christian cited a variety of scriptures to support the idea that Adam, King David, Job, Jeremiah, Moses's wife, and Jesus Christ were all "of the Black race."[27] He taught that Adam and his descendents, including the ancient Israelites, were Black. When Cain went out and dwelt in the land of Nod, people who Bishop Christian understood to be the descendents of "fallen" and "disobedient angels" expelled from heaven with Satan already inhabited the land. "I claim that the Gentiles are the increase of the fallen angels," Christian wrote, citing the Book of Job and the Book of Revelations. Although he does not say that the Gentiles were descended from Satan himself, his 1896 text is most likely the earliest written source of the belief that pious Black Christian slaves must have thought many times, and that the Nation of Islam popularized forty years hence: that the white people who tormented them were not human at all but were "devils" instead.[28]

Bishop Christian preached a race-conscious form of Christianity that directly addressed the anti-Black racism of his time and yet also overcame racialism by asserting the fundamental humanity of people of all races, despite their disparate origins. Christian inverted Blackness from a sign of the "Curse of Ham" to the mark of the covenant that God made with Abraham. "We Black people are not a thrown away people as some of our white friends pretend we are," he asserted.[29] Yet according to Christian, although Black people had sometimes intermarried with lighter-skinned people from outside the covenant, anyone could join the covenant by following his teachings. He referred to Christ as "colorless" because he had no human father and his teachings attracted followers of all races. Christian was fond of St. Paul's statement that Christianity crossed all social divisions: "There is neither Jew nor Greek, there is neither bond nor free, there is neither male nor female: for ye are all one in Christ Jesus." (Galatians 3:28). Eventhough he thought that whites and Blacks had separate origins, he believed that the Christian faith instructed people of all races to love one another. "Remember friends, Christ told us to love one another as he loved us," Christian wrote. "He never said each race love his own race; he just said love one another."[30] In order to create a biracial, antiracist church, Christian adopted biblical rituals and emphasized strict adherence to the Ten Commandments. Like the Church of God (Anderson), he instituted the ancient Near Eastern practice of foot washing, which was a mark of biblical hospitality and humility. It was also a violation of the customs of segregation, which banned bodily contact between the races, and so asserted the primacy of God's law and the inequity of racist human laws. In these and other ways, Christian was a product of his time and place. In addition to foot washing, he advocated full-immersion baptism, practiced the Lord's Supper with water rather than wine, and condemned adulterers as the vilest people on earth. Like many other biblical literalists of his day, Bishop Christian condemned fashions, vanity, and the new commercial and scientific order that had emerged after the Civil War. He asserted that the earth was flat, discouraged the use of tobacco and snuff, and threatened damnation on "vain words" and "long prayers." He likewise condemned "merchandising," citing the Book of Revelations, and predicted a sorry end for merchants and rich men, citing the Apostle James.[31]

Bishop Christian's early Black Israelite form of Holiness Christianity had a profound impact on African American religion. By 1898, Bishop Christian's teachings about the Blackness of the ancient Hebrews could be heard in ninety congregations in eleven states and territories, including Oklahoma. Christian's most famous disciple was Charles H. Mason, who spent five years in his fellowship before striking out on his own to found the Church of God in Christ (COGIC). Mason's church was the first Holiness church to organize in the South, and partly for that reason he attracted many white ministers to his organization. Mason visited the Azusa Street revival in Los Angeles in 1907, and COGIC went on to become the nation's largest Pentecostal church.[32] Meanwhile, Christian's church spread rapidly throughout the South and Midwest, and by 1906 there were sixty-eight branches and offshoots with 4,276 members in eleven states: Alabama, Arkansas, Illinois, Indiana, Kansas, Kentucky, Mississippi, Missouri, Oklahoma, Tennessee, and Texas. The heart of the church was in the upper South, with twenty churches in Arkansas and thirteen in Tennessee. By 1916, there were 192 churches with 11,635 members, and by 1926 there were 239 churches and 17,402 members, before declining to 215 churches and 9,636 adherents in 1936.[33]

William Saunders Crowdy's innovation was one of intensity, not of kind. It is unclear who was first to preach that the ancient Israelites were Black, while adopting Old Testament rituals, Bishop Christian or Bishop Crowdy, who began preaching in Guthrie, Oklahoma, five years after Bishop Christian's 1888 revelation. The two advocated very similar doctrines and rituals, although neither set down his theology in writing until much later. It is quite likely that both men's teachings did not arrive full-blown in their initial revelations but developed in the tumultuous decade of the 1890s. Bishop Christian certainly taught that the ancient Hebrews were Black, and most likely taught that contemporary African Americans were their descendants, but Crowdy began to systematically adopt the rituals of the Hebrew Bible, beginning with the seventh-day Sabbath and continuing with the Passover and the other festivals of the Hebrew calendar. Through their joint efforts, Bishops Christian and Crowdy seeded the African American religious landscape with the conviction that the ancient Israelites were Black, and attracted thousands of African American believers who had adopted some of the rites of the Hebrew Bible to go along with the conviction that the Hebrew and Christian Bibles were describing their own ancestors. In most cases, the Judaic groups that arose in northern cities before and after the First World War were lineal descendents of Bishop Crowdy's Church of God and Saints of Christ or Bishop Christian's Church of the Living God. For example, Prophet Cherry's Black Jewish sect in 1930s Philadelphia clearly wore the distinctive brown and blue costumes of the Church of God and Saints of Christ.[34] Likewise, as we shall see in Chapter 5, New York Rabbi Wentworth Arthur Matthew's attempt to create a national network of Black Jews led him to reach out to at least one minister who had received ordination from Prophet Crowdy, as well as lay people who had links to the earlier group.[35] Bishops Christian and Crowdy created an audience for alternative faiths to follow in successive decades, preparing the ground for the growth of varieties of African American Judaism and Islam.

The Pentecostal movement, like Black Israelite churches of the 1890s, could not have happened without the combination of Holiness churches and a fascination with discovering the proper identity of the Israelites. The new fields of Orientalist studies, which had themselves been inspired in part by the search for the biblical Israelites, also fueled the era's obsession with the Israelite past.[36] Much of the Holiness movement was not Orientalist, as it derived from engagement with Christian text and American communities of faith that did not refer to the Orient as a significant point of reference. But it is likewise impossible to extract nineteenth-century Christian theology from Orientalism altogether. It was commonplace for late nineteenth-century Protestants to view the Bible as an accurate map of the "Orientalisms" of the Holy Land. As the editor of the first issue of the *Oriental and Biblical Journal* proclaimed, "Oriental studies bring us into close contact with the Old Testament record."[37] For western Christians, contemporary Palestine, with its Oriental people and customs, was a window into what the dress, life, and land of the ancient Hebrews and earliest Christians must have been like. And when fervent Holiness missionaries fanned out across the globe to spread their message of perfectionism, they came face-to-face with both Africans and so-called "Orientals." It was this encounter, and the linguistic and cultural synapse it created between East and West, that sent a jolt through Holiness communities, sparking the innovation of the gift of tongues that initiated Pentecostalism. To a degree that has gone largely unappreciated, Orientalism was an important part of the theological and ritual innovations of the early Pentecostal movement.

The Pentecostal movement emerged through the efforts of a number of Holiness pastors and their students at a time around the turn of the twentieth century that was rife with millennial expectations. The world was newly stitched together with novel circuits of travel, language, and power by the emergence of the overseas empire of the United States before and after the War of 1898. Aware of how naval power had been critical to the expansion of the British Empire, the United States had set out on a quest to modernize its Navy after the publication of Alfred T. Mahan's influential 1890 book, *The Influence of Sea Power on World History*, and in light of American desires to capitalize on the trans-Pacific trade with China, Japan, and the "Orient."[38] The war against Spain, Cuba, and the Philippines that began in 1898 ended with the United States in command of the Caribbean and in possession of a string of strategic Pacific Ocean islands girding the equator along the crucial naval routes to the Philippines, Japan, and mainland Asia. Where American gunboats sailed, American engineers, traders, and missionaries soon followed, and on occasion missionaries outpaced the rest. Between the mid 1890s and the First World War, at least nine American Holiness churches established missions abroad, including some with their own publications. The largest of these, the pioneering Church of God (Anderson, Indiana), established missions throughout Europe, Jamaica, the West Indies, Panama, British Guiana, China, India, Japan, Syria, and Egypt. The Hephzibah Faith Missionary Society, founded in 1896 in Tabor, Iowa, published its periodical *Good Tidings* and spread its message through India, Japan, and South Africa. The International Apostolic Church of Cincinnati, Ohio operated in South Africa, British Guiana, and the Lesser Antilles, and multiple Holiness missions redoubled the efforts of other Holiness missionaries in China, India, Japan, and South Africa, and also sought converts in Puerto Rico, Bolivia, Guatemala, Cuba, the Cape Verde Islands, and Swaziland. By 1913, there were 27,983 Christian workers of all nationalities and denominations in the Indian subcontinent alone.[39]

Missionaries in foreign lands immediately encountered the necessity of communicating in foreign languages, but few had the linguistic gifts or advanced language training necessary to do so effectively. The growing awareness of the world's vast linguistic and religious diversity created a theological crisis for American Christians in general, and for one man in particular. As the Rev. Charles F. Parham noted in 1899, there were then 1.5 billion people in the world, but more than a billion of them had never been exposed to the Gospels or the "saving message of Christ." Parham and a host of Holiness preachers set out to change that arithmetic.[40]

The chief theologian of what became the Pentecostal movement, Parham was a Kansas preacher and faith healer who had been born in 1873 and survived a sickly childhood in the central part of the state near Wichita. He briefly enrolled in the Methodist-affiliated Southwest Kansas Conference College in Winfield,

EVANGELIST CHARLES FOX PARHAM
(From a photograph taken about the time of writing this book.)

FIGURE 3.1 Evangelist Charles Fox Parham, as a young man. Kansan Parham's Topeka-based Beth El Bible School was the first to teach that miraculously acquired foreign languages would fulfill the story of Pentecost related in Acts 2:1-11. Flower Pentecostal Heritage Center.

Kansas, in his late teens before an attack of rheumatic fever convinced him of the efficacy of divine healing and confirmed his call to the ministry (fig. 3.1). He became a Methodist minister in Linwood, Kansas, from 1893 to 1895, but his enthusiasm for the message of the Holiness movement and the anti-denominational "come-outism" of the time led him to leave Methodism and set off on his own. He lived in Lawrence, Kansas, from 1894 to 1896, preached in nearby Ottawa, and married a member of his congregation named Sarah Thistlewaite. In 1898, they founded the Beth-El Healing Home in Topeka, the state capital, and provided training and a place to stay for people interested in faith healing.[41]

The Parhams greatly desired to bridge the language barriers that plagued efforts to evangelize foreign peoples who spoke a multitude of tongues. In 1899, Parham was excited to discover an account in a Holiness periodical about Jennie Glassey, a member of Frank Sandford's Shiloh Holiness community near Durham, Maine. Glassey received a call to carry the Holiness message to Africa, and was said to have miraculously received the ability to speak in several African dialects. Parham hailed this development as "the return of the apostolic faith," referring to the account of Pentecost in Acts 2:1–11, when the Apostles had been able to converse with foreign Jews in foreign languages.[42] On that day of Pentecost, the Bible recounts, there was a "sound from heaven" like "a rushing mighty wind" and there appeared "cloven tongues like of fire." All the assembled "were all filled with the Holy Ghost, and began to speak with other tongues, as the Spirit gave them utterance." There were Jews from every nation living in Jerusalem, and when they got wind of what had happened and came to witness it for themselves, they "were confounded, because…every man heard them speak in his own language." The miracle of Pentecost, then, was not just that the Holy Ghost had given the Apostles the ability to speak in sacred tongues, but that the Holy Ghost had given them instantaneous knowledge of human languages.[43]

Thus, from its origins, the miracle of Pentecost was concerned with the problem of intercultural communication in the face of the Levant's linguistic diversity. In the Christian Bible, Pentecost was the antidote to the punishment of the babble of tongues that resulted from God's punishment to humanity for hubristically attempting to build a tower that would reach the heavens, as described in Genesis 11:1–9.[44] According to the Book of Genesis, human linguistic diversity and human dispersal across the globe are both the result of God's willful desire to thwart intercultural understanding—lest human unity lead to coordinated attempts to usurp God's place in the heavens. The story of Babel and the story of tongues at Pentecost were both about divine intervention in human language, the former to create dispersion and incomprehensibility, the other to create unity and a miraculous transcendence of linguistic barriers. Moreover, the ethnographic diversity mentioned in Acts 2 would have been recognizable to Parham and other Holiness people as part of the contemporaneous Mediterranean, Asia Minor, and the Orient, with references to such places as Mesopotamia, Asia, Egypt, Libya, and Arabia.

Interested in learning more about the appearance of African languages in New England, Parham set off on a cross-country trip on June 9, 1900, heading east from Kansas through Chicago to New York and Maine. Parham's journey knit together the major Holiness centers of his time. Parham had participated in services with members of Benjamin Irwin's Fire-Baptized Holiness Church while still a Methodist minister. Now he traveled to Zion, Illinois, north of Chicago, to hear Alexander Dowie preach, and then continued to Nyack, New York, to hear A. B. Simpson of the Christian and Missionary Alliance. Finally, he arrived at Durham, Maine, where Frank Sandford led his "Holy Ghost and Us" church in a community he dubbed Shiloh. Sandford was a native of Maine born in 1862 who accepted the Methodist sanctification teaching in the 1890s and traveled the globe as a missionary, becoming disheartened with the failures of missionary work he saw everywhere around him (fig. 3.2). He started Shiloh as a Bible school, in a large white house topped with towers and turrets, built with student labor, where students lived communally (fig. 3.4). After receiving apocalyptic messages in 1891, Sandford had increasingly focused on the Holy Land for clues to decoding God's plan for the End Times. In this he was aided by the books of C.A.L. Totten, a professor of military science at Yale University who sought to prove that the Anglo-Saxons were the Lost Tribes of Israel, using techniques of biblical exegesis and linguistic etymology. Like other Anglo-Israelites of his era, Totten believed that Anglo-American imperialism was a mark of God's favor, part of "the sacred history and independent chronology of a chosen people."[45] Sandford enthusiastically adopted the Anglo-Israelite theory. "We are Israelites but not Jews," Sandford wrote in 1896, "and our national reunion as the twelve tribes of Israel is yet to take place."[46]

FIGURE 3.2 Frank Sandford, leader of the revival at Shiloh, in Durham, Maine, where Jenny Glassey received the ability to speak in "the African dialect." Flower Pentecostal Heritage Center.

Bible School, Home of the Holy Ghosts and Us Society, Shiloh, Maine.

**FIGURE 3.3** Shiloh, Sanford's school in Durham, Maine. Note the prayer tower, site of the vigil where the ability to speak in foreign languages was first received. Flower Pentecostal Heritage Center.

The Israelite theory heightened expectations at Shiloh for the imminent millennial return of Jesus Christ, and students remained on a "tiptoe of expectation" for the next several years.[47] Moreover, the Anglo-Israelite theory supported the idea that the rapid expansion of American naval and commercial power in the 1890s was part of God's plan for the conquest of the entire globe by the alleged descendants of the ancient chosen people. Sandford called British and American imperialism part of "the sacred history and independent chronology of a chosen people," and millennial expectations at Shiloh, Maine, were only heightened with the outbreak of the War of 1898, when the warship the *USS Maine* exploded in Havana harbor, leading to war and the conquest of an American overseas empire in Puerto Rico, the Pacific, and the Philippines.[48]

Sandford's identification with the ancient Israelites and his millennial expectations were heightened by his journeys to Jerusalem, the heart of the Biblical Levant and part of the modern Orient. While the War of 1898 raged, he received a message that he interpreted to be of divine origins instructing him to go to Jerusalem, and another to "Remove the covering," a reference perhaps to Isaiah 25:7.[49] With the protection of the newly ascendant American Navy, Sandford ventured to Jerusalem with one companion, where he received the insight that not only were Anglo-Saxons the chosen people but his Shiloh settlement in Durham, Maine, with its slogan "'Till Shiloh,'" was the very Shiloh mentioned in Genesis 49:10.[50] Sandford returned from Jerusalem with a renewed faith of his own role in fulfilling biblical prophecy. In order to be sure to receive any possible divine transmissions, Sandford installed his students in a continuous prayer vigil in one of the towers. It was in this heady, pressured atmosphere, filled with identifications with the ancient Israelites and expectations of the imminent return of the messiah, that Jenny Glassey first presented the ability to speak in what Parham referred to as "the African dialect"—as if there was only one. Parham reported that Glassey had received the "African dialect" in 1895, but he did not become aware of her gifts until 1899.[51] That four-year gap is interesting in light of his patriarchal teachings, in that it would seem to indicate that speaking in tongues may have developed as part of a female counterculture within his own commune.[52]

Impressed with the speaking in tongues that he witnessed during the six weeks he spent at Shiloh, Charles Parham returned to Topeka and brought back Frank Sandford's teachings on constant prayer, Anglo-Israelism, and the possibility of miraculously acquiring knowledge of foreign languages. With the assistance of his wife, Parham started a new "Beth-El Bible School" in October 1900 in a large, grotesquely ornate Victorian mansion known as Stone's Folly that had a large tower much like the prayer tower at Shiloh (fig. 3.4).[53] Parham and his students reviewed biblical texts concerning sanctification and divine healing and began to develop an understanding that the third work of baptism in the Holy Spirit following sanctification could be known by the gift of tongues that was experienced by the apostolic church on Pentecost, as described in the Book of Acts.[54] Holiness preachers such as Charles Parham were excited about the coming of the Christian millennium, which different calendars placed anywhere between 1896 and 1901.

To mark the official start of the twentieth century according to the Roman calendar, Parham and his students held an all-night prayer vigil on December 31, 1900. As the third millennium began, a student named Agnes N. Ozman asked Parham to lay hands on her head and ask for her to be baptized in the Holy Spirit and given the gift of tongues. Sure enough, in the dawning hours of the first day of the twentieth century, Ozman began speaking in a language that the others identified as "the Chinese language." Ozman was unable to speak English for three days, and when she tried to convey her experience in writing, she wrote what others in the group recognized as Chinese characters.[55] They likewise saw Chinese characters in the shaky glyphs she wrote under the influence of the Spirit. "A Queer Faith: Strange Actions of the Apostolic Believers," read the headline in the *Topeka Daily Capital*, five days later.

**FIGURE 3.4** Stone's Folly, Topeka, Kansas, site of Parham's Beth El Healing and Bible Schools. Note the tower, site of the prayer vigil where Agnes N. Ozman first received the gift of tongues. Flower Pentecostal Heritage Center.

One scandalized former member told the newspaper that, "the members who succeed in getting it talk to each other in a sort of senseless gibberish and write a strange system of shorthand or hieroglyphics, which they say is conveyed from God personally."[56] Other newspapers derisively referred to the tongues early Pentecostals produced as "laundry talk," suggesting its similarity to the languages spoken by Chinese-born laundry workers throughout the West.[57] Indeed, thinking the sounds Ozman produced were Chinese, Parham's group took a copy of Ozman's writings to a "Chinaman" in a Topeka laundry. But he was unable to decipher the markings, saying, in the newspaper's stereotyped account: "me no understand. Takee to a Jap."[58]

Holiness people had been speaking in tongues on occasion for some time, but the Topeka outburst was the beginning of the modern Pentecostal movement, as Parham's group was one of the first to explain and spread the phenomenon as the fulfillment of Acts 2 and thus as a sign of the return of the church of the original Christian apostles.[59]

Beginning as it did with the (singular) "African dialect" and then continuing with the (singular) "Chinese language," Parham's Pentecostal phenomenon of xenoglossia occurred within the context of American Orientalism and was filtered through American ideas about Oriental and African foreignness. After Ozman received "the Chinese language," other students also received the gift of xenoglossia, claiming to have acquired "Syrian, Chinese, Japanese, Arabic and other languages," according to a skeptical account in the *Topeka State Journal* a week after the New Year's prayer vigil.[60] The Orientalist nature of the phenomenon only grew as the revival progressed. After the revivalists moved to Galena, in the ethnically diverse mining region of southeast Kansas, journalists emphasized the classical and Orientalist nature of the spiritual philology at work in tongue-speaking, reporting that members spoke in Latin, Hebrew, Chinese, and "various other tongues."[61] Soon after Parham's band packed up and took their revival to Houston, Texas, in 1905, they claimed to have summoned forth twenty different Chinese dialects.[62] At another revival the same year in Galveston, Parham's troupe spoke in an "African dialect" and "the Hindoo language."[63] Like the European and American Christian missionaries who had laboriously learned Oriental and African languages in order to evangelize their speakers, Parham and his students were in search of "missionary tongues" that would help spread the Christian message to foreign nations. Their objective was the same as that of Christian missionaries who learned Oriental languages, but they sought to achieve the same ends instantaneously through miraculous means.

Oriental languages were not the only languages the early Pentecostals claimed to speak, but such tongues make up either a plurality or a majority of the ones catalogued in the early accounts. As James R. Goff, Jr., has pointed out, Kansas at the time was a linguistically diverse place, which in 1870 had been more than 15 percent foreign born. Kansas had large numbers of Scandinavians, Bohemians, Germans, and French, and smaller numbers of Slavs, Hungarians, Bulgarians, Austrians, and Chinese. Parham's followers claimed to speak some or all of these languages, but "Oriental" tongues appeared far out of proportion to the representation of so-called Celestials (Chinese) in the population of northeast Kansas or Houston.[64] Linguist William J. Samarin studied speaking in tongues among Pentecostals fifty years after Ozman's initial discovery, and found that the predilection for Oriental tongues might be due to their exoticism and the common association between the Orient and the spirit world. But linguistic explanations are also possible; Samarin reported the identification of xenoglossia with Oriental and also Romance languages could reflect "a superficial but rather accurate observation of the phonological patterns of the glossas being uttered," noting that both language families have simpler syllabic structures than the long compound words of

Germanic languages. He also mentions a widespread belief among "occiden-tal men-in-the-street" that Oriental languages have no grammar and that they have a distinctive singsong tonal quality (reminiscent of the "laundry talk" comment, or mocking schoolyard and comedic parodies of Chinese language as a collection of random, tonal utterances). "Since the speakers could not identify their own intonational patterns with anything they knew, they could only call it oriental," Samarin writes. One of his informants reported that her glossa sounded like "an oriental chant." "Indeed," he concludes, "some tape recordings of glossolalia make one imagine romantic scenes from nineteenth-century plays of the exotic Far East."[65] Of course, it would make sense for Pentecostal tongues to remind one of nineteenth-century plays of the exotic Orient, since such plays were crucial vectors for spreading ideas about the East at the time when Pentecostal theology emerged in millennial, Holiness-infused, immigrant-rich, eastern Kansas.[66]

The Orient, Orientalism, and the ancient Israelites played an important part in Parham's thinking. He adopted Frank Sandford's identification with the ancient Israelites. Like Dowie, Sandford, and Crowdy, he claimed to be the second coming of the Prophet Elijah, and sometimes lectured in Kansas and Texas wearing "Palestinian robes," illustrating the fact that late Victorians viewed the contemporary dress and customs of the modern Orient as accu-rate depictions of the biblical past. Lecturing in the first years of his Pentecos-tal ministry in Houston wearing a white linen robe, surrounded by fourteen of his students in clothing purchased in Palestine, Parham depicted the East in Orientalist terms as static and unchanging: "These costumes," he said, "are the costumes worn in the Holy Land today as they were worn in Biblical times for the fashion never changes."[67] He then described each costume as well as "the habits of the people and the customs of the country of which the cos-tumes were representative."[68] The costumes included that of a menial worker, an "Arab Sheik," a "villager," and a "high caste lady"; two styles of "beautiful Jewish shawls,'" clothing of a "Jerusalem dude" and an official; a "garment of Ruth," a Greek Orthodox robe; and the costumes of a girl of Bethlehem and a Turk. Parham's doctrine of speaking in tongues was, in his hands, only one part of a much more comprehensive attempt to recreate "primitive Christian-ity," or the "apostolic faith," as he called it. During his time in Houston, Parham and his followers paraded down the street wearing their Palestinian costumes, holding a large banner reading "Apostolic Faith Movement."[69] Within Pentecostalism, the "apostolic faith" would come to be associated with the "Oneness" theology that taught salvation through "Jesus' name," not through the Holy Trinity.[70] Parham's embrace of "Eastern" ways suggest that

Orientalist ethnography—not simply the costumes but also the habits and customs of the Holy Land—became a central part of how he imagined the apostolic, biblical, past based on the Oriental present.

Like many Anglo-Israelites, Parham subscribed to the premillennialist doctrine that returning the Jews to the Holy Land would help initiate the messianic age, and he became obsessed with returning Jews to contemporary Palestine in order to bring the return of the messiah. Parham publicized Zionist founder Theodore Herzl's efforts to establish a Jewish homeland in Palestine, arguing that the United States owed the Jews assistance in restoring a national homeland because they were both related by blood to the ancient tribes of Israel. Citing Psalms 137:5, 6, "If I forget thee, O Jerusalem," Parham wrote, "We feel it an impossibility to describe to our readers the mingled feelings of joy and sadness…and probably no one but a Jew can understand the great love and affection that we bear Jerusalem. It amounts to a consuming passion. We long for her ancient glory, we pray for its restoration!" Parham described how he poured out his very soul in prayer for the "restoration" of Jerusalem and felt this prayer brought him "nearest to the heart of God" and into a "spirit of prophecy" like that of Ezekiel and Isaiah. "How glad we are for the work being done in the Zionist movement, under Dr. Herzel of Vienna, Austria!" Parham remarked in a book of sermons published in 1911.[71] In fact, Parham's support for Zionism was so prominent that when his band began holding meetings in Texas, the *Houston Chronicle* remarked on their tongue speaking, their faith healing, and "their peculiar gospel, that of reclaiming Zion to the Jews."[72]

Parham also sought to connect the biblical past to the Oriental present through archaeological excavations, with the aim of speeding the millennial reign of Jesus Christ. It was Parham's lifelong dream to conduct archaeological excavations in the Holy Land and to uncover Noah's Ark and the Ark of the Covenant, which he thought would be the only thing powerful enough to attract the world's Jews to Palestine and bring the return of Jesus Christ.[73] He actually set out to make a journey to Palestine in 1908, but had to return to Kansas when a thief stole his wallet in New York City.[74] And so this erstwhile Elijah who did so much to spark one of the largest religious movements of the twentieth century was undone by one of the new century's urban aggregations, places that the perfectionist-inspired Progressive movement and the Holiness-inspired Salvation Army were doing their best to reform. But the preacher persevered, and nineteen years later finally set off to see the Holy Land. When Parham finally did so, he initially found the Orient to be considerably less appealing in actuality than it had been in his imagination. Seeing the squalor of Cairo from the train window, he felt a visceral sense of revulsion, mixed with a newfound patriotism. "Something seems to bubble up inside of me," he wrote in his diary. "'Are you not glad you live in America?' I tell you, America for me!"[75] But the more time he spent, and the more he was able to map biblical narratives onto the geography of modern Palestine, the more comfortable he became. "The longer I stay the more real everything becomes," he wrote. "Now I can see each thing as it comes to me from the Bible, where it happened, the mountains, the lay of the land and towns. It makes the Bible all new."[76] The arid landscape reminded him of southern Texas, along the border with Mexico, and he was lost in a sensation of timelessness that was only interrupted by the modernization promoted by Jewish Zionist settlers. Despite the fine roads and small size of the country, "every time I go out I see something new and have to stop and think of old Bible times and pinch myself to see if I'm not living 2,000 or 3,000 years ago," he wrote. Although "the incoming Jews bring all modern machinery, yet the old settlers here keep on plodding along with old tools."[77] Using technology as the metric of modernity, Parham drew a familiar Eurocentric and Orientalist dichotomy between the new Jewish settlers, overwhelmingly from Europe, and the long-established local residents.

Parham was clearly enchanted with the allegedly timeless quality of the Palestinian present and imagined himself an expert on its culture and customs on the basis of his three months of travel there. The Kansas preacher posed for a number of photos in picturesque Arab dress, including one photo dressed as Elijah at the top of the wilderness of brook Cherith, where the Hebrew prophet was fed by ravens in 1 Kings 17:1–6. He purchased 200 slides of Palestine, "showing its people, customs, and many of the holy places," which he anticipated would allow him to give two different lectures on the Holy Land.[78]

Like Western Orientalists before and since, Parham framed the Orient within a set of received ideas about its timelessness and backwardness, a framework reinforced by the dichotomy between Zionist technological modernization and indigenous technological backwardness. This derogatory and Orientalist view of the Near East even expressed itself at the level of language: Parham referred to Arabic as "the junk of all languages," but claimed to have spoken in tongues many times in Yiddish—a mixed tongue if ever there was one—and expected "God to give me a wonderful ministry among the Jews in Jerusalem."[79] Parham's views were not simply Orientalist and Zionist but, like Anglo-Israelites who came before him, actively pro-imperialist: he wrote that Anglo-Saxons, as the descendents of the ancient Israelites, were fulfilling the imperialist prophecies that the Israelites would "push together the inhabitants of the earth to the ends thereof, possess it, yet retain the good will of him that dwelt in the bush."[80] For both Frank Sandford of Shiloh, Maine, and Charles Parham of the Great Plains, speaking in tongues was only one aspect of a return to the primitive Christianity of the Apostles within the context of the ideology of Anglo-Israelism, an ideology fueled both by sincere Christian piety and by derogatory Orientalist views about contemporary Near Eastern peoples.

The revivals led by Parham and Sandford were part of a global movement of Holiness revivals between 1898 and 1905 that featured speaking in tongues. After the initial visit during the War of 1898 that had first inspired him, Frank Sandford returned to the Orient in 1905, when he purchased a yacht and berthed off of Jaffa, Palestine, in order to begin a somewhat quixotic evangelization effort. With the press of the End Times upon him, there was no time to conduct the traditional, laborious, and slow process of evangelization. Therefore, Sandford decided to pray for God to convert the hearts of the world's peoples while anchored off the coasts of the world's continents. It was an expeditious, if chimerical, strategy. Anchored at the very spot where Jonah had set off on his ill-fated journey, Sandford's four-year voyage also hit rough seas. Increasingly authoritarian and delusional, attempting to avoid maritime authorities who threatened to arrest him if he set foot onshore, he drove the increasingly damaged ship into stormy seas, overloaded with too many passengers and not carrying enough food or water. Facing a mutiny and gale-force winds, the ship finally limped into port back in Maine. Six people died of scurvy and many more fell seriously ill. Sandford was convicted of causing their deaths and served seven years of a ten-year sentence in the federal penitentiary at Atlanta, Georgia.[81]

Christian missionary movements were some of the twentieth century's first and most significant transnational movements. International developments that shaped Pentecostalism included revivals in Wales and India in 1904 and 1905. In the words of evangelistic journalist Frank Bartleman, the Apostle Paul of the Pentecostal outburst, "The present world-wide revival was rocked in the cradle of little Wales. It was 'brought up' in India, following; becoming full grown in Los Angeles later."[82] The Welsh revival cohered around the figure of a charismatic preacher named Evan Roberts, a former miner and blacksmith who began having mystical visions in the midst of an ongoing revival in the spring of 1904. Roberts taught that the Baptism of the Holy Ghost could be realized personally, and that the revival was the beginning of a modern manifestation of the End Times spoken of in the story of

Pentecost found in Acts 2. The Welsh revival featured ecstatic worship and all of the familiar manifestations of the Spirit found in the past century of revivals: people slain in the spirit, thrown to the ground, unable to breathe, or unable to keep from singing, dancing, and weeping. Meetings lasted for hours and were almost completely spontaneous, featuring speaking and singing both in Welsh and in unknown tongues.[83]

Meanwhile, new revivals featuring speaking in tongues broke out in India, which had experienced Christian revivals since 1860. An Indian revival of 1904 broke out in the Khasi Hills in northeastern India, where Welsh Presbyterian missionaries were active in 1904, and another followed at a Christian mission for young widows and girls in Bombay run by Pandita Sarasvati Ramabai. Girls at the mission went to great lengths to induce altered states of consciousness, including singing, praying, clapping, and rolling on the floor. They beat themselves, jumped in place for hours, cried, and neither ate nor slept for days, causing school to be suspended. Those who attained trance states sustained them for as long as three or four days, and reported visions of a heavenly throne, a multitude robed in white, and blinding lights. At times, devotees spoke in tongues, and at other times colored lights seemed to appear over the heads of the ecstatic worshipers.[84] News of revivals and tongue speaking in Kansas, Maine, Wales, and Bombay spread through the Holiness movement's preexisting transnational circuits of the printed word, attracting international attention and helping to spread millennial enthusiasms.

If it is true that Israelite beliefs spread through Christian networks, and since the Christian believers in Israelite descent included white ministers such as Frank Sandford and Charles Parham in addition to African American ones such as William Christian and William Crowdy, then one would expect to find white Israelite movements in addition to Black ones. Indeed, such movements appeared around the same time as their African American contemporaries. In addition to Sandford's Shiloh community, which developed Israelite beliefs in the 1890s, Benjamin and Mary Purnell founded the Israelite House of David in Benton Harbor, Michigan, in 1903.[85] The Purnells believed themselves to be the seventh prophet in the line started by Joanna Southcott, and published a book in seven parts, each one promising to open one of the seven seals of Revelation, for the "ingathering and restoration of Israel."[86] They founded a thriving resort and sent circuit-riding preachers and bearded baseball players around the world to spread their beliefs, attracting other Southcott followers from as far away as Australia.[87]

The Pentecostal revival that broke out in Los Angeles in 1906 had many direct inspirations, inspirations that were both national and transnational, both Orientalist and anti-racist. One impetus was the introduction of Parham's Pentecostal "latter rain" theology into a city that was primed for revival. In 1906, a small Black Holiness congregation led by Julia Hutchins summoned an African-American student of Charles Parham's named William Joseph Seymour to lead a revival. Seymour had attended several months of Parham's school, sitting in the open doorway in the hall in deference to Texas's Jim Crow laws barring him from sitting among the other students.[88] Seymour had traveled west with his wife on a train ticket purchased by Parham and the other followers of the "apostolic faith" in Houston. But when he arrived in Los Angeles and preached Parham's theory that xenolalia was the sign of the baptism by the Holy Spirit, the church that had summoned him promptly threw him out. Holiness people believed they were already sanctified, and to preach that further evidence of sanctification was necessary was therefore blasphemous. Barred from formal places of worship, Seymour and his wife began to hold services where they were staying at a cottage on Bonnie Brae Street, to "a handful of colored and white saints," in the words of journalist Frank Bartleman.[89]

Los Angeles already had a large body of Holiness churches thanks to the efforts of Phineas Bresee, who had founded the Pentecostal Church of the Nazarene in 1895, and Joseph Smale, the head of the large First Baptist Church, who had visited the Welsh revival in 1905, bringing back its ardor and semi-anarchic pattern of worship. Thus, although the Seymours' message fell on deaf ears among established Black churches in Los Angeles, it found a welcome audience among the city's more radical Holiness revivalists. The crowds at the little cottage on Bonnie Brae Street quickly grew, filled with both earnest penitents and skeptical curiosity seekers attracted by the novelty of speaking in tongues.[90] When the crowds grew too large for the house, Seymour preached on the front porch, and when the weight of the excited congregants broke one of the floorboards, Seymour moved the assembly to an old church building that had been used as a warehouse in an industrial part of town, at 312 Azusa Street. There they lay planks on top of empty nail kegs and created seating for about thirty people, facing each other in a square (fig. 3.5). This was just before April 18, 1906, when 3,000 people lost their lives in the San Francisco earthquake less than four hundred miles to the north (although initial reports put the losses closer to 10,000 lives). Evangelist Frank Bartleman was among those who interpreted the San Francisco earthquake as divine retribution for the city's wickedness, and he promptly published a tract highlighting earthquakes in the Bible, spreading tens of thousands of copies throughout towns in southern California. In the weeks after the great earthquake,

**FIGURE 3.5** Leaders of the Azusa Street Mission, 1907. Seated in front (l-r): Sister Evans, Hiram W. Smith, William Seymour, Clara Lum. Second row, standing (l-r): unidentified woman, Brother Evans (reportedly the first man to receive the baptism in the Holy Spirit at Azusa Street), Jennie Moore (later Mrs. William Seymour), Glenn A. Cook, Florence Crawford, unidentified man, and Sister Prince. Florence Crawford's daughter, Mildred, is seated in the front on Hiram Smith's lap. Flower Pentecostal Heritage Center.

Bartleman brought his tract to the Azusa mission, and discovered a reverent, penitent, and interracial scene. When Bartleman first arrived, early in the revival, there were only a dozen "saints there, some white, some colored. Brother Seymour was there, in charge." According to Bartleman, the proceedings were marked by humility and earnestness, and were largely spontaneous, with worship starting of its own accord. "At 'Azusa Mission' we had a powerful time," he recalled. "The saints humbled themselves. A colored sister both spoke and sang in 'tongues.' The very atmosphere of Heaven was there."[91] As word of tongue-speaking spread throughout Holiness churches in Los Angeles, the crowds grew, and the gathering spread into a "tarrying room" upstairs, like the "upper rooms" used for prayer in Holiness communities from Shiloh to Topeka. "There were far more white people than colored coming. The 'color line' was washed away in the blood," Bartleman wrote.[92]

William Seymour was the leader of the revival, but part of why it succeeded to the extent that it did was because of his retiring nature and relaxed leadership style (fig. 3.6). Scholars who have overemphasized Seymour's centrality in the rise of Pentecostalism have intended either to recognize African American contributions to history or to claim Pentecostalism's emotional

FIGURE 3.6 William Seymour, who studied with Charles Parham in Houston and introduced Pentecostal teachings of xenolalia to Los Angeles at the revivals at Bonnie Brae and then Azusa Streets. Flower Pentecostal Heritage Center.

and spirit-filled mode of worship as part of longer cultural continuities with Africa. At their simplest, such arguments devolve into a simple invidious comparison between Charles Parham and William Seymour that largely ignore Pentecostalism's long theological continuities, social movements, and transnational revivals that spanned eras, continents, and races. Moreover, such narratives have unjustly ignored the Black women who did just as much or more than William Seymour to introduce Pentecostalism to Los Angeles. Seymour's journey west followed the trips of two African American women who had worshiped with Parham's followers in Houston and then returned to their homes in Los Angeles. Seymour came out to southern California at the behest of one of them, Mrs. Neeley Terry, a Black follower of white Holiness preacher Phineas Bresee of the Los Angeles-based Church of the Nazarene. Terry met Seymour while visiting relatives in Houston and received the gift of tongues at Parham's Bible School in Houston—long before pastor Seymour, who did not speak in tongues until the Azusa revival was well underway. Nor did Seymour find places to preach on his own: the couple that provided Seymour with a place to hold services on Bonnie Brae Street were relatives of Mrs. Terry's.[93] There was no platform or pulpit at the simple Azusa Street mission (fig. 3.7), and Seymour was a godly and humble man who was retiring to a fault and spent most of the meetings with his head inside of an empty shoe crate, in prayer. All were brothers and sisters in the spirit. "Brother Seymour was recognized as the nominal leader in charge," Bartleman reported. "But we had not pope or hierarchy. We had no human programme. The Lord himself was leading. We had no priest class, nor priest craft.... All were on a level."[94] In contrast to the segregated seating in Parham's Houston school, the Azusa Street revival boasted a form of radical egalitarianism, which during the Jim Crow era could only be found in African American neighborhoods and other communities of color. Nonetheless, the revival attracted people of all races from the very start, but met with disfavor from Los Angeles' established Black churches.

Crucially for the success of Pentecostalism, Azusa Street's revival transformed Parham's racial identification with the ancient Israelites and his Orientalist view of speaking in tongues. Influenced by its African American and interracial composition, the collective shed Parham's racial identification with the ancient Israelites, and adopted egalitarian, anarchic, and ecstatic modes of worship—not demonstrably borrowed from Africa, but rather from

FIGURE 3.7  The Azusa Street Mission, site of the revival that spread Pentecostal speaking in tongues across much of the Holiness movement. Flower Pentecostal Heritage Center.

Wales and India. The Los Angeles revival likewise shed Parham's Orientalist view of speaking in tongues as a means to acquire foreign, especially "Eastern" languages, and instead embraced even seemingly nonsensical tongues as evidence of baptism by the Holy Spirit. Both of these moves disgusted Charles Parham, and caused him to repudiate the Pentecostal movement that he did so much to inspire. At the start, this little revival bore some of the Orientalist hallmarks of its forebears: back at the cottage on Bonnie Brae Street, Seymour's future wife, Jennie Evans Moore, had impressed the stunned Los Angelenos by playing the piano and singing in a series of six languages, one of which she identified as Hebrew.[95] A young couple who visited Azusa claimed to have miraculously acquired Bengali, Hindustani, Tibetan, and Chinese.[96] But as the revival progressed, it rapidly lost its Orientalist pretensions, adopting a more egalitarian view of humanity and a more eclectic view of glossolalia as not primarily a facsimile of human language but rather as a mode of communication with the divine, not with humans. As Bartleman described it, the gift of tongues "was a spontaneous manifestation and rapture no earthly tongue can describe."[97] Bartleman, who through his journalism became the primary evangelist of the new Pentecostal movement, defended its glossolalia as a new form of wordless communication. "Was not sound given before language?" he asked. "And is there not intelligence without language also?"[98] The "new song" of the Azusa Street revival was "altogether different," Bartleman maintained, "not of human composition."[99] The skeptics seemed to agree that these new utterances were not language, even if they recognized that something newsworthy had occurred. "Breathing strange utterances and mouthing a creed which it would seem no sane mortal could understand, the newest religious sect has started in Los Angeles," reported the *Los Angeles Daily Times.*[100]

Indeed, it was this lack of correspondence to human language that drew the condemnation of Parham when he visited the Los Angeles revival. For Parham, tongues had to be intelligible human languages for them to be authentic recreations of the Pentecost of Acts 2. Only a genuine Pentecost would signal the return of apostolic times, with Anglo-Saxons as the heirs to the ancient Israelites. But the Azusa revival shared neither Parham's vision of Acts 2 nor his exclusionary racial ideology. Newspapers printed sensationalist accounts of intimate interracial contact in the "upper room" at Azusa, designed to shock racist readers. Parham, for one, was appalled by Azusa's racial integration. "I have seen meetings where all crowded together around the altar, and laying across one another like hogs, Blacks and white mingling," he commented some years later, "this should be enough to bring a blush of shame to devils, let alone angels."[101] Seymour warmly introduced his former teacher to the assembled Azusa Street participants, but Parham condemned the proceedings and did not fit in with the humble and egalitarian mood of the Los Angeles revivalists. They soon asked the first Pentecostal theologian to leave, and he established a rival revival at the local YMCA.[102]

The partial and incomplete conversion of the Holiness movement to Pentecostalism signaled an important departure from speaking in known human languages to speaking in tongues that frequently had no worldly equivalent. This shift was part of a transition from often dictatorial male Holiness preachers, prophets, and sect leaders to member-driven, female-dominated, charismatic Pentecostal ritual practices. It was precisely the eclipse of charismatic and controversial Holiness leaders that allowed the Pentecostal movement to flourish, shifting the Holiness tongues movement from authoritarian and theocratic male leaders, with narrow understandings of xenoglossia, to more democratic leadership and more inclusive practices of glossolalia. These critical shifts allowed Pentecostalism to surmount the limits and personalities of charismatic preachers and to harness raging democratic spiritual energies, spirit-filled charismatic ritual practices, and multilinguistic diversity—first of America, and then of the world. In the 1960s and 1970s, Pentecostalism inspired charismatic, tongues-filled movements within mainline Protestant denominations as well as the Roman Catholic Church. By the end of the twentieth century, Pentecostals and their charismatic fellow travelers accounted for an amazing 23 percent of the United States' population and one-quarter of the world's one billion Christians, with growing communities in the "global South" of Asia, Africa, and Latin America.[103]

Numerous scholars have attempted to make the case that Pentecostal speaking in tongues was an expression of a particularly Black form of worship with roots in African religions retained in the Americas. In truth, African American influences on Pentecostalism are far deeper and far different. It was John Wesley's journey to America, and partly his failed attempts to minister to Native Americans and African Americans, that led him to his doctrine of perfectionism that became Methodism. Africans and their descendants contributed uniquely enthusiastic forms of worship to American Christianity.[104] African Americans played key roles in spreading both Methodism and Holiness teachings throughout nineteenth-century revivals. But there is nothing explicitly or solely African about spirit possession, anarchic styles of worship, or Pentecostal speaking in tongues. In truth, the development of Pentecostalism was transnational, interracial, and polycultural.

Speaking in tongues or catching the Spirit was not something that all Black people in America knew how to do at the turn of the twentieth century, even though ecstatic worship was commonplace among enslaved Africans.[105] Rather, as Wallace Best and Milton Sernett have shown, many early twentieth-century Black churches had to learn how to catch the Spirit.[106] Although two Black women and one Black man spread Parham's teachings from Houston to Los Angeles, within days there were more whites than Blacks at the Azusa Street revival, and Pentecostalism spread through preexisting networks of (majority-white) Holiness ministers, missionaries, lay people, and journalists. Los Angeles's more established Black churches rejected the revival and its embarrassingly emotional and allegedly undignified ways of worship. Spirit possession upset the formal, even staid form of worship favored by many Black Americans since the end of slavery, when the community placed a premium on "respectability" in an effort to disprove the racist doctrine of white supremacy. A historical argument of African origins based on simple homologies between contemporary Pentecostal and contemporary African modes of spirit possession ignores similar homologies with European, Native American, and Asian spirit possession practices, overlooks the long history of theological perfectionism around the world, replaces the African past with the African present, and devalues the creativity of African-Americans, who did not live in what anthropologist Melville Herskovits termed a sterile "laboratory" simply remixing outside inputs from Europe, Africa, and Asia.[107] Instead, the Pentecostal revival demonstrates the saliency of volitional, fictive, and imagined Israelism and Orientalism in America, as well as the transnational, polycultural, and interracial nature of American cultural formation.

The popularity of the Holiness movement waned but did not disappear with the rise of its more popular Pentecostal offspring. Many Holiness people never accepted the Pentecostal teaching that speaking in tongues was evidence of baptism in the Holy Spirit. And the Holiness template of charismatic leaders invested with prophetic and quasi-messianic powers by their followers continued into the twentieth century, providing models for Sweet Daddy Grace, Elder Michaux, Father Divine, Rabbi Wentworth Arthur Matthew, and postwar Black Israelite leaders such as Ben Ami.

The Holiness camp meetings, revivals, and fiery preachers of the nineteenth century had produced a potent culture of biblical literalism and explosive theological innovations. Some results of that culture were the Israelite Holiness churches that attempted to recreate the apostolic church and that traced their ancestry back to the ancient Hebrews. Another, much larger, effect was the bloom of Pentecostal movements that took America and the world by storm. Living in the fertile intersection between biblical exegesis, Israelism, and Orientalist ethnography, early Holiness-Pentecostals imagined themselves to be communicating with people on the other side of the world, speaking in tongues that they understood to have fallen from heaven like cloven tongues of fire, as in apostolic times. As the young country sought new frontiers and conquered new peoples in the East, its spirit-filled evangelicals traced the same circuits of empire and brought a new belief system—from Maine, Chicago, Wales, Bombay, Kansas, Houston, and Los Angeles—to the world.

# 4 "OUR ONLY HOPE, OUR ONLY SALVATION AS A RACE"

## RABBI ARNOLD JOSIAH FORD, ETHIOPIANISM, AND AFRICAN AMERICAN SETTLERS IN ETHIOPIA

In previous chapters we have seen how the very idea of descent from the Lost Tribes of Israel followed a crooked trajectory: as a justification for the Anglo-American rule over foreign peoples; as a promise of the reconstitution of apostolic times; and also as an explanation of African Americans' history of bondage and liberation. This chapter describes the rise of a second generation of Black Israelite movements, which began to shift from Holiness Christianity toward the adoption of some of the language, clothing, and customs of Jews of European descent—but always as part of a complex bricolage of distinctly Black Israelite beliefs and practices. Harlem, New York City, became the epicenter of this new form of Black Israelism, which was defined as much by its politics as by its prayers. This chapter focuses on the politics of a group of Black Israelites who attempted to settle in Ethiopia in 1930, hoping to create a refuge and a colony for African Americans. They accepted, along with the colonial project, the patriarchal gender politics of "manly" Western pioneers settling and developing a continent they understood in Orientalist terms as both feminine and backwards. As Black Israelites and as Black Nationalist colonists, these settlers of Ethiopia were both lovers of Zion and practitioners of their own brand of Zionism. The Black Israelite colony in Ethiopia ultimately failed, but relayed the Israelite idea to Jamaican missionaries who returned to that island and helped spark the religious revolution of Rastafarianism, one of the most popular embodiments of Black Israelite religion in the world today.

This chapter centers on one individual, Arnold Josiah Ford, a Barbadian-born musician who befriended the Black Nationalist leader Marcus Garvey and played in the court of Ethiopia's Emperor Haile Sellasie. Ford was a man of extraordinary talent, initiative, and charisma. He was a "gentleman of parts," according to the U.S. State Department; "a musician, a 'pensman,' an artist, [who] reads writes and speaks Hebrew, and 'knows all about everything.'"[1] But this chapter is not solely Ford's story. Understanding the Israelite phenomenon, or any other intellectual trend or religious movement, requires appreciating not only the exceptional individuals like Crowdy, Christian, Parham, and Ford, but also the multifaceted networks in which those individuals functioned.

Ford is a shining example of the Ethiopianism that characterized second-generation Black Israelite thinkers. Following pioneering Bishops William Christian and William Crowdy, there were several Black Holiness churches that adopted Israelite beliefs, and several of them focused their teachings on the country of Ethiopia in the years after the modern Abyssinian nation dramatically repulsed Italian invaders at the Battle of Adwa (Adowa) in 1896. Father Elias Dempsey Smith, for example, founded a Holiness church he called "Triumph, the Church and Kingdom of God in Christ" between 1897 and 1904.[2] Like his contemporary, Bishop Crowdy, Father Smith taught strict adherence to the Ten Commandments as well as baptism by immersion and racial egalitarianism. With the rise of the Pentecostal movement in the early years of the twentieth century, Father Smith came to teach a Pentecostal faith of entire sanctification through baptism by the fire of Spirit in the form of glossolalia. Father Smith's church spread across the Eastern seaboard, and Father Smith himself left for Addis Ababa, in 1920, and later died in Ethiopia.[3]

Another bishop, R.A.R. Johnson, exemplified both the Israelite and the Ethiopianist streams of the Holiness movement. Johnson, who was born in New Bern, North Carolina, was an itinerant preacher who founded a church called "Abyssinia" around the turn of the century, and followed that with the "House of God, Holy Church of the Living God, the Pillar and Ground of Truth, the House of Prayer for All People" in 1914.[4] Johnson's church had many similarities to Crowdy's: its members kept the Sabbath on Saturday, observed some Jewish festivals, abstained from Christmas and Easter, and wore distinctive costumes, including white headdresses for female members, between the Jewish holidays of Passover in the spring and Sukkoth in the fall. Smith incorporated the church in 1918, and it soon spread to Washington, D.C., and caught on in the West Indies, West Africa, and even southern India. Johnson preached twenty-four principles, including baptism by immersion, foot washing, equality of races in the church, the investiture of female clergy, and sanctification by the Holy Spirit.[5]

The Black Israelite movement began to shift away from its roots in the Southern Holiness movement thanks to three great migrations: of Eastern

European Jews, of Southern African Americans, and of Black West Indians, who found themselves living next to each other during and after the First World War in cities across the northern United States, but especially in New York City.[6] Afro-Caribbean immigrants to the United States ballooned from a scant 411 in 1899 to 12,243 per year by 1924. Among these immigrants were many of the people who would become Ford's followers, hailing from islands such as Barbados, Jamaica, and St. Vincent. Despite the impact of restrictive immigration legislation in 1924, which constricted the flow by 95 percent, the population of foreign-born Blacks in the United States grew from 20,000 in 1900 to almost 100,000 in 1930. The majority of Black immigrants headed for New York City, where they joined the burgeoning ranks of African American migrants from Virginia and North Carolina who were rapidly transforming uptown Manhattan into a Black Mecca. On the whole, the Black Caribbean immigration was well-balanced by sex, with men composing 50.2 percent of the net arrivals from 1908–1931. By 1930, almost a quarter of Black Harlem hailed from the Caribbean.[7] Black West Indians had already proven a receptive audience for Black American Holiness churches, as Bishop Crowdy's and Bishop Johnson's success in spreading their messages internationally demonstrates. In Harlem, West Indians would become leaders and members of Black Israelite communities, which, for the first time, adopted many of the trappings and some of the beliefs of their new white Jewish neighbors.

Around the First World War, the urban north produced a second wave of Black Israelite movements with certain common elements: a focus on Ethiopia, Garveyite Black nationalism, and the incorporation of some Ashkenazi or Sephardic ritual, beliefs, and prayers into a complex bricolage of Holiness and esoteric beliefs and practices.[8] The most popular and controversial of these was the group around Elder Warien Roberson (a.k.a. E. W., Eli, Warren, or Ishi). In addition to its checkered history of scandals, Roberson's group is noteworthy for presenting themselves as Jews by imitating Yiddish-inflected Ashkenazi Jewish speech, gestures, costume, and mannerisms, and by pioneering the communal living and the deification of their leader that predated the practices of 1930s sect leader Father Divine. Roberson's group was perhaps most famous, however, for its lurid sex scandals. Born around 1880, Roberson became convinced in 1900, while working as a fishmonger in Norfolk, Virginia, that he was the second coming of Jesus Christ.[9] He founded a church called the Temple of the Gospel of the Kingdom or the Ever-Live-and-Never-Die Church.[10] Roberson conducted worship services in the style of Southern Holiness "Holy Rollers," featuring fainting, religious ecstasies, and direct revelations of God's will.[11] Evicted from Norfolk as a nuisance in 1908, he established a base in Philadelphia by 1910, at which time he came under suspicion in the murder of a church member who had left the group and revealed some of its secrets. He escaped to Mays Landing, New Jersey, where he changed his name and tried to found another group. Before he could do so, he was convicted of burglary, jumped bail, and went to New York City. In 1912 he tried and failed to form a group in New York and relocated to Atlantic City, where he brought his Philadelphia followers and finally succeeded in building the organization he desired. Roberson built up an initial following of around 300 African American and West Indian members and opened a branch in New York City in 1917, as well as branches in three other cities.[12] Roberson required members to live communally and to relinquish their possessions to the church, while Roberson accrued a substantial fortune.

The majority of Roberson's teachings would have fit into any Holiness Church. He sought to preserve health by clean living and prayer healing, and to promote peace, equality, brotherhood, and happiness through the acceptance of Christ.[13] Roberson's obsession with prayer healing extended to the denial of pain and diseases, and the elimination of death for those who believed in his teachings.[14] Like many nineteenth-century American Protestants, Roberson taught that the Bible's unfulfilled prophecies would soon reach fruition. This interest in biblical prophecy created the link to Jewish identity through identification with the covenant made to Abraham and with teachings of the Hebrew prophets.[15] According to controversial anthropologist Ruth Landes, the Church's beliefs were Jewish only in the sense that they believed that Jesus Christ was a Jew, and since they worshiped Christ, they reasoned that they were Jews.[16] Roberson taught that African Americans were descended from Esau, who was tricked out of his inheritance by Jacob, the father of the Jewish people. He claimed that African Americans were also direct descendents of King Solomon, and so were rightfully God's chosen people.[17] Roberson appointed twelve apostles to help spread his message, which included a belief in the return of the messiah in the year 1925.

Nonetheless, Roberson and his followers presented themselves as Jews, especially to European Jews on New York's East Side, to whom they appealed for charity to support apparently fictitious institutions to aid orphans and widows. At its height, Roberson's church had around 1,000 members and several businesses, including a butcher shop. They were even said to wield political power in Harlem. Followers lived in his "kingdoms," which were usually buildings owned by followers and sold to Roberson at low prices. Roberson taught his followers that the devil haunts a sleeping bed, so men slept on chairs and women on bare floors in separate rooms. Roberson's group pioneered many of the practices of the later movement of Father Divine, whose followers lived communally, practiced celibacy, invested in group-owned businesses, and worshiped their leader as God.[18] There were other ways in which Roberson's group was unique: the men grew beards, wore white robes and Jewish skull caps, and carried shepherd's staffs, referring to themselves as "Black Jews."[19] Men and women who joined the group had to foreswear marital ties and become "brother and sister." Only the groups' priests were allowed to have sexual relations with female members, and in time Roberson asserted his exclusive right to sleep with his congregants, siring numerous children who were raised communally in Absecon, New Jersey.[20]

In 1920, Roberson was again convicted of burglary, and spent the next three years in Trenton State Prison. Upon his release, his personal stature within the group only increased, as did the scale of his sexual perversity. He created a "Virgin Class" who served to bear children for himself and his closest advisors; he created a cadre of young men to seduce wealthy women; and followers knelt in front of him and kissed his feet. He expanded operations to Chicago, Philadelphia, Detroit, Atlantic City, and Absecon, New Jersey, bought a $17,000 luxury Pierce-Arrow automobile, and was accompanied everywhere by a chauffeur and a bodyguard.[21]

Roberson's real downfall, the revelation of the sect's sexual practices, and the resulting disgrace of his church, came in 1926, when he was convicted of violating the Mann Act for transporting the women of his Virgin Class between his various communities in different states. After he was released from prison this time, Roberson took a much less active role in the church until his death on June 18, 1931. Because Roberson had predicted that he would rise from the dead to destroy the world, his followers refused to relinquish his body until the authorities interceded thirty days after his death. In that time, his widow Fanny disappeared with the entire estate, which exaggerated estimates valued at $8,000,000. The fiasco confirmed the poor opinion of Black sects among many African Americans as well as Jews. In the words of Edward G. Wolf, writing in 1933, Roberson's movement preyed on the Jews of New York, and was "almost purely mercenary and lascivious, although some of the leaders were sincere in their misguided beliefs."[22] According to one prominent Black rabbi, "it sure took a long time to live that one down."[23]

Through the efforts of Father Smith and Bishop Johnson, Black Israelite movements had acquired a keen interest in Ethiopia; through Elder Roberson's hundreds of followers it had become commonplace for African Americans in Harlem to dress, speak, and act as Jews. But bringing these elements together with aspects of Judaism and linking them to the Black nationalism of Marcus Garvey's United Negro Improvement Association was the work of a different coterie of individuals, exemplified by none better than Rabbi Arnold Josiah Ford. Ford was a musician, a Freemason, and a Garveyite, who was born in Bridgetown, Barbados, on April 23, 1877. The son of an itinerant "fire and brimstone" preacher father and a Moravian mother, Ford was baptized on June 17, 1877.[24] In 1899 he joined the British Navy as a musician and spent several years on board the *H.M.S. Alert* before being stationed in Bermuda, where he worked as a clerk at the Court of General Assize. British Navy documents recorded Ford's religious affiliation as the Church of England.[25] He also studied classical languages, and would go on to acquire Latin, Greek, Hebrew, Arabic, and Amharic.[26] After studying music in London, Ford arrived in New York in 1912 at the age of thirty-four, where he passed the examination for violin administered by the New Amsterdam Musical Association (N.A.M.A.), a union for Harlem musicians, and was made an official member of the N.A.M.A. on February 16, 1916.

Ford worked as a musician in New York and belonged to the Black musicians' union until 1920.[27] Adept on a wide range of instruments, from string bass and violin to piano and banjo, Ford was a worldly, cultured, and mannerly gentleman who took great care in his appearance and possessed abundant talent, intelligence, and charisma. In New York, he made a living as a musician and music teacher and played with some of Harlem's leading ragtime bands and pioneering jazz ensembles, including the James Reese Europe Orchestra, the Vernon and Irene Castle Dance Band, and the Wilbur Sweatman Orchestra. Like many West Indians in interwar New York, Ford was also extremely active in political causes. He was sympathetic to the socialist politics of Cyril Brooks' African Blood Brotherhood (A.B.B.), and even volunteered his dance band to play at the launching of the A.B.B.'s Harlem-based magazine, *The Crusader*.[28] In Harlem, Ford met Virginia-born Olive Nurse, nine years his junior, and they married and started a family on 131st Street in Harlem.[29] Their first child, Gwendolyn Aenid Ford, was born in January 1916, and Violet Arlene Ford followed four years later.[30]

Ford lived at a time when West Indian émigrés were gaining worldwide acclaim in Harlem, and none gained more notice than his contemporary, Marcus Mosiah Garvey. Garvey was a man of humble origins who rose to become one of the most dominant personalities of his age, a man who inspired the hopes of millions. Born August 17, 1887, in St. Ann's Bay, Jamaica, Garvey learned the printing trade at the age of fourteen, and became politically aware by traveling to Central America and witnessing the desperate situation of local Blacks, many of whom had left the West Indies to work in back-breaking and poor-paying jobs building the Panama Canal or harvesting bananas for large U.S.-based corporations. Upon his return to Jamaica in 1914, Garvey started the Universal Negro Improvement Association (U.N.I.A.) with the goal of uniting the peoples of the African diaspora and advocating for the establishment of independent Black nations in Africa. The slogan of the Garvey movement was "Back to Africa," which was understood as both a philosophical and a literal return to the mother continent. Garvey came to the United States in 1916 to visit Booker T. Washington's Tuskegee Institute, but Washington died before his arrival. Garvey proceeded to Harlem, where he founded a branch of the U.N.I.A. in 1917. Through his newspaper, *The Negro World*, and by the force of his powerful oratory, Marcus Garvey captured the hearts of millions, and the U.N.I.A. blossomed, holding large parades and conventions and launching ambitious business enterprises. His headquarters in New York, Liberty Hall, was not just a site of political organizing; it was also a place that brought together people for educational and religious events. Garvey's grandiosity and his combativeness won him the enmity of much of the Black elite, who viewed him as an absurd upstart. Garvey founded the Black Star steamship line to conduct trade and transport passengers between the U.S. and West Africa, but the ship he purchased was unseaworthy, and the enterprise suffered from poor management. The shipping effort turned into a fiasco that led to Garvey's imprisonment on fraud charges in 1925. Yet despite such setbacks, Garvey and his movement embodied and expressed the militancy, nationalism, and excitement that characterized a large segment of the Black masses in the hopeful years after the First World War. Many African Americans, especially in the South, embraced Garveyism because it promoted self-respect, pride, and racial militancy.[31]

In Harlem, Ford joined the many other West Indian immigrants who were active in Marcus Garvey's movement, and "soon became one of its leading lights, a much loved and respected figure who was highly esteemed for his intelligence," according to one scholar.[32] In 1920, when Garvey's U.N.I.A. held its first large convention in New York, Ford served as an official representative and was one of the signers of the Declaration of Rights of Negro Peoples of the World.[33] The same year, he became the musical director of Liberty Hall, Garvey's headquarters, and he went on to write many of the hymns that gave the movement a spiritual identity, including co-writing its stirring anthem, "Ethiopia," or, "The Universal Ethiopian Anthem." Ford and his collaborator, Ben Burrell, were motivated to write the anthem by the murder of a Black teenager who had been raped by the head of the household for whom she worked as a domestic servant.[34] The song uses martial metaphors of onrushing armies and out-thrust swords as it urges the "children" of Ethiopia, "land of our fathers," to "Advance, advance to victory!" under the red, black, and green banner of the U.N.I.A. The song includes the stanza:

> O Jehovah, Thou God of the ages
> Grant unto our sons that lead
> The wisdom Thou gav'st to Thy Sages
> When Israel was sore in need.[35]

The choice of the Old Testament name of God and the reminder of God's covenantal relationship with the biblical people of Israel was not accidental: Ford's interest in Judaism emerged out of his involvement in political activism in general and the Garvey movement in particular.[36]

When Ford's second daughter was born in 1920, not only was she baptized in Liberty Hall but when she was confirmed in the same place, Marcus Garvey himself was her godfather. Despite her husband's intense commitment to the Garvey movement, however, Ford's wife Olive Nurse was not involved in his political activities, and his activism led to marital difficulties. "My mother was very family-oriented, and my father was very race-oriented," their daughter Arlene recalled. The Fords separated around 1924, and they sent their younger daughter to live with family in Barbados, joining her older sister, who had been in Barbados since the age of fifteen months. Both girls returned in 1926 and lived with their mother, who supported them and paid for their music lessons. They used to attend their father's synagogue on Saturdays and play music with him in local churches on Sundays. Ford's younger daughter, Arlene Ford Straw, remembers that in the late twenties "We used to play on Sunday afternoons, sort of a circuit in the local churches, my sister, my father, and myself. He played the string bass, I played the piano, and my sister played the violin. I don't remember what we played, but I know we did it for quite a while."[37]

Ford was also a 33° Freemason, and was a member and Master of Memmon Lodge, Number 51, of a local branch of the Scottish Rite Masons.[38] One of his brother Masons, and the president of the U.N.I.A. choir, was a Jamaican immigrant named Samuel Valentine, who shared Ford's interests in Hebrew and Judaism.[39] Valentine was an expert plasterer who came to America from Jamaica in 1919. Like Ford and many other West Indians, Valentine served on the high seas, in his case as a cook.[40] As noted above, Marcus Garvey's Liberty Hall headquarters was a place that brought together people for educational and religious events. With its grand providential themes and elaborate rituals, the Garvey movement attracted many of Harlem's religious innovators. Another Garveyite who shared Ford's interests was Mordecai Herman, a peddler who sold his wares from a horse and wagon and specialized in dolls and Jewish liturgical items. Like the members of Elder Roberson's "Ever Live" faith, Herman wore a beard, spoke some Yiddish, and was well known in Jewish neighborhoods in New York. Herman started a short-lived Masonic offshoot called the Moorish Zionist Movement in July 1921, which split up in 1922.[41] Like Ford and Valentine, Herman was also involved in Freemasonry, which may have been a factor in their shared interest in Judaism, in light of Masonry's investment in the legends of the Hebrew Bible and Jewish cabbalistic magic. The handsome, gregarious, and personable Ford helped out with Herman's business ventures, using his knowledge of Yiddish to act as an intermediary between Herman and some of his Jewish manufacturers.[42]

Ford "learned Hebrew from Jews in the Garment District," according to Eliezer Brooks, a Black Jew who was a longtime cantor and rabbi in various New York Black Israelite synagogues. "What he learned of Judaism he learned from Jews."[43] Ford, however, claimed to have studied Hebrew and Talmud with Egyptian teachers.[44] Ford, Valentine, and Herman held classes in Hebrew and other subjects every Sunday at Garvey's headquarters, Liberty Hall. Further evidence of his interest in Judaism comes from records of the 1922 U.N.I.A. convention, where Ford spoke for the advocates of Judaism on a committee on the "Future Religion of the Negro."[45] But although Garvey's ideas continued to influence Ford, he did not remain under Garvey's umbrella for long; in 1923, when the Federal government convicted Garvey on charges of mail fraud connected with the sale of Black Star Line stock, Ford viewed it as his own personal destiny to lead the Black race.[46] In 1925, Ford brought successful lawsuits against Garvey and the U.N.I.A. for not paying him royalties from recordings and sheet music of his compositions.[47]

Ford and Valentine left the U.N.I.A. in 1923 and started a congregation called Beth B'Nai Israel.[48] The pair then joined Herman in forming a synagogue they called the Moorish Zionist Temple (M.Z.T.) (fig. 4.1). Both served as religious leaders and teachers, while Samuel Valentine was the president of the school, Talmud Torah Beth Zion.[49] Ford took the title of rabbi and was able to attract support from local white Jews, in addition to bringing many members of his U.N.I.A. choir with him to the new Judaic organization— notably Eudora Paris, its lead singer.[50] But the M.Z.T. would be short lived. There was friction between Ford and his collaborators that continued in 1924, when he and Herman argued over Ford's use of the title "rabbi" and his

**FIGURE 4.1** Rabbi Mordecai Herman and the Moorish Zionist Temple of the Moorish Jews in 1920s Harlem, photographed by James Van Der Zee. © Donna Mussenden VanDerZee.

desire to take his choir on professional concert tours. Herman had no popular following of his own; he was overshadowed by Ford's intelligence and charisma, and felt that Ford took advantage of him.[51] Just as they had once left the U.N.I.A. to join the M.Z.T., Ford and Valentine left the M.Z.T. to establish their own congregation, Beth B'nai Abraham (B.B.A.), attracting the choir and a number of other followers (see figs. 4.2–4.5).

In the B.B.A., Ford, Valentine, and their congregants created a synagogue that practiced a form of Judaism that was much closer to European Jewish liturgy and rituals than those of the Black Israelite churches—based on the Holiness movement—that had come before. Whereas the Holiness Black Israelite founders had derived Judaic practices from Christian and Masonic texts and practices, Ford and his collaborators were not trying to use Christian scriptures to "reverse engineer" the Hebraic practices of the early Christian church. Instead, they rejected Christianity and practiced Jewish rituals with Jewish prayer books. As Ford put it in a letter to a white Jewish correspondent, "The Congregation Beth B'nai Abraham is a number of Black Jews (Hebrews, we call ourselves) who have resolved to found a Synagogue or temples

FIGURE 4.2 Rabbi Ford and the BBA Choir in front of the BBA's storefront in Harlem, June 30, 1925. The original caption for this photo said that the congregation "is gathered from all parts of Africa and also from South America and the West Indies. In addition to his religious duties, Rabbi Ford conducts a vocal and instrumental music group, particular attention being given to Hebrew and Arabic melodies." © Underwood & Underwood/Corbis.

among their racial brethren in Harlem for the purpose of congregating and worshipping the One Supreme Being pursuant to the Laws and Customs of Ancient Israel."[52] Ford's preference for the terms "Hebrew" and "Israelite" rather than "Jew" helped to carve out an autonomous identity separate from white Jews. "We are Africans," he declared, in a bold, three-word sentence.[53] Ford used the category of "race," but not to signify skin color or geographical origin but rather "culture and human virtues evolved through generations of obedience to certain Laws, Statutes and traditions."[54]

Ford proclaimed that no "Caucasian" Jews ever taught his congregation—"Caucasian," he wondered, "(is that a nice name?)"[55]—but Ford's close associate, Samuel Valentine, did indeed accept the tutelage of Ashkenazi Jews. In 1927, a white Jewish reporter attended a *bris* for Valentine's son, and noted that the Black Jews wanted to be recognized as Jews but depended on white Jews for liturgical and cultural guidance. "The negroes felt at once humiliated and exalted," the reporter wrote. "They receive so much attention and yet they had to yield to the few white Jews who knew ever so much more about this ceremony."[56]

FIGURE 4.3 Samuel Valentine and male members of Beth B'Nai Abraham. Reproduced from B. Z. Goldberg, "A Negro Bris," *B'Nai B'rith Magazine* (New York) 41, no. 11 (August 1927): 465.

One obnoxious white Jew "embarrassed the negroes by making too plain their lack of knowledge," and later insisted, fairly absurdly, that pickled herring was essential for the completion of the ceremony.[57] Yet despite such intrusiveness, other white Jews participated in the ceremony more cooperatively: the *mohel* was a white Jew, and a white rabbi was among the handful of white Jews in attendance.[58] Valentine later led a group that split off from Ford's B.B.A., wanting an observance that was more similar to Judaism of European derivation, so it is possible that his willingness to accept the guidance of white Jews was not representative of Ford or his following.[59] On one occasion, however, Rabbi Ford reportedly officiated at a wedding of members of the congregation with the assistance of a white rabbi.[60] Whether the white rabbi truly served as an assistant, or whether he was present as a teacher, is impossible to discern.

Ford's Hebrews, for their part, were sincere in their desire to practice Judaism. They would not say they had converted to Judaism; instead, they insisted that they had returned to Judaism, and that their families had long traditions of practicing Jewish customs.[61] Ford insisted that Judaism itself was originally

**FIGURE 4.4** Barbardian-born Rabbi Arnold Josiah Ford, musician, leader of the UNIA choir, rabbi of Beth B'Nai Abraham, and Ethiopian pioneer, from the frontispiece of *The Universal Ethiopian Hymnal*, (New York: Beth B'Nai Abraham Publishing Company, 1922). Manuscripts, Archives and Rare Books Division, Schomburg Center for Research in Black Culture, New York Public Library, Astor, Lenox and Tilden Foundations.

African, and that contemporary West Africa was not only Semitic but Mosaic. It was the Romans who had "severed Africa completely from the recognized Jewish economy."[62] Yet he ascribed most of the origins of contemporary Black Hebrews to contact and descent from Sephardic Jews in the West Indies in recent history. Ford believed that his congregation's teachings came through its members' parents, but believed that their ancestors had suffered side by side with their "Caucasian brethren" during the Inquisition and the trans-Atlantic slave trade.[63] According to Ford, 600 Sephardic Jews fleeing the Spanish Inquisition were shipwrecked off St. Thomas and the Virgin Islands, where they remained, intermarried with free Africans, and passed on their names and customs to their descendants.[64]

**FIGURE 4.5** Rabbi Ford in a turban. Turbans were commonly used in Black Spiritual churches and signified the mystical East when used by Black religious-magical workers. Reproduced from B. Z. Goldberg, "A Negro Bris," *B'Nai B'rith Magazine* (New York) 41, no. 11 (August 1927): 465.

"The negroes are very serious about being Jews," the reporter noted of Samuel Valentine's family. "They observe the least *mitzva* as the most important."[65] Ford declared that their intention was to observe the Sabbath and all holy days, along with all laws of the *bris* and laws governing the household and families, "as nearly as our deplorable economic conditions will allow us." Moreover, Ford and his congregation wanted to train their children to observe Hebraic laws and customs and to grow up "as Israelites." "Although in ritualism we may differ and perhaps be found wanting," he declared, "in heart and custom we are Hebraic and nothing else." Beth B'nai Abraham also had a universalistic perspective, wanting to teach respect for the laws of the land and to "disseminate Love, good will and Peace to all mankind."[66]

Between 1927 and 1929, the congregation succeeded in acquiring two torahs. They held services on Friday and Sunday nights and not on Saturday, because too many members had to work Saturdays to allow a *shabbos* service. But they continued to aspire to be as faithful to Jewish customs as possible. Their services were "a mixture of Reform and Orthodox Judaism, but when they practice the old customs they are seriously orthodox," wrote another white Jewish observer.[67] They claimed eighty-five members, excluding children, and at one point as many as seventy-five children ages five to fourteen were taking Hebrew classes taught by the rabbi.[68] Twenty-eight adults and two children took classes in Hebrew and Arabic on Sunday mornings, so that they could better understand the original sources of their ancestral history.[69]

Politics, not simply prayers, were discussed in the pews of the B.B.A. When Ford left the U.N.I.A. to found his own Jewish synagogue, he took a lot of the U.N.I.A. with him. The fact that the initials of the B.B.A. were the inverse of the African Blood Brotherhood (A.B.B.) was probably not coincidental, as Ford was a sympathizer of that group, a Socialist organization with many West Indian members, and his band played at A.B.B. events. The link between Ford and the

A.B.B. may help to explain why the A.B.B. chose the term "Negro Sanhedrin" to describe its summit in 1924, as the term "Sanhedrin" is borrowed from the Jewish rabbinical councils of ancient times. When the left-leaning Intercollegiate Cosmopolitan Club and the Fellowship of Reconciliation toured radical headquarters in 1925 and 1927, Beth B'nai Abraham made the cut.[70] The F.B.I. reported that many of the members expressed "communistic leanings."[71] As a former seaman, Ford would have been a prime candidate for the communist policy of recruiting merchant seamen, and might have been influenced by Communist Party organizing drives carried out through organizations such as the Harlem Workers' Center, the American Negro Labor Congress, and the League of Struggle for Negro Rights.[72]

The most thorough outside observer of Ford's congregation concluded that Garvey's nationalism was "the essential matrix of the B.B.A.," and that "Judaism had touched the B.B.A. only as an arabesque, a signature of Ford's genius."[73] A more charitable estimation would be that Judaism, for Ford, was only one part of a much broader concern with the progress of the race, understood in Romantic terms. We can see the tenor of Ford's lofty concerns, and his somewhat florid manner of expressing them, in the précis he wrote to one of his compositions, entitled "Africa." "With the unassuming demeanour of the humble widow casting, ungrudgingly, her only two mites into the Jewish treasury, I dedicate this sincere though feeble effort, in the service of the Great Supreme, to the scatter'd millions of native souls of the dark, yet the brightest, richest, and most prospective continent of this our terrestrial globe," Ford wrote, with both exaggerated humility and the language of uplift that trained its high-flying adjectives on the so-called dark continent. Using a Masonic term for God, Ford continued, "The Divine Architect has glorified our race by bestowing on us stalwart physical structures and powerful intellects, for the purpose of soaring *ad libitum* to the highest summit of civilization and immortal glory allotted to sons of earth." This is the discourse of civilization, wielded on behalf of the Black race. For Ford, who himself had a dark complexion, Blackness was not a mark of ignominy, as in the Curse of Ham, but was rather a marker of election. "The Divine Artist knew and did what was best when He decorated our section of His wonderful creation with the darker and stronger shades of His palette," Ford wrote. "What He has done is well done. Then for all things let us praise Him. Let us live in direct conformation to His Supreme will. Not to be ashamed of, or try to shun the banner under which He has placed us," Ford concluded, "but to take it up, wave it high, go forward and upward singing the praises of the most High, for He alone is God."[74]

Ford's themes are redemption, progress, and uplift. Ford depicts Africa's descendants as scattered and ashamed, but they have the potential to rise, "soaring," as they climb "forward and upward," to the "highest summit of civilization and immortal glory." Like the Reverend Edward Wilmot Blyden before him, Ford transforms Blackness—the "darker and stronger shades"—into a preferential sign.[75] Although there is no explicit reference to Marcus Garvey, the focus on Africa, the allusions to collective struggle, and the general tone are all hallmarks of the Garvey movement, which exercised great influence not only on Ford but also on many of his fellow practitioners of alternative religious faiths in Harlem, Chicago, Detroit, Boston, and other destinations on the over-ground railroad that took African Americans and West Indians to the north during and after the First World War.

Ford conjoined racial Romanticism with advocacy for science and progressive "scientific" methods. "We do not merely think we are from the original Jews, but we know as a matter of exact scientific knowledge that we are," the rabbi asserted, explaining that there was no racial difference between Ethiopians and Semites.[76] Ford likewise encouraged his congregants to interrupt him and debate him if they could prove anything he said to be untrue, for "Our seeking of Truth is no gesture."[77] The congregation did not believe in the stories of Jonah as literally true, but they did believe in "Jehovah, God of Israel," who was "a God of Truth. This universe is run by certain laws which we must investigate scientifically," Rabbi Ford believed. "It is only in living in accordance with these laws that we can gain freedom and happiness."[78]

Ford was a masterful public speaker, capable of drawing on his wit, eloquence, erudition, humor, and racial pride to win over an audience. "The Negro must turn his thoughts and energies to his own miserable condition on this earth," Ford once proclaimed, decrying African Americans' lack of real, material, wealth. "He puts on a bold front of prosperity as he walks up Lenox Avenue, but this is only a surface prosperity." Extolling the beauty of "the Ethiopian woman" as one of "the finest specimens of womanhood in the world," who was currently unjustly the "scrubwoman of civilization," Ford declared that his duty as rabbi was "to brush away some of the superstition and ignorance that has checked our progress."[79]

Through close reading of the Hebrew Bible, Ford and the B.B.A. developed the teaching that ancient Africans were Hebrews, and that Christianity was an oppressive legacy of enslavement. Ford also developed elaborate genealogical theories to explain how this occurred, variously claiming that the original Hebrews originated in Nigeria and migrated eastward through Egypt to Palestine, and also that the original Hebrews were the Carthaginians. He purported to have received the secret Carthaginian traditions from his mother, whom he variously claimed as either Carthaginian or Mende.[80] In ancient times, Carthage was located on the southern edge of the Mediterranean in modern Morocco and Tunisia. It had famously been the home of the elegant queen Dido in Virgil's Aeneas, as well as the home of Hannibal, who conquered Rome, but it had not been a force since the end of the seventh century of the Common Era. Ford's construction of a Judaic identity based on classical antiquity reflects the classical education that was widespread in Britain and its empire in Ford's era. His remembrances of secret familial traditions passed down through his mother could reflect a range of prior traditions, which could bear resemblance to Hebraic ones, from Jewish traditions passed down from an Ashkenazi or Sephardic ancestor in the Caribbean, to African folkways, or to the Sabbath-keeping and dietary regulations of Seventh Day Adventism.[81] Whatever those customs might have been, he said that it was not until he observed Jews of European descent in Harlem that he realized the practices he had grown up with were Jewish.[82] The congregation employed several local European-descended Jews as teachers, and Ford was innovative in that his congregation was the first Black Israelite group to follow some of the liturgical standards of European Jews.[83]

In the twenties, Beth B'nai Abraham flourished, rapidly becoming the largest Black Israelite synagogue in Harlem, and attracting visitors such as Wentworth A. Matthew, who was still using the title Bishop, not Rabbi. Harlem's Christian ministers were frequent guests at the B.B.A.'s Sunday evening services, in which members would customarily rise and deliver testimonials affirming their identities as Jews and the falsity of Christianity. Ministers would often rise to object to something Rabbi Ford had said, and when they did Rabbi Ford was always ready with an eloquent rejoinder. His public speaking was spellbinding: he held his audience "almost like a magician...now swaying them to laughter with a joke, now making them serious with a sober discussion of a Biblical point."[84] Each point that Rabbi Ford made met with a murmur of assent from his congregants, and each affirmation of Judaism met with a wave of assent "like a roll of thunder."[85]

By accepting the practices of the Jewish faith, Arnold Josiah Ford might be termed the father of Black Judaism, as opposed to the Black Israelism of his predecessors who attempted to recreate the apostolic Christian church and did not model their rituals on contemporary Jewish practices. He was exceptional in that he rejected Christianity and Jesus, whereas previous forms of Black Israelism had adopted an Israelite identity while still maintaining the prominence of Jesus Christ.[86] In part, the religious ritual of the congregation followed the model of Jewish synagogues. The congregation's Hebrew Torah scrolls were housed in a special case, or ark. On either side of the ark there stood two menorahs, and the pulpit was covered with the Zionist flag—a white field with blue bands framing a blue six-pointed Star of David. Men covered their heads either with hats or Jewish skullcaps, and some men wore prayer shawls. Men and women sat in separate sections, except in the choir, and women wore colorful head coverings. Music continued to be a major focus of Ford's congregation as it was in his U.N.I.A. activities—a photograph of the time shows him with his upright bass and members of the choir in front of the Beth B'nai Abraham synagogue (see fig. 4.2). B.B.A. held services at their Harlem synagogue, partly in Hebrew and partly in English. The congregation used Ashkenazi European Jewish prayer books but sang hymns with Christian melodies. The Sunday night services reminded one observer of a "modern revival meeting." The prayer service was followed by an "open forum" that featured testimonials from the congregants reaffirming their faith by recounting their experiences with Judaism, in the manner of the testifying practices found in many Protestant denominations. Ford was an adept orator and a charismatic preacher, able to project both gravitas and humor in his speeches and in his witty rejoinders to incredulous visitors who challenged his claims about Black history and religion.[87]

Ford's papers and personal effects were lost during the 1930s, so few writings survive, but it seems that Ford, like Matthew and the other innovators of Black Judaism, crafted a polycultural religion that drew from many sources—including aspects of Judaism, Freemasonry, Garveyism, Theosophy, Christianity, and Islam. Rabbi Ford's polycultural theology combined these elements with a millenarian, internationalist, and Black Nationalist political agenda. He taught that Hebrew and Arabic were the original African languages, and each member received a Hebrew name when they joined the congregation to complement their Christian "slave" name.[88] Ford's theological debt to esoteric and Islamic religious practitioners active during the Harlem Renaissance, with whom he had come into contact through the Garvey movement, can be seen in the fact that he integrated some Islamic practices such as the observance of the fast of Ramadan along with his Jewish ones.[89] According to an early account, it was through the Garvey movement that Ford had become friendly "with these 'voodoo men' and glorifiers of Mohammedanism and thus taught a mixture of Mohammedanism and Judaism."[90] Ford once opened a letter to another Black Israelite rabbi with "greetings to yourself, your family and your Congregation and the blessings of Allah."[91] His son explained, "his basic philosophy was that the religious schism between Judaism, Christianity, and Islam was a result of political machinations of man and should not be tolerated."[92] Even his personal dress reflected this ecumenical philosophy, as he wound a turban over a Jewish skullcap.[93]

Ford's roots in the mystical milieu of Harlem's esoteric religious communities can also be seen in the general tone of his theology. In 1927, an observer wrote:

> The Negro Jews have a mystical conception of religion.... They speak in the language of the Book of Daniel. Their phraseology reminds one of the theosophic writings—words, phrases, generalizations that in themselves do not say anything specific but are the expression of an urge, a striving of the 'dumb tongue' and limited brain to lay bare that which is beyond words.[94]

The mysticism of the teachings, the prophetic tone, and their relatedness to esoteric theosophy all are characteristic of the culture of popular African American esoteric religions in Harlem of the 1920s.

The B.B.A. continued to thrive through 1928. Ford organized classes in Hebrew and the Bible as well as subjects such as mechanical drawing and mathematics at Beth B'nai Abraham. He organized the B'nai Abraham Progressive Corporation in November 1928 in order to purchase a property to house the congregation and its classes. However, with the onset of the Great Depression after the stock market crash of 1929, the corporation struggled with high rates of vacancies in its building and became insolvent when it could not cover the mortgage. Amid great dissension among the officers of the corporation, the bank foreclosed on the property in October 1930.[95] In the same period, the B.B.A began to fall apart amid allegations that the rabbi had engaged in financial improprieties and had affairs with some of the female members of his congregation. A theological rift also developed between Jamaican and Barbadian-born members, with the Jamaicans, led by Samuel Valentine, splitting off into their own congregation, which used the Germanic Jewish language of Yiddish and adhered more closely to conventional Ashkenazi Judaism.[96] But whereas Ford was not interested in following the conventional Jewish liturgy, he, like Garvey, was very interested in using Jewish nationalism as a template for returning Blacks to their African motherland. In 1930, just as the bank foreclosed on the B.B.A.'s property, Ford led a group of settlers to the Black Zion of Ethiopia.

Understanding how and why Ford's Harlem-based Black Jews set out to "colonize" the ancient land of Ethiopia requires a closer look at Garveyism's complex relationship with Jews and Zionism. Although Garvey's program has frequently been called "Black Zionism," Garvey respected Zionism and admired Jews while also professing anti-Semitic beliefs later in life.[97] The affinity between Garveyism and Zionism is important for understanding Rabbi Ford's abortive attempt to found an American settlement in Ethiopia, which became a defining moment in his own life and in the development of Rastafarianism. Those concerned with national self-determination for peoples of African descent had long admired the Jewish Zionist movement, which found political expression with the First Zionist Congress in Basel, Switzerland, in 1897. Liberian scholar and statesman Edward Wilmot Blyden, one of those who inspired Marcus Garvey, commended "the marvelous movement called Zionism," which he saw as a kindred spirit to the goal of creating a colony for African Americans in Africa. "The question, in some of its aspects, is similar to that which at this moment agitates thousands of the descendants of Africa in America, anxious to return to the land of their fathers," he wrote in his 1898 pamphlet, "The Jewish Question."[98] Garvey, who grew up a British subject, saw his movement as one of a range of nationalist movements that sought independence from the British Empire after the First World War. Garvey repeatedly cited Jewish Zionism, as well as other nationalist political movements, as justifications for his own nationalist program. What made Garvey's an unconventional nationalist movement was that he was attempting to mobilize people scattered across a wide diaspora while asserting a claim to another land in their name. Garvey thought of Zionism and his own movement as being different manifestations of the same impulse following the carnage of the First World War. "A new spirit, a new courage, has come to us simultaneously as it came to the other peoples of the world," he told an audience of thousands at his New York City Liberty Hall headquarters on Saturday, July 11, 1920. "It came to us at the same time it came to the Jew. When the Jew said, 'We shall have Palestine!' the same sentiment came to us when we said, 'We shall have Africa!'"[99] Indeed, the similarity between Garvey's nationalism and Jewish Zionism was noted by friend and foe alike; at one convention, Garvey read a letter of support from a Los Angeles Jewish Zionist, and the 1925 Communist Party platform impugned Garveyism by equating it with "reactionary" Jewish Zionism.[100] As late as 1937, Garvey told a Canadian audience, "We want to work out a plan like the Zionists so as to recover ourselves."[101] Garvey frequently described his cause in relationship to both Jewish Zionism and Irish nationalism: "Our obsession is like that of the Jews," he told another Canadian audience in the same year. "They are working for Palestine. We are working for Africa, like the Irishman, he is working for Ireland."[102]

But while Garvey modeled his program in part on Zionism and had respect for Jewish accomplishments and perseverance in the face of oppression, he also had an inflated view of Jewish power that developed into conspiratorial anti-Semitism when his own fortunes soured. During Garvey's early and most influential period, he expressed mostly positive sentiments toward Jews. Like Blyden, who also grew up among Jews in the West Indies, Garvey had a close Jewish friend as a boy. Like many of his contemporaries, Garvey believed that Jewish financial capital ran the world, dictated the First World War, and even brought the Jewish-born communist revolutionary Leon Trotsky to power in the Soviet Union.[103] When the Federal government convicted Garvey of violating securities and postal laws in using the mail to sell stock for his *foundering* Black Star Line and sent him to prison in 1923, the embittered U.N.I.A. founder blamed his troubles on a Jewish conspiracy, and compared his fate to the betrayal and crucifixion of Jesus. An F.B.I. informant reported that Garvey believed Jews in Harlem were against him because "he was organizing the negroes and advising them to buy only t[hrough] negroes and because of this they had influenced the Judge against him."[104] Garvey was tried and convicted by Judge Julian Mack, a founder of the Harvard Law Review who was also president of the Zionist Organization of America in 1918 and the American Jewish Congress in 1919.[105] Garvey later wrote, in 1928, "When they wanted to get me, they had a Jewish judge try me, and a Jewish prosecutor (Mattucks). I would have been freed but two Jews on the jury held out against me ten hours and succeeded in convicting me, whereupon the Jewish judge gave me the maximum penalty."[106] Garvey was convinced he had been betrayed by a powerful Jewish conspiracy. "Truly I may say 'I was going down to Jeric[h]o and fell among friends,'"[107] he wrote in 1923 from New York City's Tombs Prison. Five years later, his anti-Semitism had hardened and he was quoting the forgery *The Protocols of the Elders of Zion*, which had been popularized in America by Henry Ford's paper, *The Dearborn Independent*. In a 1928 interview from London with Jamaican-American writer Joel Augusts Rogers, Garvey said, "I wish to say, emphatically, that the Negro must beware of the Jew. The Jew is no friend of the Negro, though the Negro has been taught to believe that.... The *Elders of Zion* teach that a harm done by a Jew to a Gentile is no harm at all, and the Negro is a Gentile."[108] In Garvey, then, we can see the paradox of a man who admired Jews and modeled his program in part on Jewish Zionism, but who harbored conspiratorial views of Jewish influence that became more sinister as his own fortunes flagged.

Still, Marcus Garvey's anti-Semitism did not prevent him from drawing parallels between Jewish history and Black history. In Garvey's view, African

Americans and European Jews suffered from similar forms of oppression. After the Nazis rose to power, Garvey would write that Zionism had developed too late to save the Jews from the envy that was the natural consequence of a minority race accumulating wealth in the midst of a majority. "This is a good lesson for Negroes, and particularly those in the United States," Garvey wrote, in light of Nazi persecution of German Jews. "The Negro in America has no wealth, and so is worse off than the Jew, but should he ever accumulate wealth in the United States he would ultimately find himself in the same position the Jew finds himself in today, realizing the only safe thing to do is to go after and establish racial autonomy."[109] Garvey saw Jewish persecution as a lesson for Blacks, and felt assured that one day Blacks in America would face the same pressure as Jews had in Hitler's Germany.

As a Black Israelite and as a Garveyite, Rabbi Ford had thus positioned himself between two identities that both had a strong Zionist component, ideologies that required gathering a scattered diasporic population to a national home with ancestral ties in the distant past. "As Garveyites, the Hebrews' Ethiopianist identification was underscored," writes William R. Scott, "for Ethiopianist ideas and themes also played a significant part in UNIA ideology."[110] In 1925, Rabbi Ford's congregation contributed to the Palestine Foundation Fund, and the rabbi showed movies in the synagogue extolling the Zionist project in Palestine. Ford believed that Palestine was a place "from which Hebraic idealism and culture can come," according to a contemporary report.[111] In the twenties, Rabbi Ford expressed the double Zionism of his Garveyism and his Judaism by organizing a subsidiary of Congregation Beth B'nai Abraham whose purpose was to encourage migration of Africans in the diaspora to some as-yet-unidentified promised land. The Aurienoth Club, named after the Hebrew for "angel of light," assembled 600 members who were mostly British West Indians residing in Harlem or Cleveland.[112] Members each paid annual dues of one dollar, in addition to other gifts, donations, and fees, for which they were to receive land, livestock, and other benefits.[113] The club's activities were mostly religious, but they also held a Sunday forum to which anyone could come, and Rabbi Ford was able to attract some of Harlem's doctors, lawyers, dentists, and schoolteachers in addition to the more common working-class West Indian immigrants who composed the rank and file of the Garvey movement. Through this club, Ford preached a version of Garvey's doctrine of nationalism and colonization of Africa, with a Socialist bent toward collective action.[114] Ford's home was often the site of political discussions concerning the future of "the race."[115] The B.B.A. school taught a number of subjects that would be useful for eventual resettlement in

Africa, such as mathematics, mechanical drawing, Arabic, and Hebrew. Through the activities of the Aurienoth Club, and in light of the surge of excitement among African-descended peoples surrounding the 1930 coronation of a new emperor of Ethiopia, the only independent African nation, Ford and his followers identified their new promised land in a famous corner of the African continent.

The biblical land of Ethiopia had long been a source of hope and inspiration for Christians of African descent, for whom Psalms 68 verse 31 held special resonance: "Princes shall come out of Egypt; Ethiopia shall soon stretch out her hands unto God." The term "Ethiopianism" came to be applied to segments of the independent church movement in Africa during the late nineteenth century, when Africans, discontented with segregation and lack of control in the Protestant churches of Southern Africa, and influenced by African-American missionaries, started forming their own "Ethiopian" churches. With the popularity of Alexander Dowie's Holiness church, based in Zion, Illinois, and with the evolution of the Holiness movement into the Pentecostal movement at the start of the twentieth century, a new stream of prophetic, spirit-filled, apocalyptic churches emerged among African Americans and, through their missionizing, among Africans as well, calling themselves "Zionist." Often spread by Seventh Day Adventists and their spiritual children in the Jehovah's Witness and Watchtower movements, "Zionism" among African churches did not mean the return of a diasporic people to their native land, but it designated Saturday as the Sabbath, identified with the Old Testament and the ancient Israelites' liberation from slavery, and called for independence from European rule. Thus it should not be surprising that at least some of the hundreds of Ethiopian and Zionist sects that emerged in Africa began to identify themselves as Israelites, particularly since Bishop Crowdy's Church of God and Saints of Christ had sent missionaries to South Africa as early as 1903.[116]

Ethiopia has held a special place in the Black diaspora's invention of Africa, first as a synonym for the mythic continent, and then as a specific country after its consolidation under the rule of Sahle Maryam (1844–1913) as Emperor Menelik II.[117] When Ethiopia defeated Italian armies in the battle of Adwa in 1896, "it was the most significant victory of an African military during the era of European high imperialism." And added new luster to the ancient biblical symbol of Ethiopia. The victory "conjured up the symbol of Ethiopia as the Zion of Africa in the minds of vast numbers of Afro-Americans, as well as Africans living under colonial rule," in the words of scholar William A. Shack.[118] With the victory, Ethiopia became the "Zion of Africa," that is, the symbol of Africa as a whole, and the homeland to which many diasporic Blacks hoped to return. Marcus Garvey, who frequently referred to Ethiopia to signify the entire continent of Africa, used Ethiopia's status as the only African country to have successfully resisted colonization to inspire African-Americans that their dreams of independence and self-rule would soon come to fruition. In one typical statement, Garvey proclaimed: "We Negroes believe in the God of Ethiopia, the everlasting God—God the Son, God the Holy Ghost, the one God of all ages. That is the God [in] whom we believe, but we shall [see him] through the spectacle of Ethiopia."[119]

Adding even greater potency to this web of overlapping associations around Ethiopia, Zionism, and Israelism was the fact that Ethiopia's national epic rooted the country's founding in the biblical story of the union of King Solomon and the Queen of Sheba. Much as Virgil's *Aeneid* claimed the mantle of civilization for the Romans by linking them to the illustrious glories of Greek civilization that had come before them, the Ethiopian national epic linked the country to the glories of the biblical past. In the fourteenth century of the Common Era, during the literary renaissance that accompanied the reign of Ethiopian King Amba Sion, the ruler commissioned the *Kebra Nagast* (The Glory of Kings), several millennia after the events it chronicles. The epic relates the founding of the Ethiopian royal dynasty by Menilek I, the son of King Solomon and the Queen of Sheba. According to the narrative, King Solomon sent his son to rule Ethiopia with a copy of the Ark of the Covenant. But Menilek's men switched the copy for the actual Ark, which was installed in a replica of the Temple built in the Ethiopian capital.[120]

Chapter 2 reviewed some of the debates over the origins of Ethiopian Jews, known as Falashas or, more properly, Beta Israel (House of Israel). But whatever their origins may have been, the Beta Israel's religious identities were radically altered by nineteenth- and twentieth-century contact with both Christian and Jewish missionaries, as well as their deliberate cultural "modernization." Historian David Francis Kessler relates that "when the Falashas were first visited by European Jews in the nineteenth and early twentieth centuries they were surprised to find that they were not the only Jews left in the world."[121] The Beta Israel became familiar with European standards of Jewish identity and ritual through Protestant efforts to convert them to Christianity and Jewish counter-efforts to repel Christian evangelization. In 1860 and again in 1862, Henry Stern, a converted Jew and a missionary for the London Society for Promoting Christianity among the Jews, traveled to Ethiopia and proselytized among the Falashas. Concerned at the success of Protestant groups in converting the Falashas, French Jewish linguist Joseph Halevy visited them in 1867, and sent a few of them abroad for study. Halevy's work was continued by his student Jacques Faitlovitch, who first traveled to Ethiopia in 1904 on behalf of the Parisian Société de l'Alliance Israélite Universelle, and worked tirelessly on behalf of Ethiopian Jewry until his death in 1955. Supported by the European Jewish Rothschild banking family, his purpose was to thwart the efforts of Christian missionaries operating among the Beta Israel. To do so, he decided he needed to reform Ethiopian Judaism to make it conform to contemporary European Jewish practices. Faitlovitch found himself in the tenuous position of trying to change the culture of the Beta Israel in order to preserve their community. "Their religion was under attack by Protestants and Western Jews," James Quirin summarizes. "Ironically, both agreed on some of their agenda, such as abolishing Beta Israel sacrifice."[122] Faitlovitch introduced elements of rabbinic Judaism, and discouraged Beta Israel customs outside of the Jewish rabbinical tradition.

On a visit to New York in connection with his work as head of the pro-Falasha committee in the 1920s, Faitlovitch heard of New York's own Black Jews. He paid a visit to Rabbi Ford, but decided the group had no connection to Ethiopia. Some authors report that it was through this interaction that the Israelites of New York learned of the Falashas, which seems unlikely, as Abyssinian Jews had been subjects of reports in Black newspapers since at least 1913.[123] In any case, the Falashas and the Ethiopian account of descent from King Solomon and the Queen of Sheba soon became crucially important to New World Israelites. By 1927, some groups of Israelites in New York represented themselves as Falashas, and Harlem's Black Israelites were referred to as Falashas in the popular press until the 1960s. In addition to his story about Carthaginian Black Jewish origins, Rabbi Ford taught that all Blacks were descendents of King Solomon and the Queen of Sheba, but that in Africa and the United States the heritage had been lost.[124] In summary, then, as Garveyites, Jews, and Zionists in several senses, Rabbi Ford and his followers had multiple reasons for their interest in establishing a colony in Ethiopia.

In 1919, an Ethiopian delegation visited Harlem and the United States, and in the twenties a small group of African Americans settled in the Ethiopian highlands.[125] Interest in settling in Ethiopia peaked, however, with the coronation of Ras Tafari Makonnen as Emperor Haile Selassie I in 1930. By 1933 there were approximately 100 African American settlers in Abyssinia, another name for Ethiopia.[126] Other factors besides Garveyism and Israelite identity compelled African Americans to want to find a new home for themselves in Africa. Significant among these were the sense of alienation born of struggle in a country that was infused with racism and was changing rapidly as industrialization, urbanization, and immigration swelled bustling northern cities in the late nineteenth and early twentieth centuries. Edna Jackson of Buffalo, New York, wrote President Franklin D. Roosevelt in 1933 asking for help in transporting African Americans who wished to settle in Africa. She pleaded, "I guess you think I am crazy to but my plea is this. I want to go home where I belong and that is Africa my nation home." Alienation stemming from industrialization was a major factor in her desire to return to Africa, and specifically the land she referred to as Abyssinia. "You know that this is a machine age and…we are all caught up and the South every year is getting worse and worse so that [I want to] let you know that our time is out and we can go home and catch frogs and such like and live happy." Mrs. Jackson's letter illustrates that even people of modest education were interested in going to Ethiopia, which was seen in this case as an idyllic pastoral respite from discrimination and the grind of life in the industrial age. Writing to President Roosevelt in 1935, James Moody argued that it would save the government millions of dollars to send willing African Americans to Ethiopia, and would save white labor organizations, farmers, and congressional representatives the hassles of treating Blacks fairly, since they had proven their inability or unwillingness to do so. He referred to Blacks as "discarded citizens" who were "abridged of all rights of a citizen and privileges almost to the end of living existence."[127]

When one of the Ethiopian delegates who had visited in 1919 returned to the United States in 1931, this time as minister of foreign affairs, the U.S. State Department strove to "prevent any embarrassment on account of his color," such as he had suffered just after the First World War.[128] Addison Southard, the head U.S. official in Addis Ababa wrote, "should he arrive in Washington dressed European style I would suggest that if such can be tactfully done he be persuaded to don Ethiopian garb, which would give him very much less of the appearance of an American darky."[129] The same racism that made travel in the United States uncomfortable for an Ethiopian official made Ethiopia seem like a haven for many of the African Americans whom Southard crassly referred to as "darkies."

The Ethiopianist Zionism of Ford's society found an outlet when Kantiba Gabrou, the mayor of the Ethiopian capital of Addis Ababa, and Taamarat Emanuel, a Beta Israel who had received an education in Europe under the auspices of the Société de l'Alliance Israélite Universelle, visited the United States as part of an official mission in the summer of 1930, and encouraged African Americans to emigrate to Ethiopia.[130] At the time, the Ethiopian government was seeking to develop a dam on Lake Tsana, and Ethiopians hoped they could avoid European domination of large-scale engineering projects by engaging the help of skilled African Americans.[131] In addition, Kantiba Gabrou probably saw an opportunity for personal advantage in attracting settlers to clear and open up considerable tracts of poor agricultural land that he had received from the Ethiopian government. To Ford and his followers, Gabrou's offer must have seemed like a godsend, the answer to their long-held hopes of African colonization. Taking only a few short months to prepare for the enterprise in an era when a letter could take over a month to reach Ethiopia, Ford neglected to plan adequately, and the Black Israelite colonization of Ethiopia foundered in the gulf that separated the mythical, millennial, and providential Ethiopia of the African American imagination from the actual Ethiopian country of contemporaneous Africa.

With the support of the hundreds of members of his Aurienoth Club, Ford and three followers left for Ethiopia carrying a formidable petition to Emperor Haile Selassie in November 1930, with Ford promising to negotiate a deal with the Ethiopian government for land grants of 125 acres of land to the family of each settler, along with cattle, horses, and the added benefit of "soldiers to help clear the land."[132] The enterprise ran into trouble before they even arrived in Ethiopia, when one of the party died en route. In addition, Ford was far from a light traveler: in addition to bringing a considerable amount of furniture, he amazingly brought three pianos, which were held for a year at the railway station against payment of various charges before being auctioned when Ford failed to pay the fees in time. Ford's customs troubles were an apt metaphor for the barriers and friction that ensued when his group's Zionist dreams of the imagined Ethiopia of legend met the realities and challenges of the actual place. Not only were the material circumstances of the country different from what Ford and his allies expected, but the ways Ethiopians and African-Americans viewed each other were incompatible, as well.[133]

Travelers expecting Ethiopia to be a slow-moving, idyllic place would have been sorely disappointed. Addis Ababa in the early thirties was a city set in the mountains and surrounded by cool eucalyptus forests. The houses on the outskirts of town were either straw *tukuls*, capped with upside-down green Perrier and Chianti bottles, or wood frame and plaster houses with sloping roofs of imported corrugated iron. The city center boasted a large and magnificent railroad station, grand squares with gilded statues of the Lion of Judah, and narrow streets and broad avenues crowded with people, mules, the occasional racing automobile, and innumerable mangy dogs. Buildings made of wood, mud, or rubble and topped with corrugated iron surrounded the bustling streets. Men typically wore white jodhpurs, white shirts, and scarves, while women wore loose white tunics, belted at the waist with many dangling crosses and other amulets. Wealthier men rode mules and wore heavy black capes and broad-brimmed felt hats, accompanied by barefoot servants who ran alongside carrying firearms.[134]

In the early months of the enterprise, Ford was filled with an irrepressible enthusiasm, as well as the conviction that his efforts were the historic continuation of Garvey's policies and the only salvation for the Black race. Six months after his arrival, when his small group of settlers numbered only seven people, he described riding his saddled mule with an Ethiopian servant in the crowded streets of Addis Ababa when His Highness Ras Hailu drove past in an automobile surrounded by about one hundred guards. The prince stopped and Ford rode up to his car. "I dismounted, gave the reins to my servant and bowed most respectfully to him," Ford described the encounter in a letter to his associate, Black Israelite Rabbi Wentworth Arthur Matthew. "He put his hand out to me, I shook it and he greeted me most cordially as all his guards stood to attention," Ford continued. "Believe me they are depending for good works from us. They have all received me in audience graciously, do not fail them, for we will be failing ourselves."[135] The facts that Ford was riding a mule and attended by a servant, and was conversing with princes, all indicate that the Barbadian-born musician, rabbi, and mystic was well connected, but not extraordinarily well off in a country where retinues often numbered in the dozens.

Ethiopian noble Kentiba Gebrou offered leases of one-half *gasha* of land (about fifty acres) to "my Afra-American friends…that my friends may have some place for residential quarters when coming from America."[136] However, despite Gebrou's willingness to provide land, Ethiopian law barred foreigners from buying land and put severe restrictions on their even leasing land. These and other obstacles had delayed the consummation of a deal throughout Ford's first year in Ethiopia, while the members of the Aurienoth Club back home had received only reassuring letters filled with reports on his halting progress, along with appeals for additional funds. The lack of success and lack of funds led to divisions among the Black settlers, and several complained to the American Diplomatic Legation of Ford's "shifty practices, particularly in matters of finance."[137]

The colonization scheme faced severe structural economic problems that would have even foiled organizers with far more experience and practical skills than Rabbi Ford possessed. His enterprise was a little quixotic, with his high-flown schemes, exaggeratedly proper manners, and his man-servant. The United

States Legation in Addis Ababa estimated that farming in Ethiopia would be practically impossible unless one had enough capital to be independently wealthy in the United States. Local prices for farm produce were very low because of a small domestic market and poor transportation networks, as well as the need to compete with indigenous farm laborers who lived on a wage of less than a quarter of a dollar for each twelve-hour day. American diplomat Addison Southard conceded that living in Ethiopia might provide the Black colonist of means with "at least a temporary satisfaction of living in a good climate surrounded by a ruling people of his own color."[138] But resettling Black Americans in Ethiopia as agriculturalists was never viable in economic terms.[139]

In June 1931, Ford sent a certificate of ordination to Rabbi Matthew signed by priest Alaika Barnabas of the Church of Dabreh Michoo in Gondar, which Matthew would proudly display in his office for many decades and offer as proof of his ordination as an Ethiopian Hebrew rabbi.[140] Ford also appealed to Matthew to become his representative in America, and to send colonists to help the effort. "Tell your people to work. Build large farms and homes here. Prepare to settle in the most wonderfully beautiful and the richest climate on earth.... We need money for building and development. Do wake up." Referring to Emperor Haile Selassie and notables Ras Kasa, Ras Hailu, and Kentiba Gebrou, Ford wrote, "these most wonderful gentlemen of ancient Aethiopia want to see what Aethiopian America is going to do for the development of a modern Aethiopia.... This is our only hope, our only salvation as a race."[141] Ford had the zeal and fervor of the visionary that he was, and he clearly believed that he was carrying on the work of Marcus Garvey in creating an outpost for African Americans in the symbolic heart of Africa.

Ford sought a mixture of African land and American-style religious freedom: "I have told them, we want homes for ourselves and our generations for ever, we want religious freedom, we want farms, horses, mules, cattle, poultry and opportunity for work on the great [Tsana] dam, we want land in that vicinity. All of these things they have granted us. Yes, with love and goodwill, they have answered *Yes. Go ahead. Come. Build. Occupy*."[142] Ford's movement was an occupation, not simply an immigration; it was a colonization scheme in the mold of the Garveyite dreams of returning African Americans to their ancestral homes in Africa.

Ford's letter also conveyed the strain created by the grandeur of his vision and the lack of means to bring it to fruition. "Now with all this bigness I have got the responsibility of building a headquarters to house Americans here," he told Rabbi Matthew. "Do help me. I have got seven with me now. Some landed without a cent; but they are alright and happy. The burden though is on me," he wrote in increasingly urgent tones. "Try and wake up interest in building homes here among Americans who want to come. Save your money and your people's money to come....Do not turn back now. The thing is too big. God will bless us, love to all."[143] In Ford's mind, he was not simply the head of a small band of pioneers but was at the vanguard of the only hope for the Black race: returning to Africa via Ethiopia. "The thing is too big," he wrote, and indeed it was.

Perhaps an even bigger source of disappointment than the economic obstacles to establishing a viable American colony in Ethiopia was the disjuncture between the way African Americans viewed Ethiopia and the way Ethiopians viewed African Americans. Rather than finding Black confraternity, the settlers discovered a multitiered system of racial privilege and discrimination in Emperor Haile Selasie's empire. The government allowed only the most elite Ethiopian nobles on the streets after a seven o'clock curfew, whereas white Europeans and Americans were allowed to travel unencumbered. Haile Selassie was keen to use Europeans and Americans to modernize his country's institutions, and he was even willing to establish a separate police force made up of Belgian Hessian soldiers to police Europeans who might object to being handled by Africans.[144] Ethiopians not only provided concessions to white racism, but they practiced their own forms of discrimination against dark-skinned peoples, as well. Enslavement of dark-skinned Africans was common, and ruling-class Ethiopians took offense at the suggestion that they were Black at all, with Selassie and many others taking pride in their Arabian ancestry.[145] Although Selassie attempted to attract talented African-Americans to help build the Tsana Dam, many Ethiopians looked down on African-Americans and treated them poorly on account of their slave ancestry, and sometimes their skin tone. In certain cases, cultural misunderstandings could escalate into violence. In one incident, two African Americans who were attempting to run a farm a hundred miles from Addis Ababa were severely beaten by their Ethiopian laborers because they paid only the men who had worked for them and not everyone who had applied for jobs. One of the African American settlers was brought to the American hospital in Addis Ababa, where both of his legs were amputated.[146]

Ford and many of his followers had begun to self-identify as Ethiopian Jews in Harlem, so it must have been a hard blow when Ethiopian Jews rejected the Harlem immigrants. Wanting to reach out to the Jews of Ethiopia, Ford brought along a Torah to present to them as a gift. But they rejected his offering because the Torah was written in Hebrew, and they used a Torah written in the language of Ge'ez. Ford ended up giving the Torah to his supporter Eudora Paris, who eventually returned it to the United States.[147] Ford's exhortation to "Come. Build. Occupy" would have rankled Ethiopians busy warding off the challenge of Italian imperial occupations in East Africa.

Compounding the difficulties in Ethiopia was the fact that the man Ford chose as his successor as head of the Aurienoth Club, F. A. Cowan, embezzled money from the club treasury and was replaced by the vice president, one Mrs. Thomas.[148] Although Thomas, originally from the Danish West Indies, was a friend and student of Rabbi Ford, Ford's inability to produce an official land grant document signed by Ethiopian officials soon tested the patience of the club members, who were supporting their rabbi in Ethiopia as well as his daughters in New York.[149] The Aurienoth Club drew up a petition "of great import" in triplicate, demanding that the rabbi produce a charter in Arabic, with an authorized translation in English, duly signed and sealed by legitimate Ethiopian officials, granting the club members all that Rabbi Ford had promised. Thomas, Mignon Innis, Mary Lynch, and a Brother Sandeford brought a copy of the petition with them when they sailed to join Rabbi Ford in November 1931.[150] Ford acknowledged receipt of the petition with another one of his upbeat letters, encouraging his followers to have faith and remain in good spirits, as he would deliver the promised concessions, although he was typically vague on the specifics or timing. Discouraged by Ford's lack of success and by the financial scandals, and stripped of the charismatic presence of their leader, the Aurienoth Club began to lose members.[151]

In Ford's absence, the embezzler Cowan founded another group, called the Pioneers of Aethiopia, which similarly aimed to send colonists to Ethiopia.[152] Cowan appears to have been sincerely interested in promoting colonization of Ethiopia, although his methods were fraudulent. He wrote a German firm based in Addis Ababa requesting quotations on a long list of machinery of various kinds needed for sawmills, brick making, tanning, and other industries for use in "colonizing a tract of land in Abyssinia," indicating that he was perhaps influenced by Booker T. Washington's emphasis on developing industrial and trade skills among African Americans. Cowan was full of bluster and braggadocio, and appealed to prospective settlers' race pride and sense of manliness. One person swayed by Cowan's appeal was Lawrence Beckford, a West Indian living in Puerto Cabezas, Nicaragua, who traveled as far as Djibouti en route to Ethiopia at Cowan's behest. When Beckford approached American consular officials, he was carrying a letter from Cowan dated September 29, 1931. "Aethiopia stretches out her hand for you, calling you to come. The possibilities are verily unlimited," Cowan wrote. With no basis of support, Cowan claimed that Ethiopia had a great demand for tradesmen, and that the pioneers had access to enough land to offer their members "all the land that you can intelligently handle, free, and tax free for seven years."[153] No superlative was too great for Cowan, and his wildly imaginative depictions of Ethiopia are reminiscent of the inflated claims that provoked land settlement swindles on the arid plains of the American West. "The land is rich beyond mention," he wrote. "Most of the food that you must plant in the West Indies and in Central America are indigent (*sic*) to the soil of Africa. Sugar cane grows wild. Bees make honey in the trunk of trees and in caves in abundance. Coffee, cotton, ginger, oranges, plantains etc grow wild. It is a veritable heaven."[154] For advocates of African colonization such as Cowan, Africa existed in the imagination as a kind of Eden, an unspoiled paradise of milk and honey, just waiting for the manly hands of Western pioneers to master its fecundity.

The "Pioneers of Aethiopia" may have been of African descent, but their colonization program mimicked the civilizing discourse that animated European colonization efforts. As scholars from Judith Stein to Kevin Gaines have demonstrated, African American elites often shared the same assumptions of European elites when it came to "civilizing" the "backwards" peoples of the "dark continent."[155] "The country needs building up, and that is the reason that we are going in such large numbers, to live there and build industries and cities," Cowan wrote. What Africa most needed was precisely what it was thought to lack: industries and cities in the pattern of Europe and the United States. No matter that Ethiopia had both cities and one of the oldest recorded civilizations on the globe; in Cowan's imagination it was an African Eden, feminine and untrammeled, just waiting for Western penetration to bring it into the ranks of the civilized. Writing in all caps, Cowan emphasized that the job would require virility: "WE ARE PIONEERS. WE ARE BUILDERS. WE WORK HARD. WE LIVE HARD. WE PLAY HARD. WE EAT HARD. WE FIGHT HARD. It will be a glorious life for the sincere hard working and honest man."[156] Manliness was integral to the era's view of the civilizing mission, and one can see in Cowan's appeal the use of the manly ideal in order to inspire his particular vision of colonization.[157]

According to the gender politics of African colonization, not only were the pioneers virile and manly, but Africa itself was depicted as female, as a damsel in distress. Arnold J. Ford's most famous composition, the Garvey anthem, included the verse:

> Arise, O Aethiop's daughter rise,
> From thine Aionian sleep.
> And to the Heaven's lift thine eyes.

Thy tryst with Allah keep.
"Not dead; but sleeping," Angels said
"Those hands stretch'd forth shall be
Afric shall once more raise her head
Her children shall be free."[158]

In one verse, Ford depicts Africa as daughter, lover, and mother. Patriarchal gender politics were central to the way these African American pioneers conceived of their mission and structured their project. Indeed, it was a politics that was reinforced in many ways from the Ethiopian side of the equation, as well. In a letter to one perspective settler, Kantiba Gabrou wrote, "I hope you're coming with your husband, as it is difficult for a lady to travel such a long way alone."[159] Upon their arrival in Ethiopia, many of the African-American male settlers began to act out their ideas of virile, hard-living adventurers, images that were inflected both by their experiences in Jim Crow America and by their ideas about African patriarchy and polygamy. Rabbi Ford, who was rumored to pursue the female members of his congregation in New York, took four wives in Ethiopia, according to the U.S. legation. Other members of the African American expatriate community made waves by making passes at the white nurses at the American Presbyterian Hospital in Addis Ababa, or by courting Ethiopian women regardless of whether they already had Ethiopian spouses.[160]

African American expatriates typically did not bring sufficient funds to support themselves for very long, and desperate Americans wanting funds for the return voyage back to New York soon besieged the U.S. legation in Addis Ababa.[161] One petitioner, Cornell graduate Headley Edmund Bailey, had gone to Ethiopia hoping to find a position as a schoolteacher, but was unable to find any employment and regretted his decision to go. Ford's ambition soon outstripped his funds, and when that happened, his main Ethiopian contact Kantiba Gabrou severed their friendship. In any case, Gabrou probably never had it in his power to fulfill his promises—the chief of the American legation, Addison E. Southard, described him as "a man of no great standing or influence here," whom the Emperor used on missions abroad because of his knowledge of foreign languages and customs. "Gabrou is generally looked upon as a visionary and a hypocrite," the U.S. diplomat wrote. Southard concluded that Gabrou either had a very poor grasp of economics, or, more likely, that his real motive in having African Americans attempt to colonize his land was his "well-known avarice."[162]

Floundering economically in Ethiopia, Ford fell back on his musical talents, eking out a living doing carpentry, tuning pianos, or playing the drum, fiddle, or banjo to the accompaniment of follower Hattie Coffie on piano—although Coffie complained that Ford kept more than his fair share of their earnings. Coffie was extremely disenchanted with Ethiopia. "It's the last stop before Hell," she was said to exclaim, "and the only thing that keeps me here is no money." Ford and Coffie provided "the only reasonably good dance music available in Addis Ababa," according to Southard, "but the demand for that commodity is not great here and the fees to be earned are modest."[163] Emperor Haile Selassie himself occasionally employed Ford and Coffie for his parties, but payment for such services at the palace were usually months, if not years, behind schedule. For a time, Ford and Coffie were the featured attractions of the most exclusive nightclub in Addis Ababa, the Tambourine, which was run by an "affable and unctuous little Corsican,"[164] and employed two Somali waiters to cater to an all-white clientele of Europeans and Americans. Coffie taught herself dance music by borrowing and improvising upon the latest records to arrive in Ethiopia, and her long fingers "performed miracles upon the nervous system of the Tambourine's piano," in the words of an American visitor. "No longer young, she preserved the youthful air and, to a certain extent, the appearance of a musical immortal."[165] The musical program was an eclectic mix of German waltzes and other European Continental favorites, but after eleven in the evening Coffie and Ford cut loose with Southern spirituals and syncopated "jazzed" music, or entertained the patrons with square dances and Virginia reels.

The era of revelry at the Tambourine Club was short lived, however, because although its white customers were happy to be entertained by Black Americans as if inside a Harlem nightclub, the club barred Ethiopian patrons. One evening, a group of twenty young Ethiopians, many of whom were employed by the government, decided to challenge the color line, and fighting broke out when they were refused entrance to the inner dance room. Within an hour, a company of Ethiopian soldiers arrived, ejected the patrons, and shuttered the Tambourine Club. The appearance of Cotton Club-type Jim Crow segregation in Addis Ababa's nightlife was too great an affront to Ethiopian pride to last for very long.[166]

Of the approximately one hundred African Americans and West Indians in Ethiopia by 1932, only eleven can be confirmed as Ford's followers, although there may have been more.[167] Nonetheless, Ford was a powerful influence and a leader in the expatriate community of Addis Ababa. A "confidential and under-cover source" told the local U.S. governmental officials that Ford was "behind" the emigration.[168] Despite his difficulties, Ford managed to convey the impressive, refined bearing of the worldly and talented man that he was, and his home became a salon and gathering place for the

expatriate African Americans and West Indians in the Ethiopian capital.
Ford associated with younger progressive Ethiopians who were in favor of
Selassie's modernization program, and the rabbi wrote voluminously in this
period, though his writings and other possessions were lost during the Italian
invasion of Ethiopia in 1935.[169] He always greeted American officials with a
cordial manner and attempted to cultivate ties with the American diplomats
by reporting "international political propaganda" that Ethiopians were being
convinced to distrust Americans of all races because they "had taken America and killed the Indians and were now bent on taking Ethiopia and killing
the Ethiopians." Whether true or false, the American legation saw only financial ambition in Ford's eagerness to provide information, and kept him at
arm's length.[170]

In Ethiopia, Ford married and started a family with his follower Mignon
Innis, and together they had two boys, Yoseph, born in 1934, and Abiyi, born
in 1935. Ford died soon after, reportedly of a heart attack, on September 17,
1935, just before Italy invaded and conquered Ethiopia. But when he was on
his deathbed he made his wife swear not to leave the country.[171] Mrs. Ford
and the sons suffered through the Italian occupation and remained in Ethiopia.
In the early 1940s, Mignon Innis Ford and two other West Indian women
founded the Princess Zännäbä Wärq school, which became the most elite
school in Ethiopia.[172]

In the wake of the Italian invasion, most of the few remaining African
Americans found means to return home, and ten who could not afford the
cost of passage were resettled in the United States with the help of the International Red Cross, paid for by the American government.[173] The Paris family
returned to the United States with Rabbi Ford's Torah and a two-year-old
Ethiopian boy they called Hailu. The ship stopped in Hamburg, where Nazis
searched it. "Nazis were on board checking out everybody, looking for Jews,"
says Hailu Paris. "They didn't expect Blacks to have Jewish artifacts, or that
there would be Black Jews, so they hid the Torah, and nobody saw it."[174]
A ship list manifest from 1936 clearly shows that Hailu Paris first entered the
country as the two-year-old adopted son of Eudora E. Paris, 44, on the SS St.
Louis, which sailed from Hamburg on September 12, 1936, and that they
traveled on passports issued in Addis Ababa, Ethiopia.[175] The St. Louis would
become infamous a few years later when its Jewish passengers fleeing the Ho-
locaust were refused entry by the United States, and the ship had to return to
Germany.[176] Hailu would grow up to become a rabbi of Black Israelite
synagogues in New York, using the very Torah that accompanied him as a
toddler. He left behind the wreckage of his war-torn homeland, and the

dashed dreams of African-American independence and salvation that it had inspired for a few heady years in the infancy of Haile Selassie's reign.

The Black Israelite colonization of Ethiopia had failed but, all was not lost. The Black Israelite engagement with Ethiopia proved critical to the formation of Rastafarianism, which lives on today as Jamaica's most visible artistic culture. Rastafarianism repeated and amplified the Israelite teaching that Africans in the Americas are descended from the Lost Tribes of Israel, a belief grounded in biblical exegesis and contemporary history. Rastafarianism goes further, to claim that Emperor Haile Selassie, born Ras Tafari Makonnen, is the living embodiment of Jesus Christ, with Marcus Garvey as a kind of latter day Paul who allegedly prophesized the return of the messiah who would lead oppressed Black people toward their African redemption.[177]

The efforts of Black Israelites like Rabbis Ford and Matthew in both Harlem and Ethiopia were critical to the development of Rastafarianism in Jamaica. The Black Israelites of Harlem and Ethiopia doubly influenced Leonard Percival Howell, the man most responsible for the emergence of Rastafarianism in Jamaica in the early thirties. Howell, the eldest of ten children, was born on June 16, 1898, to a peasant farming family in the Bull Head Mountain district of Jamaica.[178] He signed up as a cook with the U.S. Army Transport service during the First World War, and arrived in New York in 1918. He worked on a total of five U.S. Army vessels before being discharged in 1923. Like many other Jamaican immigrants in the United States, he took manual labor jobs as a porter and a construction worker. He later opened a tea room in the heart of Black Harlem on 136th Street, where he is said to have served potent concoctions of ganja (marijuana) tea.[179] Like Rabbis Matthew and Ford, Howell was very much involved in the dense culture of Harlem healers and mystics that coalesced around the Garvey movement. An acquaintance described him as a "mystic man," and his brother said that he had "excellent hands with sickness and helped many people."[180] Like Rabbi Matthew and many others of the "mystic scientists," Howell found inspiration in the magical books of the Lauron William de Laurence Company, a popular publisher of occult texts. Scholar Vijay Prashad reports that Howell utilized *The Great Book of Magical Art, Hindu Magic and East Indian Occultism* by de Laurence, an author who was a great favorite with the self-proclaimed "mystic scientists" who haunted Liberty Hall and other Harlem hot spots.[181] Howell was hardly unique in this regard among the founders of the Rastafarian movement; his peer Joseph Nathaniel Hibbert specialized in occultism and the secrets of the de Laurence publications.[182] As with many of the 1920s self-proclaimed "mystic scientists," Howell had a hint of sinister magic about him, and rumors circulated that he practiced obeah, or black magic. Robert Hill found evidence that Howell had been censured by the U.N.I.A. in New York for being both a con man and a "samfie [obeah] man."[183] Howell maintained his reputation as a healer and "scientist" later in life, as well.[184] In addition to being involved in Garveyism and the mystical religious underground of Harlem in the twenties, Howell, like Ford, was also influenced by the radical Socialist politics of the era. He knew and corresponded with the Trinidad-born communist George Padmore, and described his Rastafarian commune outside of Kingston as practicing "a socialistic life."[185]

Not only did Howell share important elements of biography and cultural influences with New York Israelites and probably learned the basic tenets of Israelite ideology from them, but two incidents in particular involving Rabbi Ford's expedition to Ethiopia pointed Howell specifically toward Ethiopia and the worship of Haile Selassie. The first came when a contingent of Matthew's and Ford's followers marched in a Garvey parade in New York City on Sunday, January 4, 1931. Rabbi Ford was in Ethiopia at the time and Garvey had been deported, but some of the hundreds of Black Israelites who remained carried a life-size portrait of Emperor Haile Selassie side by side with a portrait of Marcus Garvey at the head of the march.[186] Photographs of this event were some of important clues that convinced Howell and others of the Providential link between the two iconic figures. When Howell returned to Jamaica around 1931, he met two Israelite missionaries who had recently returned from a long stay in Ethiopia. David and Annie M. Harvey had followed a vision telling them to go to Abyssinia in 1925, where they remained for five and a half years. In Ethiopia they would have surely met the dapper rabbi, Arnold Josiah Ford, whose parlor was a center for the small community of African-American expatriates in Addis Ababa. As his son recalled, "many learned Ethiopians came to our house. They looked at him as a tutor. It was a ritual: on Sundays people would gather to discuss things. It was a place of learning."[187] Upon returning to Jamaica in 1931, the Harveys founded a sect called The Israelites, and distributed photographs of Ras Tafari. Henry Dunkley, a peer of Howell's who also spread the doctrine of Ras Tafari's divinity, explained that Howell had "copied all of what they [the Israelites] were doing and launched out himself and formed a body of people, Back-to-Africa movement.... Howell went round to their headquarters at Paradise Street after he came back from New York and catch hold of one of the photographs and developed on it and brought it forward to the public, and let the public know that is the Eternal Messiah come back."[188] Howell started a community called Pinnacle outside Kingston, and in 1935 he published *The Promise Key*, under the name Gangunguru (or G.G.) Maragh. His pen name either comes from one of the Hindustani titles, Gyanguru Maharaj, "Venerable Teacher of Knowledge," or Gyanguru Marg, meaning "The Road of the Venerable Teacher."[189] The British need for labor on the sugar plantations of the Caribbean after the emancipation of Black slaves had introduced almost half a million Indian indentured laborers in the years 1834–1916.[190] Following others, Vijay Prashad makes the case that contact with this population gave Rastafarianism some of its enduring traditions, such as the ritual use of marijuana, known by its Hindi name, *ganja*, or in the growing of matted dreadlocks, like the *jata* of the Indian holy men known as *jatadharis*.[191]

Yet Howell's thought was also influenced by another stream of the Black mysticism of the New York area in the 1920s, as his *Promise Key* is cribbed almost entirely from a 1924 publication called *The Holy Piby*, or *The Blackman's Bible*.[192] Robert Athlyi Rogers, who immigrated to the Newark area from the Caribbean island of Anguilla in the nineteen-teens, wrote the *Piby*. Rogers took the title "Shepherd," a common designation among practitioners of the Afro-Caribbean Revival religion, and founded a church he called the "Afro-Athlycan Constructive Gaathly." Like the other mystic scientists of the time, Rogers was drawn to Marcus Garvey's U.N.I.A., and he declared Garvey to be a divine apostle sent to redeem the children of Ethiopia. Rogers traveled widely, spreading his teachings as far away as the Caribbean, Central and South America, and Kimberly, South Africa.[193] The *Piby* is a fascinating document in its own right, written in the cadence of the King James Bible, with a rich panoply of comets, angels, encounters with God, and an angel named Douglas. While many Black prophets of the period identified African Americans with the children of Israel, Rogers predicted a millennial salvation of the "Children of Ethiopia," whom he distinguished from the "Children of Israel": "Again did the Lord stretch forth his hands over Ethiopia and Canaan and the offsprings of Ham became mighty and the lands became prosperous in animals, fruits and grains. Great cities sprang up among them and the women as well as men mastered ships upon the waters."[194] Like Black religious thinkers such as Edward Wilmot Blyden, Prophet Robert Athlyi Rogers reworked the curse of Ham into a Providential mission for all descendants of Africa.

Rogers' millennial Black religious interest in outer space and interplanetary colonization might be the earliest manifestation of what would become an important theme in African American mysticism and musical culture. Many alternative religious practitioners treated the passing of Haley's Comet as a divine omen, and it appears to have sparked an interest in celestial portents in Rogers's text, which, in its final book, makes a range of predictions tied to the passing of a mighty comet called "Satter," which would pass two miles from earth, raising new lands in the Pacific and Atlantic Oceans. There would be a new era of interplanetary space travel, with "laborers in Mars, strike-breakers on earth and my daughter in college in Jupiter."[195] In the twentieth century, space became a place where African Americans could remap society in a manner that would correct some of the racism and social ills of this planet. The Nation of Islam incorporated the idea that an intergalactic Mother Ship was waiting to wreak vengeance on whites and rescue Blacks, ideas that led various splinter groups to craft their own versions of Black religious interplanetary millennialism. Interplanetary mystical visions expressed themselves in the 1960s and 1970s in the work of a number of Black musicians such as Sun Ra, who claimed to be a space alien.[196]

To be sure, there were other roots of Rastafari, such the indigenous Jamaican religious movement known as Revival and the customs of East Indians in Jamaica—not to mention peripatetic Bishop R.A.R. Johnson, an itinerant preacher whose Israelite teachings found a following in Harlem and in the West Indies. Yet Harlem Black Israelite culture was indispensable to the formation of Rastafarianism. Most scholars of Rastafarianism offer no explanation for the simultaneous emergence of the Israelite doctrine among four different Jamaican prophets, and ignore the continuity between the earlier Black Israelites and the later Rastafarians.[197] It is a reasonable inference that without the transmission of Black Israelite doctrines through Ford, Matthew, and others, there would have been no Rastafarianism, and without the brief episode of African American colonization of Ethiopia, the beatification of Ras Tafari probably would not have taken place.

In the decades since, Rastafarianism has developed into a truly major cultural force, not only in Jamaica but also around the world. Through emissaries such as Bob Marley, Burning Spear, and Buju Baton, the doctrines of Rastafarianism have spread worldwide in reggae music.[198] How ironic it is that Rabbi Ford spent his last days in Ethiopia struggling to play music, his Ethiopian movement in shambles. When he died it appeared that the fire of Israelite Ethiopianism had been extinguished, but somehow an ember from that adventure managed to smolder long enough and give off just enough heat to ignite another major cultural conflagration. Long after the demise of the Black Israelite colony in Ethiopia, Rastafarian reggae music would broadcast Ethiopianist Black Israelite teachings worldwide.

# 5  "I SAW YOU DISAPPEAR WITH MY OWN EYES"

## HIDDEN TRANSCRIPTS OF RABBI WENTWORTH A. MATTHEW'S BLACK ISRAELITE BRICOLAGE

With Rabbi Arnold Josiah Ford's death in Ethiopia in 1935, another West Indian, Wentworth Arthur Matthew, became the Black Israelite torchbearer. From the 1930s to the 1970s, a visitor to the Ethiopian Hebrew Commandment Keepers congregation in Harlem on a Saturday morning would have found Rabbi Matthew leading a room of African Americans engaged in Hebrew prayer, the men wearing Jewish prayer shawls and skull caps, the women sitting in a separate section at the rear. At the midpoint of the service the diminutive, bearded rabbi would remove the Torah from its enclosure and lead others around the synagogue as the congregation sang the hymn "We Are Marching to Zion," a favorite of the Wesleyan camp meeting revival movement of the nineteenth and early twentieth centuries.[1] For the most part, these worshipers were not converts to Judaism, nor did they even describe themselves as Jews, preferring the terms "Hebrew" or "Israelite" (see fig. 5.1). By the 1930s, their congregation was the oldest remaining Israelite synagogue in New York, a holdover from the First World War years, and it included former members of Rabbi Ford's congregation. One evening after Friday night services had concluded, Matthew turned to the dozen worshipers in the audience and began speaking on the familiar theme of his magical abilities. Turning to Brother William, Matthew asked for corroboration that he had made himself invisible with a wave of the hand.

> "Yes, you did," corroborated Brother William. "I saw you disappear with my own eyes."
>
> Immediately, the rest of the worshippers (all women) rose from their seats and shouted ecstatically, "Hallelujah, the Lord loves our teacher."
>
> "Let us sing 'Adon Olam'," the Rabbi roared. "Let us sing so that all our enemies will know that we are the chosen sons and daughters of Jehova"[2]

FIGURE 5.1 Rabbi Matthew and the rabbis and members of the Commandment Keepers of Harlem. The women's headdresses and robes are similar to those worn in Black Spiritual churches and in the Church of the Living God, while the men's head coverings are like those worn in Ashkenazi and Sephardic synagogues. New York Historical Society. Photograph by Alexander Alland.

Rabbi Matthew's "Commandment Keepers Church of the Living God the Pillar and Ground of Truth and the Faith of Jesus Christ" began as a Christian church in 1919, and progressively incorporated more Jewish rituals and decreased the prominence of Jesus as the decades passed. There were many sects of Black Jews during the 1920s, in a range of American cities, and many of these had more members than Matthew's Ethiopian Hebrews or gained more wealth and notoriety. But like Rabbi Ford, Matthew practiced a religion that was not only Black Israelite but was explicitly Jewish. He preached descent from the ancient Israelites while incorporating Jewish ritual, Hebrew language, and kosher dietary practices.[3] During the five decades Matthew was active, he ordained a dozen or more rabbis, making him the torchbearer for Black Judaism in the United States. Yet despite this long career, his movement probably never numbered more than a few thousand followers at the most, split among a handful of small congregations.

Black Jews did not simply imitate white Jews, but rather they were bricoleurs who constructed a polycultural religion that creatively reworked threads from religious faiths, secret societies, and magical *grimoires*. This microhistory of the development of Rabbi Matthew's theology reveals how the Jewish ritual that he presented to the world was undergirded by Holiness Christianity and magical practices borrowed from esoteric sources such as Freemasonry and Spiritualism. When one combines the study of Rabbi Matthew's Black Israelism with similar studies of Black Israelism, Black Islam, Rastafarianism, Father Divine's Peace Mission movement, and various New Thought-based Black religions operative in the 1920s, it is possible to appreciate a remarkable wave of overlapping esoteric religious creativity that accompanied the much more famous artistic creativity of the Harlem Renaissance.[4] Like other religions of the African diaspora, Black Israelism drew on Caribbean carnival traditions, Pentecostal Christianity, Spiritualism, magic, Kabbalah, Freemasonry, and Judaism, in a polycultural creation process dependent not on imitation or inheritance of Judaism as much as on innovation, social networks, and imagination.

Understanding Rabbi Wentworth Arthur Matthew, who died as "Chief Rabbi of the Ethiopian Hebrews of the Western World," is made more difficult because of what scholar James Scott called the public, partial, and hidden transcripts, Matthew's rhetoric when whites were present was different from that when his audience was exclusively African American, and it was different again when his audience were all Black Israelites; one of the items he taught at his religious school was "speech in front of mixed congregations."[5] Similarly, what he told a Black newspaper was different from what he told a white newspaper. Toward the end of his life, frustrated at what he perceived as the injustices dealt him by reporters and scholars, he refused to make statements to outsiders at all. Moreover, Rabbi Matthew left few papers or interviews, and he protected the secrets of his past even from his followers. It is, therefore, necessary to unearth and decipher the partial and hidden transcripts in order to understand the cultural world of early Black Israelites, the intellectual wells from which they drew, and the social meanings they gave to their practice and identity.[6] Like other subaltern histories without abundant written sources, the task of reconstructing and interpreting Rabbi Matthew's religion forces the scholar himself to be something of a bricoleur, piecing together an intellectual history from a handful of clues gleaned from a small body of surviving documents, membership lists, and pamphlets, as well as a limited number of secondhand accounts.[7]

The amount of Judaic ritual in Matthew's church and the importance of Jewishness to his faith rose as the number of white Jews in Harlem declined. In 1923 he celebrated his first Passover; in 1929 his synagogue was receiving some financial aid from white synagogues; and in 1930 "Bishop" Matthew celebrated Rosh Hashanah with six Jews of European origins among the 175 congregants. In the same year the congregation purchased a Torah.[8] What made "bishop" and then "rabbi" Matthew's Black Israelism different from many other varieties of Black Israelism that arose in Memphis, New Orleans, Philadelphia, Chicago, Jamaica, South Africa, and even New York in later decades was the fact that Matthew, like Rabbi Ford before him, adopted the ritual forms of Judaism to augment his Israelite identity. The congregation retained a belief in the divinity of Jesus, but began to incorporate elements of Jewish worship, including the use of Jewish prayers such as the *Shemma* and the observance of holidays such as Rosh Hashanah and Yom Kippur. A newspaper story from 1929, entitled "Negro Sect in Harlem Mixes Jewish and Christian Religions," described how Matthew ate kosher meat, wore a skullcap and a prayer shawl, and used some Hebrew. However, the congregation thought of Jesus either as a prophet of the rank of Moses or as divine, and the service itself resembled that of the sanctified church more than that of a Jewish synagogue.[9]

In addition to mixing beliefs, Matthew was actively combining Jewish rituals with customs and rituals derived from African American Christianity—as well as from conjuring, as we shall see. For example, Rabbi Matthew's observance of the Jewish holidays mixed in aspects of African-American religious culture not usually found in Jewish practice (fig. 5.2). On Rosh Hashanah, each congregant received a small bottle of oil. The Tashlich ceremony, in which Jews throw breadcrumbs into a body of water, symbolizing the release of their sins, became embellished by placing petitions into apples and throwing them into the river. On Rosh Hashanah and Yom Kippur alike, the Commandment Keepers burned incense, filled a bowl with oil, and placed two silver coins into the oil. On the festive holiday of Simchat Torah, a glass of whiskey was given to each reader before the reading of the Torah. On Passover, Matthew convened a community seder and feast, and chose a "beloved son of the year." In a nod to his past in sanctified churches, Matthew also incorporated foot washing into the Passover ritual.[10]

There is no doubt that as the twenties progressed, Matthew and his followers sincerely came to believe themselves to be Jews, the physical and spiritual descendents of the ancient Israelites. Bishop Matthew attended services at Rabbi Ford's congregation, Beth B'nai Abraham, and interacted with other Israelite teachers in Harlem. Eventually, Matthew adopted the Israelite teaching himself. Near the end of his life, looking back on this period during a rare conversation about his Christian past, Matthew emphasized

**FIGURE 5.2** Members of Harlem's Commandment Keepers Church of the Living God, the Pillar and Ground of Truth. New York Historical Society. Photograph by Alexander Alland.

the individual nature of his religious odyssey: "I got tired of Christianity, of going from church to church," he said. "Got the spirit it wasn't right. Just found this by myself because I wanted Hebrew. Like I was reaching out and discovered this."[11]

When Rabbi Matthew died on December 3, 1972, his death certificate matched the story he had told as far back as 1937—that he had been born in Lagos, Nigeria, on June 23, 1892, to a Falasha father and a West Indian mother. However, government documents hidden from public view tell a very different story. In 1918, 1920, and even as late as 1969, when he applied for a social security number, Matthew reported that he was born on June 23, 1892, on St. Kitts in the British West Indies, and immigrated to New York in 1913.[12] Community leader Rabbi Hailu Moshe Paris reported that members were upset to discover that Matthew was not born in Africa. "Later when he passed on a lot of people did not like that he was from St. Kitts," Paris related.[13]

Matthew's parents, Frances Cornelious and Joseph Matthew, raised him as a Methodist, and he later belonged to a "Jesus-only" Pentecostal church in the West Indies.[14] As an adult, he later described a deep religious faith that was a part of daily life in the Caribbean, writing that "the people of the islands were among the most enlightened, biblically," and, in accordance with biblical prohibitions, would not eat animals that had died of strangulation or drowning.[15] For Matthew, as for many working-class Protestants of the nineteenth and early twentieth centuries, the Bible not only was a holy document to be read by a religious authority on Sunday but was also part of the fabric of daily life, a mystical roadmap that promised to guide one through the past, the present, and the afterworld. Like many other devout Protestants, Rabbi Matthew and the people who became his followers committed large portions of the Bible to memory.[16]

Matthew's Caribbean childhood provided the first of many opportunities to perform and embody biblical identities. Commenting on a passage from the book of Exodus, Matthew once wrote:

> Here I am reminded of the Patriarchal plays at Christmas time, also of David and Goliath and the children of Israel, by which the people of [the] islands were reminded from year to year that they were the children of the house of Israel. In the stories of Joseph in Egypt, Solomon and Sheba, strictly Biblical, are vividly portrayed the same people in America who are "Negroes" and in most part of the British domain [are known] as "darkies."[17]

The plays to which Matthew referred were a feature of Christmas celebrations in Nevis and St. Kitts, when roving bands of a dozen or more actors would act out various themes to the accompaniment of several types of music. When Matthew was growing up, Bible stories were part of the living, breathing life of the Caribbean islands. As a historian of the Christmas diversions in Nevis St. Kitts commented, one of the striking things about them was "the dimension of biblical knowledge that is suggested that these 'unschooled' rural folk possessed, particularly at a time when there were no common media like the radio. The long passages from the Bible, or other narrative or verse that they memorized, are a credit to these artists, many of whom perhaps never had a chance to go to school."[18] The Christmas plays that Matthew later credited with forming the genesis of his Israelite identity were part of a rich tradition of weaving the Bible not only into the daily lives but also into the very identities of its readers. The celebrations were polycultural, popular, and riotously heterogeneous: topics ran the gamut of popular culture from the Bible to Hollywood movies, and had titles such as "Children of Israel," "Clowns," "Indians and Cowboys," "Cakewalk with Japanese Girls," "Samson and Delilah,"

"Julius Caesar," and "Tarzan of the Apes." Matthew referred to two of these plays in particular that transmitted the knowledge of Afro-Israelite identity—"David and Goliath" and "Children of Israel." These biblical stories were adapted from plays by Hannah More, an English writer of the late eighteenth and early nineteenth centuries, and were notable for their overwrought language. A small boy was usually picked to play David, which made his feat of memorization all the more impressive, especially when he had to deliver convoluted lines such as: "I bring of your aged Sir the gifts of such plain plates and rural vivands as suits his frugal fortune." No doubt the strangeness of More's turgid language must have added to the pleasure and the power of their enunciation for performers and audience members alike.[19]

These Christmastime plays were a local Nevian variant of carnivalesque masquerade, which polyculturally recombined heterogeneous materials made available to local people by the transnational currents that delivered Hollywood movies and English poetry alike as flotsam on global cultural currents. As in many other forms of masquerade, actors became the characters they portrayed, and the entire community was drawn into the performance through the act of participating in the retelling of familiar biblical stories. When David slew Goliath, or when the Israelites escaped Egypt, the actors and their audience became identified with the time, space, and race of the pageants. The theatrical alchemy of Christmas productions provided one site where Afro-Caribbean peoples incorporated biblical identities not only into their religion but also into their very bodies.[20]

Rabbi Matthew's insistence that he had unwittingly practiced a form of Judaism in the Caribbean suggests that some piece of Afro-Caribbean religiosity had become identified with Judaism. Perhaps Seventh Day Adventism spread Judaic practices along with the Saturday Sabbath, or perhaps elements of Afro-Caribbean religions became identified with Judaism. In the middle of the nineteenth century, an occult practice known as Myal emerged in Jamaica that combated obeah, the sinister form of African spiritual power often equated with malevolent witchcraft. With the infusion of spiritual energies during the Great Revival in 1860, Myal was transformed into two variants, Zion and Pukumina (or Pokomania), both under the rubric of "Revival." Of the two, Zion appeared first and retained more of the forms of Christianity. Adherents of Zion adamantly refused to show respect for dangerous spirits but sought to control them through ritual symbolism. In contrast, followers of Pukumina acknowledged the power of all spirits, good and bad.[21] One source reports that followers of Pukumina were also known as "Black Jews." Whether it was by observing certain dietary laws and taboos, by keeping the

Seventh Day Sabbath, by preserving memory of Caribbean Jewish ancestry, or by actually referring to themselves as "Black Jews," some West Indian people thus developed religious identifications with Judaism before immigrating to the United States.[22]

The Caribbean was not just a border zone where cultures met and meshed; it was also a place whose people frequently left in search of jobs and opportunity. In the first decades of the twentieth century, the catastrophic collapse of world sugar prices, soil exhaustion, natural disasters, and population growth on the older British colonies of Barbados, Jamaica, and Nevis-St. Kitts led to mass migrations from the islands.[23] Many West Indian sailors escaped the poverty of the Caribbean by traveling the world for a time in the merchant marine, and since Matthew claimed to have visited Palestine, Egypt, and Haiti, perhaps he was among them. Matthew was a stocky, powerfully built young man, 5'4" in height, and he once indicated he was trained as a carpenter. Steady work in the Caribbean was increasingly hard to find, however, and on May 9, 1913, just shy of his twenty-first birthday, Matthew once again boarded a ship, leaving St. Kitts on the SS *Parima* and arriving at Ellis Island in New York after a brief, two-day journey.[24] It was probably in New York that Matthew met and married Florence Docher Liburd, also a native of the British West Indies, and together they had four children. In his first years in New York, Matthew earned a living by performing odd jobs, and by competing as a boxer and a wrestler.[25]

Meanwhile he studied to become a Christian minister. He studied theology in Harlem at a place he identified as the "Hayden Seminary" and received ordination. On April 15, 1919, he founded The Commandment Keepers Church of the Living God, the Pillar and Ground of Truth. At the beginning, when he incorporated the church with the State of New York in 1921, the name included the phrase: "and the faith of Jesus Christ" an appellation that remained until the late 1960s. Matthew's church shared its long compound name with several other churches, all of which taught Ethiopianism, adherence to the Ten Commandments, and Black descent from ancient Israelites.[26]

The earliest of these, an offshoot of Bishop Christian's "Church of the Living God" active in Harlem after the First World War, was the "Church of the Living God, the Pillar and Ground of Truth," founded by Mother Mary L. Tate in Tennessee in 1903. Mother Tate's church practiced foot washing, justification, and eventually incorporated sanctification by the Holy Spirit through glossolalia, or speaking in tongues. The *Decree Book* of Mother Tate's church related the biblical story of the Israelites' Exodus from Egypt to the "land that flowed with milk and honey" and God's anger at the Israelite's fickleness, saying, "Let the present Church of the Living God, the Pillar and Ground of the Truth use the commandments of God given through the anointed leaders of God which was appointed to lead Israel as a guide in our present and future state of conditions of times and in changes of times and places."[27] Notice that Israel is referred to in the present, the possessive, and the first person plural—*our* present and future state. Like Matthew's later Commandment Keepers Congregation, the Church of the Living God taught literal, not simply allegorical, identification with Israel, and blended biblical and contemporary time. In outlining the faith, Mother Tate's *Decree Book* stated, "we believe that eyes have not seen, neither have ears heard, what is in store in that city for those that love the Lord, do his will and keep His commandments."[28] It was certainly a sentiment that would have resonated with Matthew's church, which came to call themselves the "Commandment Keepers."

Another Black Israelite pioneer with a "Church of the Living God" was Bishop R.A.R. Johnson. Johnson, who was born in New Bern, North Carolina, was an itinerant preacher based in Florida and a one-time follower of Mother Tate's who founded a church called Abyssinia before the First World War.[29] In 1914, in Beaufort, South Carolina, Johnson founded the House of God, Holy Church of the Living God, the Pillar and Ground of Truth, the House of Prayer for All People. The church was incorporated in 1918 and the same year spread to Washington, D.C. Soon the movement spread to the West Indies, West Africa, and southern India, bringing its twenty-four principles, including immersion, foot washing, women ministers, equality of races in the church, and sanctification by the Holy Spirit. The church practiced Pentecostal Christianity and observed some Jewish festivals. Church members observed the Sabbath on Saturday and did not celebrate Christmas or Easter. Women wore white, including white headdresses, from Passover to Sukkoth, the harvest festival.[30]

In 1927, Bishop Johnson organized the Sister's Unity Gideon Band in Avenel, New Jersey. Wentworth A. Matthew retained the minutes of that first meeting, in which a West Indian-born fifty-seven-year-old woman named Annie Matthew, a dedicated evangelist, was named pastor of the small congregation, which consisted of seven women and two men. Evangelist Annie Matthew led the congregation in prayer and song at the start of each meeting, "After which the Commandments were repeated." Evangelist Matthew preached on topics such as "Unity," "Be Steadfast" and "The Effects of Unity." This was very much a Christian church—the opening song at the May 7, 1928, meeting was "Since Christ My Soul Set Free."[31] Repeating the Ten

Commandments would become a standard part of Rabbi Matthew's Harlem Commandment Keepers' practice, if it was not already. As an itinerant preacher of some talent and ability, and as an early pioneer of both Ethiopianism and Israelism, Bishop R.A.R. Johnson played an important and under-recognized role in the development and spread of the Ethiopian Israelite teaching from his base in Florida along the routes of African American migration.[32]

Despite Matthew's attraction to Jewish rituals and practices, his private records demonstrate his general practice of Holiness rituals and his acceptance of Holiness and esoteric patterns of affliction and healing, including belief in the danger posed by doctors, and belief in the hazards that could befall those who spoke ill of the minister. Baptism and a second baptism in the Holy Spirit were part of the practice of the early Commandment Keepers. All this is revealed in a record of deaths of members, where he noted that Philip Ellis "was not a Commandment Keeper. Only he was baptized in Jesus Name, but not in Holy Ghost."[33] In other words, the deceased had been baptized, but he had not received an experience of sanctification, the central experience of Wesleyan perfectionism that had led to a century of the Holiness movement. His interest in divine healing and a taboo against Western medicine, common to many Holiness, Pentecostal, and Spiritual ministers, is revealed when he wrote of Agnes Miles, who died in 1924, "She was a Holy and harmless child. She died from heart disease after taking doctors medicine." According to Matthew's cosmology, not all supernatural power was benevolent. Irene Aleide died in 1922, and Matthew tersely noted next to her name and date of death, "She spoke abusively of the Minister and fell dead."[34] Reinforcing the church's Christianity, Matthew displayed a placard in the sanctuary reading, "Wait for the Power that Fell Pentecost," and another one that proclaimed: "People Prepare to Meet Thy God. Jesus Saves."[35]

Matthew, who used the title "Bishop" in the first decade of the Commandment Keepers, was part of a community of ministers that stretched across the Eastern seaboard and extended to the Caribbean. Matthew's personal correspondence and the congregation's record books demonstrate that he corresponded with these ministers and sometimes co-officiated with them at baptisms, which were a part of his ministry in its first decade. In 1926 he even co-officiated a baptism with Bishop R. C. Lawson, the founder of the "Church of Our Lord Jesus Christ of the Apostolic Faith," which would become one of the major African-American Pentecostal denominations.[36]

In the first decade of the Commandment Keepers' existence, Matthew, like many sanctified church ministers, incorporated syncopated "jazzed" music into the prayer service. In at least the first decade of the Commandment Keepers, Matthew played guitar during services, and others played saxophone, piano, tambourines, triangles, and cymbals. A visitor in 1929 described how worshipers played tambourines, cymbals, triangle, saxophone, and piano.

> The woman in the white smock ran a few scales on the saxophone. The Bishop [Matthew], removing his cap and putting on a black skull-cap, picked up a guitar. The girl at the piano struck a few chords; the Bishop tuned up. The tambourines, the triangle and the cymbals were passed out to the women. Some one in the audience called the number of a song in the hymnal. "106!" The Bishop sat in [the] rear of the pulpit, his hymn book on a small music stand, the guitar in his lap.[37]

The group started into the hymn, "The Cloud and the Fire," which relates the exodus of the ancient Israelites through the desert—"So the sign of the fire by night. And the sign of the cloud by day; Hov'ring O'er—Just before—As they journey on their way." As the hymn progressed, traces of syncopation slipped into the even march tempo, with the tambourines rattling and the triangle striking the off beats. On the third verse the pace quickened and the volume grew. "The piano gives a run in the bass chords—a trace of syncopation. The song rises louder. Bodies begin swaying to the time. It picks up, up to a quick-step." The song continued with its tale of the deliverance of the Exodus: "Shall a guide and a leader be, Till the wilderness be past; For the Lord our God—in his own good time—Shall lead to the light at last." "Over and over they sang it," the visitor recounted. "They ran out of verses, and still they sang. The chorus again and again. Their feet beat time on the floor. They were jazzing it; evenly, an infectious swing. A large negress in a black fur coat rose from her seat and began slowly swaying in the aisle. There were shouts of 'Hallelujah!' 'Praise the Lord.' The music beat faster, faster." Finally the music stopped and they pitched into another hymn, again starting slowly and working up to a cathartic peak.[38] The predominance of women among the worshipers, the use of band instruments, and syncopation of the music, the swaying of the faithful, even the woman standing, swaying in her fur coat, are all descriptive of African American churches in general but of Holiness churches in particular, where band instruments, syncopated music, and physically demonstrative worship all found more acceptance than they did at the larger, older, and more prestigious Black churches. As the decades passed, the Commandment Keepers' instrumentation became simpler—the piano remained, but the congregation discontinued use of the guitar, saxophone, and cymbals.[39]

The curricula of two schools Matthew ran show his religious evolution toward Judaism, as he labored to train new rabbis and build relationships with other Black Israelite leaders. In 1934, a decade after his first Passover seder, "Bishop" Matthew ran the "Bishops' Ecclesiastical School of the Commandment Keepers Church of the Living God, the Pillar and Ground of the Truth, Inc.," which was "open to churchmen, and men of, and from educational centers." In 1940, then using the title "rabbi," Matthew published the similar "Curriculum of the Ethiopian Hebrew Rabbinical College of the Royal Order of Ethiopian Hebrews and the Commandment Keepers Congregation of the Living God, Inc.," along with a statement of the beliefs of the Commandment Keepers. The rabbinical school curriculum was essentially the same as that of the earlier ecclesiastical curriculum, except that it replaced "Jesus Christ" with "the cultural house of Israel" or "the kingdom to come." Significantly, Matthew's later lesson plan replaced "Jews" in most places with "Israelites," and "Israelitish ancient and medieval history" replaced "Jewish ancient and medieval history." The new curriculum added "Hebraic ancient history" in addition to "Jewish ancient history," thus making a distinction between the ancient Hebrews and the ancient Jews.[40] These changes suggest that in the late thirties Matthew and his congregation were Judaizing their Christian beliefs. By the middle of the 1930s, Matthew's congregation celebrated all the major Jewish holidays, including Rosh Hashanah, Yom Kippur, Succoth, and Passover; they also identified as "Negro Jews."[41] By 1944 the transition was complete, and Matthew had jettisoned his one-time belief in Jesus altogether, as when he brushed off questions about Jesus with the rebuke, "Your Jesus has been a long time dead."[42]

Conjuring was for a long time part of the bricolage of the the Commandment Keepers' beliefs. For decades after they began practicing elements of Judaism, they retained esoteric practices common to peers in the Holiness movement. And in the early fifties, observers recorded four elements of Matthew's belief system: healing and "cabalistic science," a belief in Hebrew angels, theosophy, and cosmology. His claim to be able to make himself invisible was part of his mastery of what he called conjuring or "cabalistic science." The best exposition of Matthew's belief in Kabbalistic science comes from Howard Brotz's work, published in 1952. He quotes from one of Matthew's sermons:

Years ago I gave a complete course in cabalistic science. I am a doctor of metaphysics and studied mental telepathy. I can tell your thoughts. It took seven years to complete the course: learned how to stop rain, heal the sick. I was in Charlottesville, Virginia, and I said, "I hear a voice speaking to me right now." Then I said, "Mother Johnson, please go see Mother Hubbard right now." When I got back to New York I saw Mother Johnson who said, "I was working on my laundry when I heard the rabbi's voice to go see Mother Hubbard and it was a good thing I went because she was in trouble." Is that conjuring? Is that sorcery?

Conjure, by the way, is a good word, meaning compel. Here, I take this match and strike it and compel it to light. The Negroes call it *cunjur*, the whites call it *conjoor*. The atomic bomb is a matter of conjuring, and so are all the forces. The word isn't so bad. But the poor Negro from Africa was made afraid by the Gentile master. That was the only secret he had and the Gentile taught him to be afraid of 'spirits.'

Cabalistic science is one of the branches of mental telepathy. Those who thought it conjuring had a dark cell in their minds. This is an angelic science—has nothing to do with rabbit's foot, spiritualism, or conjuring spirits out of a graveyard. The spiritualists set you against your best friends, lead you into the numbers racket. Use dirt and filth— dead man's fingers, grave dirt. Cabalistic things are parchment. The science of Israel is a big thing. It's why we use *talesim* [a Jewish prayer shawl with knotted fringes], candles, and incense. The Catholics faintly imitate us. Do you think the three Hebrew boys who went into the fiery furnace went in saying, "Lawdy Jesus?" They knew how to pray. They went into the furnace anointed with the oil of life, which we can't take up tonight, and they tell me that when they came out they didn't even smell of smoke.[43]

The two intertwined belief systems that Matthew referenced are spiritualism and African religions of the Caribbean. In truth it is not possible to speak of spiritualism and Afro-Caribbean religions as distinct heritages, because after spiritualism's efflorescence in upstate New York in 1848, it has entered many forms of Afro-Atlantic religions, becoming a major part of Cuban Santeria, Haitian Vodou, and African American Black Spiritual churches. In the first paragraph, Matthew described a number of attributes of spiritualism. Mental telepathy, that is the transmission of thoughts from one person to another without the use of the five senses, is one aspect of the paranormal that is associated with spiritualism. Similarly, Matthew claimed the power of clairvoyance as well as the power to hear by means other than the ear. Healing was one of the major focuses of spiritualism, and spiritualism helped to spawn the divine healing movement of the late nineteenth century.

Indeed, healing practices are a major part of many Afro-Atlantic religions, and such religions give Matthew's words further context. In the second paragraph, Matthew defends the concept of conjuring, defines "conjure" as "compel," and chides the taboo against conjuring. There are, in fact, two parallel African spiritual traditions in the Caribbean, which are conjoined in Haitian Vodou but are separate and antagonistic in Cuban Santeria and in African-derived spiritual systems of the British West Indies, where Matthew grew up. In Vodou, this division is between the cool, familiar *rada* spirits, of West African (Fon) lineage, and the fiery, petulant *petwo* spirits, of Central African (Congo) heritage.[44] In other parts of the Caribbean, these two pantheons of African gods do not share the same house, but are worshiped by separate and mutually antagonistic parties. Thus, when Matthew says that conjuring is simply compelling, what he means is that conjuring is simply the efficacious way of working the spirits. When he says, "the poor Negro from Africa was made afraid by the Gentile master. That was the only secret he had and the Gentile taught him to be afraid of 'spirits,'" what he means is that the African practice of serving the gods was stigmatized by Europeans, and Africans lost a key part of their religious heritage—"that was the only secret he had."

But while Matthew was willing to defend conjuring and even, secretly, to use it, the Kabbalistic science as he understood it was part of the "good" or morally unambiguous side of African spiritual power. This is what he means in the third paragraph when he says that Kabbalistic science is an "angelic science." Moreover, the items he singles out for condemnation, such as human remains and dirt from a graveyard, are recognizably part of the petwo or obeah side of the spiritual pantheon. Even as Matthew practiced mental telepathy and other aspects of spiritualism, there were certain aspects of "black magic" such as communing with the dead, from which he disassociated himself. These paragraphs seem contradictory, and to a certain extent they are. Yet it is a contradiction that is consistent with Afro-Caribbean culture in the Spanish, Dutch, or British Caribbean, where few would admit to using sinister magic. At the same time, one might hint that one knew how to do so if necessary. In Jamaica in the late nineteenth and early twentieth centuries, it was not at all unusual for Revival Shepherds to also practice obeah, either openly or secretly.[45]

"Cabalistic things are parchment," Matthew says. "The science of Israel is a big thing. It's why we use *talesim*, candles, and incense." Waitzkin correctly noted that there is no special use of candles or incense in Jewish Kabbalah. Parchment held the words of the Torah, but while the words themselves were treated as almost animate objects, the parchment was endowed with no special significance. In contrast, Waitzkin notes, "parchment, candles, and incense have been very significant materials in voodoo, where they possess magical qualities," a statement he supports with a quote from Zora Neal Hurston's work on Hoodoo in the American South. Both Brotz and Waitzkin interpret this passage ("This is an angelic science...") as an example of an attempt by Matthew to differentiate himself from his African-American neighbors. Here is Brotz writing in *Phylon* in 1952: "The Cabalistic science, too, like the rest of their practices, is the basis of explicit self-differentiation from the stereotype of the Southern, rural Negro."[46] Although it is true that Matthew extolled middle-class values and in his later years referred to emotionalism in worship as "niggeritions," Rabbi Matthew was not distancing himself from the cultures of his Southern and Caribbean-born neighbors by emphasizing the positive aspects of Kabbalistic science, but in fact was clearly and unambiguously embedding himself in those very cultures.[47]

Rabbi Matthew's "cabalistic science" drew on the stream of New Thought philosophy within Harlem's esoteric Holiness practitioners—especially those who gathered in the orbit of Marcus Garvey's Liberty Hall.[48] One of the most important of the Garveyite esoteric religious circle was named Bishop John Hickerson, who also went by the names "The Rev. St. Bishop the Vine" and "Bishop Eshof Bendoved." Before coming to Harlem, Hickerson had lived and collaborated with George Baker, the future Father Divine, in Baltimore.[49] There they developed a New Thought-based doctrine that God dwelled inside the individual. New Thought was a philosophy of positive thinking that had developed in nineteenth-century New England, and which taught, according to historian Jill Watts, "that God existed in all people, that the channeling of God's spirit eradicated problems, and that unity with God guaranteed salvation."[50] In 1914 Hickerson founded yet another version of the "Church of the Living God, the Pillar and Ground of the Truth" in Harlem—five years before Matthew founded his version. Hickerson, whose Hebrew name meant "son of David," identified himself as an Ethiopian, and taught a variation of New Thought. One of his chants was: "God in you, God in me, You God, I God, Everybody be God." Hickerson's students showed a similar pattern of New Thought beliefs. Hickerson claimed that he had taught Hebrew to Arnold Josiah Ford, and that Ford had then taught Matthew "everything he knows about Hebrew."[51] The association between Judaism and New Thought that Hickerson helped to establish can be seen in his most famous associate, Father Divine, whose "reputedly 'Jewish' doctrine was simply 'God is within man'," according to anthropologist Ruth Landes.[52] In sum, Hickerson helped to spread the New Thought idea that God dwelled inside charismatic leaders and their followers, a concept that was at the heart of the "Jewish," "Hebrew" or Black Israelite beliefs of his followers and associates.

This Black Israelite/New Thought theology utilized the works of Lauron William de Laurence, a former hypnotist based in Chicago who made his name by publishing English translations of magical esoteric works from around the world. His books have been widely circulated and remain highly respected among practitioners of Afro-Atlantic religions such as Santeria, Vodou, Rastafarianism, and other Afro-Atlantic religions. De Laurence's works played critical roles in the genesis of twentieth-century alternative African American religions such as the Moorish Science Temple's Black Islam, Rabbi Matthew's Black Judaism, and Leonard Howell's Rastafarianism. The central theme in de Laurence's introductions and glosses, like the central theme in the beliefs of Bishop Hickerson, Father Divine, and Rabbi Matthew, is the New Thought concept of the immanence of God. De Laurence favored biblical quotations such as "The Kingdom of God is within you," "You are the temples of the Living God," "The Father is in me, I in Him and we in you," all of which are strikingly similar to Father Divine's slogans, or other New Thought-based esotericism.[53]

Rabbi Matthew used an esoteric book to create magical rituals and a "Hebraic" creed that allowed him to be filled with God's spirit. He based what he

FIGURE 5.3 Children of the Commandment Keepers study Hebrew letters and the Hebrew language. New York Historical Society. Photograph by Alexander Alland.

called his "cabalistic science" on the most popular of De Laurence's books, *The Sixth and Seventh Books of Moses*, a manual of magical seals and spells wildly popular among African American conjurers, which claims to divulge the cabbalistic secrets of the ancient Hebrews. The work purports to be a collection of ancient Hebraic sacred texts, diagrams, incantations, and prayers attributed to Moses and other biblical patriarchs, and includes instructions on the effective uses of the Psalms in between long glosses written by De Laurence.[54] De Laurence's 1910 edition republished a German popular manuscript, or *volksbuch*, that had circulated since medieval times and been published in Stuttgart in 1849 and in the United States in the 1860s.[55] The book was translated into English in four separate 1880 American editions, and it began to appear among West Indian obeah men the following decade.[56] There were four undated editions in addition to the four 1880 versions, de Laurence's 1910 version, and a 1938 reissue. All told, the book was so popular among African Americans that the great folklorist and novelist Zora Neale Hurston estimated that there were "millions" of copies "being read and consulted in secret because the readers believe in Moses."[57] Another folklorist estimated that sales of the book were "enormous" and that it was widely used among Southern African Americans in the 1920s.[58] De Laurence's edition of the text appeared throughout Africa and the Afro-Atlantic world, and many colonial and postcolonial governments banned the work as subversive. According to scholar Patrick Polk, the acceptance of the *Sixth and Seventh Books of Moses* in the African diaspora is due in part to the prestige of Moses within Afro-Atlantic spiritual traditions, as well as the suspicion that whites have not shared the whole Bible but have hidden the most powerful portions for their own use.[59] As a product of print culture, de Laurence's book helped create the imagined community of Black Israelism, while it was also a ritual manual that gives instructions for performing transformative, magical rites. Thus it was singularly effective in helping Matthew and others both to imagine and to inhabit Israelite identities.

Matthew's personal papers include two amulets combining diagrams and Hebrew words from *The Sixth and Seventh Books of Moses* with Hebrew incantations for drawing God within oneself, in a manner consistent with New Thought theology. These amulets offer an unparalleled view into the hidden transcript and the private settings where Rabbi Matthew performed the most secret transformative rituals at the hidden heart of Black Israelism. The square amulet in Matthew's personal papers (fig. 5.4) was modified from "The Second Table of the Spirits of Fire," found on page 16 of *The Sixth and Seventh Books of Moses* (fig. 5.5). What makes the derivation of Matthew's dia-

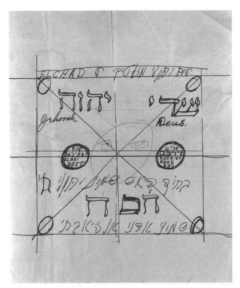

**FIGURE 5.4** Square Hebrew Diagram, n.d. Wentworth A. Matthews Collection, Manuscripts, Archives and Rare Books Division, Schomburg Center for Research in Black Culture, New York Public Library, Astor, Lenox and Tilden Foundations.

**FIGURE 5.5** Table of Fire. From Lauron William de Laurence, ed., *The Sixth and Seventh Books of Moses*, 2nd ed. (Chicago: de Laurence Company, ca. 1900), 16.

gram from de Laurence's diagram indisputable is the fact that de Laurence has included a calligraphic error in the Hebrew that Matthew has repeated. The word at the bottom, חבכ *Ha-ko-ach*, meaning "The Power," has been miswritten. An errant vertical line closes the gap of the middle letter, כ *kaph*, making it look like an uppercase "D." In fact, there is no Hebrew letter with that shape, but in Matthew's diagram חבה is in the exact same place, underneath the intersection of the diagonals, and Matthew has repeated the same mistake in the letter *kaph*, demonstrating that he used de Laurence's text as a source for his "cabalistic science."

The two amulets shed light on Matthew's esoteric theology, part of the secret knowledge at the heart of his Black Israelite belief.[60] Matthew wrote several phrases in fractured Hebrew on the diagram, the top one of which can be translated: "Rise and give me good luck." Just below the median line the Hebrew can be translated: "Within the eighth fire you should give me life," and the bottom line may read either: "The eighth God should be my father," or "The eighth God, my God, my father."[61] At the simplest level, this diagram appears to be a good luck charm. But at a deeper level, this amulet amplifies and expands on Matthew's theology. In later decades, Matthew taught that there were seven "spirits" or elements of God, and twelve heavens, which his daughter explicated in the congregational newspaper in 1965:

> Do you know how few of us, *the Black Jews*, know that G-d is *Wind, Water, Fire, Life, Light, Power,* and *Mind*? This is G-d—the seven elements. Each one of these elements are all gods among themselves, but the creator of these—the one ruler of these, is the one and only. He is G-d. He is in us, out of us, and is all about us; and without Him we wouldn't exist. Without any one of these gods we would not exist.[62]

Given that Matthew believed in seven elements of God, this diagram appears to have been used to worship and invoke the power and presence of the supreme Creator God, an eighth god who appears through the medium of fire. The repetition of the number eight, the image of fire, and a personal filial relationship with God are noteworthy. Again, the amulet can be translated: "Rise and give me good luck/Within the eighth fire you should give me life/the eighth God, my God, my father." Remembering that Matthew began in the sanctified church, he may have borrowed this fiery conception of God from the common "fire-baptized" Holiness-Pentecostal conception of God.[63] The multiple "god-elements" in his theology, however, are what make Matthew's creed most like the pantheistic religions of the Black Atlantic.[64]

Moreover, the ritual use of these diagrams seems to have allowed Matthew to be filled with the presence of God, and to relate to the Creator God as a son relates to a father. The second, round, amulet (fig. 5.6) repeats and amplifies this sense of God's immanence and Matthew's own power. The diagram consists of several Hebrew sentences printed over a Mogen David, literally a

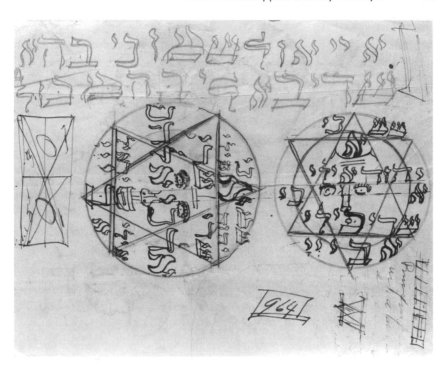

FIGURE 5.6 Round Hebrew Diagram, n.d. Wentworth A. Matthews Collection, Manuscripts, Archives and Rare Books Division, Schomburg Center for Research in Black Culture, New York Public Library, Astor, Lenox and Tilden Foundations.

"Shield of David" or six-pointed star, which is a common cabbalistic referent. After some undecipherable words at the beginning of the prayer, the sentence continues: "Eighth God…come God, come to me in the flood." The words overlaid on top of the Mogen David itself can be translated: "The Name of God is in me, the Lord my God Exalted Lord God is in me, my God will see me, my father God."[65] In this second amulet Matthew emphasizes and underlines the immanence of God in a manner that is consonant with the New Thought teachings of the de Laurence source text. After asking God to enter him "in a flood," he triumphantly proclaims, "the name of God is in me!" What is especially notable here is not just the idea that God is inside Matthew, but his almost messianic connection with God. It is even possible that through the ritual use of these amulets and incantations, Matthew believed himself able to unify the triune parts of the Holiness-Pentecostal Godhead: God is the Father, he is the Son, and they meet via the medium of "the eighth fire," or the Holy Spirit.

We know that Matthew used these and other diagrams and prayers; they did not simply end up among his personal papers. In 1938, a European Jewish visitor mentioned "a prayer that the Rabbi has composed himself and which he speaks before he lifts the Torah. The sentences have lost their sense almost entirely because of the most impossible distortions, changes and confusions."[66] A reporter in 1946 described the Commandment Keepers congregation on the corner of 128th and Lenox as "a dingy three-story red brick building, every window of which displays the Star of David. Some of these stars have an eye in the center with the inscription underneath, 'Royal Order of Ethiopian Jews.'"[67] There is also a 1959 picture of Matthew's son-in-law Norman Dore pointing out a similar Mogen David with circular elements to Matthew's grandson Dovid Dore. Matthew's polycultural version of Judaism may have been unorthodox, but the fact that he began to practice Judaism distinguished him and his followers from the Holiness-based charismatic leaders who had come before.

During the interwar years, the Kabbalistic diagrams that Matthew based in part on the publications of de Laurence seem to have provided a ritual blueprint for the embodiment of divine power in a manner consistent with the "reputedly Jewish" New Thought–based practices of Bishop Hickerson and some of the other religious bricoleurs of the time. The "cabbalistic science" that could make one disappear or make God appear inside oneself was a form of both spiritual and temporal power, power that was particularly attractive to Matthew and his congregants.

There undoubtedly were other elements of Matthew's faith that escaped comment altogether. A visitor in 1966 gave the following account of Matthew's work environment:

> His office is a jumble round a desk with an antique typewriter, a photograph of a grand-daughter in her graduation mortar-board, framed Hebrew prayers, two Coca-Cola bottles wrapped in tinfoil and holding the Stars and Stripes. "That's my *smichah*": he points to his rabbi's certificate on the wall; it has been approved and signed in Gondar, Abyssinia.[68]

This description of the rabbi's office combines the mundane—a photograph of a grandchild—with the truly extraordinary—the certificate from Ethiopia. But the most highly charged objects in the room might be the tinfoil-wrapped Coca-Cola bottles holding the American flags. Both flags and covered bottles are not neutral items in Afro-Atlantic religions but in fact are highly potent means for attracting and containing spirits. There is a long history of their use in Haitian Vodou as well as in other African-based religions of the Caribbean.

In fact, American flags are commonly used in the altars of Black Hawk shrines among the Black Spiritualists of New Orleans, whose female members also wear white habits similar to those worn by female members of Matthew's congregation. Those flags and Coca-Cola bottles on Matthew's desk may have simply been patriotic emblems, but in the hidden transcript they could have been pledges of allegiance to the alternative religiosity of Black Spiritual churches.[69]

Like other forms of Black religion that upended Western history and placed Black people at its very center, Black Judaism was inherently political, and Black Jews joined in the political movements of their day. Like many of his working-class peers of Caribbean extraction, Matthew was a supporter of Marcus Garvey's United Negro Improvement Association (U.N.I.A.). As we have seen in the previous chapter, Garvey took to the streets and the lecture halls and captivated a large segment of Black America with a vision of a free Africa supported by a strong diaspora.[70] Garvey's mixture of racial pride, Black nationalism, and messianism inspired thousands of Black men and women who considered alternatives to conventional Black Christianity in their search for economic and cultural self-sufficiency. As we have seen, the U.N.I.A.'s New York City headquarters, Liberty Hall, was a center for people interested in Black Judaism. It was through the U.N.I.A. and Freemasonry that Matthew's predecessors Arnold Josiah Ford, Mordecai Herman, and Samuel Valentine met each other and founded the Moorish Zionist Temple and Beth B'nai Abraham (B.B.A.), and it was the U.N.I.A. that brought Matthew in touch with his mentor, Rabbi Ford. Black Israelite identity was a spiritual means of cultural empowerment in the context of both racist discrimination and Black nationalist attempts to organize and uplift the race. Rabbi L. A. McKethan, Matthew's student, wrote in 1966 that Matthew had carried on the work of great race leaders such as Booker T. Washington, Hubert Harrison, and Marcus Garvey, as well as earlier Black Israelite teachers. "All these were great and learned men in the days of our Rabbi W. A. Matthew, within a space of 20 years they all died, and thus the full responsibility of rehabilitation, and salvaging of which was lost, was placed upon his shoulders," McKethan wrote. "Many brilliant men fell by the wayside, and some committed suicide under the depression. It is here our leader, our emancipator, proved to be not just a man, but The man. Many have referred to him as being seven men in one, TRULY ANOTHER GREAT MOSES."[71] As in the *Sixth and Seventh Books of Moses*-based diagrams, we see the repetition of the number seven and the implication that Matthew is the successor to the great Moses. At times, Matthew's congregants seemed to view his powers as supernatural. One female member is known to have shouted ecstatically: "Our Rabbi is an Angel! He will lead us all to Heaven."

The majority of Matthew's followers were women, as has been the case historically with most churches, Black and white. Matthew instituted separate seating for men and women, with men in the front and women in the rear. This was a physical manifestation not only of patriarchy but also of the separate spheres for men and women mandated by the discourse of civilization. To be civilized meant to segregate the sexes; the alternative religions of Harlem in the 1920s inscribed within themselves the patriarchy of their time.[72] Much as Jim Crow relegated African Americans to the balconies of New York's Broadway theaters and downtown movie palaces, the Black Israelites relegated women to the rear of the congregation, as was commonly done among all Jewish congregations at the time. African Americans may have suffered the indignity of segregation in public spaces, but within the zone of their own alternative churches, Black Israelites asserted their respectability by creating separate spaces for men and women.

Likewise, Black Israelites' membership in the ancient mytho-historical community of Israel functioned as a form of anti-racism, an antidote to the virulent white supremacy, violence, and economic discrimination that people of African descent encountered in the Americas. Lawrence Levine has usefully employed Mircea Eliade's concept of the sacred in traditional societies to argue that "the slaves created a new world by transcending the narrow confines of the one in which they were forced to live. They extended the boundaries of their restrictive universe backward until it fused with the world of the Old Testament, and upward until it became one with the world beyond."[73] A very similar phenomenon is seen in the case of Rabbi Matthew and his followers, who were not only thinking with the Bible, but in a very real sense embodying the Bible and living in biblical time. The weekly ritual of the congregation reflected this journey as Matthew and his assistant rabbis would march around the congregation with the Torah, singing the Holiness revival favorite, "We Are Marching to Zion."

Matthew's theology also had an apocalyptic edge, and the imagery of the end of days found in the book of Revelation took on a racial cast. A visitor to the congregation in 1938 observed that Matthew was preaching about a coming racial apocalypse:

> Injustices which we (Negroes? Jews?) have suffered in the course of centuries will be atoned for at the end of the days. This idea gives the speaker new impetus; his eyes glow, the audience is gripped by attention.

There follows a fantastic, very primitive description of a war at the end of the time between the black and white world, a gruesome picture of the last judgment and of the final victory of the black skinned people."[74]

The congregation participated in the call and response of the lecture with frequent "amens" and "that's rights", binding the rabbi and the congregation into one insurgent whole: "Every word is accepted with devotion and faithfulness. Whatever the Rabbi says is valid. For all his statements he refers to the Bible. Everything that he desires he proves triumphantly by interpretation from the Bible. The biblical stories are easily identified with contemporary events as if they all had happened in the recent past."[75]

For Matthew, Blackness was itself the mark of God's covenant with God's chosen people, and white Jews were necessarily usurpers or imitators. As Rabbi Matthew developed religious practices that were increasingly indebted to Judaism, he simultaneously became more embittered toward New York's white Jews and developed an ethnological theory that claimed that Black Israelites were the only authentic Jews. He taught that Black Jews were the real Jews, descended directly from Jacob, who was Black because the Bible says his skin was smooth. White Jews were descended from Esau, who was hairy, and like Esau, they had intermarried and assimilated Gentile ways.[76] Furthermore, all Blacks were descended from the Ten Lost Tribes of Israel, whom, he claimed, had been driven from Canaan and settled in Ethiopia.[77] Indeed, numerous accounts report that Matthew taught that European Jews were descended from Edomites, the offspring of Esau who were ancient enemies of the Israelites. One careful observer remarked that "this topic was selected for the guests," which explains why it shows up disproportionately in public transcript accounts of Matthew's theology.[78]

In addition to book groups, churches, salons, and Black Nationalist clubs, one of the new forms of sociability in Jazz Age Harlem was the flowering of benevolent associations and new varieties of secret societies. The Garvey movement provided a powerful mechanism for acting out new identities in the public sphere through its massive parades that wound through the streets of Harlem before its annual conventions during the 1920s. In these displays, proud Black men and women wearing flashy black uniforms or white nurse's outfits pulled their bodies erect in military bearing and marched with heads held high through the streets. On several occasions, Rabbi Matthew's followers joined other Black Israelites marching in these processions with thousands of spectators, and so publicly paraded their identities as Israelites, as Garveyites, and as political actors.[79]

Matthew also tapped into the organizational structures and mythology of Freemasonry, which lay like a vast aquifer just below the surface of Jazz Age popular culture.[80] Many founders of Black Israelite orders were either Masons or were strongly influenced by Masonic ideas, and almost all early Israelite orders incorporated the signs and symbols of Masonry in their rituals and organizations.[81] Matthew, who founded the Commandment Keepers Church of the Living God in 1919, in 1924 launched the Royal Order of Ethiopian Hebrews, the Sons and Daughters of Culture, Inc., as a Masonic order and benevolent association linked to the congregation's religious education program. In time, as the church de-emphasized its Christian past, the church and its Masonic affiliate became conflated, and the congregation became known as "The Commandment Keepers Royal Order of Ethiopian Hebrews." In 1936, a newspaper reported that "In connection with the Commandment Keepers, there is the Royal Order of Ethiopian Hebrew Sons and Daughters of Culture, one of the oldest branches of the Masonic order." Not surprisingly, African American Prince Hall Masons did not treat the Royal Order with the same respect. Harry A. Williamson, the preeminent Prince Hall historian, lists Matthew's synagogue in his index of "bogus" Masonic organizations.[82]

Freemasonry itself has a system of graduated "degrees" by which the initiate learns the secret mysteries of the order. The primary role of Matthew's Royal Order was as a mechanism to educate lay people and to train clergy members, as in the following account of the Beth Hamidrash or religious school that Matthew held after the Shabbat service (fig. 5.3). After drills on simple Hebrew phrases, the subjects were the Bible, civics, and, interestingly, architecture:

> The biblical Books are enumerated and the contents of the individual Book defined. Some care is given to dates: How many years did such and such live, what are the names of the children of such and such, who followed King such and such (never: Why?). Then like in a catechism, important sentences from the Bible, ethical rules, confessions, laws, are being recited in Hebrew and English. The Bible is followed by the study of civics—Declaration of Independence, The Constitution, more important Presidents, forms of Administration, Regional Structure of New York, more important buildings. Nobody knew when the Brooklyn Bridge was built. The Rabbi laughed a great deal about this but he did not give any answer but offered to return "to this question the next time."[83]

This obviously was not a typical Hebrew school curriculum, and it is that last detail, the date of the construction of the Brooklyn Bridge, that is most askew.

Why would Hebrew school students be drilled on statistics of "more important buildings" and bridges? Why, indeed, would they be drilled on civics, judicial documents, and "more important Presidents"? The form of this recitation ("like a catechism") as well as the content—the Bible, presidents, civics, and major buildings, are borrowed from Freemasonry. Masons, as their name implies, imagined themselves to be part of a mythic community of builders stretching from the Egyptian pyramids to the present. Freemasons use such catechisms of facts and figures drawn from the Bible, civics, and architecture as a means of transmitting the secrets that comprise the graduated degrees of their orders. The catechisms are printed in books, as well as memorized and rehearsed orally, much as Matthew conducted his Hebrew school.

The seamless inclusion of Masonic trivia along with Hebrew phrases shows that Freemasonry provided not only the form but also some of the content of Matthew's teaching. Freemasonry's emphasis on cooperating economically with other Masons became for Matthew one of the most "Jewish" aspects of his religious worldview. One visitor described the economic element of Matthew's ideology: "In defense of his program, Rabbi Matthew explains that the philosophy of the Jews is to acquire wealth and command respect. It is this religion, he says, which impels a Jew to walk several miles from the Bronx to the Battery to spend a dollar with another Jew."[84] Matthew equates Jewish economic behavior with Jewish religion in a way that accords with Masonic principles of economic solidarity and uplift.

The Royal Order was a means of communication and proselytizing in addition to being an educational vehicle. In 1943, journalist Roi Ottley wrote, "Through membership in Masonic lodges, affiliated with the Royal Order of Ethiopian Hebrews, they also march in colorful parades that provide the community with highlights during its marching season (from April to October). Through these lodges also they are in constant touch with other Black Jews throughout the country."[85] The Royal Order was one of the primary means that Matthew spread the Commandment Keepers' Black Israelism to other cities, as Matthew explained in 1968, looking back on his creation at the Fifty-First Annual Conference of the Ethiopian Hebrew Congregations:

> The President, Rabbi W. A. Matthew...then gave a short history of the existence of this great work. In the year 1919 only eight (8) members were present. In 1923 the first Passover observance was held. In 1924–25 robes and costumes were ordered for the Royal Order and then the work began to spread from one State and City to another among the Black People of America.[86]

The observation that mysteries transmitted by irregular branches of Prince Hall Masonry could have played an important role in the creation of Black Israelite sects makes sense, given the many similarities between Prince Hall Freemasonry and Black Israelism. Both systems of thought are exercises in counter-history: they replace common derogatory images of African Americans and the African past with an exalted identity rooted in the heroics of the ancient biblical past.[87]

Matthew built both a local and a national network of Black Israelites. In the thirties, Matthew claimed 250 active members and 650 total followers in New York, with offshoots in Brooklyn and Arverne-by-the-Sea (just beyond Far Rockaway, in Nassau County, Long Island).[88] He also maintained ties with congregations in Pennsylvania, Ohio, and Virginia.[89] Matthew built his network of congregations in part by recruiting Black Israelite churches and synagogues that had come out of different streams of the Holiness movement. Whereas Matthew had roots in the Church of the Living God, the Pillar and Ground of Truth, the rabbi of the Youngstown, Ohio, branch, W. O. Dickens, had been ordained by Prophet William Saunders Crowdy of the venerable Church of God and Saints of Christ.[90]

Like the benevolent and fraternal organizations on which he partly modeled his organization, Matthew convened annual conventions during which Israelite leaders from around the country met one another. In 1934, Matthew welcomed nine Black rabbis to the thirteenth annual convention, held in September during the Jewish holiday of Rosh Hashanah. The fact that those rabbis were not tending their own flocks during the Jewish "high holidays" indicates that Rabbi Matthew's tradition of celebrating Jewish holidays was not then widespread among his Israelite peers.[91] In 1936, the congregation received Rabbi E. J. Berson of Media, Pennsylvania, Rabbi A. W. Clark of Philadelphia, Rabbi H. C. Scott of Youngstown, Ohio, Rabbi Charles Harrel of Cullen, Virginia, and Rabbi Henry Forrest of Cincinnati, Ohio.[92] In 1938 *The New Yorker* noted a congregation in Baltimore, Maryland, as well.[93] In 1942 there were new reports of congregations in Salt Lake City, Newark, and St. Louis.[94] Rabbi Matthew did not found all of these synagogues or train their rabbis, but he was an organizer who kept in touch with the other rabbis and occasionally brought them together for conventions, reinforcing his claim of being "Chief Rabbi of the Black Jews in the Western Hemisphere."

A detailed record of the twenty-eighth annual convention in 1948 demonstrates that Christian hymns helped to knit together disparate congregations that probably differed significantly in terms of theology and liturgy. The three-day gathering was punctuated by nineteen songs, two of which were

Hebrew hymns—"Adon Olom" and "Lkol Adonoy." The other seventeen songs were hymns that were commonly used in many Christian denominations, such as "Guide Me O Thou Great Jehovah," "Nobody But You Lord Can Make Me Holy," "I'm Feeling All Right No Condemnation in My Heart," and "O How Lovely."[95] The fact that these songs were shared among many denominations meant that members from all over the country and members who had once belonged to diverse Christian churches could all sing together in one voice at the convention of the Commandment Keepers. Matthew met with some limited success in spreading his version of Black Judaism to places such as Columbus, Ohio, and the West Indies, and by 1951 claimed six branches across the country.[96] The following year, he visited Chicago to found a Hebrew school, which he put in the charge of a local rabbi, Abihu Reuben. In 1956 Rabbi Matthew started an official branch of his Commandment Keepers synagogue in Chicago, under the direction of Rabbi Joseph Lazarus.[97]

As Harlem lost its luster and became one of New York's most depressed neighborhoods in the 1930s, the Black Judaism it produced also changed. After the 1920s, the period of intellectual, religious, and political ferment known as the Harlem Renaissance that generated Rabbi Ford's colonization effort and Rabbi Matthew's emergence as a polycultural Black Israelite rabbi, the subsequent decades saw Matthew attempt to normalize and institutionalize his faith, build bridges to Black Israelite rabbis in other cities, and establish a suburban foothold outside of the depressed inner city. Yet he could not quite pull it off: Black Jews like Rabbi Matthew lost the prominence they had once held in the Black alternative religious tableaux, and they watched related alternative religious movements attain newfound prominence. With the emergence of Father Divine's "heavens" in the 1930s and the increasing popularity of the Nation of Islam in the late 1950s, newer and more overtly millenarian movements better addressed the anger of Black ghettos and the growing perception that Jews were white oppressors, not people to be emulated.[98] Meanwhile, Detroit's Rev. Albert Cleage popularized the idea that Jesus Christ and other Hebrews were Black, an idea that spiritualists and Israelites had preached in Detroit since at least the First World War. But by stripping the concept of its spiritualist and Judaic trappings, Cleage made it more Christian, and therefore more palatable for a Black mass audience.[99]

Although in the later years of his life Matthew hid all of his non-Jewish practices and influences, we have seen that his religious practice was far more complex, and far more interesting. Hidden transcripts demonstrate that Matthew used personal networks and print culture to create a polycultural religion, drawing on such sources as New Thought, Pentecostalism, Caribbean pageantry, and Kabbalah. Arising as his religious practice did out of the radical culture of the mystic scientists of the Harlem Renaissance, Matthew inverted the discourse of civilization and turned his religion into one of Black supremacy. Jewish ideas and rituals did not simply float into the Commandment Keepers by osmosis, heredity, or institutional affiliation. Rather, Rabbi Wentworth A. Matthew was a bricoleur who, in several gradual and halting steps, and under the influence of ideas and mentors drawn from a variety of sources, transitioned from "Bishop" to "Rabbi" and from Holiness Christianity to Judaism. Israelite identity drew heavily from the culture of the 1920s mystic scientists. Matthew's congregants imagined and performed their religious identities through lectures on sidewalks and conversations about African history in Garveyite halls; they embodied them through Caribbean pageants, and acted them out through Garveyite and Masonic parades. Black Israelism was lived through secret spiritualist and Kabbalistic rituals, and taught openly through Masonic affiliates and Sunday schools. Finally, it was an identity that was formed and performed in a mixture of Holiness-Pentecostal and Jewish rites. Print culture, performance, and complex social networks were all important to the imagination and realization of this new Israelite identity.

Since Rabbi Matthew's passing in 1973, the rabbis he taught have gradually standardized their liturgical practice to match the version of Judaism practiced by Ashkenazi and Sephardic Jews. Twenty years after his passing, one of Matthew's successors even called a *beit din*, or rabbinical council, to scrub the Commandment Keepers' liturgies of the polycultural idiosyncrasies that Matthew had introduced. Rabbi L. A. McKethan, who had once called his teacher "another great Moses" changed his name to "Levi Ben Levy," and called a series of rabbinical courts "to correct possible error committed in traditions applied to torah law" that had arisen out of following Rabbi Matthew's customs.[100]

Matthew's influences may have been disparate and polycultural, but the religious identity he helped to create was cohesive and persuasive for its hundreds of members. In 1999, one of the oldest remaining members of the Commandment Keepers remembered that in the late 1920s Rabbi Matthew preached to passersby from a stepladder, just like Harlem's more famous street speakers such as Hubert Harrison and Marcus Garvey. "It was 1927 when I first saw Rabbi Matthew on Lenox Avenue," she recalled. "He was standing on a ladder with a yarmulke on, and he was speaking to a crowd of people. He was preaching that we were not Christians as they had told us, but that we were the lost house of Israel." Matthew's message resonated with the then-twenty-four-year-old woman, who spent her days scrubbing floors and making beds in Jewish households in the Bronx, and described conditions for Black people as "atrocious." "I heard the call. And when I went to the temple on 128th Street I realized I was in the right place. I did not join the Hebrew faith—I returned.... In the Bible Jeremiah says he is Black. Solomon says he is Black. And David was and Samuel was and Jacob was. That's where I come from."[101]

# CONCLUSION

Despite a brief resurgence in the Black Power era of the 1960s, American Black Israelite movements never regained the popularity they held before the Great Depression. Partly this was because of general changes in the religious and social zeitgeist. Black Christianity in the twentieth century transitioned from the Old Testament God of collective deliverance from slavery to the New Testament Jesus of individual, otherworldly salvation.[1] With this shift, the ancient Israelites lost their prominent place in the Black religious imagination. In addition, Black conjuring practices that had fueled identification with Moses began to lose their popularity. Furthermore, the concept of Black Jews may have begun to appear increasingly incongruous as the decline of the inner cities and the rise of the Black freedom struggles brought waves of violent unrest to the nation during the long hot summers of the 1960s. Some white Jews who had moved out of Black neighborhoods in the twenties and thirties retained a presence in those same neighborhoods as merchants and landlords, and white Jews saturated the social service professions in large cities like New York. Both capacities brought Blacks and white Jews into daily, face-to-face contact, and sometimes conflict.

Other, more immediate causes of the decline of Black Israelite faiths were personal: the fortunes of small sects tend to rise and fall with the abilities of charismatic leaders. After Bishop Crowdy's death in 1908, the Church of God and Saints of Christ split into two factions, which then splintered even further. With the passing of Elder Roberson in 1931 and Rabbi Ford in 1935, the New York Israelites lost two of their most able advocates. Rabbi Matthew continued for many decades until his passing in 1973, ordaining a few dozen rabbis to carry on the work, yet his movement was always small, torn by numerous schisms.

Moreover, in the decades following the twenties, other movements arose, led by more capable leaders who borrowed from the same sources as the Israelites and crowded them out in the competition for the hearts and minds of the Black public. In the 1930s, Father Divine borrowed the communal structure of Elder Roberson's "heavens" as well as the Living God theology pioneered by Bishop R.A.R. Johnson and the Black Israelites, and built an extremely popular church, which attracted thousands of members during the

Depression. After the Second World War, the Nation of Islam popularized a polycultural African American version of Islam, which drew from the dense religious culture of the Harlem Renaissance, incorporating Masonic and esoteric lore, and benefited from the charismatic leadership of Elijah Muhammad and Malcolm X. Islam had always outweighed Israel in the Masonic imaginary. Furthermore, with a potent tradition of Orientalism but relatively few actual Muslims in America before 1964, Islam was a signifier that could be claimed and filled by African Americans. Meanwhile, in the Caribbean, under the leadership of Leonard Howell and others, the Israelite idea spread through Rastafarianism.

This book has endeavored to discuss Black Israelites in terms of wider and deeper communities, networks, and contexts. Although Black Israelites and their white detractors have often mobilized opposing narratives of authenticity and inauthenticity, purity and impurity, this book has argued that Black Israelite movements draw on genealogies that are primarily intellectual, literary, and social, not genetic, organic, or natural. Understanding Black Israelite faiths requires comprehending their relationship to much larger movements: Freemasonry, Anglo-Israelism, African American conjuring, New Thought, and the Garvey movement, among others. The popularity of tracing contemporary genealogy to the ancient Israelites was one effect of a century of social dislocation and spiritual enthusiasm. In England, the idea of the Lost Tribes of Israel gained new currency in the religions of the poor and dispossessed, and a line of prophets beginning with Joanna Southcott preached that the English were literal descendants of the Lost Tribes of Israel. These modern-day Israelites, or Later-Day Saints, as the Mormons also called themselves, were a small but significant part of the religious movements of the nineteenth century. The idea that the British were descendants of the Israelites gained its greatest exposition from the Anglo-Israelite movement, composed largely of British elites in London, who viewed the British Empire as a proof that they were descended from the chosen people of the Hebrew Bible. Anglo-Israelism became a rationale not only for conquest but also for oppressing and killing indigenous peoples, even as its tenets became widespread in Masonic publications in certain Christian churches.

The first generation of Black Israelite churches arose from the Holiness movement among the Methodist followers of John Wesley's teachings. This book has argued that the particular conditions of geographic dispersion, biblical literalism, and doctrinal innovation in the American West helped to produce Hebraic practices. Those Holiness churches that adopted Hebraic practices originally intended not to mimic Judaism but to emulate the apostolic church. Furthermore, Anglo-Israelite beliefs and Orientalist views of language led to the initial outbreaks of Pentecostal speaking in tongues. The ecstatic form of worship and the emphasis on inducing states of spirit possession overlapped with African-descended patterns of worship among African Americans, though they had even more direct antecedents in contemporary revivals in India and Wales.

Black Israelism helps us to see that the Black nationalism that flowered in the late 1960s as the Black Power movement had much deeper roots in the soil of Black separatist and emigration movements going back at least as far as Reconstruction. The Great Migration that produced Black Harlem, Chicago, and Detroit had been preceded by many years of other migrations, such as the Exodusters' migration of the 1870s and the independent Black town movement in Kansas and Oklahoma of the 1880s and 1890s. Black towns of the upper South and Great Plains produced the first African American Holiness preachers; in efforts to recreate the early Christian church, much like others in the Holiness movement, Bishops William Christian and William Saunders Crowdy taught that Blacks were the true children of Israel. The idea that African slavery in the Americas was not a mark of shame but instead a mark of distinction as God's chosen people appealed to some African Americans, who appreciated the way the doctrine gave them pride and dignity in the context of Jim Crow segregation that sought to subordinate and humiliate them at every turn.

Rabbis Arnold Josiah Ford and Wentworth Arthur Matthew were part of the wider culture of Black religious innovators and they inherited previous traditions of Black Israelism, although Rabbi Ford was far more independent of Holiness Christianity than was Matthew. A "gentleman of parts," Ford was part of networks of Black Israelite practitioners, but he also learned Hebrew and Judaism from white Jews and became a prominent figure in Marcus Garvey's United Negro Improvement Association. In Ford's story we can see the way his belief in Black Zionism, and a return to Africa, makes sense in the context of a discourse of civilization that advocated colonization of "less developed" continents. Ford's organization activated the patriarchal language of the discourse of civilization to support his cause: manly pioneers would redeem the violated honor of female Africa, depicted as a mother and lover. Ford set out for an imaginary country, and his enterprise floundered when it met with reality on Ethiopian soil. Yet Ford's sojourn in Ethiopia probably played a crucial role in the formation of Rastafarianism, when Jamaican missionaries returned from Ethiopia with the Israelite doctrine and passed it on to Leonard Howell, who had participated in the culture of Harlem's religious innovators of the 1920s. In this new context, the Israelite teachings and focus on returning to Ethiopia gained new popularity.

Considered in the larger contexts of the migration of rural peoples into the quickened pace of northern cities after Reconstruction, the rise of Black Judaism suggests that there was a rich substratum of working-class cultural creativity that deserves to be read into the history of the "New Negro" Renaissance that has become most associated with Harlem. It challenges us to think of working-class African Americans not merely as workers or migrants but also as organic intellectuals, capable of voicing their own dreams, mysticism, and religions in ways that were articulate responses to the key concerns of the modern age.

Rabbi Ford's student, Rabbi Wentworth Arthur Matthew, affords us the opportunity to parse many of the diverse influences on Black Israelite theology. Matthew started as a Christian minister, and slowly incorporated elements of Jewish worship long before he disavowed the divinity of Jesus. He learned much from other ministers and prophets such as Bishop R.A.R. Johnson and Bishop Saint John the Divine. Mind power, New

Thought, and the Theosophist-flavored teaching that God resides inside each individual were central to the theologies of the Israelite prophets of the Harlem Renaissance. Likewise, spells and conjuring gleaned from sources such as de Laurence's *Sixth and Seventh Books of Moses* played an important role in Matthew's religion, as did the teachings and rituals of Freemasonry. Matthew's evolution illustrates that new African American urban sects were polycultural bricolages of numerous influences, ideas, and ritual systems, constructed by networks of creative individuals. As such, these religions are more idiosyncratic and polycultural than they are acculturative and syncretic.

Anthropologist Melville Herskovits depicted the Americas as a "social laboratory" in which history mixed the "pure" cultures of Africa and Europe, using the principle of "syncretism" to describe the degree of mixture along the putative "acculturative continuum." Little about that model works in Matthew's case. It is important to note, however, that Matthew himself constructed his own biography according to the tropes that Herskovits established—hence the legend he fabricated, claiming to be born in West Africa of an Ethiopian Jewish father. But such reductive fictions reduce the complexity and the inventiveness of Matthew and his peers in similar Black Orientalist Muslim, Rastafarian, and New Thought movements. The syncretic theory of Black religion misses the true genius of practitioners of alternative African American religions who delved deep into the treasure house of the Atlantic World and recombined the sparkling cultural artifacts therein, not according to any "mechanistic and materialistic" syncretic logic, as Herskovits once put it, but using a heterodox polycultural bricolage and aesthetics that were distinctly American, in the broadest sense of the term.[2]

Polyculturalism allows us to depict cultural invention not as a syncretic confrontation between dissimilar, concrete, pure types, but as the reblending of the already blended; the splicing together of diverse elements made possible not by their differences but by their overlapping similarities. The microhistorical treatment of Rabbi Matthew's faith enables us to observe a process of cultural creation at the individual level. What emerges is the intelligent, individualistic, historically contingent, and creative bricolage of multiple ideas and processes, which are always similar, constructed, and "impure." Each extraordinary but ordinary individual person is not the exception to the rule of cultural purity—instead, the exceptions are the rule.

An example of polyculturalism can be seen in the practice of the occult. African American communities in slavery and afterward practiced forms of divination and conjuring that had African antecedents. These patterns continued in the twentieth century, but much indigenous African knowledge had been augmented or even replaced by magical practices from other sources entirely. *The Sixth and Seventh Books of Moses* originated in the mysticism of late seventeenth-century Europe. The "weapons of the weak" developed by certain people in one time and place were available in a completely different context for different populations of oppressed peoples. Polyculturalism can explain how these kinds of borrowings occur at overlapping sites of cultural similarities rather than as antagonistic syncretisms along a bipolar acculturative continuum.

"Polyculturalism" is a better term than "syncretism" for describing the process by which African Americans have created new religions in the twentieth century. Melville J. Herskovits's training in laborious physical measurement of human beings colored his view of syncretism in conservative, biological terms. His idea of culture has a holism and rigidity that few anthropologists would defend any longer. Polyculturalism offers a better metaphor to describe the process of cultural creation, dependent on individual choices and creativity, not automatic reactions. These new cultural formations come about through the bricolage of impure and porous cultures, not the bipolar encounter between brittle, hostile, or holistic ones.

Polyculturalism challenges us to look at the world, its peoples, and cultures as riotously impure. It suggests that we ourselves are inheritors of unstable racial and cultural identities that are historically contingent and informed by the entire spectrum of humanity. Who can delineate a boundary between the emotionalism of the worship of the English working class and the emotionalism of the worship of enslaved Africans in the Americas? Who can separate the occultism of European Americans and the occultism of African Americans? On close examination, boundaries between "racial" cultures disappear into a continuum of humanity. Imagination, invention, and individuality are indispensable aspects of cultural creation that we too often depict in essentialist terms as belonging to one racial group or another. By disrupting the notion that racial identities are monolithic and natural, polyculturalism can help to view ourselves and others as fully human.

## SHORT HISTORY OF THE CONGREGATION BETH B'NAI ABRAHAM, NEW YORK, N.Y. BY RABBI ARNOLD JOSIAH FORD

## Our Aims

The Congregation Beth B'nai Abraham is a number of Black Jews (Hebrews, we call ourselves) who have resolved to found a Synagogue or temples among their racial brethren in Harlem for the purpose of congregating and worshipping the One Supreme Being pursuant to the Laws and Customs of Ancient Israel.

To observe, as nearly as our deplorable economic condition will allow us, Sabbath, Holidays, Fast Days and all other ritualistic observances and Laws of the Brith, the Laws of the household women and children.

To train our children to observe these laws and customs and to bring them up as Israelites.

To teach respect for Law and Order in the various communities in which we may be domiciled, to disseminate Love, good will and Peace to all mankind.

## Our Origin

We are Africans. We do not believe as some people do, that it is necessary to be a Caucasian before you can lay claim to the Jewish faith; our belief is that the Jewish race is one of culture and human virtues evolved through generations of obedience to certain Laws, Statutes and traditions, and not one to be determined by the color of the skin or modern geographical classification and restrictions.

Here is a very significant fact, that those of us here never even had a Caucasian teacher to instruct us into the principles of our faith up to the present, this alone is evidence that as regards our faith as original.

However, we ourselves do not hasten to take advantage of the forgoing as a proof of our Jewish originality, because although our teaching came through our parents, our parents might have had theirs from our Caucasian brethren with whom they suffered side by side during the horrible years of the Christian Inquisition and the Christian slave-trade in Africa, the West Indies and South America. This is a fact that can be proven by us.

It is not customary for Caucasian (is that a nice name?) Hebrew brethren to admit that behind the African mind there are originally the roots of Hebrew culture; but this is our contention; and although in ritualism we may differ and perhaps be found wanting; in heart and in custom we are Hebraic and nothing else.

## Our History

Added to this is the contact, through family life with free Africans in the West Indies and dispersed Jews from Spain during the Inquisition who had settled in the West Indies and South America. In one instance a shipload of Sephardim Jewish youths over 600 of them exiled from Spain where shipwrecked on St. Thomas and the Virgin Islands, now owned by the United States. They never left there. They grew up, intermarried with the Africans, propagated, and their descendants bear their names, customs and blood to the present day. These are facts.

In Barbados and other ports, deserted synagogues bear silent but unmistakable testimony to that which had been.

In South America the Jewkas of Surinam Guiana tell another Jewish story and may well augment real Jewish history.

In 1863 the Dutch Government finding the natives hostile to the Christian Religion which had enslaved them, gave them the alternative in Parimaribo, Dutch Guiana, of becoming Jews before obtaining their freedom. They were freed thereby.

Christian suppression and proselytism was carried out vigorously, relentlessly even cruelly after these events, but nothing has ever yet destroyed the Jewish faith when rightly founded.

The Diaspora, the last great catastrophy of the Jewish Empire brought about by this Roman age in which we are now living, severed Africa completely from the recognized Jewish economy. It was and it is a well laid out plan by the Ancient Roman Empire. Dividem et tandem. Africa must be cut off.

The destruction of Africa and the rise of Europe. The destruction of Judaism and the Jew and the rise of Romanism and the Roman.

To accomplish this, the dis-franchisement of Africa in religious activities other than that which was sponsored by the Roman regime was of paramount importance. This was accomplished hand in hand with the destruction of Jerusalem, Egypt, Carthage and all of North African States and Empires, in the wars of subjugation prior to and after the Diaspora. The Crusades completed it.

The Jews fell into a trap. Whereas the promise to Abraham by Israel's God was, that his seed would be numberless as the sands upon the seashore; the Diaspora cut them all asunder and the ancient Divine promise declared null and void.

The New Roman Gods declared that the Jews should not be numerous or numberless; but should be confined only to a small number of people actually organized through Roman permission by Jochanan Ben Zakkai, immediately after or co-incident with the Diaspora. These were two divisions only the Sephardim who were forced into exile under the Vizi-Gotts (or Western Gods) and the Ashkenazim who were forced into exile or proselyted by consent of the Ostra-Gotts (or Eastern Gods). These constituted but a small minority of the great Israelitish peoples and the great majority were scattered abroad in the earth.

The motherland Africa is still today the home of millions of these descendants of ancient Jerusalem, and West Africa whence our forebears came may yet be proud that in native customs and traditions she can boast of not being only Semitic but Mosaic.

An impartial sociological survey will reveal much that West African may yet contribute to the human race for morality, culture and peace, and we declare these attributes will be found to be based on Hebraic culture.

Mr. Geo. De Lachevotier who has just recently returned to the West Indies from Africa, in his booklet on West Africa says—"The Hausas are a race of many tribes which, through black with curly hair, do not possess the distinctive characters of the true Negro." The origin of the people still remains unknown; not is it known whence their civilization came.

Their language has been placed in the Semitic group and is the most universally spoken in West Africa and the Soudan, which facts account, I think, for the reasoning that "Hausa" more correctly describes an African tongue than a people, since everyone is termed a "Hausa" who has knowledge of the Hausa language.

The Hausas are an industrious people, they are agriculturists, spinners and weavers, tanners and dyers metal workers, potters, builders, hunters and above all traders. Hausas are "bloods"—a dressy people—and are very dignified in appearance.

The origin of the race remains doubtful, but it is supposed that these people migrated from the East and settled themselves in the Soudan.

They are of Semitic stock and probably of the same race as the Jallof in Senegal. Albeit they succeeded in establishing themselves as the ruling race in the Hausa states and remained conquerors for over 200 years and founded the great Filane Sokoto Dynasty.

Mr. de Lachevotier also in his booklet speaks of the Moslem converts, but mentions nothing of the religion of these peoples who are not classified as Moslem converts.

But we who are here say to you that we are B'nai Yisroale. The fact is;

Our true history has never been written in this Christian age. To the contrary; "We have been taken into captivity, our history everywhere suppressed and destroyed, and destruction aimed mercilessly at our very existence." This is true of us Africans, this is true of the Jews. Then to pick us up, blinded stunned, half conscious, robbed of all we possessed and ask us, who are we, from whence we came and wither we are going may be fair as a matter of routine, but it is unethical and unreasonable to demand from us immediate answer.

You who are conscious must help to restore us first to consciousness, you who can see must help us to regain our sight, you who have recovered your history must help us to get back and write ours and then the Great Light shall dawn in us and we shall find out that we are a mighty people, indestructible, indivisible. On that day we shall be one. A Light to lighten the Gentiles and the Glory of our people Israel. Our God One.

Source: Rabbi Arnold Josiah Ford to Jacques Faitlovitch, "Short History of the Congregation Beth B'nai Abraham, New York, N.Y." n.p., n.d. (c. 1924–1930), Jacques Faitlovitch Collection, folder 82, Sourasky Central Library, Tel Aviv University.

# NOTES

1. Bishop William Christian was an important leader of the Black Holiness movement who founded a church that would come to preach Black Israelite ideas, although it is not clear that Christian actually preached such beliefs before Crowdy. William Christian, *Poor Pilgrim's Work in the Name of the Father, Son and Holy Ghost* (Texarkana: Joe Erlich Print, 1896); Clarence E. Hardy, "From Exodus to Exile: Black Pentecostals, Migrating Pilgrims, and Imagined Internationalism," *American Quarterly* 58, no. 3 (September 2007): 743–749, 756; David D. Daniels, "Charles Harrison Mason: The Interracial Impulse of Early Pentecostalism," in *Portraits of a Generation: Early Pentecostal Leaders,* ed. James R. Goff, Jr. and Grant Wacker (Fayetteville: University of Arkansas Press, 2002), 259; James E. Landing, *Black Judaism: Story of an American Movement,* (Durham, N.C.: Carolina Academic Press, 2002), 46–50, 81; Cheryl J. Sanders, *Saints in Exile: The Holiness-Pentecostal Experience in African American Religion and Culture* (New York: Oxford University Press, 1996), 21, 137.
2. On the etymology and history of the word "culture," see Raymond Williams, *Keywords: A Vocabulary of Culture and Society,* rev. ed. (New York: Oxford University Press, 1976, 1983), 87–93; Tony Bennett, "Culture," in *New Keywords: A Revised Vocabulary of Culture and Society*, rev. ed., ed. Tony Bennett, Lawrence Grossberg, and Meaghan Morris (Oxford: Wiley-Blackwell, 2005), 63–69.
3. White Black Israelites do exist, such as white Rastafarians, or the white bishop and early members of Prophet Crowdy's Church of God and Saints of Christ, but although there are and have been a few such people, their numbers are small and their places within Black religious movements have seldom been uncontested.
4. Hoyt W. Fuller, interview with Asiel Ben Israel, "An Interview: The Original Hebrew Israelite Nation" *The Black World*, May 1975, 63. This denial that a religion is a religion points to the fact that "religion" has been defined as primarily concerned with interiority and the individual believer and less with community and practice. Ben

Israel stressed, in contrast, the collective nature of a belief based in a historical claim, as well as the practice of Biblical laws. See Bruce Lincoln, *Holy Terrors: Thinking about Religion after September 11* (Chicago: University of Chicago Press, 2006), 1–3.

5. Schisms have created at least four rival Churches of God and Saints of Christ: one headquartered in Belleville, Virginia; a branch headquartered in Cleveland, Ohio; another branch headquartered in New Haven, Connecticut; and a Caribbean branch headquartered in Morant Bay, St. Thomas, Jamaica. Of these, only the Belleville group does not believe that Jesus is the messiah; all teach adherence to the Ten Commandments and various laws of the Hebrew Bible.

6. Prominent examples of the roots metaphor applied to African American history include: Lawrence W. Levine, *Black Culture and Black Consciousness: Afro-American Folk Thought from Slavery to Freedom* (New York: Oxford University Press, 1977); Sterling Stuckey, *Slave Culture: Nationalist Theory and the Foundations of Black America* (New York: Oxford University Press, 1987); Michael A. Gomez, *Exchanging Our Country Marks: The Transformation of African Identities in the Colonial and Antebellum South* (Chapel Hill: University of North Carolina Press, 1998).

7. Gilles Deleuze and Félix Guattari, *A Thousand Plateaus: Capitalism and Schizophrenia* trans. and forward by Brian Massumi (Minneapolis: University of Minnesota Press, 1987), 21, 8.

8. University of California Berkeley, March 11, 2007, "Gene Transfer between Species Is Surprisingly Common," *ScienceDaily*, retrieved December 19, 2007, from http://www.sciencedaily.com–/releases/2007/03/070308220454.htm; Rice University, "Does Evolution Select for Faster Evolvers? Horizontal Gene Transfer Adds to Complexity, Speed of Evolution," January 29, 2007, retrieved December 19, 2007, from http://www.sciencedaily.com–/releases/2007/01/070129114638.htm.

9. Deleuze and Guattari, *A Thousand Plateaus*, 10–11.

10. The concept of a "meme" is problematic in that it uses an organic and biological metaphor for culture and thus reprises the weaknesses of older metaphors for cultural formation based on biological models. I use it here only for rhetorical purposes, for those who prefer such models to more flexible discursive ones. The first use of the term "meme" was by Richard Dawkins, *The Selfish Gene* (New York: Oxford University Press, 1976). The phrase "horizontal meme transfer" turned up a scant 188 times in a Google search performed on May 4, 2007. There was one blog calling itself "horizontal meme transfer," http://nftb.net/. The metaphor "Black Atlantic Dialogue" is borrowed from J. Lorand Matory, *Black Atlantic Religion* (Princeton: Princeton University Press, 2005).

11. Jean Comaroff and John Comaroff, *Modernity and Its Malcontents: Ritual and Power in Postcolonial Africa*, ed. Comaroff and Comaroff (Chicago: University of Chicago Press, 1993), xv–xxii.

12. Jacob S. Dorman, "Black Orientalism and Black Gods of the Metropolis," in *The New Black Gods: Arthur Huff Fauset and the Study of African American Religions*, ed. Edward E. Curtis IV and Danielle Brune Sigler (Bloomington: Indiana University Press, June 2009), 116–142.

13. To be sure, this tendency has already been surpassed in some more recent works, but for examples of criminal depiction of Black Orientalist faiths, See Edward Wolf, "Negro Jews: A Social Study," *Jewish Social Service Quarterly* 9 (June 1933): 314–319; C. Eric. Lincoln, *The Black Muslims in America*, rev. ed. (Westport, Conn: Greenwood, 1973). See also David Levering Lewis, *When Harlem Was in Vogue,* 2nd ed. (New York: Penguin, 1997), 221–222; Susan Nance, *How the Arabian Nights Inspired the American Dream, 1790–1935* (Chapel Hill: University of North Carolina Press, 2009), 205–255.

14. Here my debt is to ethnographer Wallace Zane's conception of one particular Black religion as reflecting "human biology and human ways of living in the world." Wallace W. Zane, *Journeys to the Spiritual Lands: The Natural History of a West Indian Religion* (New York: Oxford University Press, 1999), 11.

15. For African American debates about the American relationship to Africa in the interwar years, see Clare Corbould, *Becoming African Americans: Black Public Life in Harlem, 1919–1939* (Cambridge: Harvard University Press, 2009). For Herskovits, see notes below.

16. The Jewishness and the political progressiveness of a long string of noted scholars of African American Studies profoundly influences their work. A partial list includes Franz Boas, Melville Herskovits, Herbert Aptheker, the Arthurs Schlessinger, Philip Foner, August Meier, Lawrence Levine, Richard Newman, Leon Litwack, Eric Foner, Martin Bernal, and Merrill Singer. Whereas African Americans are often described with a racial adjective, Jewish scholars are seldom identified as Jews as well as scholars, which masks their backgrounds and perpetuates the normative universalism of whiteness. Nor could I shake the question, borrowed from my Black peers' discussions of their responsibility to the Black community, of whether I bore a similar responsibility to speak about the misjudgments of a member of my natal community, even when his work was foundational to a half century of work in the field of African American Studies. The role of Jews in the development of African American Studies has been explored by August Meier and John Bracey, "Towards a Research Agenda on Blacks and Jews in United States History," in *Strangers and Neighbors: Relations between Blacks and Jews in the United States* (Amherst: University of Massachusetts Press, 2000), 27–34; for Jews and anthropology, see Gelya Frank, "Jews, Multiculturalism, and Boasian Anthropology," *American Anthropologist* 99, no. 4 (December 1997): 731–745. On "Warlockian" anthropology, see John L. Jackson, *Real Black: Adventures in Racial Sincerity* (Durham: Duke University Press, 2005), 256, 260.

17. Stefan Kuhl, *The Nazi Connection: Eugenics, American Racism, and German National Socialism* (New York: Oxford University Press, 1994).

18. Sidney W. Mintz, introduction to *The Myth of the Negro Past* by Melville J. Herskovits (1941, 1958; Boston: Beacon, 1990), xii–xv; André Droogers and Sidney M. Greenfield, "Recovering and Reconstructing Syncretism," in *Reinventing Religions: Syncretism and Transformation in Africa and the Americas*, edited by Sidney M. Greenfield and André Droogers (New York: Rowman & Littlefield, 2001), 24–27.

19. Melville J. Herskovits, "Acculturation and the American Negro," *Southwestern Political and Social Science Quarterly* 7, no. 3 (December 1927), 7.

20. Herskovits, *The Myth of the Negro Past*, 6. For the original call to study African nostrils, lips, facial forms, bodily proportions, and "functional processes," see Melville J. Herskovits, "The Negro in the New World: The Statement of a Problem," *American Anthropologist* 32 (1930), reprinted in Herskovits, *The New World Negro: Selected Papers in Afroamerican Studies*, ed. Frances S. Herskovits (Bloomington: Indiana University Press, 1966), 9.

21. See, for example, the critical essays on syncretism in the journal *Historical Reflections/Reflexions Historiques* 27, no. 3 (Fall 2001), especially A. J. Droge, "Retrofitting/Retiring 'Syncretism,'" 375–388, and Bruce Lincoln, "Retiring Syncretism," 453–460. The quote is from Lincoln, "Retiring Syncretism," 454. Also see Charles Stewart and Rosalind Shaw, eds., *Syncretism/Anti-Syncretism: The Politics of Religious Synthesis* (London: 1994); André Droogers and Sidney M. Greenfield, "Recovering and Reconstructing Syncretism," in *Reinventing Religions: Syncretism and Transformation in Africa and the Americas*, ed. Sidney M. Greenfield and André Droogers, 21–42 (New York: Rowman & Littlefield, 2001). See also Sidney M. Greenfield, "Recasting Syncretism . . . Again: Theories and Concepts in Anthropology and Afro-American Studies in Light of Changing Social Agendas," in *New Trends and Developments in African Religions*, ed. Peter B. Clarke (Westport, Conn.: Greenwood, 1998); Andrew Apter, "Herskovits' Heritage: Rethinking Syncretism in the African Diaspora," *Diasporas* 1 (1999): 261–284; Paul Christopher Johnson, *Diaspora Conversions: Black Carib Religion and the Recovery of Africa* (Berkeley: University of California Press, 2007), 263–265.

22. Melville J. Herskovits, "Social Pattern: A Methodological Study," *Social Forces* 4, no. 1 (September 1926): 61.

23. Ibid.

24. Herskovits, "The Negro in the New World," 8.

25. Ibid., 7.

26. Melville Herskovits, "What Has Africa Given America?" (1935), in *The New World Negro*, 170.

27. Herskovits, *The Myth of the Negro Past,* 164.

28. Ibid., 6.

29. Ramon Ortiz, *Cuban Counterpoint, Tobacco and Sugar*, trans. Harriet De Onís, intro. Bronislaw Malinowski; prologue Herminio Portell Vila, new intro. Fernando Coronil (Durham: Duke University Press, 1995), 99, 101.

30. Robin D. G. Kelley, "People in Me," *ColorLines Magazine* 1, no. 3 (Winter 1999): 5–7.

31. Seeing anthropological "others" as fully coeval helps us to view earlier eras as being just as dynamic, if not more dynamic, than our own. Johannes Fabian, *Time and the Other: How Anthropology Makes Its Object* (New York: Columbia University Press, 1983).

32. Vijay Prashad, *Everybody Was Kung Fu Fighting: Afro-Asian Connections and the Myth of Cultural Purity* (Boston: Beacon, 2001), xi–xii.

33. Please note that in theorizing "polycultural religions" in this manner, I am not trying to suggest that there are some religions that are not polycultural and by inference pure. Rather, polyculturalism's great strength is that it pictures a world in which there are no "pure" cultures and every tradition is constantly recreated through bricolage. Here I differ with Richard Werbner, who has similarly defined syncretism as "religious hybridization" but has also tried to develop a distinction between 'religious' syncretism and 'cultural' bricolage. Richard Werbner, "Afterword," in Stewart and Shaw, *Syncretism/Antisyncretism: The Politics of Religious Synthesis* (London: Routledge, 1994), 215.

34. James Clifford, *The Predicament of Culture: Twentieth-Century Ethnography, Literature, and Art* (Cambridge: Harvard University Press, 1988), 388.

35. This arachnidian image owes an obvious debt to Clifford Geertz; the concept owes a less obvious debt to Mary-Jane Rubenstein of Wesleyan University, who helped clarify the idea that people are constituted by culture. The spider web metaphor could be continued *ad infinitum* if not for the danger of reaching *absurdum* first. For Geertz's famous web metaphor, see Clifford Geertz, *Interpretation of Cultures* [1973] (New York: Basic Books, 2000), 5. The spider-web analogy is spun between Marx's base/superstructure dialectic, found in "Preface to *A Critique of Political Economy*" in *Karl Marx: A Reader*, ed. Jon Elster [1859] (New York: Cambridge University Press, 2006), 187. The idea of bricoleurs spinning webs of meaning on the protean webs of other bricoleurs is akin to the idea of the dialogic found in Mikhail Bakhtin, *The Dialogic Imagination: Four Essays*, ed. Michael Holquist and trans. Caryl Emerson and Michael Holquist (Austin: University of Texas Press, 1981), which has been put to productive use in religious history by Evelyn Brooks Higginbotham, *Righteous Discontent: The Women's Movement in the Black Baptist Church, 1880–1920* (Cambridge: Harvard University Press, 1993), 16, 236, 281.

36. Michel de Certeau, *The Practice of Everyday Life,* trans. Steven Rendall (Berkeley: University of California Press, 1984), xiv–xv.

37. The concept of "bricolage" entered scholarly literature in Claude Lévi-Strauss, *The Savage Mind* (Chicago: University of Chicago Press, 1966), 16–23. See also Jacques

Derrida, *Of Grammatology*, trans. Gayatri Chakravorty Spivak (Baltimore: Johns Hopkins University Press, 1998), xviii–xxi, 138–139. On bricolage in relation to subcultures, see Dick Hebdige, *Subculture: The Meaning of Style* (London: Methuen, 1979), 104; George McKay, *Senseless Acts of Beauty: Cultures of Resistance* (London: Verso, 1996), 12, 47, 78, 87–88. Jean Comaroff offers a theory of "subversive bricolage" that demonstrates how the bricolage of South African Zionist churches destabilizes power structures; see Jean Comaroff, *Body of Power, Spirit of Resistance: The Culture and History of a South African People* (Chicago: University of Chicago Press, 1985), 12. Also see the discussion of conjuring as bricolage in David H. Brown, "Conjure/Doctors: An Exploration of a Black Discourse in America, Antebellum to 1940," *Folklore Forum* 23, nos. 1–2 (1990): 20.

38. Robin D. G. Kelley, "Notes on Deconstructing 'The Folk'," *American Historical Review* 97, no. 5 (December 1992): 1402.

39. Antonio Gramsci, *The Antonio Gramsci Reader: Selected Writings 1916–1935*, ed. David Forgacs (New York: New York University Press, 2000), 211–218, 427; see also Raymond Williams, "Base and Superstructure in Marxist Cultural Theory," in *Problems in Materialism and Culture: Selected Essays*. London: Verso, 1980, 31–49; T. J. Jackson Lears, "The Concept of Cultural Hegemony: Problems and Possibilities," *American Historical Review* 90, no. 3 (June 1985): 567–593.

40. George Lipsitz, *Time Passages: Collective Memory and American Popular Culture* (Minneapolis: University of Minnesota Press, 1990), 122–123.

41. Mikhail M. Bakhtin, *Rabelais and His World*, trans. Helene Iswolsky [1968] (Bloomington: Indiana University Press, 1984); Mary Douglas, *Purity and Danger: An Analysis of Concepts of Pollution and Taboo* [1966] (New York: Routledge, 2001); Peter Stallybrass and Allon White, *The Politics and Poetics of Transgression* (Ithaca: Cornell University Press, 1986); Eric Lott, *Love and Theft: Blackface Minstrelsy and the American Working Class* (New York: Oxford University Press, 1993); Kevin J. Mumford, *Interzones: Black/White Sex Districts in Chicago and New York in the Early Twentieth Century* (New York: Columbia University Press, 1997).

42. Although I am quite sympathetic to the notion that Ashkenazi and Sephardi Jewish communities invented themselves and their traditions through frequent borrowing from neighboring peoples, and that those identities and customs did not cohere until well into the Common Era, such debates lie outside my own academic expertise. It is clear, however, that recent genetic studies of Jewish populations have overreached when they claim to demonstrate the veracity of Biblical accounts of Jewish history. European Jewish customs, from the baking of braided poppy-seed-covered *challah* bread to the lighting of *yartzheit* candles, were themselves "invented" in recent historical times, and modern Jewish identities, and identification with the ancient Israelites, are similarly constructed. For some of the debate surrounding the origins of European Jews, see Paul Wexler, *The Ashkenazic Jews: A Slavo-Turkic People in Search of a Jewish Identity* (Columbus, Ohio: Slavica Publishers, 1993), idem., *The Non-Jewish Origins of the Sephardic Jews* (Albany:

State University of New York Press, 1996); Shlomo Sand, *The Invention of the Jewish People*, trans. Yael Lotan (London: Verso, 2009). For a critique of Wexler's work, see Dovid Katz, "A Late Twentieth Century Case of *Katoves*," in *History of Yiddish Studies: Papers from the Third Annual Oxford Winter Symposium in Yiddish Language and Literature*, ed. Dov-Ber Kerler (Philadelphia: Harwood Academic Publishers, 1991), 141–164.

43. See, for example, Roberta S. Gold, "The Black Jews of Harlem: Representation, Identity, and Race, 1920–1939," *American Quarterly* 55, no. 2 (June 2003): 179–225; Sylvester A. Johnson, "The Rise of Black Ethnics: The Ethnic Turn in African-American Religions, 1916–1945," *Religion in American Culture: A Journal of Interpretation* 20, no. 2 (Summer 2010): 125–163.

44. Karen Brodkin, *How Jews Became White Folks and What That Says about Race in America* (New Brunswick: Rutgers University Press, 1998); Matthew Frye Jacobson, *Whiteness of a Different Color: European Immigrants and the Alchemy of Race* (Cambridge: Harvard University Press, 1999); Jacobson, *Roots Too: White Ethnic Revival in Post-Civil Rights America* (Cambridge: Harvard University Press, 2006); Thomas A. Guglielmo, *White on Arrival: Italians, Race, Color, and Power in Chicago, 1890–1945* (New York: Oxford University Press, 2003); Eric L. Goldstein, *The Price of Whiteness: Jews, Race, and American Identity* (Princeton: Princeton University Press, 2006); Melanie Kaye/Kantrowitz, *The Colors of Jews: Racial Politics and Radical Diasporism* (Bloomington: Indiana University Press, 2007).

45. Martha Biondi, *To Stand and Fight: The Struggle for Civil Rights in Postwar New York City* (Cambridge: Harvard University Press, 2003), under "Note on Usage."

CHAPTER 1

1. Walker, *Life and Works of Crowdy*, 1–3; Wynia, *The Church of God and Saints of Christ*, 19.

2. Though St. Mary's County was too isolated to have been a battleground in the Civil War, the northern part of the state took center stage in 1862, when General Robert E. Lee and the Confederate Army of Northern Virginia invaded Maryland north of Washington, culminating in the Union victory in the battle of Antietam Creek by the village of Sharpsburg on September 17, 1862. Antietam was the bloodiest single day of the bloodiest war in American history, leaving 12,401 dead and wounded Union soldiers and 10,318 dead and wounded Confederates. Yet despite the high cost, Lee's defeat ended the very real possibility that England and France would recognize the Confederacy and provided Lincoln with the victory he had been waiting for to announce the Emancipation Proclamation. Lincoln had presented the measure to his cabinet in July as a military necessity: "We must free the slaves or be ourselves subdued," he told his cabinet. "The slaves [are] undeniably an element of strength to those who [have] their service, and we must decide whether that element should be with us or against us." Notes kept by Secretary of the Navy

Gideon Welles, July 22, 1862, in James M. McPherson, *Battle Cry of Freedom: The Civil War Era* (New York: Oxford University Press, 1988), 504; for casualty totals, see McPherson, ed., *The Atlas of the Civil War* (New York: Macmillan, 1994), 80.

3. "Murder of a Negro Recruiting Officer in Maryland," *New York Times*, October 22, 1863, p. 1. On Crowdy, see Sherry Sherrod DuPree, African-American Holiness and Pentecostal Collection, Box 10, Folder 8, Schomburg Center for Research in Black Culture, New York Public Library, Astor, Lenox and Tilden Foundations (hereafter, Schomburg Center); Church of God and Saints of Christ Collection, Kansas State Historical Society, Topeka, Kansas; Beersheba Crowdy Walker, *Life and Works of William Saunders Crowdy* (Philadelphia: Elfreth J. P. Walker, 1955); Elly Wynia, *The Church of God and Saints of Christ: The Rise of the Black Jews* (New York: Garland, 1994); James E. Landing, *Black Judaism: Story of an American Movement* (Durham, N.C.: Carolina Academic Press, 2002), 50–61.

4. Record keeping during the Civil War was imperfect for troops and camp followers on both sides, and William Saunders Crowdy does not appear in extant U.S. Military or Freeman's Bureau records. His brother Daniel, who also served in the war, does appear on the books of the Freedman's Bank. The most extensive source for biographical details of Crowdy's life is the one passed down through his family and recorded by his daughter, Beersheba Crowdy Walker. Walker, *Life and Works of Crawdy*; Rabbi Curtis Caldwell, telephone interview by author, May 7, 2007.

5. Nell Irvin Painter, *Exodusters: Black Migration to Kansas after Reconstruction* (New York: Knopf, 1977), 158; Quintard Taylor, *In Search of the Racial Frontier: African Americans in the American West 1528–1990* (New York: W. W. Norton, 1998), 136.

6. Taylor, *Racial Frontier*, 95–96; Roger D. Cunningham, "Welcoming 'Pa' on the Kaw: Kansas's 'Colored' Militia and the 1864 Price Raid," *Kansas History* 25 (Winter 2000/2001); 89.

7. Richard White, *"It's Your Misfortune and None of My Own": A History of the American West* (Norman: University of Oklahoma Press, 1991), 143–145.

8. Painter, *Exodusters*, 147.

9. Taylor, *Racial Frontier*, 97.

10. Norman L. Crockett, *The Black Towns* (Lawrence: Regents Press of Kansas, 1979), 6–7.

11. Painter, *Exodusters*, 146–147.

12. Ibid., 147.

13. Ibid., 159; Albert Castel, "Civil War Kansas and the Negro," *Journal of Negro History* 51, no. 2 (April 1966), 135; and Randall B. Woods, "Integration, Exclusion, or Segregation? The 'Color Line' in Kansas, 1878–1900," *Western Historical Quarterly* 14, no. 2 (April 1983), 196–197.

14. Woods, "Integration, Exclusion, or Segregation?" 196–197; Taylor, *Racial Frontier*, 136–137.

15. Painter, *Exodusters*, 160.
16. Samuel W. Winn, "Enterprise, Mississippi, New Orleans," *Southwestern Christian Advocate*, May 29, 1879, in Painter, *Exodusters*, 190.
17. Painter, *Exodusters*, 170–171.
18. Ibid., 184.
19. For a critical take on Painter's thesis, see David J. Peavler, "Creating the Color Line and Confronting Jim Crow: Civil Rights in Middle America: 1850–1900" (Ph.D. dissertation, University of Kansas, 2008), 193–291. My own reading of Nell Irwin Painter's Papers, now housed at Duke University, does not support her thesis that those who fled without enough funds to complete the journey comfortably were "millennials" who believed they were being delivered from the South by an act of God. What is more clear from those papers, and her excellent book, is the amount of planning that went into many of the emigration clubs, and the depths of terror and economic oppression African Americans suffered in the Deep South with the collapse of Reconstruction. The Kansas Exodus is a poor fit for Norman Cohn's five-part definition of millennialism that Painter employed to cast the Exodusters as millennialists: the migrants who attempted to gain passage up the Mississippi sought to travel by steam boat, not by divine agency, and they did not expect perfection in Kansas, only the chance to live lives free of continual existential and actual terror. Norman Cohn, "Medieval Millenarism: Its Bearing on the Comparative Study of Millenarian Movements," in Sylvia L. Thrupp, ed., *Millennial Dreams in Action: Studies in Revolutionary Religious Movements* (New York: Schocken, 1970), 31; cited in Nell Irvin Painter, "Millenarian Aspects of the Exodus to Kansas of 1879," 15, in Nell Irvin Painter Papers, Box 94, Duke University Rare Books, Special Collections, and Archives Library.
20. "Africa's Exodus: Alarming Emigration of Destitute Negroes from the South. They Are Coming Here by Hundreds, En Route for Kansas: A Perplexing Difficulty Which Must Be Met," *St. Louis Globe-Democrat* 8 no. 2–3 (March 14, 1879) in Painter Papers, Box 97.
21. St. Louis *Globe-Democrat*, March 19, 1879, in Painter, *Exodusters*, 195. It is possible that the Exodus metaphor was especially appealing to the very old, who had the longest experiences of enslavement. I have translated the quote from the original nineteenth-century ethnographic rendering of Black speech, adding final consonants while keeping verb tenses constant and retaining unique words: "chile" and "a'wavering" remain, while "de" becomes "the," "chillun" becomes "children," and "jes" becomes "just." Lawrence Levine pointed out that no one speaks the way language is written, and discussed the problem of whether or not to translate such passages in *Black Culture and Black Consciousness*; I felt that doing so in this case removed an unnecessary barrier to comprehension. See Lawrence W. Levine, *Black Culture and Black Consciousness: Afro-American Folk Thought from Slavery to Freedom* (New York: Oxford University Press, 1977), xvi–xvii.

22. John Solomon Lewis, "From Louisiana to Kansas: As Told by an Ex Soldier: from the Boston *Traveller*," *Southwestern Christian Advocate* 1 no. 5–6 (June 10, 1873), in Painter Papers, Box 96.

23. Painter, *Exodusters*, 195–201.

24. Michael Walzer, *Exodus and Revolution* (New York: Basic Books, 1985); Albert J. Raboteau, *Slave Religion: The "Invisible Institution" in the Antebellum South* (New York: Oxford University Press, 1978); Eddie S. Glaude, Jr., *Exodus! Religion, Race, and Nation in Early Nineteenth-Century Black America* (Chicago: University of Chicago Press, 2000).

25. This account, based on city directories and census reports, differs from the chronology of Crowdy's life out West in previous works. James Landing and Elly Wynia, following Beersheba Crowdy Walker's 1955 account, claim that Crowdy moved first to Guthrie, Oklahoma, then "around the mid 1890's" moved to Kansas City, Missouri and had three children but returned to Guthrie by 1893 and was already married. See Walker, *Life and Works of Crowdy*, 1–3; Wynia, *The Church of God and Saints of Christ*, 19–20; Landing, *Black Judaism*, 50–51. See, however, *Marriages of Arapahoe County, Colorado, 1859–1901: Including Territory that became Adams, Denver, and other counties* (Colorado: Colorado Genealogical Society, 1986), digital image, Ancestry.com, http://www.ancestry.com (hereafter: Ancestry.com).

26. 1880 U.S. census, Denver, Arapahoe County, Colorado, Enumeration District 13, sheet 32, 664 Blake Street, William Crowdy household, Family History Film 1254088, roll 88, page 280D; Corbett, *Hoye & Co.'s Fifth Annual City Directory City of Denver 1877* [Crowdy, William, (col'd), lab., r. Wewatta, ne. cor. 12th]; *Corbett, Hoye & Co.'s Eighth Annual City Directory City of Denver 1880* [Crowdy, William S., lab., r. Wazee, ne. cor. 23d]; *Corbett & Ballenger's Ninth Annual Denver City Directory City of Denver 1881* [Crowdy William S., col'd, cook, r 670 Blake]; all digital images, Ancestry.com.

27. Family histories record Lovey's maiden names as Yates Higgins. See: Walker, *Life and Works of Crowdy*, 3. Marriage license for William S. Crowdy and Lovey J. Higgins, Marion County Marriage Book, April 2, 1882, 99, *Missouri Marriage Records* (Jefferson City: Missouri State Archives); digital image, Ancestry.com.

28. 1880 U.S. Census, Kansas City, Jackson County, Missouri, Enumeration District 10, Page 45, Family History Film: 1254693, Roll 693, Page 313A, Image 0055; digital image, Ancestry.com.

29. *Bushnell's Des Moines Directory 1882–83* [Crowdy William, cook, bds 1021 Vine]; *R. L. Polk & Co.'s Sioux City Directory 1884–5* [Crowdy Wm S (col'd), cook Madison House]; digital images, Ancestry.com.

30. The first two children are listed in the following census: Iowa State Census 1885, Sioux City, Woodbury County, Iowa, Roll IA1885_281, Line 24, Family Number 380' digital image, Ancestry.com.

31. *Hoye's City Directory of Kansas City, Mo. 1886–87* [Crowdy William H. col'd, cook, r. 1412 Walnut]; *Hoye's City Directory of Kansas City, Mo. 1887–88* [Crowdy, William S. col'd, cook, r. 1825 Grove]; *Hoye's City Directory of Kansas City, Mo. 1888–89* [Crowdy, William S. cook, r. 1825 Grove]; *Hoye's City Directory of Kansas City, Mo., 1889–1890* [Crowdy, William D. *c* cook r 1825 Grove]; *Hoye's City Directory of Kansas City, Mo., 1890–91* [Crowdy William S. *c* r 1825 Grove]; digital images, Ancestry.com. For a slightly different version of this story as preserved in family and church histories, see Walker, *Life and Works of Crowdy*, 1–3.

32. Charles E. Coulter, *Take up the Black Man's Burden: Kansas City's African American Communities 1865–1939* (Columbia: University of Missouri Press, 2006), 21.

33. Ibid., 26.

34. U.S. Census Bureau, *Abstract of the Twelfth Census of the United States, 1900* (Washington, D.C.: United States Census Office, 1900), 101.

35. Angie Debo, *And Still the Waters Run: The Betrayal of the Five Civilized Tribes* (Princeton: Princeton University Press, 1980); Donald Grinde and Quintard Taylor, "Red vs. Black: Conflict and Accommodation in the Post Civil War Indian Territory, 1865–1907," *American Indian Quarterly* 8:3 (Summer 1984): 212–213; Thomas F. Andrews, "Freedmen in Indian Territory: A Post-Civil War Dilemma," *Journal of the West* 4, no. 3 (July 1965): 367–376; Daniel F. Littlefield, Jr., *The Cherokee Freedmen: From Emancipation to American Citizenship* (Westport, Conn.: Greenwood, 1978), 8–10; Jimmie Lewis Franklin, *Journey toward Hope: A History of Blacks in Oklahoma* (Norman: University of Oklahoma Press, 1982); Taylor, *Racial Frontier*, 114–121.

36. Taylor, *Racial Frontier*, 114.

37. Franklin, *Journey toward Hope*, 9; George O. Carney, "Oklahoma's All-Black Towns," in *African Americans of the Western Frontier*, ed. Monroe Lee Billington and Roger D. Hardaway (Niwot: University Press of Colorado, 1998), 147–159.

38. Monroe Lee Billington, "Buffalo Soldiers in the American West, 1865–1900," in *African Americans of the Western Frontier*, ed. Monroe Lee Billington and Roger D. Hardaway (Niwot: University Press of Colorado, 1998), 63; William H. Leckie, *The Buffalo Soldiers: A Narrative of the Negro Cavalry in the West* (Norman: University of Oklahoma Press, 1967), 245–251.

39. Carney, "Oklahoma's All-Black Towns," 148; United States Department of the Interior, Bureau of the Census, *Twelfth Census of the United States, 1900: Population* (Washington, D.C.: United States Government Printing Office, 1903), 553.

40. United States Department of the Interior, Bureau of the Census, *Compendium of the Eleventh Census: 1890* (Washington, D.C.: United States Government Printing Office, 1893), 503.

41. Crockett, *The Black Towns*, 168; Carney, "Oklahoma's All-Black Towns," 150.

42. Works Progress Administration (hereafter, WPA), *Oklahoma: A Guide to the Sooner State: Compiled by Workers of the Writers' Program of the Work Progress Administration in the State of Oklahoma* (Norman: University of Oklahoma

Press, 1941), 358. In 1903, the Fort Smith and Western Railroad extended its track from Arkansas to intersect with the Santa Fe at Guthrie. Crockett, *The Black Towns*, 21, 34.

43. WPA, *Oklahoma: A Guide to the Sooner State*, 358, maps, back pocket.

44. Ibid., 26.

45. Ibid., 358.

46. Kaye M. Teall, ed., *Black History in Oklahoma: A Resource Book* (Oklahoma City: Oklahoma City Public Schools, 1971), 169. For more on Langston, Oklahoma, see Kenneth Marvin Hamilton, "The Origin and Early Developments of Langston, Oklahoma," *Journal of Negro History* 62 (1977): 270–282; Martin Dann, "From Sodom to the Promised Land: E. P. McCabe and the Movement for Oklahoma Colonization," *Kansas Historical Quarterly* 40 (1974): 370–378; Daniel F. Littlefield and Lonnie E. Underhill, "Black Dreams and 'Free' Homes: The Oklahoma Territory, 1891–1894," *Phylon* 34 (1973): 342–357. The locations of the Indian reservations are given in B. F. Watson, "Oklahoma Inquiries Answered," *Christian Recorder* (Philadelphia), April 9, 1891.

47. Carney, "Oklahoma's All-Black Towns," 150; Crockett, *The Black Towns*, 20.

48. Crockett, *The Black Towns*, 20. 20.

49. "How Long?" *Langston City Herald*, November 14, 1891.

50. On Langston Hughes's name, see Langston Hughes, *The Big Sea: An Autobiography* ([1940] (New York: Hill and Wang, 1963), 12–13; Faith Berry, *Langston Hughes: Before and Beyond Harlem* (Westport, Conn.: L. Hill, 1983), 3.

51. "The Blacks in Oklahoma: Flocking to the Territory in Large Numbers: The Colonists Industrious and Ready to Push Their Way Forward—A War of Races with Plows and Hoes in Prospect," *New York Times*, April 9, 1891, 9.

52. Crockett, *The Black Towns*, 23.

53. Ibid., 23–24.

54. "Never!! We Cannot Ignore the Needs of Our Race" *Langston City Herald*, December 19, 1891.

55. "The Blacks in Oklahoma," 9; Crockett, *The Black Towns*, 22, 178.

56. "Oklahoma Investments," *Langston City Herald*, November 14, 1891.

57. E. P. McCabe, "Freedom! Peace, Happiness and Prosperity, Do You Want All These? Then Cast Your Lot with Us and Make Your Home in Langston City," *Langston City Herald*, February 6, 1892; Crockett, *The Black Towns*, 115, 120.

58. *Langston City Herald*, November 17, 1892, August 10, 1895, cited in Crockett, *The Black Towns*, 41.

59. WPA, *Oklahoma: A Guide to the Sooner State*, 10.

60. "The Blacks in Oklahoma," 9.

61. WPA, *Oklahoma: A Guide to the Sooner State*, 255–256; Crockett, *The Black Towns*, 178, 164.

62. "The Blacks in Oklahoma," 9.

63. Crockett, *The Black Towns*, 185.

64. Ibid., 43.

65. Ibid.

66. Booker T. Washington, "Boley, a Negro Town in the West," *Outlook* 88 (January 1908): 28–31.

67. *Langston City Herald*, June 15, 1893, cited in Crockett, *The Black Towns*, 40.

68. Church of God and Saints of Christ publication, n.d., 65, Dupree African-American Pentecostal and Holiness Collection, Schomburg Center, Box 10, folder 8.

69. Crockett, *The Black Towns*, 65.

70. Franklin, *Journey Toward Hope*, 153–156; Zella J. Black Patterson, *Churches of Langston* (Oklahoma City: Western Heritage Books, 1982).

71. "Numerical Index, City and Town Lots, Langston," Logan County Courthouse, Guthrie, Oklahoma.

72. See Milton Sernett, *Bound for the Promised Land: African American Religion and the Great Migration* (Durham: Duke University Press, 1997), 161–164. See Chapter 3, below.

73. Watson, "Oklahoma: Inquiries Answered."

74. Rev. S. S. Atkins, "The Oklahoma District: Compliments Its Presiding Elder and Takes on New Life," *Christian Recorder* (Philadelphia), May 16, 1895.

75. Crockett, *The Black Towns*, 150.

76. Walker, *Life and Works of Crowdy*, 20.

77. Ibid., 4.

78. Crockett, *The Black Towns*, 49.

79. "And I took a little book out of the angel's hand, and ate it up; and it was in my mouth sweet as honey: and as soon as I had eaten it, my belly was bitter." Revelation 10:10 *KJV*.

80. The Seven Keys: First Key—The Church of God and Saints of Christ. 1st Cor. 1:1–2. Second Key—Wine forbidden to be drunk in the Church of God forever. Lv. 10:0–10. Third Key—Unleavened bread and water for Christ's body and blood. Matthew 26:26–27. Fourth Key—Foot washing is a commandment. Saint John 13:1 to 17. Fifth Key—The disciples' prayer. Saint Matthew 6:9 to 14. Sixth Key— You must be breathed upon and saluted in the Church of God with a holy kiss. Saint John 20:21–22. Romans 16:16. Seventh Key—The ten commandments. Exodus 20:1 to 18. "The Seven Keys," DuPree Collection, Box 10, folder 8, Schomburg Center.

81. The Holiness Movement developed from Methodist circles in the Northeast in the 1830s and spread rapidly after the Civil War. Theologically, Holiness people believed that intense faith and divine grace could lead to a "baptism of the Holy Spirit" and obliterate the appeal of sin. The movement sponsored numerous revivals, where hundreds and thousands of people of all races worshiped and caught the spirit. For more on the Holiness movement, see Chapter 3.

82. Crowdy, *Church of God and Saints of Christ*, DuPree Collection, Box 10, folder 8, Schomburg Center.

83. Walker, *Life and Works of Crowdy*, 9–10.

84. Ibid., 11.

85. Ibid., 10.

86. Ibid.

87. Wynia, *The Church of God and Saints of Christ*, 21.

88. For example, "Christ is the end of the law," Romans 10:4; "you are under no law," Romans 6:14; "when there is a change of the priesthood, there must also be a change of the law," Hebrews 7:12.

89. Crockett, *The Black Towns*, 76. *Western Age*, April 9, 1909. For another example of the Black-town attitude toward Jews, see *Clearview Patriarch*, December 21, 1911.

90. Walker, *Life and Works of Crowdy*, 11.

91. Elfreth John Prince Walker, ed. *The Armor Bearer: Bishop Groves as I Knew Him* (Philadelphia: Elfreth John Prince Walker, c. 1925), 1–8.

92. Ibid., 9.

93. David J. Peavler, "Creating the Color Line and Confronting Jim Crow: Civil Rights in Middle America: 1850–1900" (Ph.D. dissertation, University of Kansas, 2008), 3–4.

94. Department of the Interior, Census Office. *Compendium of the Eleventh Census: 1890*. Part I: *Population*. (Washington, D.C.: Government Printing Office 1892), 164, 548. The term "colored" was not exclusive to those of African descent, but did not include the two Chinese people or the one "civilized Indian." Statewide, Black people of African descent made up 98.4 percent of the total "colored" population. *1890 Census*, Part I, ciii, 469. The population of Lawrence's Douglas County had grown from 8,083 in 1860 to 20,592 in 1870 and 23,961 in 1890, over 90 percent of whom were native-born. Census Office, *Compendium of the Eleventh Census: 1890*, I, 19.

95. Peavler, "Creating the Color Line," 9. The great majority of Lawrence's Douglas county was white (20,443) but there were also 3,076 residents of African descent, 12.8 percent of the population, along with two Chinese people and 440 "civilized Indians." Census Office, *Compendium of the Eleventh Census: 1890*, I, 468, 518, 530, 605. There were more men than women among the colored population as well as in the white population, reflecting the gender imbalance of many frontier societies. Statewide there were 752,112 men as compared to 674,984 women, and the "colored" population of African descent totaled 49,710, 3.5 percent of the total population statewide. These figures included "colored" people not of African descent.

96. The largest block was the Methodists, with 1,529 congregations, including 65 African Methodist churches. Next were the half dozen variations of Baptists, with 1,220 congregations. This figure no doubt included many Black Baptists, perhaps listed among the 6 Regular Baptists (South), the 20 Primitive Baptists, or the 3 "other" Baptists. There were 1,042 Presbyterian churches, 410 Lutheran, and 367

Roman Catholic congregations, along with 355 United Brethren in Christ churches, 9 Spiritualist meetings, 26 Mormon temples, 6 Jewish synagogues, and many small Protestant and Holiness Protestant sects. Department of the Interior, Census Office, *Report on Statistics of Churches in the United States at the Eleventh Census: 1890* (Washington, D.C.: Government Printing Office, 1894), 2–7.

97. Wynia, *The Church of God and Saints of Christ*, 23.

98. "But when I speak with thee, I will open thy mouth, and thou shalt say unto them, Thus saith the Lord GOD; He that heareth, let him hear; and he that forbeareth, let him forbear: for they are a rebellious house." Ezekiel 3:27, KJV.

99. Walker, *Life and Works of Crowdy*, 11.

100. Ibid.

101. Ibid.

102. Ibid.; Walker, *The Armor Bearer*, 9.

103. Walker, *The Armor Bearer*, 9.

104. Walker, *Life and Works of Crowdy*, 14; Wynia, *The Church of God and Saints of Christ*, 23.

105. "Weird Religion: 'Bishop' Crowdy Making Things Boom out West—He's as Black as Can be" *Broad Ax* (Salt Lake City, Utah), August 6, 1898.

106. Ibid.; "Something New" *Fair Play* (Fort Scott, Kansas), July 22, 1898.

107. William Saunders Crowdy, *The Bible Gospel Told; The Revelation of God Revealed; Set Forth by Bishop W. S. Crowdy of the Church of God and Saints of Christ; The World Evangelist; My Teacher is the Father, Son, and Holy Ghost* (Philadelphia: The Church of God Publication House, 1902), 26–28.

108. Ibid., 30. Crowdy used thirty scriptures to show that water, not wine, represented Christ's body in the Eucharist, using such verses as: Mark 9:42; John 4:15; Revelation 22:-17.

109. For the 1899 Seven Keys, see Wynia, *The Church of God and Saints of Christ*, 25. On the drive for prohibition in western all-Black towns, see Crockett, *The Black Towns*, 101.

110. For further New Testament verses emphasizing the importance of the Mosaic law, see also Romans 3:31, Romans 7:12, and James 1:25.

111. Crowdy, *The Bible Gospel Told*, 21–25.

112. Ibid., 31–33.

113. Ibid., 33, 34.

114. Ibid., 36.

115. See, for example, William Saunders Crowdy, "Great Prophetic Sermon," March 9, 1903, Lawrence, Kansas, in *Prophet William Saunders Crowdy's Great Prophetic Sermon, Epistles of Warning and Consolation, Induction Sermon with Revelation, Slite History of His Beginning and End,* (Philadelphia, Charles B. H. McNeill, n.d.), 15.

116. Walker *Life and Works of Crowdy,* 21; Elmer T. Clark, *The Small Sects in America* (New York: Abingdon-Cokebury Press, 1937), 151–152; U.S. Bureau of the Census, *Religious Bodies: 1906,* 201–202, quoted in Landing, *Black Judaism*, 53.

117. Wynia, *The Church of God and Saints of Christ*, ix–x.

118. Solomon, "D.C.'s Well-kept Secret," 4.

119. Rabbi Curtis Caldwell, telephone interview by author, May 7, 2007.

120. Wynia, *The Church of God and Saints of Christ*, 23. *Prophet William Saunders Crowdy's Great Prophetic Sermons*, March 9, 1903, 21.

121. Walker, *Life and Works of Crowdy*, 23; Wynia, *The Church of God and Saints of Christ*, 30.

122. Walker, *Life and Works of Crowdy*, 23.

123. Ibid.

124. Ibid.

125. Ibid.

126. Ibid. Indeed, the 1900 census records a fifty-year-old former slave named Lizzie Lavender in Utica, New York, whose profession was "Evangelist." I have been unable to find similar corroboration for George Labiel or Flora Walker, who went on to become esteemed elders in the church, but there was a woman in Oneida who might have been the Mrs. Titus referred to in the official church history. See: 1900 U.S. Census, New York State, Oneida County, Utica Ward 4, Enumeration District 55, sheet 2, Roll T623_1133, page 2A [Lavender, Lizzie]; 1900 U.S. Census, New York State, Madison County, Oneida Village, Enumeration District 12, sheet 22, Roll T623_1072, page 22A [Titus, Diana J—60 year old Black female, 3 living children].

127. Walker, *Life and Works of Crowdy*, 23. On conjuring, see David H. Brown, "Conjure/Doctors: An Exploration of a Black Discourse in America, Antebellum to 1940," *Folklore Forum* 23, nos. 1–2 (1990): 3–46; Yvonne Chireau, *Black Magic: Religion and the African American Conjuring Tradition* (Berkeley: University of California Press, 2003), Jeffrey E. Anderson, *Conjure in African American Society* (Baton Rouge: Louisiana State University Press, 2005).

128. 1900 United States Census, Philadelphia Ward 4, Philadelphia, Pennsylvania, Enumeration District 89, sheet 7, roll T623_1453, page 7B; digital image, Ancestry.com.

129. Walker, *Life and Works of Crowdy*, 23.

130. The first Passover was actually observed in Kansas in 1899; the East church followed in 1901. Walker, *Life and Works of Crowdy,* 32.

131. The membership numbers come from Walker, *Life and Works of Crowdy*, 44, but such large figures are corroborated by a U.S. Department of Commerce finding that the Church of God and Saints of Christ had 3,311 members in 1916 and 6,781 members in 1927. "Church of God in Christ (*sic*) Has 6,741 Members: Denomination Founded by Prophet Crowdy; Now Led by Bishop Plummer," *Norfolk Journal and Guide*, December 3, 1927, 5.

132. Although Elly Wynia's account and an earlier article of my own report that Christian was Xhosa sailor and former Baptist missionary, passenger lists from the United States in 1903 and 1906 and England in 1906 identify him as West Indian.

*Philadelphia Passenger Lists, 1800–1945*, Roll T840_42, Line 29 [Mr. Albert Christian, May 5, 1903, 35 years old, estimated birth year: abt 1868, Gender Male, Calling Minister, Nationality West Indian, Race West Indian, Port of Departure Liverpool, England, Ship Name Noordland, Port of Arrival Philadelphia, Friend's Name Mr. Edward Philips, Last Residence Port Elizabeth, S. Africa. Line 30: Mrs. Eva Christian, Wife, Nationality West Indian, Race West Indian]; *UK Incoming Passenger Lists, 1878–1960*, Class BT26, piece 254, Item 39 [Albert Christian, January 6, 1906, Durban, South Africa to Dover, England]; digital images, Ancestry.com; Walker, *Life and Works of Crowdy*, 51; Wynia, *The Church of God and Saints of Christ*, 40; Jacob S. Dorman, "Black Israelites aka Black Jews aka Black Hebrews: Black Israelism, Black Judaism, Judaic Christianity," in *Introduction to New and Alternative Religions in the United States*, ed. Eugene V. Gallagher and W. Michael Ashcraft (Westport, Conn.: Praeger, 2006), 78.

133. *New York Passenger Lists, 1820–1957*, Year: 1906, Microfilm Serial T715, Microfilm Roll T715_658, Line 27, Page 8 [Christian, Albert B. Age 38, Occupation Minister, Friend Mrs. A. Christian, Portsmouth, Virginia], digital image, Ancestry.com.

134. Walker, *Life and Work of Crowdy*, 51. Revelation 19:10 reads: "And I fell at his feet to worship him. And he said unto me, See [thou do it] not: I am thy fellow servant, and of thy brethren that have the testimony of Jesus: worship God: for the testimony of Jesus is the spirit of prophecy," KJV.

135. Walker, *Life and Work of Crowdy*, 51–52.

136. Walker, *Life and Works of Crowdy*, 52.

137. Landing, *Black Judaism*, 161–164.

138. Walker, *Life and Works of Crowdy*, 52; for another retelling based on Walker, see Landing, *Black Judaism*, 57, 161, 339. Since the A.M.E. church had been active in South Africa since 1896 (see below), and since Christian was affiliated with that body after his return to the country, between 1903 and 1906, it seems quite likely that he had been affiliated with the A.M.E. church prior to his acceptance of Crowdy's teachings—which also might help explain his trip to Philadelphia, as the City of Brotherly Love was the birthplace and headquarters of the A.M.E. church.

139. J. Lorand Matory, *Black Atlantic Religion: Tradition, Transnationalism, and Matriarchy in the Afro-Brazilian Candomblé* (Princeton: Princeton University Press, 2005).

140. Walker, *Life and Work of Crowdy*, 11–14; Wynia, *The Church of God and Saints of Christ*, 23.

141. The church remembers the disease as smallpox, but it could have been polio, as cases of polio were 30 percent higher than normal in the summer of 1908. Wharton Sinkler, M.D., "Epidemics of Poliomyelitis in Philadelphia," *Journal of Nervous and Mental Disease* 35, no. 4 (April 1908): 260; Walker, *Life and Works of Crowdy*, 46.

142. Walker, *The Armor Bearer*, 10.

143. Ibid., 10–11.

144. The Historical Committee of the Church of God and Saints of Christ, *The Re-Establishing Years, (1847–1908) History of the Church of God and Saints of Christ*, Vol. 1 (Suffolk, Va.: Church of God and Saints of Christ, 1992), 69. Thus far, no historian of the Church of God and Saints of Christ has reported this connection, although Pentecostal archivist Sherry Sherrod DuPree has confirmed the existence of Black Israelite teachings within Bishop Mason's theology. Sherry Sherrod DuPree, telephone interview by author, April 1998.

145. More work needs to be done on the diversity of beliefs among Prophet Crowdy's followers and the exact timing and rationales of the various schisms among them. My own cursory reading of COGASOC newsletters indicates that its leaders did not start using the title "rabbi" until the 1930s, which suggests that the church began to emphasize Judaic practices around the same time as Wentworth Arthur Matthew made his own transition from "Bishop" to "Rabbi," as discussed in Chapter 5.

146. Henne Pretorius and Lizo Jafta, "'A Branch Springs Out': African Initiated Churches," in *Christianity in Southern Africa: A Political, Cultural, and Social History*, ed. Richard Elphick and Rodney Davenport (Berkeley: University of California Press, 1997); Norman Etherington, "The Historical Sociology of Independent Churches in South East Africa," *Journal of Religion in Africa* 10, no. 2 (1979): 113–115, 120.

147. Pretorius and Jafta, "A Branch Springs Out," 214–215.

148. Ibid., 217.

149. Walter J. Hollenweger, *Pentecostalism: Origins and Development Worldwide* (Peabody, Mass.: Hendrickson, 1997), 41–53; Pretorius and Jafta, "A Branch Springs Out," 217; Edith Bruder, *The Black Jews of Africa: History, Religion, Identity* (New York: Oxford University Press, 2008), 174.

150. Nicole Anderson and Scott London, "South Africa's Newest 'Jews': The Moemedi Pentecostal Church and the Construction of Jewish Identity," *Nova Religio: The Journal of Alternative and Emergent Religions* 13, no. 1 (August 2009): 95.

151. Landing, *Black Judaism*, 161–164; Bruder, *The Black Jews of Africa*, 174.

152. Landing, *Black Judaism*, 165–169; Landeg White, *Magomero: Portrait of an African Village*, (Cambridge: Cambridge University Press, 1987).

153. Bruder, *The Black Jews of Africa*, 176–177; Mark Ellyne, "The Black Jews of Africa," http://www.mindspring.com/~jaypsand/rusape6.htm.

154. Landing, *Black Judaism*, 161–169.

155. Arye Oded, "The Bayudaya of Uganda: A Portrait of an African Jewish Community," *Journal of Religion in Africa* 6, no. 3 (1974): 167–186; Landing, *Black Judaism*, 165–169.

CHAPTER 2

1. Edward Wilmot Blyden, *The Jewish Question* (Liverpool: Lionel Hart, 1898), 16.

2. See, for example: Allen H. Godbey, *The Lost Tribes a Myth: Suggestions towards Rewriting Hebrew History* (Durham: Duke University Press, 1930); Rudolph R. Windsor, *From Babylon to Timbuktu: A History of the Ancient Black Races Including the Black People in America Today* (Philadephia: Windsor's Golden Series Publications, 1988); Shaleak Ben Yehuda, *Black Hebrew Israelites from America to the Promised Land: The Great International Religious Conspiracy against the Children of the Prophets* (New York: Vantage, 1975); Morris Lounds, *Israel's Black Hebrews: Black Americans in Search of Identity* (Washington, D.C.: University Press of America, 1981); James E. Landing, *Black Judaism: Story of an American Movement* (Durham, N.C.: Carolina Academic Press, 2002); Jacob S. Dorman, "Black Israelites aka Black Jews aka Black Hebrews: Black Israelism, Black Judaism, Judaic Christianity," in *Introduction to New and Alternative Religions in the United States*, ed. Eugene V. Gallagher and W. Michael Ashcraft (Westport, Conn.: Praeger, 2006), 59–84.

3. Edith Bruder, *The Black Jews of Africa: History, Religion, and Identity* (New York: Oxford University Press, 2008), 116.

4. Publius Cornelius Tacitus, *The History of Tacitus*, Book V [1]: 2, trans. Alfred John Church and William Jackson Brodribb (Cambridge: Macmillan, 1864), 265.

5. See, for example: Shlomo Sand, *The Invention of the Jewish People*, trans. Yael Lotan (London: Verso, 2009).

6. Bruder, *Black Jews of Africa*, 102–103.

7. Ibid., 20.

8. Ibid., 106, 116.

9. Ibid., 107.

10. Ibid., 133–134.

11. Tudor Parfitt and Emanuela Trevisan Semi, eds., *Judaising Movements: Studies in the Margins of Judaism* (London: RoutledgeCurzon, 2002), 4–7.

12. Ibid., 11–16.

13. Joseph J. Williams, *Hebrewisms of West Africa: From Nile to Niger with the Jews* [1930] (New York: Biblo and Tannen, 1967); Godbey, *The Lost Tribes a Myth*. In the late 1960s, African American scholars picked up these themes, as discussed in Chapter 7. See Windsor, *From Babylon to Timbuktu*; Yosef Ben-Jochannan, *Black Man of the Nile and His Family*, 2nd ed. [1972] (Baltimore: Black Classic Press, 1989).

14. Dierk Lange, *Ancient Kingdoms of West Africa: Africa-Centered and Canaanite-Israelite Perspectives: A Collection of Published and Unpublished Studies in English and French* (Dettelbach: J. H. Röll, 2004).

15. Bruder, *Black Jews of Africa*, 133–134.

16. Eric Hobsbawm and Terence Ranger, eds. *The Invention of Tradition* (Cambridge: Cambridge University Press: 1993); Benedict Anderson, *Imagined Communities:*

*Reflections on the Origin and Spread of Nationalism* (London: Verso, 1983); Gilles Deleuze and Félix Guattari, *A Thousand Plateaus: Capitalism and Schizophrenia* (1987), 3–25.

17. Although recent genetic studies have purported to show that contemporary Ashkenazi Jews can trace their ancestry back to the "Middle East," two Tel Aviv University professors have disputed the idea that contemporary diasporic Jewish populations can trace their language, religion, or ancestry back to the ancient Israelites. See Sand, *Invention of the Jewish People*; Paul Wexler, *The Ashkenazic Jews: A Slavo-Turkic People in Search of a Jewish Identity* (Columbus, Ohio: Slavica Publishers, 1993), Wexler, *The Non-Jewish Origins of the Sephardic Jews* (Albany: State University of New York Press, 1996). For a critique of Wexler's work, see: Dovid Katz, "A Late Twentieth Century Case of *Katoves*," in *History of Yiddish Studies: Papers from the Third Annual Oxford Winter Symposium in Yiddish Language and Literature*, ed. Dov-Ber Kerler (Philadelphia: Harwood Academic Publishers, 1991), 141–164. For recent genetic studies, see Gil Atzmon, Li Hao, Itsik Pe'er, et al., "Abraham's Children in the Genome Era: Major Jewish Diaspora Populations Comprise Distinct Genetic Clusters with Shared Middle Eastern Ancestry," *American Journal of Human Genetics* 86, no. 6 (June 11, 2010): 850–859; Doron M. Behar, Bayazit Yunusbayev, Mait Metspalu, et al., "The Genome-Wide Structure of the Jewish People" *Nature* 466 (July 8, 2010): 238–242.

18. On the Beta Israel, see Wolf Leslau, *Falasha Anthology* (New Haven: Yale University Press, 1951); David Kessler, *The Falashas: The Forgotten Jews of Ethiopia* (London: George Allen & Unwin, 1982); Steven Kaplan, "A Brief History of the Beta Israel," in *The Jews of Ethiopia: A People in Transition* (New York: Jewish Museum, 1986), 11–29; Louis Rapoport, *Redemption Song: The Story of Operation Moses* (New York: Harcourt Brace Jovanovich, 1986); James Quirin, *The Evolution of the Ethiopian Jews: A History of the Beta Israel (Falasha) to 1920* (Philadelphia: University of Pennsylvania Press, 1992); Steven Kaplan, "Beta Israel Studies toward the Year 2000," in *Between Africa and Zion: Proceedings of the First International Congress of the Society for the Study of Ethiopian Jewry*, ed. Steven Kaplan, Tudor Parfitt, and Emanuela Trevisan Semi (Jerusalem: Ben Zvi Institute, 1995), 9–20; Tudor Parfitt and Emanuela Trevisan Semi, eds., *Jews of Ethiopia: The Birth of an Elite* (London: Routledge, 2005).

19. Arye Oded, "The Bayudaya of Uganda: A Portrait of an African Jewish Community," *Journal of Religion in Africa* 6, no. 3 (1974): 167–186; Bruder, *The Black Jews of Africa: History, Religion, Identity* (New York: Oxford University Press, 2008); Robert G. Weisbord and Arthur Stein, *Bittersweet Encounter: The Afro-American and the American Jew* (Westport, Conn.: Negro University Press, 1970), 19. See also studies of white Jews in the South, such as David J. Hellwig, "Black Images of Jews: From Reconstruction to Depression," *Societas* 8, no. 3 (1978): 205; Arnold Shankman, "Friend or Foe? Southern Blacks View the Jew 1880–1935," in *Turn to the South*, ed. Nathan M. Kaganoff and Melvin Urofsky (Charlottesville: University Press of Virginia, 1979), 107.

20. Seymour Drescher, "The Role of Jews in the Transatlantic Slave Trade," *Immigrants and Minorities* 12, no. 2 (1993): 113–125.

21. Franklin W. Knight, *The Caribbean: The Genesis of a Fragmented Nationalism*, 2nd ed. (New York: Oxford University Press, 1990), 73.

22. Jacob Rader Marcus, *The Colonial American Jew, 1492–1776,* vol. 3 (Detroit: Wayne State University Press, 1970), 80.

23. Ibid., 115.

24. Ibid., 114, 120. Jews won the right to vote in the British West Indies in 1830, and the right to hold political office in Jamaica in 1831, twenty-seven years before they could hold office in England. So many won posts that in 1849 the Jamaican Assembly adjourned for Yom Kippur. Knight, *The Caribbean,* 149; Malcolm H. Stern, "Portuguese Sephardim in the Americas," *American Jewish Archives* 24, no. 1 (Spring/Summer, 1992): 151.

25. Stern, "Portuguese Sephardim in the Americas," 152.

26. Ibid., 154. I use the term "white Jew" in the section that follows, when Jews of European origin benefit from the race-based caste system associated with African slavery in the Americas.

27. Marcus, *Colonial American Jew,* 91. Marcus speculates that Haiti's liberator, Pierre Dominique Toussaint "L'Ouveture," was a descendant of Jacob Toussaint, one of Saint-Domingue's Jewish planters in the mid-1700s.

28. Ibid., 121.

29. For more on sex, race, and the color line during slavery and Reconstruction, see Martha Hodes, *White Women, Black Men: Illicit Sex in the Nineteenth-Century South* (New Haven: Yale University Press, 1999); Hodes, ed., *Sex, Love, Race: Crossing Boundaries in North American History* (New York: New York University Press, 1999); Elizabeth Dillon, *The Gender of Freedom: Fictions of Liberalism and the Literary Public Sphere* (Palo Alto: Stanford University Press, 2004).

30. Rabbi Dobrin, *Hayehudi* 21 (1911): 13, quoted in Arthur Dobrin, "A History of the Negro Jews in America" (unpublished paper, City College of New York, microfilm, Schomburg Library for the Study of Black Culture, New York Public Library, 1965), 15; Lisa Douglass and Raymond Thomas Smith, *The Power of Sentiment: Love, Hierarchy, and the Jamaican Family Elite* (Boulder, Colo.: Westview, 1992), 91, 98.

31. Stern, "Portuguese Sephardim in the Americas," 146.

32. Marcus, *Colonial American Jew,* 186.

33. Isaac Samuel Emmanuel and Suzanne A. Emmanuel, *History of the Jews of the Netherland Antilles* (Cincinnati: American Jewish Archives, 1970), 482.

34. G. W. van der Meiden, "Governor Mauricius and the Political Rights of the Surinam Jews," in *The Jewish Nation in Surinam: Historical Essays*, ed. R. Cohen (Amsterdam: S. Emmering, 1982), 49.

35. Marcus, *Colonial American Jew,* 160, 186; Dobrin, "A History of Negro Jews," 15.

36. Z. Loker and R. Cohen, "An Eighteenth-Century Prayer of the Jews of Surinam," in *The Jewish Nation in Surinam,* ed. R. Cohen, 76.

37. Robert Cohen, *Jews in Another Environment: Surinam in the Second Half of the Eighteenth Century* (Leiden: E. J. Brill, 1991), 161–163; Cohen, "Patterns of Marriage and Remarriage among the Sephardi Jews of Surinam, 1788–1818," in *The Jewish Nation in Surinam,* ed. R. Cohen, 93.

38. Stern, "Portuguese Sephardim in the Americas," 143, Marcus, *Colonial American Jew*, 153–155, 161, 200.

39. Cohen, *Jews in Another Environment*, 156–174.

40. Anemona Harocolis, "God's Chosen People?: Having Rejected Christianity as a Slave Religion, the Israelites Have Seized on an Identity That Is Almost as Old as Time," *New York Newsday*, July 28, 1993, 78.

41. Rabbi Eliezer Brooks, interviews by author, August 14 and 22, 1996, Bronx, New York, tape recordings.

42. J. David Bleich, "Black Jews: A Halakhic Perspective," *Tradition: A Journal of Orthodox Thought* 15, no. 1–2 (Spring/Summer 1975): 48–79.

43. Graenum Berger, *Graenum: An Autobiography by Graenum Berger* (Pelham, N.Y.: John Washburn Bleeker Hampton, 1987): 300.

44. Bertram Wallace Korn, *Jews and Negro Slavery in the Old South, 1789–1865* (Elkins Park, Pa.: Reform Congregation Keneseth Israel, 1961), 26. On Jews and slavery in the South, see also Bertram Wallace Korn, *American Jewry and the Civil War* (Philadelphia: Jewish Publication Society of America, 1951); Hugh H. Smythe and Martin S. Price, "The American Jew and Negro Slavery," *Midwest Journal* 7 (1956): 315–319; Bertram Wallace Korn, "Jews and Negro Slavery in the Old South, 1789–1865," in *Jews in the South*, ed. Leonard Dinnerstein and Mary Dale Palsson (Baton Rouge: Louisiana State University Press, 1973), 89–134; Nathan M. Kaganoff and Melvin Urofsky, eds., *Turn to the South: Essays on Southern Jewry* (Charlottesville: University Press of Virginia, 1979); Samuel Proctor and Louis Schmier, eds., *Jews of the South: Selected Essays from the Southern Jewish Historical Society* (Macon: Mercer University Press, 1984); Abraham J. Peck, "That Other 'Peculiar Institution': Jews and Judaism in the Nineteenth Century South," *Modern Judaism* 7 (1987): 99–114; Howard N. Rabinowitz, "Nativism, Bigotry and Anti-Semitism in the South," *American Jewish History* 77, no. 3 (1988): 427–451; Jason H. Silverman, "Ashley Wilkes Revisited: The Immigrant as Slaveholder in the Old South," *Journal of Confederate History* 7 (1991) 123–135; Eli Farber, *Jews, Slaves, and the Slave Trade: Setting the Record Straight* (New York: New York University Press, 1998); Saul S. Friedman, *Jews and the American Slave Trade* (New Brunswick, N.J.: Transaction, 1998).

45. Korn, *Jews and Negro Slavery*, 57. Silverman disputes this assertion somewhat, arguing that Germans and Jews had better reputations as slave masters than Irish immigrants. Silverman, "Ashley Wilkes Revisited," 135.

46. Benjamin Kaplan, "Judah Philip Benjamin," in Dinnerstein and Palsson, eds., *Jews in the South*, 75–88; Richard S. Tedlow, "Judah Benjamin," in Kaganoff and Urofsky, "*Turn to the South*," 44–54; Eli N. Evans, *Judah Benjamin: The Jewish Confederate* (New York: Free Press, 1988).

47. There is a vast and rich literature on whiteness studies. The salient ones for the topic of Jews and whiteness are: Karen Brodkin, *How Jews Became White Folks and What That Says about Race in America* (New Brunswick: Rutgers University Press, 1998); Matthew Frye Jacobson, *Whiteness of a Different Color: European Immigrants and the Alchemy of Race* (Cambridge: Harvard University Press, 1998); Thomas A. Guglielmo, *White on Arrival: Italians, Race, Color, and Power in Chicago, 1890–1945* (New York: Oxford University Press, 2003); Matthew Frye Jacobson, *Roots Too: White Ethnic Revival in Post-Civil Rights America* (Cambridge: Harvard University Press, 2006); Eric L. Goldstein, *The Price of Whiteness: Jews, Race, and American Identity* (Princeton: Princeton University Press, 2006); Melanie Kaye/Kantrowitz, *The Colors of Jews: Racial Politics and Radical Diasporism* (Bloomington: Indiana University Press, 2007).

48. Korn, *Jews and Negro Slavery*, 67–68.

49. Silverman, "Ashley Wilkes Revisited," 135.

50. Lenora E. Berson, *The Negroes and the Jews* (New York: Random House, 1971): 10–26; Berger, *Graenum*, 26–27.

51. Cited in Shankman, "Friend or Foe?" 122.

52. Ibid. Of course, separation was never total. James McBride's best-selling 1996 memoir chronicled his mother's childhood as the daughter of a Southern Jewish merchant who married two African American men in New York. James McBride, *The Color of Water: A Black Man's Tribute to his White Mother* (New York: Penguin Putnam, 1996).

53. Ralph Melnick, "Billy Simons: The Black Jew of Charleston," *American Jewish Archives* 32, no. 1 (1980): 6.

54. Ibid., 4.

55. Obituary in the *Weekly Gleaner*, a San Francisco Jewish newspaper, quoted ibid., 7.

56. Ibid.

57. Ibid., 5.

58. Marion Anderson, *My Lord, What a Morning* (New York: Avon, 1956), 19.

59. Korn, *Jews and Negro Slavery*, 49.

60. Shankman, "Friend or Foe?" 107.

61. Jayme A. Sokolow, "Revolution and Reform: The Antebellum Jewish Abolitionists," *Journal of Ethnic Studies* 9, no. 28 (1981): 28.

62. John Hope Franklin, *From Slavery to Freedom: A History of Negro Americans* (New York: World Publishing, 1961), 1. Numbers at the time of the Civil War given as 150,000 Jews, 400,000 Free People of Color, and 4,000,000 Black slaves in John Bracey and August Meir, "Towards a Research Agenda on Blacks and Jews in United States History," in the *Journal of American Ethnic History* 12, no. 3 (1993): 60; Korn, *American Jewry and the Civil War*, 19.

63. Leonard Dinnerstein, Roger L. Nichols, and David M. Reimers, *Natives and Strangers, Blacks, Indians, and Immigrants in America*, 2nd ed. (New York: Oxford University Press, 1990): 62.

64. Korn, *American Jewry and the Civil War*, 30. Blake Touchstone, "Planters and Slave Religion in the Deep South," in *Masters & Slaves in the House of the Lord: Race & Religion in the American South 1740–1870*, John B. Boles, ed. (Lexington: University Press of Kentucky, 1988), 100–101.

65. Sokolow, "Revolution and Reform," 27.

66. Ibid., 28, 33.

67. Ibid., 28.

68. Louis Schmier, "For Him the 'Schwartzers' Couldn't Do Enough: A Jewish Peddler and His Black Customers Look at Each Other," *American Jewish History* 73, no. 1 (1983): 48.

69. Ibid.

70. See Timothy L. Smith, "Slavery and Theology: The Emergence of Black Christian Consciousness in Nineteenth Century America," *Church History* 41, no. 4 (1972): 497–512; Katherine L. Dvorak, "After Apocalypse, Moses," in *Masters & Slaves in the House of the Lord: Race & Religion in the American South 1740–1870*, ed. John B. Boles (Lexington: University Press of Kentucky), 175; Michael Walzer, *Exodus and Revolution* (New York: Basic Books, 1985); Albert J. Raboteau, *Slave Religion: The "Invisible Institution" in the Antebellum South* (New York: Oxford University Press, 1978); Eddie S. Glaude, Jr., *Exodus! Religion, Race, and Nation in Early Nineteenth-Century Black America* (Chicago: University of Chicago Press, 2000).

71. Ulysses Santamaria, "Black Jews: The Religious Challenge or Politics versus Religion," *Archives Europeennes de Sociologie* (Paris) 28, no. 2 (1987): 220–221.

72. Smith, "Slavery and Theology"; Vincent Harding, "Religion and Resistance among Antebellum Negroes, 1800–1806," in *The Making of Black America,* vol. 1, ed. August Meir and Elliot Rudwick, 179–197 (New York: Athenaeum, 1969).

73. Smith, "Slavery and Theology."

74. Cecil Roth, *A History of the Jews in England* (Oxford: Clarendon Press, 1949), 150.

75. Ibid.

76. Craig Rose, *England in the 1690s: Revolution, Religion, and War* (Oxford: Blackwell, 1999), 20–28, 75–78, 86, 146, 160, 178.

77. Edward P. Thompson, *The Making of the English Working Class* (New York: Pantheon, 1963), 386, 392.

78. Iain McCalman, *Radical Underworld: Prophets, Revolutionaries and Pornographers in London, 1795–1840* (New York: Cambridge University Press, 1988).

79. Henry Blaine Foster, *Rise and Progress of Wesleyan-Methodism in Jamaica* (London: Wesleyan Conference Office, 1881); Gayraud S. Wilmore, *Black Religion and Black Radicalism* (Garden City, N.Y.: Doubleday, 1972), 146.

80. Judges 12:6. See Robert G. Kissick, *The Irish Prince and the Hebrew Prophet: A Masonic Tale of the Captive Jews and the Ark of the Covenant* (New York: Masonic Publishing, 1896), 9.

81. William L. Ingram, "God and Race: British Israelism and Christian Identity," in *America's Alternative Religions*, ed. Timothy Miller (Albany: State University of New York Press, 1995), 119.

82. Thompson, *The Making of the English Working Class,* 386, 392.

83. Edward Said, "Michael Walzer's *Exodus and Revolution*: A Canaanite Reading," *Grand Street* 5, no. 2 (Winter 1986): 86–106; Michael Walzer, *Exodus and Revolution* (New York: Basic Books, 1985).

84. Edward Hine, *Forty-Seven Identifications of the British Nation with the Lost Ten Tribes of Israel* (London: S. W. Partridge, n.d.); Michael Barkun, *Religion and the Racist Right: The Origins of the Christian Identity Movement* (Chapel Hill: University of North Carolina Press, 1997), ix–x, 8–15, 48–54, 63, 79–85, 112–116, 139.

85. Rev. Robert Pegrum, "Mannaseh's Identification," in *The Banner of Israel: A Weekly Journal, Advocating the Identity of the British Nation with the Lost Ten Tribes of Israel* (London), vol. 5 (July 20, 1881): 298–299; Barkun, *Religion and the Racist Right*; Edward J. Blum, *Reforging the White Republic: Race, Religion, and American Nationalism, 1865–1898* (Baton Rouge: Louisiana State University Press, 2005), 91–97, 103. Beecher's involvement with the First Identity Church is given in Kissick, *The Irish Prince*, 7. See also "City and Suburban News," *New York Times*, February 8, 1882, 8.

86. Pegrum, "Mannaseh's Identification," 298–299.

87. See J. Thomson, "More Blind Evidence on Gen. IX, 25–27," in *The Banner of Israel*, vol. 5 (July 6, 1881), 285, for the identification of the Jews as the House of Judah.

88. Frances A. Yates, *The Rosicrucian Enlightenment* (London: Routledge, 1972). For critiques of Yates's work, see Brian Vickers, "Frances Yates and the Writing of History," *Journal of Modern History* 51, no. 2 (June 1979): 287–316; Wouter J. Hanegraaff, "Beyond the Yates Paradigm: The Study of Western Esotericism between Counterculture and New Complexity," *Aries* 1, no. 1 (2001): 5–37.

89. David Stevenson, *The Origin of Freemasonry: Scotland's Century, 1590–1710* (New York: Cambridge University Press, 1988), 222.

90. The literature on Freemasonry is vast, and includes a large quantity of apocrypha. For an introduction to academic studies of Freemasonry in Europe, see Stevenson, *The Origin of Freemasonry*; and Margaret C. Jacob, *Living the Enlightenment: Freemasonry and Politics in Eighteenth Century Europe* (New York: Oxford University Press, 1991).

91. Steven C. Bullock, *Revolutionary Brotherhood: Freemasonry and the Transformation of the American Social Order, 1730–1840* (Chapel Hill: University of North Carolina Press, 1998); Margaret C. Jacob, *The Origins of Freemasonry: Facts and Fictions* (Philadelphia: University of Pennsylvania Press, 2006).

92. Joseph A. Walkes, Jr., *Black Square and Compass: 200 Years of Prince Hall Freemasonry* (New York: Writer's Press, 1979); Corey D. B. Walker, *A Noble Fight: African American Freemasonry and the Struggle for Democracy in America* (Urbana: University of Illinois Press, 2008); David G. Hackett, "The Prince Hall Masons

and the African American Church: The Labors of Grand Master and Bishop James Walker Hood, 1831–1918," *Church History* 69, no. 4 (December 2000): 770–802; Craig Wilder, *In the Company of Black Men: The African Influence on African American Culture in New York City* (New York: New York University Press, 2001); Theda Skocpol, Ariane Liazos, and Marshall Ganz, *What a Mighty Power We Can Be: African American Fraternal Groups and the Struggle for Racial Equality* (Princeton: Princeton University Press, 2006); Martin Summers, *Manliness and Its Discontents: The Black Middle Class and the Transformation of Masculinity, 1900–1930* (Chapel Hill: University of North Carolina Press, 2004); Stephen Kantrowitz, "'Intended for the Better Government of Man': The Political History of African American Freemasonry in the Era of Emancipation," *Journal of American History* 96, no. 4 (March 2010): 1001–1026.

93. On secret societies in Sierra Leone, see John Thornton, *Africa and Africans in the Making of the Atlantic World, 1400–1680* (Cambridge: Cambridge University Press, 1992), 252.

94. Rachel Beauvoir-Dominique, "Underground Realms of Being: Vodoun Magic," in *Sacred Arts of Haitian Vodou*, ed. Donald J. Cosentino, 159–161 (Los Angeles: UCLA Fowler Museum, 1995). On the Abakua and Arara, see Ivor Miller, *Voice of the Leopard: African Secret Societies in Cuba* (Jackson: University of Mississippi Press, 2009).

95. Scott Trafton. *Egypt Land: Race and Nineteenth-Century American Egyptomania* (Durham: Duke University Press, 2004), 70–72.

96. Mary Ann Clawson, *Constructing Brotherhood: Class, Gender, and Fraternalism* (Princeton: Princeton University Press, 1989), 114–115.

97. Susan Nance, *How the Arabian Nights Inspired the American Dream, 1790–1935* (Chapel Hill: University of North Carolina Press, 2009), 84–85, 92.

98. Piers Mackesy, *British Victory in Egypt, 1801: The End of Napoleon's Conquest* (London: Routledge, 1995); Trafton, *Egypt Land*.

99. See Tony Fels, "Religious Assimilation in a Fraternal Organization: Jews and Freemasonry in Gilded-Age San Francisco," *American Jewish History* 74, no. 4 (1985): 369–403, 378; Samuel Oppenheim, "The Jews and Masonry in the United States before 1810," *Publications of the American Jewish Historical Society* 19 (1910): 1–94; Walkes, *Black Square and Compass*, 140–141. On Jews and Freemasons in Europe, see: Daniel Beresniak, *Juifs et francs-maçons* (Paris: Bibliophane, 1989); Jacob, *Living the Enlightenment*, 66, 80, 102, 130, 154–155, 173–174, 230, 240; Jacob Katz, *Jews and Freemasons in Europe 1723–1939*, tr. Leonard Oschry (Cambridge: Harvard University Press, 1970).

100. Charles W. Ferguson, *Fifty Million Brothers: A Panorama of American Lodges and Clubs* (New York: Farrar & Rinehart, 1937), 247–262.

101. Fels, "Religious Assimilation," 386–390. See also Frances A. Yates, *Giordano Bruno and the Hermetic Tradition* (Chicago: University of Chicago Press, 1964), 273–274; and Gershom Scholem, *Kabbalah* (New York: New American Library

1978), 196–201. Of course, not everyone has agreed that freemasonry is built on a Jewish foundation. One Masonic author, J.S.M. Ward, in *Freemasonry and the Ancient Gods* (London: Simpkin, Marshall, Hamilton, Kent, 1921), wrote that "Freemasonry could not have originated among the orthodox Jews of King Solomon's days.... Not only were they not builders, but their conception of God was and still is entirely different from that which underlies the Masonic ritual" (135). However, Ward does list four avenues of Jewish influence on freemasonry. Moreover, the real issue is not whether or not freemasonry was in fact greatly influenced by Judaism but whether it could be interpreted as such. Numerous authors were willing to answer that question in the affirmative.

102. "Freemasonry and Religion: A Concise View of the Origins, Progress, and Ultimate Aims of the Masonic Institution," *The Hebrew* (San Francisco), August 25, 1865, 4, quoted in Fels, "Religious Assimilation," 390.

103. Rabbi Isaac M. Wise, *The Israelite*, August 3, 1855.

104. James Webb, *The Flight from Reason*, Vol. 1 of *The Age of the Irrational* (London: Macdonald, 1971), 140.

105. Ibid., 140–141.

106. On the Hebraicism of Rosicrucianism, see Yates, *Rosicrucian Enlightenment*, 220–228.

107. Robert Morris, *Freemasonry in the Holy Land, a Narrative of Masonic Explorations Made in 1868, in the Land of King Solomon and the Two Hirams* (La Grange, Ky.: published for the author, 1879); Joseph A. Walkes, Jr., *History of the Shrine: Ancient Egyptian Arabic Order Nobles of the Mystic Shriner, Inc. Prince Hall Affiliated: A Pillar of Black Society* (Detroit: Ancient Egyptian Arabic Order Nobles of the Mystic Shrine of North and South America, 1993), 18.

108. William Carpenter, *The Israelites Found in the Anglo-Saxons* (London: George Kenning, 1874), 1–2.

109. Ibid., 193; Isaiah 42:6.

110. Isaiah 60:2–3 (KJV): "For, behold, the darkness shall cover the earth, and gross darkness the people: but the LORD shall arise upon thee, and his glory shall be seen upon thee. And the Gentiles shall come to thy light, and kings to the brightness of thy rising."

111. On the civilizing mission and the "discourse of civilization" in the United States, see Matthew Frye Jacobson, *Barbarian Virtues: The United States Encounters Foreign Peoples at Home and Abroad 1876–1917* (New York: Hill & Wang, 2000); Evelyn Brooks Higginbotham, *Righteous Discontent: The Women's Movement in the Black Baptist Church, 1880–1920* (Cambridge: Harvard University Press, 1993).

112. William Christian, *Poor Pilgrim's Work* (Texarkana, Ark: Joe Ehrlich's Print, 1896), Preface. The 1916 version is cited in Landing, *Black Judaism*, 49.

113. George W. Stocking, Jr., *Victorian Anthropology* (New York: Free Press, London: Collier Macmillan, 1987); Richard G. Fox and Barbara J. King, eds., *Anthropology*

*beyond Culture.* (Oxford: Berg, 2002); Eric Hobsbawm, *The Age of Empire 1875–1914* (New York: Pantheon, 1987).

114. On Jewish immigration, see: John Higham, *Send These to Me: Immigrants in Urban America*, rev. ed. [1975] (Baltimore: Johns Hopkins University Press, 1984); and Dinnerstein et al., *Natives and Strangers*, 136–137. On the Great Migration, see Joe William Trotter, ed., *The Great Migration in Historical Perspective: New Dimensions of Race, Class & Gender* (Bloomington: Indiana University Press, 1991).

CHAPTER 3

1. Iain MacRobert, *The Black Roots and White Racism of Early Pentecostalism in the USA* (New York: St. Martin's Press, 1988); Ithiel C. Clemmons and Adrienne M. Israel, *Bishop C. H. Mason and the Roots of the Church of God in Christ* (Bakersfield, Cal.: Pneuma Life, 1996).

2. There is now a long literature on Orientalism's impact in American culture in general and African American culture specifically. For the former, see note 36 below. On Orientalism within African American culture, see Reginald Kearney, *African American Views of the Japanese: Solidarity or Sedition?* (Albany: State University of New York Press, 1998); Vijay Prashad, *Everybody Was Kung Fu Fighting: Afro-Asian Connections and the Myth of Cultural Purity* (Boston: Beacon, 2001); Robin D. G. Kelley, *Freedom Dreams: The Black Radical Imagination* (Boston: Beacon, 2002); Bill V. Mullen, *Afro-Orientalism* (Minneapolis: University of Minnesota Press, 2004); Jayna Brown, *Babylon Girls: Black Women Performers and the Shaping of the Modern* (Durham: Duke University Press, 2008).

3. Amiri Baraka considered the African inheritance in African American culture, suggesting that tangible attributes of African cultures did not survive the Middle Passage, but that African *aesthetic* sensibilites remain in Black music. For more on the debates over African "retentions" in the Americas, see the introduction. Amiri Baraka, *Blues People: Negro Music in White America* (New York: W. Morrow, 1963).

4. Vinson Synan, *The Holiness Pentecostal Tradition: Charismatic Movements in the Twentieth Century* (Grand Rapids, Mich.: William B. Eerdmans, 1997), xi, 6–7, 15.

5. Ibid., 4–5.

6. John Wesley, *Journal of John Wesley*, vol. 1, p. 455, cited ibid., 4.

7. John Wesley, *The Works of John Wesley*, vol. 1, p. 103, cited ibid., 4–5.

8. Ibid., 7.

9. David Hempton, *Methodism: Empire of the Spirit* (New Haven: Yale University Press, 2006), 19.

10. Synan, *The Holiness Pentecostal Tradition*, 28; Kathryn T. Long, "Palmer, Phoebe Worrall," in *Historical Dictionary of the Holiness Movement*, ed. William C. Kostlevy (Lanham, Md.: Scarecrow Press, 2001), 196–198.

11. Hempton, *Methodism*, 1–2.

12. David D. Daniels, III, "Pentecostalism," in *Encyclopedia of African American Religions*, ed. Larry G. Murphy, J. Gordon Melton, and Gary L. Ward (New York: Garland, 1993), 586.

13. Synan, *The Holiness Pentecostal Tradition*, 16–20.

14. Robert Maples Anderson, *Vision of the Disinherited* (New York: Oxford University Press, 1979), 29–30.

15. Synan, *The Holiness Pentecostal Tradition*, 23, 26, 31–34.

16. Ibid., 35, 42.

17. Grant Wacker, *Heaven Below: Early Pentecostals and American Culture* (Cambridge: Harvard University Press, 2001), 1.

18. Daniels, "Pentecostalism," 587; Synan, *The Holiness Pentecostal Tradition*, 40; James T. Campbell, *Songs of Zion: The African Methodist Episcopal Church in the United States and South Africa* (New York: Oxford University Press, 1995), 44–51. The first African American Holiness denomination was the Zion Union Apostolic Church, founded in 1869 and reorganized in 1881. See: United States Bureau of the Census, *Religious Bodies . . . : Separate Denominations: History, Description, and Statistics* (Washington, D.C.: Government Printing Office, 1910), 483–484.

19. The Christian Faith Band eventually became a Pentecostal church, The Church of God (Apostolic). See Daniels, "Pentecostalism," 586. Merle D. Strege, "Church of God (Anderson, Indiana)," in *Historical Dictionary of the Holiness Movement*, ed. William C. Kostlevy (Lanham, Md: Scarecrow Press, 2001), 51–52.

20. James R. Goff, Jr., *Fields White unto Harvest: Charles F. Parham and the Missionary Origins of Pentecostalism* (Fayetteville: University of Arkansas Press, 1988), 19–20.

21. Noting the strained ecological and economic setting that gave rise to radical Holiness groups is intended not to assert the existence of a more fundamental economic or material reality underlying theological movements, but rather to note the hardships that accompanied them and perhaps made hard-pressed farmers more interested in radical other-worldly doctrines promising relief from worldly suffering.

22. Synan, *The Holiness Pentecostal Tradition*, 36–37.

23. Daniels, "Pentecostalism," 588; Synan, *The Holiness Pentecostal Tradition*, 54–58.

24. James E. Landing, *Black Judaism: Story of an American Movement* (Durham, N.C.: Carolina Academic Press, 2002), 46.

25. David D. Daniels, "Charles Harrison Mason: The Interracial Impulse of Early Pentecostalism," in *Portraits of a Generation: Early Pentecostal Leaders*, ed. James R. Goff, Jr., and Grant Wacker (Fayetteville: University of Arkansas Press, 2002), 259.

26. Alexander Campbell, *The Christian System: In Reference to the Union of Christians, and a Restoration of Primitive Christianity, as Plead in the Current Reformation* (Cincinnati: Standard Publishing, 1839), 118.

27. Bishop Christian cited Psalms 119:83, Job 30:30, Jeremiah 8:12, Numbers 12:1, and other scriptures in support of the assertion that the ancient Hebrews were Black.

28. William Christian, *Poor Pilgrim's Work, In the Name of the Father, Son and Holy Ghost on Christian Friendship Works No. 3, First Man and Woman: Fallen Angels, or Gentiles in the Land of Nod; Adam and Eve are the Starting Point of the Black People: And Other Important Things* (Texarkana, Ark.: Joe Ehrlich's Print, 1896), 2, 4. Christian cites Job 1:6–12, Job 2:1–6, Rev. 12:7–9 to support the idea that whites were descended from fallen angels.

29. Ibid., 6.

30. Ibid., 19.

31. Ibid., 23–24, 8. Christian cites Rev. 18: 1–24 and James 5:1–3.

32. Ithiel C. Clemmons and Adrienne M. Israel, *Bishop C. H. Mason and the Roots of the Church of God in Christ*, centennial ed. (Bakersfield, Cal.: Pneuma Life, 1996).

33. Landing, *Black Judaism*, 45–50; Elmer T. Clark, *The Small Sects in America* (New York: Abingdon-Cokebury, 1937), 120–121.

34. To the best of my knowledge, no one has noted this link between Bishops Crowdy and Cherry in print. Arthur Huff Fauset, *Black Gods of the Metropolis: Negro Religious Cults of the Urban North* [1944] (Philadelphia: University of Pennsylvania Press, 2002), 34.

35. Ordination certificate for W. O. Dickens, in "Miscellaneous" folder of the W. A. Matthew Collection, Schomburg Center for Research in Black Culture, New York Public Library, Astor, Lenox and Tilden Foundations.

36. There is now much literature on Orientalism's impact on American culture. See Edward Said, *Orientalism* (New York: Pantheon, 1978); William Leach, *Land of Desire: Merchants, Power, and the Rise of a New American Culture* (New York, Vintage, 1993); John Kuo Wei Tchen, *New York before Chinatown: Orientalism and the Shaping of American Culture 1776–1882* (Baltimore: Johns Hopkins University Press, 1999); Holly Edwards, ed., *Noble Dreams, Wicked Pleasures: Orientalism in America, 1870–1930* (Princeton: Princeton University Press, 2000); Timothy Marr, *The Cultural Roots of American Islamicism* (New York: Cambridge University Press, 2006); Susan Nance, *How the Arabian Nights Inspired the American Dream, 1790–1935* (Chapel Hill: University of North Carolina Press, 2009).

37. Rev. Stephen D. Peet, ed., "The Scope of Our Journal" (unsigned editorial), *Oriental and Biblical Journal* (Chicago) 1, no. 1 (January 1880): 22–23.

38. Alfred Thayer Mahan, *The Influence of Sea Power on World History, 1660–1783* (Boston: Little, Brown, 1890).

39. Foreign Missions Conference of North America, *Foreign Missions Conference of North America: Being the Report of the Twenty-Fifth Conference of Foreign Mission Boards in the United States and Canada* (Garden City, N.Y.: Foreign Missions Conference, 1918), 434–436, 275–276.

40. Goff, *Fields White unto Harvest*, 72.

41. Anderson, *Vision of the Disinherited*, 49; Goff, *Fields White unto Harvest*, 72; Sarah E. Parham, ed., *The Life of Charles F. Parham: Founder of the Apostolic Faith Movement* [1930] (New York: Garland, 1985).

42. Charles Parham, *Apostolic Faith* (Topeka) 1 (June 21, 1899): 4, cited in Goff, *Fields White unto Harvest*, 73.

43. "And they were all amazed and marvelled, saying one to another, Behold, are not all these which speak Galilaeans? And how hear we every man in our own tongue, wherein we were born? Parthians, and Medes, and Elamites, and the dwellers in Mesopotamia, and in Judaea, and Cappadocia, in Pontus, and Asia, Phrygia, and Pamphylia, in Egypt, and in the parts of Libya about Cyrene, and strangers of Rome, Jews and proselytes, Cretes and Arabians, we do hear them speak in our tongues the wonderful works of God." Acts 2:1–6; Acts 2:7–11 (KJV).

44. "And the LORD said, Behold, the people is one, and they have all one language; and this they begin to do: and now nothing will be restrained from them, which they have imagined to do. Go to, let us go down, and there confound their language, that they may not understand one another's speech. So the LORD scattered them abroad from thence upon the face of all the earth: and they left off to build the city. Therefore is the name of it called Babel; because the LORD did there confound the language of all the earth: and from thence did the LORD scatter them abroad upon the face of all the earth." Genesis 11:6–9 (KJV).

45. William Charles Hiss, "Shiloh: Frank W. Sandford and the Kingdom: 1898–1948,"(Ph.D. dissertation, Tufts University, 1978, 166–169.

46. Ibid., 170. Wacker, *Heaven Below*, 5, 256.

47. Hiss, "Shiloh", 170.

48. Ibid., 168–169, 181.

49. Isaiah 25:7: "And he will destroy in this mountain the face of the covering cast over all people, and the veil that is spread over all nations." Shirley Nelson and Rudy Nelson, "Frank Sandford: Tongues of Fire in Shiloh, Maine," in *Portraits of a Generation: Early Pentecostal Leaders*, ed. James R. Goff, Jr., and Grant Wacker (Fayetteville: University of Arkansas Press, 2002), 62. The Nelsons reproduce the scriptural reference slightly differently. They also place Sandford's acceptance of Totten's Anglo-Israelite theory in Jerusalem, which is belied by the fact that he espoused the theory in print as early as 1896. See Hiss, *Shiloh*, 168–170.

50. Genesis 49:10: "The sceptre shall not depart from Judah, nor a lawgiver from between his feet, until Shiloh come; and unto him shall the gathering of the people be." Nelson and Nelson, "Frank Sandford," 63.

51. Goff, *Fields White unto Harvest*, 73.

52. Wacker, *Heaven Below*, 28, 172.

53. Anderson, *Vision of the Disinherited*, 49.

54. The passages are Acts 2:4, 10:46; 19:6; 1 Corinthians 14:1–33. Synan, *The Holiness-Pentecostal Tradition*, 91; Anderson, *Vision of the Disinherited*, 52–57; Goff, *Fields White unto Harvest*, 66–72.

55. Charles F. Parham, "The Later Rain: The Story of the Origin of the Original Apostolic or Pentecostal Movements," in Parham, *The Life of Charles F. Parham*, 52–53.

56. "A Queer Faith: Strange Actions of the Apostolic Believers: Are Inspired From God: The Believers Speak a Strange Language and Write a Strange Hand – S.J. Riggins' Extraordinary Statement," *Topeka Daily Capital*, January 6, 1901, 2.

57. "Converts in Zion City Get 'Gift of Tongues,'" miscellaneous news clippings in Parham Family Scrapbook, personal possession of Mrs. Pauline Parham, Dallas, Texas, cited in Goff, Jr., *Fields White unto Harvest*, 37.

58. "A Queer Faith," 2; Wacker, *Heaven Below*, 47.

59. Synan, *The Holiness-Pentecostal Tradition*, 91; Anderson, *Vision of the Disinherited*, 53.

60. *Topeka State Journal*, January 7, 1901, 4, 7.

61. "Wonderful Cures in Kansas," from *Cincinnati Enquirer and Joplin News Herald* (Galena, Kan.), January 27, 1904, in Parham, *The Life of Charles Parham*, 98.

62. Synan places the outbreak of multiple "Chinese" tongues in Houston; Parham's own account, written some years later, places the account of twenty Chinese dialects in the original Topeka revival. Synan, *The Holiness-Pentecostal Tradition*, 94; Parham, "The Later Rain," 54.

63. Parham, *The Life of Charles F. Parham*, 131.

64. Although Parham and later Pentecostals believed that the tongues they received were spiritual gifts, some scholars have explained the phenomenon through a process known as cryptomnesis, in which the brain stores hidden memories of language in the brain, which are only dislodged under stress. Linguists have also determined that glossas are neither gibberish nor language, properly speaking, as they lack grammar, syntax, and systematic connections to the world. William J. Samarin, *Tongues of Men and Angels: The Religious Language of Pentecostalism* (New York: Macmillan, 1972), 115–128.

65. Ibid., 108–109.

66. Marr, *The Cultural Roots of American Islamicism*; Michael B. Oren, *Power, Faith and Fantasy: America in the Middle East: 1776 to the Present* (New York: W. W. Norton: 2007); Nance, *How the Arabian Nights Inspired the American Dream*.

67. Parham, *The Life of Charles F. Parham*, 133.

68. Ibid.

69. Rufus G. W. Sanders, *William Joseph Seymour: 1870–1922* (Sandusky, Ohio: Xulon Press for Alexandria Press, 2003), 68.

70. Allan Anderson, *An Introduction to Pentecostalism: Global Charismatic Christianity* (Cambridge: Cambridge University Press, 2004), 50.

71. Charles F. Parham, *A Voice Crying in the Wilderness* (Baxter Springs, Kan.: R. L. Parham, 1944), reprinted in *The Sermons of Charles F. Parham, "The Higher Christian Life" Sources for the Study of the Holiness, Pentecostal, and Keswick Movements*, ed. Donald W. Dayton (New York: Garland, 1985), 101.

72. "Houstonians Witness the Performance of Miracles. Mysticism Surrounds Work of Apostles of Faith—Speak in All Tongues Known to Man," *Houston Chronicle*, August 13, 1905, in Parham, *The Life of Charles F. Parham*, 122.

73. Parham, *A Voice Crying*, 103.

74. Goff, *Fields White unto Harvest*, 146.

75. Parham, *The Life of Charles F. Parham*, 361.

76. Ibid., 373.

77. Ibid., 376.

78. Ibid., 396. Parham's ambition to make a living from the cultural capital gained through travels in the Orient followed an established model in American popular culture, whereby even travelers who had spent very little time in the Orient represented themselves as experts and made good livings on the lecture circuit. See Nance, *How the Arabian Nights Inspired the American Dream*, 58–82.

79. Charles F. Parham, *The Everlasting Gospel* (Baxter Springs, Kan.: Apostolic Faith Bible College, 1911) in *The Sermons of Charles F. Parham*, 66–67.

80. Parham, *A Voice Crying*, 107.

81. Nelson and Nelson, "Frank Sandford," 66–67.

82. Frank Bartleman, *Azusa Street* (Plainfield, N.J.: Logos International, 1980), 19.

83. Keith Robbins, *England, Ireland, Scotland, Wales: The Christian Church 1900–2000* (Oxford: Oxford University Press, 2008), 93–94; Anderson, *An Introduction to Pentecostalism*, 36; Eifon Evans, *The Welsh Revival of 1904* (Bridgend: Evangelical Press of Wales, 1969), 190–196; Wacker, *Heaven Below*, 21, 102, 256.

84. Bartleman, *Azusa Street*, 35; Anderson, *An Introduction to Pentecostalism*, 37; Wacker, *Heaven Below*, 43.

85. Goff, *Fields White unto Harvest*, 57, 101; Clare Adkin, Jr., *Brother Benjamin: A History of the Israelite House of David* (Berrien Springs, Mich.: Andrews University Press, 1990).

86. Benjamin Franklin Purnell and Mary Purnell, *The Seven Books of Wisdom* (Benton Harbor, Mich.: Israelite House of David, c. 1914), ii; accessed on http://hdl.handle.net/2027/mdp.39015071584125.

87. Adkin, *Brother Benjamin*; Elaine Cotsirilos Thomopoulos, *Images of America: St. Joseph and Benton Harbor* (Charleston, S.C.: Arcadia Publishing, 2003), 117–122; Rebecca Alpert, *Out of Left Field: Jews and Black Baseball* (New York: Oxford University Press, 2011).

88. Wacker, *Heaven Below*, 232.

89. Bartleman, *Azusa Street*, 43.

90. Vinson Synan, "Frank Bartleman and Azusa Street," in Bartleman, *Azusa Street*, xi; Bartleman, *Azusa Street*, 19.

91. Bartleman, *Azusa Street*, 51–52.

92. Ibid., 53. Ironically, Pentecostal scholars have frequently cited Bartleman's vivid phrase about the color line without his preceding sentence, which significantly alters its import.

93. Sanders, *William Joseph Seymour*, 68–73.

94. Bartleman, *Azusa Street*, 57–58.

95. Synan, *The Holiness-Pentecostal Tradition*, 96.

96. Wacker, *Heaven Below*, 49.

97. Bartleman, *Azusa Street*, 56.

98. Ibid.

99. Ibid., 57.

100. "Weird Babel of Tongues: New Sect of Fanatics Is Breaking Loose—Wild Scene Last Night on Azusa Street—Gurgle of Worldless Talk by a Sister," *Los Angeles Daily Times*, April 18, 1906, 1.

101. Parham, *Sermons of Charles F. Parham*, 72.

102. Wacker, *Heaven Below*, 42.

103. *Spirit and Power: A 10-Country Survey of Pentecostals* (Washington, D.C.: Pew Forum on Religion and Public Life, October 2006), 3–10.

104. Albert Raboteau, *Slave Religion: The "Invisible Institution" in the Antebellum South* (New York: Oxford University Press, 2004), 10–11, 17, 19, 20, 27–28, 35–36, 44–92; Charles Joyner, *Down By the Riverside: A South Carolina Slave Community* (Urbana: University of Illinois Press, 1984), 141–144.

105. Milton C. Sernett, *Black Religion and American Evangelicalism: White Protestants, Plantation Missions, and the Flowering of Negro Christianity, 1787–1865* (Metuchen, N.J.: Scarecrow Press and the American Theological Library Association, 1975), 104–105. Iain MacRobert is not the only one to reductively equate emotionalism with Africanism in Black worship; see also Walter F. Pitts, Jr., *Old Ship of Zion: The Afro-Baptist Ritual in the African Diaspora* (New York: Oxford University Press, 1993).

106. Milton Sernett, *Bound for the Promised Land: African American Religion and the Great Migration* (Durham: Duke University Press, 1997), 4, 29, 190; Wallace D. Best, *Passionately Human, No Less Divine: Religion and Culture in Black Chicago, 1915–1952* (Princeton: Princeton University Press, 2005), 57–59, 98–101.

107. Melville Jean Herskovits, *The Myth of the Negro Past* (Boston: Beacon, 1941), 10, 93.

CHAPTER 4

1. State Department Memo, Washington D.C., to Addis Ababa, Ethiopia, NE HLD/GC No. 231, no date (c. 1934), State Department Series 884.55/2, National Archives and Records Administration, College Park, Maryland (hereafter NARA), 4.

2. James E. Landing, *Black Judaism: Story of an American Movement* (Durham, N.C.: Carolina Academic Press, 2002), 66.

3. E. T. Clark, *The Small Sects in America* (Nashville, Tenn.: Abingdon, 1949), 129; Hans A. Baer, *The Black Spiritual Movement: A Religious Response to Racism* (Knoxville: University of Tennessee Press, 1984), 83; Landing, *Black Judaism*, 65–66.

4. Sherry Sherrod DuPree, ed., *Biographical Dictionary of African-American Holiness-Pentecostals, 1880–1990* (Washington, D.C.: Middle Atlantic Regional

Press, 1989), 136; DuPree, ed., *African-American Holiness Pentecostal Movement: An Annotated Bibliography* (New York: Garland, 1996), 141, 148.

5. DuPree, *Biographical Dictionary*, 136; DuPree, *Annotated Bibliography*, 141, 148.

6. On the Jewish immigration, see John Higham, *Send These to Me: Immigrants in Urban America* [rev. ed., 1975] (Baltimore: Johns Hopkins University Press, 1984); Leonard Dinnerstein et al., *Natives and Strangers: Blacks, Indians, and Immigrants in America*, 2nd ed. (New York: Oxford University Press, 1990), 136–137; Ruth Gay, *Unfinished People: Eastern European Jews Encounter America* (New York: W. W. Norton, 2001). On Jews and Blacks in Harlem, see Gilbert Osofsky, *Harlem: The Making of a Ghetto: Negro New York, 1890–1930* (New York: Harper Torchbooks, 1963); Jeffrey S. Gurock, *When Harlem Was Jewish, 1870–1930* (New York: Columbia University Press, 1979). On the West Indian immigration, which was concentrated on New York City, see Irma Watkins-Owens, *Blood Relations: Caribbean Immigrants and the Harlem Community 1900–1930* (Bloomington: Indiana University Press, 1996), 4, 45, 55; Winston James, *Holding Aloft the Banner of Ethiopia: Caribbean Radicalism in Early Twentieth-Century America* (London: Verso, 1998), 12–13, 355–364. On the African American Great Migration, see *The Great Migration in Historical Perspective: New Dimensions of Race, Class & Gender*, ed. Joe William Trotter (Bloomington: Indiana University Press, 1991); James R. Grossman, *Land of Hope: Chicago, Black Southerners, and the Great Migration* (Chicago: University of Chicago Press, 1991); Milton Sernett, *Bound for the Promised Land: African American Religion and the Great Migration* (Durham: Duke University Press, 1997); Eric Arneson, ed., *Black Protest and the Great Migration: A Brief History with Documents* (New York: Bedford/St. Martin's, 2002).

7. James, *Holding Aloft the Banner of Ethiopia*, 12–13, 355–364; Osofsky, *Harlem: The Making of a Ghetto*, 113, 128–130, 141; Jervis Anderson, *This Was Harlem, 1900–1950* (New York: Farrar, Straus, Giroux, 1981), 301.

8. James Landing depicts the continuities between different generations of Black Israelite groups as the result of direct transfer, whereas I see them as influencing one another but less directly connected. See Landing, *Black Judaism*, 121.

9. Edward Wolf, "Negro 'Jews': A Social Study," *Jewish Social Service Quarterly* 9 (June 1933): 314. Wolf refers to Robinson using the pseudonym "Abraham."

10. Ruth Landes, "Negro Jews in Harlem," *Jewish Journal of Sociology* 9, no. 2 (December 1967): 178.

11. Ibid., 178; Wolf, "Negro 'Jews,'" 314–315; Landing, *Black Judaism*, 121.

12. Wolf, "Negro 'Jews,'" 314–315, Landes, "Negro Jews in Harlem," 178.

13. Wolf, "Negro 'Jews,'" 315.

14. Landing, *Black Judaism*, 122.

15. Ibid.; Wolf, "Negro 'Jews,'" 315.

16. Landes, "Negro Jews in Harlem," 178. Landes's assessment of Rabbi Ford's movement as being nothing more than a version of Black nationalism is suspect, making her assessment of other groups' beliefs to be suspect as well. J. Lorand

Matory's discusses Landes's inadvertent impact on Afro-Brazlian religion: J. Lorand Matory, *Black Atlantic Religion: Tradition, Transnationalism, and Matriarchy in the Afro-Brazilian Candomblé* (Princeton: Princeton University Press, 2005), 188–223. See also Gelya Frank, "Jews, Multiculturalism, and Boasian Anthropology," *American Anthropologist* 99, no. 4 (December 1997): 736–737.

17. Landing, *Black Judaism*, 122.

18. Jill Watts, *God, Harlem U.S.A.: The Father Divine Story* (Berkeley: University of California Press, 1992). James Landing makes a similar comparison: Landing, *Black Judaism*, 128.

19. Landing, *Black Judaism*, 125.

20. Wolf, "Negro 'Jews,'" 315.

21. Landing, *Black Judaism*, 126.

22. Wolf, "Negro 'Jews,'" 315, 319.

23. Rabbi Wentworth Arthur Matthew, quoted in Howard Brotz, *The Black Jews of Harlem: Negro Nationalism and the Dilemmas of Negro Leadership* (New York: Free Press of Glencoe, 1964), 11. For an excellent lengthy account of Elder Roberson and his movement, see Landing, *Black Judaism*, 121–129.

24. Arnold Josiah Ford, Certificate of Baptism, June 17, 1877, Barbados, copied and issued September 6, 1972, in author's possession, copied from Abraham (Abiyi) Ford; Abraham (Abiyi) Ford (son of Arnold Josiah Ford), interview by author, Washington, D.C., May 10, 1999.

25. "Certificate of the Service of Arnold Ford in the Royal Navy," in author's possession, copied from Abraham (Abiyi) Ford. See also J. F. Heijbroek, "Ford, Arnold Josiah," in *American National Biography*, ed. John A. Garraty and Mark C. Carnes (New York: Oxford University Press, 1999), 217–218.

26. Abraham (Abiyi) Ford, interview by author, Washington, D.C., May 11, 1999.

27. Biographical details come from the 1920 United States Census (F630, Enumeration District 1335, Sheet 22, Line 48); *Who's Who in Colored America: A Biographical Dictionary of Notable Living Persons of Negro Descent*, ed. Joseph J. Boris (New York: Who's Who in Colored America Corp., 1927), 131; and the minutes of the New Amsterdam Musical Association, found in the Samuel Edwin Heyward Jr. Papers, Box 3, "Minute Book, 1906–1915," Schomburg Center for Research in Black Culture, New York Public Library, Astor, Lenox and Tilden Foundations (hereafter Schomburg Center).

28. Ted Vincent, *Keep Cool: The Black Activists Who Built the Jazz Age* (London: Pluto Press, 1995), 62, 107. 137–141; Arlene Ford Straw, interview by author, May 18, 1999, Coney Island, New York, notes. On the A.B.B., see Robert Hill, "Racial and Radical: Cyril V. Briggs, THE CRUSADER Magazine, and the African Blood Brotherhood, 1918–1922," introduction to *The Crusader: September 1918-August 1919*, vol. 1, ed. Robert A. Hill (New York: Garland, 1987), v–lxvi; James, *Holding Aloft the Banner of Ethiopia*, 156–162, 173, 178–180, 190; Minkah Makalani, *In*

*the Cause of Freedom: Radical Black Internationalism from Harlem to London, 1917–1939* (Chapel Hill: University of North Carolina Press, 2011).

29. "Ford, Arnold" and "Ford, Olive" (38 West 131st Street, New York New York), *Fourteenth Census of the United States, 1920* (Series T625, Roll 1221, Page 265, Enumeration District 1335, Sheet 22, Lines 98, 99).

30. Arlene Ford Straw, interview by author, May 18, 1999.

31. Marcus Garvey, *Philosophy and Opinions of Marcus Garvey*, ed. Amy Jacques Garvey (New York: Arno Press, 1968); Theodore G. Vincent, *Black Power and the Garvey Movement* (Berkeley: Ramparts Press, 1971); John Henrik Clarke, ed., *Marcus Garvey and the Vision of Africa* (New York: Vintage Books, 1974); Judith Stein, *The World of Marcus Garvey: Race and Class in Modern Society* (Baton Rouge: Louisiana State University Press, 1986); Mary G. Rolinson, *Grassroots Garveyism: The Universal Negro Improvement Association in the Rural South, 1920–1927* (Chapel Hill: University of North Carolina Press, 2007); Colin Grant, *Negro with a Hat: The Rise and Fall of Marcus Garvey* (New York: Oxford University Press, 2008).

32. Heijbroek, "Ford, Arnold Josiah."

33. Sholomo B. Levy, "Ford, Arnold Josiah," in *Harlem Renaissance Lives: From the African American National Biography*, ed. Henry Louis Gates and Evelyn Brooks Higginbotham (New York: Oxford University Press, 2009), 205.

34. Randall K. Burkett, *Garveyism as a Religious Movement: The Institutionalization of a Black Civil Religion* (Metuchen, N.J.: Scarecrow Press, 1978), 36, 44.

35. Ben Burrell and Arnold Josiah Ford, "The Universal Ethiopian Anthem," in *The Universal Ethiopian Hymnal* (New York: Beth B'Nai Abraham Publishing, 1922). Manuscripts, Archives and Rare Books Division, Schomburg Center.

36. Landes, "Negro Jews," 184; Arlene Ford Straw, interview by author, May 18, 1999.

37. Arlene Ford Straw, interview by author, May 18, 1999.

38. "Ford, Arnold Josiah," in *Who's Who in Colored America*, 131.

39. Interview with Vertella S. Gadsden, Valentine's daughter, August 12, 1995; Heijbroek, "Ford, Arnold Josiah," 276; Landing, *Black Judaism*, 130.

40. "Jewish Girl Honored," *New York Amsterdam News*, December 20, 1933.

41. Wolf, "Negro 'Jews,'": 316; Landing, *Black Judaism*, 130.

42. In 1925 Ford spoke to a judge in Yiddish. See "Negro Jews Win in Rent Suit," *New York Amsterdam News*, December 23, 1925, in Black Jews Vertical File, Schomburg Center. The account of Ford serving as a middleman for Herman comes from Wolf, "Negro 'Jews,'" 316.

43. Rabbi Eliezer Brooks, interview by author, August 14, 1996, Bronx, New York, tape recording.

44. "Ford, Arnold Josiah," in *Who's Who in Colored America*, 131.

45. Levy, "Ford, Arnold Josiah," 206.

46. Landes, "Negro Jews in Harlem," 180.

47. Levy, "Ford, Arnold Josiah," 206.

48. Ibid.

49. Landing, *Black Judaism*, 130.

50. By this time Noble Drew Ali's Moorish Science Temple had gained some notoriety, and Herman's choice of the similar-sounding Moorish Zionist Temple (MZT) could not have been accidental. Herman's story that the organization had been founded by a rabbi with the curiously French name "Richelieu" in 1899 was most likely an apocryphal attempt to claim an origin older than the MZT's more famous Islamic counterpart. The similarity of their names is also indicative of the fact that Black Israelites and Black Muslims of the 1920s were close cousins who shared similar influences, beliefs, and even rituals. The MZT's claim to date from 1899 is highly implausible. If there was a "Moorish" rabbi in New York at the turn of the century, why would he carry such a European name? Second, the origin date claimed predates the influx of Black Israelite faith with the spread of Prophet Crowdy's Church of God and Saints of Christ. Third, it is highly unlikely that such a group could have operated unnoticed in New York for twenty-five years, especially when New York's active Yiddish-language press carried stories about other Black Jewish sects, such as Elder Roberson's Black Jews. I have been able to find only one press account of "Negro Hebrews" in New York from before the First World War era. That account, from 1898, was of a twenty-five-year-old African American named Samuel Muskowitz, called before a New York City court, who claimed not to speak English and was alleged to be able to speak and write Hebrew. Muskowitz's interpreter claimed there were 300 "Negro Hebrews" in New York, and "they all come from Jerusalem." "Race Flashes: Negro Hebrews in New York: Three Hundred in the City—All Come From Jerusalem," *Fair Play* (Kansas) (November 4, 1898), 1. This story is no more plausible than that of the Moorish rabbi Richelieu. On similarities between Black Jews and Black Muslims in the interwar period, see Jacob S. Dorman, "Black Orientalism and Black Gods of the Metropolis," in *The New Black Gods: Arthur Huff Fauset and the Study of African American Religions*, ed. Edward E. Curtis IV and Danielle Brune Sigler (Bloomington: Indiana University Press, June 2009), 116–142.

51. Landes, "Negro Jews," 182.

52. Rabbi Arnold Josiah Ford to Jacques Faitlovitch, "Short History of the Congregation Beth B'nai Abraham, New York, N.Y." n.p., n.d. (c. 1924–1930), Jacques Faitlovitch Collection, folder 82, Sourasky Central Library, Tel Aviv University.

53. Ibid.

54. Ibid.

55. Ibid.

56. B. Z. Goldberg, "A Negro Bris," *B'Nai B'Rith Magazine* (New York) 41, no. 11 (August 1927): 465.

57. Ibid., 466; B. Z. Goldberg, Untitled, in *Negro and Jew: An Encounter in America*, ed. Shlomo Katz (New York: Macmillan, 1967), 56.

58. Goldberg, "A Negro Bris," 466.

59. Vertella Gadsden, interview by author, August 12, 1995; Landing, *Black Judaism*, 135.
60. Sidney Kobre, "Rabbi Ford," *Reflex* 4, no. 1 (January 1929), 26.
61. Goldberg, "A Negro Bris," 466.
62. Ibid.
63. Ford to Faitlovitch, "Short History of the Congregation Beth B'nai Abraham," n.p.
64. Ibid.
65. Goldberg, "A Negro Bris," 466.
66. Ford to Faitlovitch, "Short History of the Congregation Beth B'nai Abraham," n.p..
67. Sidney Kobre, "Rabbi Ford," 25.
68. Sidney Kobre, "Rabbi Ford," 26, 28.
69. Ibid., 28.
70. State Department Memo, Washington, D.C., to Addis Ababa, Ethiopia, NE HLD/ GC No. 231, no date (c. 1934), State Department Series 884.55/2, NARA, 5.
71. Special Agent L. A. Mullen, February 19, 1932, State Department Records Series FW 884.55/2, NARA, 6; Ted Vincent, *Keep Cool: The Black Activists Who Built the Jazz Age* (London, CT: Pluto Press, 1995), 62, 107, 137–141; interview with Arlene Ford Straw, May 18, 1999; Earl E. Titus, FBI Report, January 18, 1924, Case Number 190–1781–6, NARA.
72. Robert A. Hill, "Dread History: Leonard Howell and Millenarian Visions in Early Rastafari Religion in Jamaica," *Epoché: Jounal of the History of Religions at UCLA* 9 (1981): 38.
73. Landes, *Negro Jews*, 184.
74. Arnold Josiah Ford, "Africa," Sheet Music Collection, Schomburg Center; Sylvester A. Johnson, *The Myth of Ham in Nineteenth-Century American Christianity: Race, Heathens, and the People of God* (New York: Palgrave Macmillan, 2004).
75. Edward Wilmot Blyden, "Mohammedanism and the Negro Race," in *Christianity, Islam, and the Negro Race* [1888] (Baltimore: Black Classic Press, 1994), 19.
76. Kobre, "Rabbi Ford," 26.
77. Ibid., 27.
78. Ibid.
79. Ibid.
80. Landing, *Black Judaism*, 135.
81. J. Gordon Melton, "Bible Sabbath Association" and "Sabbatarianism," in *Encyclopedia of Protestantism* (New York: Facts on File, 2005), 85–86, 477–479.
82. Landing, *Black Judaism*, 133.
83. Ibid., 129.
84. Kobre, "Rabbi Ford," 25.
85. Ibid.
86. On the B.B.A.'s rejection of Jesus, see Goldberg, "A Negro Bris," 465–466.

87. Kobre, "Rabbi Ford," 25–29.

88. Landes, "Negro Jews," 182–185.

89. Landing, *Black Judaism*, 135.

90. Wolf, "Negro 'Jews,'" 317.

91. Personal correspondence, Rabbi Arnold J. Ford to Rabbi W. A. Matthew, June 5, 1931, Wentworth A. Matthew MS, Schomburg Center.

92. Abiyi Ford, interview by author, May 10, 1999.

93. Ibid.

94. Goldberg, "A Negro Bris," 465–466.

95. "Court Halts Sale of Harlem Stock by Negro Jews: B'nai Abraham Progressive Corp., Insolvent since October, Bows to Order," *New York Herald Tribune*, December 9, 1930, 19.

96. Vertella Gadsden, interview by author, August 12, 1995; Landing, *Black Judaism*, 135.

97. Arnold Rose, *The Negro's Morale: Group Identity and Protest* (Minneapolis: University of Minnesota Press, 1949), 43–44; Colin Legum, *Pan-Africanism: A Short Political Guide, Revised Edition* (New York: Praeger, 1965), 14, 17, 33; Essien Udosen Essien-Udom, *Black Nationalism: A Search for An Identity in America* (Chicago: University of Chicago Press, 1971), 250. Harry Haywood defined cooperation with one's enemies as "a characteristic feature of zionist type nationalist movements," and discussed Garvey and Herzel in this light; Haywood, "The Nation of Islam: An Estimate" *Soulbook* 6 (Winter–Spring 1967): 140. See also Ernest Allen, Jr., "Religious Heterodoxy and Nationalist Tradition: The Continuing Evolution of the Nation of Islam," *Black Scholar* 26, no. 3–4 (Fall–Winter 1996): 5; Ibrahim K. Sundiata, *Brothers and Strangers: Black Zion, Black Slavery, 1914–1940* (Durham: Duke University Press, 2003).

98. Edward Wilmot Blyden, *The Jewish Question* (Liverpool: Lionel Hart, 1898), 7.

99. "Thousands Pack Liberty Hall to Hear Messages of Inspiration and Hope," *Negro World*, July 17, 1920, Report of U.N.I.A. Meeting, July 11, 1920, New York City, in Hill et al., *Garvey Papers*, 2: 411.

100. Robin D. G. Kelley, "Afric's Sons with Banner Red," in *Race Rebels: Culture, Politics and the Black Working Class* (New York: Free Press, 1994), 107.

101. Marcus Garvey, speech in Toronto on August 29, 1937, in Robert A. Hill, Barbara Bair, and Edith Johnson, eds., *The Marcus Garvey and Universal Negro Improvement Association Papers*, vol. 7 (Berkeley: University of California Press, 1990), 774.

102. Marcus Garvey, speech in Nova Scotia c. October 1, 1937, ibid., 792. See also "Sacrifice and Success the Theme at Liberty Hall," *Negro World*, March 6, 1920, in Hill et al., *Garvey Papers*, vol. 2 (Berkeley: University of California Press, 1983), 235–236.

103. Marcus Garvey, "A Barefaced Coloured Leader," editorial in the *Black Man*, London, July 1935, in Hill et al., *Garvey Papers*, 7: 632.

104. "Confidential Informant 800 to George F. Ruch," c. November 25, 1921, in Hill et al., *Garvey Papers*, vol. 4 (Berkeley: University of California Press, 1985), 217.

105. Biography of Julian William Mack (1866–1943), in Hill et al., *Garvey Papers*, vol. 5 (Berkeley: University of California Press, 1986), 301.

106. *Philadelphia Tribune*, September 27, 1928, quoted in J. A. Rogers, "Additional Facts on Marcus Garvey and His Trial for Using the Mails to Defraud," Negroes of New York Writers Program, New York, 1939, cited in Hill, et al., *Garvey Papers*, 5: 367.

107. Marcus Garvey, "Message from Marcus Garvey" Tombs Prison, New York City, June 19, 1923, in Garvey, *The Philosophy and Opinions of Marcus Garvey*, vol. 1, 218.

108. Rogers, "Additional Facts on Marcus Garvey" in Hill et al., *Garvey Papers*, 5: 367.

109. Marcus Garvey, "The Jews on the Run," editorial, *The Black Man* (March 1936), in Hill et al., *Garvey Papers*, 7: 667.

110. William R. Scott, *The Sons of Sheba's Race: African-Americans and the Italo-Ethiopian War, 1935–1941* (Bloomington: Indiana University Press, 1993), 181–182.

111. Kobre, "Rabbi Ford," 28.

112. State Department Memo, Washington, D.C., to Addis Ababa, Ethiopia, NE HLD/GC No. 231, no date (c. 1934), State Department Series 884.55/2, NARA, 2; William R. Scott, "Rabbi Arnold Ford's Back-to-Ethiopia Movement: A Study of Black Emigration, 1930–1935," *Pan-African Journal* 8, no. 3 (Summer 1975): 194.

113. State Department Memo, NE HLD/GC No. 231, 2.

114. Special Agent L. A. Mullen, February 19, 1932, State Department Records Series FW 884.55/2, NARA.

115. Arlene Ford Straw, interview by author, May 18, 1999.

116. George Shepperson, "Ethiopianism and African Nationalism," *Phylon* 14, no. 1 (1953), 9–18; Landing, *Black Judaism*, 339.

117. Landing, *Black Judaism*, 339; Scott, *Sons of Sheba's Race*; James, *Holding Aloft*; Robin D. G. Kelley, "This Ain't Ethiopia, But It'll Do," chapter 6 in *Race Rebels: Culture, Politics, and the Black Working Class*, 129.

118. William A Shack, "Ethiopia and Afro-Americans: Some Historical Notes, 1920–1970," *Phylon* 35, no. 2 (1974): 145.

119. Burkett, *Garveyism as a Religious Movement*, 34–35, 85–86, 122, 125, 134–135; G. A. Nelson, "Rastafarians and Ethiopianism," in *Imagining Home: Class, Culture and Nationalism in the African Diaspora*, ed. Sidney Lemelle and Robin D. G. Kelley (New York: Verso, 1994), 69.

120. Tudor Parfitt, *The Lost Ark of the Covenant: Solving the 2,500-Year Old Mystery of the Fabled Biblical Ark* (New York: Harper Collins, 2008), 182.

121. David Francis Kessler, *The Falashas: A Short History of the Ethiopian Jews*, 3rd rev. ed. (London: Routledge, 1996), 15.

122. James Quirin, *The Evolution of the Ethiopian Jews: A History of the Beta Israel (Falasha) to 1920* (Philadelphia: University of Pennsylvania Press, 1992), 199.

123. Israel J. Gerber, *The Heritage Seekers: American Blacks in Search of Jewish Identity* (Middle Village, N.Y.: Jonathan David, 1977), 16. For an early example of an article on Ethiopian Jews in a Black newspaper, see M. A. Majors, "Black Jews Black Irishmen Black Dutchmen," *Chicago Defender*, July 19, 1913, 2. On Faitlovitch's visit to New York, see Quirin, *Evolution of the Ethiopian Jews*, 191–200; Emanuela Trevisan Semi, "The 'Falashisation' of the Blacks of Harlem: A Judaising Movement in 20th-century USA," in *Judaising Movements: Studies in the Margins of Judaism*, ed. Tudor Parfitt and Emanuela Trevisan Semi (London: Routledge, 2002), 87–110.

124. Goldberg, "Negro Bris," 466.

125. Shack, "Ethiopia and Afro-Americans," 147.

126. Jerrold Robbins, "The Americans in Ethiopia," *American Mercury* 29 (May 1933): 69.

127. Edna Jackson to Franklin D. Roosevelt, April 13, 1933, State Department Series 884.55/13, NARA; James Moody to President Franklin D. Roosevelt, June 21, 1935, State Department Series 884.55/11/3, NARA. Note that this James Moody was not the jazz saxophonist, who was born in 1925.

128. Addison E. Southard, U.S. Consul, Addis Ababa, to Wallace Murray, Department of State, Washington, D.C., October 20, 1931, State Department Series 033.8411/80, NARA.

129. Ibid.

130. James L. Park, Chargé d'Affaires, Ethiopia, to the Secretary of State, Washington, D.C., July 1, 1930, State Department Series 884.51 A/1, NARA.

131. Shack. "Ethiopia and Afro-Americans," 142–155.

132. State Department Memo, Washington, D.C., to Addis Ababa, Ethiopia, NE HLD/GC No. 231, no date (c. 1934), , State Department Series 884.55/2, NARA, 2.

133. Addison E. Southard to the Secretary of State, May 7, 1932, State Department Series 884.55/8. NARA.

134. Carleton S. Coon, *Measuring Ethiopia and Flight into Arabia* (London: Jonathan Cape, 1936), 64–68.

135. Personal correspondence, Rabbi Arnold J. Ford to Rabbi W. A. Matthew, June 5, 1931, Wentworth A. Matthew MS, Schomburg Center.

136. Addison E. Southard to the Secretary of State, May 7, 1932, State Department Series 884.55/8, NARA.

137. Ibid.

138. Addison E. Southard to the Secretary of State, June 15, 1933, State Department Records Series 884.55/15, NARA.

139. R. B. Shipley to William A. Newcome, Ira F. Hoyt et al., passport agents, January 20, 1932, State Department Records Series 884.55/2, NARA.

140. Personal correspondence, Rabbi Ford to Rabbi W. A. Matthew, June 5, 1931. Wentworth A. Matthews Collection, Schomburg Center.
141. Ibid.
142. Ibid.
143. Ibid.
144. Coon, *Measuring Ethiopia*, 136.
145. John H. Spencer, *Ethiopia at Bay: A Personal Account of the Haile Selassie Years* (Hollywood, Cal.: Tsehai Publishers, 2006), 306.
146. Coon, *Measuring Ethiopia*, 148.
147. Rabbi Hailu Moshe Paris, interview by author, May 1999, New York, New York.
148. State Department Memo, Washington D.C., to Addis Ababa, Ethiopia, NE HLD/ GC No. 231, no date (c. 1934), State Department Series 884.55/2, NARA, 2–3.
149. Ibid., 3–4.
150. Ibid., 3.
151. Ibid.
152. Addison E. Southard to the Secretary of State, October 8, 1932, Dispatch No. 1056, State Department Series 884.55/12, NARA.
153. Ibid. See also Robert F. Fernald, American Consul, Puerto Cabezas, Nicaragua, to the Secretary of State, Washington, D.C., December 21, 1931, State Department Series 884.55/2, NARA.
154. Southard to the Secretary of State, October 8, 1932, Dispatch No. 1056.
155. Judith Stein, *The World of Marcus Garvey: Race and Class in Modern Society* (Baton Rouge: Louisiana State University Press, 1986), 7–23; Kevin K. Gaines, *Uplifting the Race: Black Leadership, Politics, and Culture in the Twentieth Century* (Chapel Hill: University of North Carolina Press, 1996), 37, 39, 74, 84, 126, 240, 257.
156. F. A. Cowan to Lawrence Beckford, September 29, 1931, Department of State Series 884.55/9, NARA.
157. Gail Bederman, *Manliness & Civilization: A Cultural History of Gender & Race in the United States, 1880–1917* (Chicago: University of Chicago Press, 1995); Gaines, *Uplifting the Race*, 126.
158. Burrell and Ford, "The Universal Ethiopian Anthem."
159. Kantiba Gebrou to Mrs. Edna Jackson, June 1933, State Department Series 884.55/13, NARA.
160. Coon, *Measuring Ethiopia*, 137; Addison Southard, Addis Ababa, "Enclosure with Dispatch No. 545," October 6, 1930, Department of State Series 166.121, NARA; Southard to the Secretary of State, November 2, 1931, Department of State Series 884.55/3, NARA.
161. Wallace Murray to Mr. Castle, January 18, 1932, Department of State, Division of Near Eastern Affairs, FW.884.55/1/4, NARA; L. A. Mullen to Mr. A. R. Burr, February 19, 1932, Department of State, Division of Near Eastern Affairs, FW 884.55/2, NARA.

162. Addison Southard to the Secretary of State, June 15, 1933, Department of State Series 884.55/15, NARA.

163. Addison Southard to the Secretary of State, May 7, 1933, Department of State Series 884.55/8, NARA..

164. Coon, *Measuring Ethiopia*, 140.

165. Ibid.

166. Ibid.

167. According to the U.S. State Department, "approximately 100 American and West Indian negroes emigrated from the United States to this country [Ethiopia]." William M. Crump, U.S. vice consul, Addis Ababa, Ethiopia, to Secretary of State, Washington, D.C., April 18, 1935, State Department Series 884.55/1, NARA.

168. State Department Memo, Washington D.C., to Addis Ababa, Ethiopia, NE HLD/ GC No. 231, no date (c. 1934), State Department Series 884.55/2, NARA, 2.

169. Abiyi Ford, interview by author, May 10, 1999.

170. Ibid.; Addison Southard to the Secretary of State, May 7, 1933, Department of State Series 884.55/8, NARA.

171. Abiyi Ford, interview by author, May 10, 1999; death certificate: Arnold Josiah Ford, "Rabbi and Professor of Music. British subject by birth in Barbados, British West Indies" Died September 17, 1935, Addis Ababa, registered October 13, 1939, Frank Stannard Gibbs, Acting British Consul General.

172. Coon, *Measuring Ethiopia*, 137; Kenneth J. King, "Some Notes on Arnold J. Ford and New World Black Attitudes to Ethiopia," in *Black Apostles: Afro-American Clergy Confront the Twentieth Century*, ed. Randall K. Burkett and Richard Newman (Boston: G. K. Hall, 1978), 53.

173. William Phillips, Under Secretary of State, Washington, D.C., to Harry L. Hopkins, Federal Emergency Relief Administrator, Washington, D.C., June 17, 1935, State Department Series 384.1115/6, NARA; Louise White, Ethiopia, to U.S. State Department, Washington, D.C., July 25, 1932, State Department Series 384.1115 White, NARA.

174. Hailu Moshe Paris, interview by author, May 17, 1999, Harlem, New York City.

175. Alien Ship List Manifest, *SS St. Louis*, Hamburg—New York, September 12, 1936, NARA Northeast Regional Branch, New York City. See also Richard Yaffe, "Future Bleak for Bronx Black Jews," *Heritage* (Los Angeles), March 23, 1973, 9, 12. Rabbi Isaac Trainin, a pivotal figure in the New York Jewish Federation in the sixties, erroneously claimed that Paris's Ethiopian nativity is fictitious and that he was actually from Jamaica. Rabbi Isaac N. Trainin, interview by author, August 31, 1995, New York, New York, tape recording.

176. Gordon Thomas and Max Morgan Witts, *Voyage of the Damned* (New York: Stein and Day, 1974).

177. See, for example Leonard E. Barrett, Sr., *The Rastafarians* (Boston: Beacon, 1997), 104–111.

178. Hill, "Dread History," 37.

179. Ibid., 37.

180. Ibid., 38; Ennis Barrington Edmonds, *Rastafari: From Outcasts to Culture Bearers* (New York: Oxford University Press, 2003), 39.

181. Vijay Prashad, *Everybody Was Kung Fu Fighting: Afro-Asian Connections and the Myth of Cultural Purity* (Boston: Beacon, 2001), 90–91.

182. Barry Chevannes, *Social Origins of the Rastafari Movement* (Mona, Jamaica: Institute of Social and Economic Research, 1978), 132.

183. Hill, "Dread History," 38.

184. Chevannes, *Social Origins*, 132.

185. Hill, "Dread History," 38.

186. Ibid., 33. Hill cites the *Amsterdam News*, January 4, 1931, which is not part of the only extant microfilm of that newspaper, produced by the New York Public Library.

187. Yoseph Ford, interview by author, May 11, 1999, notes. For more on the society of African-American expatriates in Addis Ababa between the coronation of Haile Selassie I and the Italian invasion of 1935, see Scott, *Sons of Sheba's Race*.

188. Hill, "Dread History," 39.

189. Madhukar Shah, cited in Murrell et al., *Chanting down Babylon*, 386–387; Prashad, *Everybody Was Kung Fu Fighting*, 91.

190. Prashad, *Everybody Was Kung Fu Fighting*, 87.

191. Ibid., 89. The first published speculation regarding Rastafarianism's indebtedness to East Indians in Jamaica was Ajai Mansingh and Laxmi Mansingh, "Hindu Influences on Rastafarianism," in *Caribbean Quarterly Monographs: Rastafari*, ed. Rex Nettleford (Kingston: Caribbean Quarterly, 1984), 96–115; Ajai Mansingh, "Rasta-Indian Connection," *Daily Gleaner* (Kingston, Jamaica), August 8, 1982 and July 18, 1982.

192. Ras Sekou Sankara Tafari, "Introduction," in Shepherd Robert Athlyi Rogers, *The Holy Piby: The Blackman's Bible* [1924] (Kingston, Jamaica: Headstart, 2000), 17.

193. Ras Michael (Miguel) Lorne, "Preface," in Rogers, *The Holy Piby*, 7–8; Sankara Tafari, introduction to *The Holy Piby*, 10.

194. Rogers, *The Holy Piby*, second book, chapter 10, page 61.

195. Rogers, *The Holy Piby*, fourth book, chapter 1, page 91.

196. Elijah Muhammad, *Message to the Blackman* (Philadelphia: Hakim's Publications, 1965), 291; Kathleen Malone O'Connor, "Alternative to 'Religion' in an African American Islamic Community: The Five Percent Nation of Gods and Earths," in *Introduction to New and Alternative Religions in America*, ed. Eugene V. Gallagher and W. Michael Ashcraft (Westport, Conn.: Greenwood, 2006), 23–58; John Szved, *Space Is the Place: The Lives and Times of Sun Ra* (New York: Pantheon, 1997); Graham Lock, *Blutopia: Visions of the Future and Revisions of the Past in the Work of Sun Ra, Duke Ellington, and Anthony Braxton* (Durham: Duke University Press, 1999).

197. See, for example: Barry Chevannes, *Rastafari and Other African-Caribbean Worldviews* (London: Macmillan, 1995), 31; Edmonds, *Outcasts to Culture Bearers*, 37. Robert Hill is the notable exception.

198. On the spread of Rastafarianism through reggae music, see the following essays in Murrell et al., *Chanting down Babylon*: Frank Jan Van Dijk, "Chanting Down Babylon Outernational: The Rise of Rastafari in Europe, the Caribbean, and the Pacific," 178–198; Verena Reckord, "From Burru Drums to Reggae Ridims: The Evolution of Rasta Music," 231–252; William David Spencer, "Chanting Change around the World through Rasta Ridim and Art," 266–283.

CHAPTER 5

1. The hymn was performed by a thousand-voice chorus at Methodist meetings at Ocean Park, New Jersey, in Matthew's time. See Samuel Freuder, *A Missionary's Return to Judaism: The Truth about the Christian Missions to the Jews* (New York: Sinai Publishing, 1915), 151.

2. Arnold Sherman, "The Black Jews of Harlem," *Chicago Jewish Forum* (Spring 1957): 173.

3. The name of the church is taken from 2 Timothy. By far the most exhaustive and authoritative compendium of Black Jewish movements in the United States and around the world is James E. Landing, *Black Judaism: Story of an American Movement* (Durham, N.C.: Carolina Academic Press, 2002).

4. On Black Islam, see Edward E. Curtis IV, *Islam in Black America: Identity, Liberation, and Difference in African-American Islamic Thought* (Albany: State University of New York Press, 2002); Mattias Gardell, *In the Name of Elijah Muhammad: Louis Farrakhan and the Nation of Islam* (Durham: Duke University Press, 1996). On Rastafarianism, see Ennis Barrington Edmonds, *Rastafari: From Outcasts to Culture Bearers* (New York: Oxford University Press, 2003); Hélène Lee, *The First Rasta: Leonard Howell and the Rise of Rastafarianism*, trans. Lily Davis and Hélène Lee, ed. Stephen Davis (Chicago: Lawrence Hill Books, 2003); Vijay Prashad, *Everybody Was Kung Fu Fighting: Afro-Asian Connections and the Myth of Cultural Purity* (Boston: Beacon, 2001), 90–91; Leonard E. Barrett, Sr., *The Rastafarians* (Boston: Beacon, 1997); Robert A. Hill, "Dread History: Leonard Howell and Millenarian Visions in Early Rastafari Religion in Jamaica," *Epoché: Journal of the History of Religions at UCLA*, 9 (1981): 30–71. Works on Father Divine include Jill Watts, *God, Harlem, USA: The Father Divine Story* (Berkeley: University of California Press, 1992); Robert Weisbrot, *Father Divine and the Struggle for Racial Equality* (Urbana: University of Illinois Press, 1983).

5. James C. Scott, *Weapons of the Weak: Everyday Forms of Peasant Resistance* (New Haven: Yale University Press, 1985); Wentworth A. Matthew, "Bishop's Ecclesiastical School Curriculum prescribed and divided according to the various capacities and diverse callings in the Ministry of the Word of God," page 2 of 4-page

pamphlet (Wentworth A. Matthew Collection, Schomburg Center for Research in Black Culture, New York Public Library, Astor, Lenox and Tilden Foundations [hereafter "Schomburg Center"]).

6. Paying attention to micropolitics, hidden transcripts, and subversive bricolage also challenges definitions of Black protest religion that would exclude esoteric forms of African American religion. See, for example, Sherman Jackson, *Islam and the Black American: Looking toward the Third Resurrection* (New York: Oxford University Press, 2005), 29–32.

7. In the mid-1990s, Sholomo B. Levy, a scholar and rabbi from the New York Ethiopian Hebrew community, and Howard Smythe, an archivist at the Schomburg, collected the papers of Rabbi Matthew and the congregations he inspired. Those papers provide the core archival source of the present study.

8. Carl Helm, "Negro Sect in Harlem Mixes Jewish and Christian Religions," *New York Sun*. January 29, 1929, Black Jews Vertical File, Schomburg Center; "Commandment Keeper Meeting Minutes," April 7, 1930, "Ledger," page 55, Kohol Beth B'nai Yisrael Collection, Box 2, Schomburg Center.

9. 1920 U.S. Census, M300, vol. 286, Enumeration District 1411, Sheet 7, Line 26, reel 1223. The dating of the first Passover in 1923 is given by Matthew in 1968. See Rabbi W. A. Matthew, "The 51st Annual Conference of the Ethiopian Hebrew Congregations," June 30, 1968, Beth Ha-Tefilah Collection, Schomburg Center.

10. "Chief Rabbi Wentworth Arthur Matthew and the International Israelite Board of Rabbis Inc., Customs and Traditions of the Black Jews of America (Harlem USA)," Bet Din #011793, January 5, 1993, p. 4, Beth Elohim Commandment Keepers Collection, folder "I.B.R.," Schomburg Center.

11. J. David Bleich, "Black Jews: A Halakhic Perspective," *Tradition: A Journal of Orthodox Thought* 15, no. 1–2 (Spring/Summer 1975): 65.

12. Wentworth A. Matthew, application for Social Security Number, June 1969. Darrell Blevins, Social Security Administration, correspondence with author, August 30, 1999.

13. Hailu Moshe Paris, interview by author, Harlem, New York, May 17, 1999. Indeed, Matthew's African origins were still part of the biography written by Rabbi Sholomo Ben Levy, the son of one of Rabbi Matthew's students. See Rabbi Sholomo Ben Levy, "Biography of Rabbi W. A. Matthew," www.Blackjews.org/Bio_of_Black_Rabbis/Biographies_of_Black_Rabbis_in_America.htm.

14. Matthew's Methodist upbringing comes from Edward Wolf, "Negro 'Jews': A Social Study," *Jewish Social Service Quarterly* 9 (June 1933): 316. Matthew mentioned his affiliation with the Jesus-only Pentecostal church in a private letter: W. A. Matthew to Bishop C. H. Brown, March 25, 1947, 2; Wentworth A. Matthew Papers, Schomburg Center).

15. Rabbi Wentworth A. Matthew, "The Truth about Black Jews and Judaism in America," part 1, *New York Age*, May 17, 1958, Black Jews Vertical File, Schomburg Center.

16. Carlo Ginzburg, "Latitude, Slaves and the Bible: An Experiment in Microhistory," paper delivered at UCLA European History Colloquium, June 5, 2000, 9; Howard M. Brotz, "Negro 'Jews' in the United States," *Phylon* 13 (December 1952): 334.

17. Matthew, "The Truth about Black Jews and Judaism in America."

18. Frank L. Mills, S. B. Jones-Hendrickson, and Bertram Eugene, *Christmas Sports in St. Kitts–Nevis: Our Neglected Cultural Tradition* (no city, no publisher, 1984), 38.

19. Ibid., 13, 38. More's written original was slightly different—*cates*, not plates, and *viands*, not vivands; see Hannah More, *The Works of Hannah More: First Complete American Edition*, vol. 1 (New York: Harper and Brothers, 1843), 85.

20. There is a voluminous literature on ritual, performance, and embodiment, including the groundbreaking Erving Goffman, *The Presentation of Self in Everyday Life* (New York: Anchor Books, Doubleday, 1959); Victor W. Turner, *The Ritual Process* (Chicago: Aldine, 1969).

21. Barry Chevannes, *Rastafari and Other African-Caribbean Worldviews* (London: Macmillan, 1995), 20.

22. Donald William Hogg, "Jamaican Religions: A Study in Variations," Ph.D. dissertation, Anthropology, Yale University, 1964, iii.

23. See Winston James, *Holding Aloft the Banner of Ethiopia: Caribbean Radicalism in Early Twentieth-Century America* (London: Verso, 1998).

24. Alien Ship List Manifest, *SS Parima*, May 11, 1913, National Archives and Records Administration, New York City, microfilm.

25. "Black Israel: Harlem Jews Keep the Fast of Yom Kippur," September 29, 1934, Black Jews Vertical File, Schomburg Center; J. F. Heijbroek, "Matthew, Wentworth Arthur" in *American National Biography*, ed. John A. Garraty and Mark C. Carnes (New York: Oxford University Press, 1999), 275–276.

26. On Ethiopianism, see George Shepperson, "Ethiopianism and African Nationalism," *Phylon* 14, no. 1 (1953): 9–18; Robin D. G. Kelley, "This Ain't Ethiopia, But It'll Do," chapter 6 in *Race Rebels: Culture, Politics, and the Black Working Class* (New York, Free Press, 1994), 129.

27. *The Decree Book* of the Church of the Living God, the Pillar and Ground of Truth, 61, found in the Sherry S. DuPree Collection, Box 6, folder 25, Schomburg Center.

28. Ibid.

29. Sherry Sherrod DuPree, ed., *Biographical Dictionary of African-American Holiness-Pentecostals, 1880–1990* (Washington, D.C.: Middle Atlantic Regional Press, 1989), 136; DuPree, ed., *African-American Holiness Pentecostal Movement: An Annotated Bibliography* (New York: Garland, 1996), 141, 148.

30. Ibid.

31. I have been unable to confirm whether Annie Matthew was related to Wentworth Matthew, who was twenty-four years her junior. See "Sister's Unity Gideon Band Notebook, 1927–8," Commandment Keepers Ethiopian Hebrew Congregation,

Box 1(1), Schomburg Center. On Annie Matthew's place of birth, see U.S. Department of the Interior, Census Office, 1920 Census, Borough of Manhattan, New York County, New York, Series T625, Roll 1201, p. 70, s.v. "Anna Matthew."

32. Historian Robert Hill, editor of the Marcus Garvey Papers Project at UCLA, reports that Bishop Johnson influenced the early Jamaican Rastafarians, which makes sense, given that Rastafarianism shares the belief in descent from the ancient Israelites and a reverence and identification with Ethiopia, or Abyssinia, as Johnson named his first church. Conversation with Robert Hill, August 1999.

33. W. A. Matthew, *Commandment Keepers Log*, 1919–, Commandment Keepers Ethiopian Hebrew Congregation MS, Box 1(1), Schomburg Center.

34. Ibid.

35. Carl Helm, "Negro Sect in Harlem Mixes Jewish and Christian Religions: Come from Abyssiania, Eat Kosher Meat and Have Three Synagogues in Which They Worship." *New York Sun*, Tuesday, January 29, 1929.

36. Matthew, *Commandment Keepers Log*, 22, Commandment Keepers Ethiopian Hebrew Congregation MS, Box 1(1), Schomburg Center. Coincidentally, Lawson later became the head of the Ethiopian World Federation, in which capacity he often clashed with Rastafarians who had been inspired in part by photos of Rabbi Matthew and his followers marching in a Garveyite parade in the 1920s. See: "Ethiop Meet Marks Return of Eritrea," *New York Amsterdam News*, January 6, 1951, 4.

37. Helm, "Negro Sect in Harlem."

38. Ibid.

39. See also "Judaizing Sects are Increasing among the Negroes in Harlem: Mix Elements of Christianity with Jewish Rites; Believe Themselves Descendants of Judah," *Jewish Daily Bulletin*, February 18, 1929, 3.

40. Compare the 1934 "Bishop's School Curriculum," Matthew MS, Schomburg Center, to the 1940 "Curriculum of the Ethiopian Hebrew Rabbinical College of the Royal Order of Ethiopian Hebrews and the Commandment Keepers Congregation of the Living God, Inc.," reproduced in Roi Ottley, *New World A-Coming* (New York: Houghton Mifflin, 1943), 138–140. The dating of the Bishop's School to 1934 is derived from the "record book," Commandment Keeper's Collection, Schomburg Center.

41. "Jewish Negroes," *Foto*, April 1938, Black Jews Vertical Clipping File, Schomburg Center.

42. Harry Bucalstein, "'Black Jews' in Brooklyn," *Religious Digest* (Grand Rapids, Mich.), January 1945, 84.

43. Matthew sermon quoted in Brotz, "Negro 'Jews,'" 332–333.

44. Karen McCarthy Brown, *Mama Lola: A Vodou Priestess in Brooklyn* (Berkeley: University of California Press, 1991): 100–101, 188, 246, 261, 324–325; Maya Deren, *Divine Horsemen: The Living Gods of Haiti* (New York: Thames and Hudson, 1953), 60–70.

45. Jean Besson, *Martha Brae's Two Histories: European Expansion and Caribbean Culture-Building in Jamaica* (Chapel Hill: University of North Carolina Press, 2002), 242; Arvilla Payne-Jackson, Mervyn C. Alleyne, *Jamaican Folk Medicine: A Source of Healing* (Mona, Jamaica: University of West Indies Press, 2004), 133, 233–274.

46. Brotz, "Negro 'Jews,'" 332.

47. "Niggeritions": Brotz, "Negro 'Jews' in the United States," 336; Albert Raboteau, "The Black Church: Continuity within Change," *A Fire in the Bones: Reflections on African-American Religious History* (Boston: Beacon, 1995), 109.

48. Randall K. Burkett, *Garveyism as a Religious Movement: The Institutionalization of a Black Civil Religion* (Metchuen, N.J.: Scarecrow Press, 1978); Susan Nance, "Respectability and Representation: The Moorish Science Temple, Morocco, and Black Public Culture in 1920's Chicago," *American Quarterly* 54, no. 4 (December 2002): 630–631; Yvonne Chireau and Nathaniel Deutsch, *Black Magic: Religion and the African American Conjuring Tradition* (Berkeley: University of California Press, 2003), 143.

49. On Father Divine, see Watts, *God, Harlem, USA*; Weisbrot, *Father Divine*.

50. Jill Watts, *God, Harlem, USA*, 21–24; Richard Weiss, *The American Myth of Success: From Horatio Alger to Norman Vincent Peale* (New York: Basic Books, 1969), 144–145, 172–188.

51. T. R. Poston, "'I Taught Father Divine' Says St. Bishop The Vine: 'And He is Not Doing Right by Theory,' Prophet Holds," *New York Amsterdam News*, November 23, 1932, 1. Roberson also turns up in David Levering Lewis, *When Harlem Was in Vogue* [1979] (New York: Penguin 1997), 222–224, although Lewis gives a stereotyped portrayal of the Black Jews as "weird" cultists and products of "religious hysteria."

52. Ruth Landes, "Negro Jews in Harlem," *Jewish Journal of Sociology* 9, no. 2 (1967), 187.

53. De Laurence's *The Book of Magical Art, Hindu Magic and Indian Occultism* (Chicago: De Laurence, 1904, and in slightly different form, 1915) was a signal influence on Leonard Howell, one of the principal founders of Rastafarianism; see Prashad, *Kung Fu Fighting*, 90.

54. Lauron William de Laurence, comp., *The Sixth and Seventh Books of Moses* (Chicago: De Laurence, 1910).

55. Kevin J. Hayes, *Folklore and Book Culture* (Knoxville: University of Tennessee Press, 1997), 17.

56. Johann Scheible, and Joseph Ennemoser, *The Sixth and Seventh Books of Moses: or, Moses' magical spirit-art, known as the wonderful arts of the old wise Hebrews, taken from the Mosaic books of the Cabala and the Talmud, for the good of mankind. Translated from the German, word for word, according to old writings* (New York, 1880); Hayes, *Folklore and Book Culture*, 17.

57. Zora Neale Hurston, *Moses: Man of the Mountain* (Urbana: University of Illinois Press, 1984), 8.

58. Newbell Niles Puckett, quoted in Hayes, *Folklore and Book Culture*, 18.

59. Patrick A. Polk, "Other Books, Other Powers: *The 6th and 7th Books of Moses* in Afro-Atlantic Folk Belief," *Southern Folklore* 56, no. 2 (1999), 128; W. F. Elkins, "William Lauron de Laurence and Jamaican Folk Religion," *Folklore*, 97 no. 2 (1986), 215–218. The fixation with Moses in the occult world was reinforced by his association with Hermes Trismegistus, the legendary figure who was alleged to have compiled a body of ancient Egyptian mysticism known as the Hermetica. Scholars have dated *The Sixth and Seventh Books of Moses* to an anonymous *grimoire* produced in Germany in 1797. However, the nameplate of the book lists a date of 1686, which would place it in the era of the fervent messianism that followed the career of the false messiah Sabbatai Sevi as well as the uproar in Europe surrounding the rumors of a Rosicrucian conspiracy in the seventeenth century. Francis Yates, *Giordano Bruno and the Hermetic Tradition* (Chicago: University of Chicago Press, 1964), 3, 11–28, 40, 42–50, 55, 84, 110–116, 141, 152, 173, 177, 182, 184, 223, 250, 267, 268, 351, 371, 378, 403, 404, 425, 437, 442; Yates, *The Rosicrucian Enlightenment* (London: Routledge, 1972), chapter 7; Gershom Scholem, *Sabbatai Sevi: The Mystical Messiah, 1626–1676*, trans. R. J. Zwi Werblowsky (Princeton: Princeton University Press, 1973); Jacob Barnai, "From Sabbateanism to Modernization: Ottoman Jewry on the Eve of the Ottoman Reforms and the Haskala Sephardi and Middle Eastern Jewries," in *History and Culture in the Modern Era*, edited by Harvey Goldberg (Bloomington: Indiana University Press, 1996), 75.

60. W. A. Matthew, Hebrew Diagrams, Wentworth A. Matthew Collection, Box 1 (folder 13), Schomburg Center. In the upper right hand corner over the Greek "Deus" is written שדי a name of God that implies God's magical power and is a common kabbalistic referent. In the upper left corner is יהוה, also known as the tetragrammaton, the unpronounceable Hebrew name of God, which is also a common kabbalistic referent. In English יהוה has been translated as Jehovah, which appears in the diagram below the Hebrew. See figures 2 and 3.

61. My great thanks goes to Professor David Myers of UCLA for his translation of the fractured Hebrew of these diagrams. The top line (reading from right to left) is: מצלטוב The middle line is: בחיך הָאיש שמונ יתנלי חי The bottom line is: אבותי קוס ותנלי שטוני אדני אל יהי.

62. Shirley Dore, "Who is this G-d We Worship?" *Malach*, (September 1965), 3–4; quoted in Howard Waitzkin, "Black Judaism in New York," *Harvard Journal of Negro Affairs* 1, no. 3 (1967): 41.

63. In 1895, B. H. Irwin of the Fire-Baptist Holiness Church began to preach in Iowa that baptism by the "fire" of the Holy Ghost was a separate third step after conversion and sanctification. See Vinson Synan, *The Holiness-Pentecostal Movement in the United States* (Grand Rapids, Mich.: William B. Eerdmans, 1971), 61–68.

64. Similarity alone does not suggest an evolutionary link between twentieth-century Black Israelism and African religions of prior centuries. On theology and god

concepts in the Black Atlantic, see, for example, Joseph M. Murphy, *Working the Spirit: Ceremonies of the African Diaspora* (Boston: Beacon, 1994).

65. The first sentence is: איי אול שטוני בהא שדי באלי בהמבול The sentence overlaid on the Mogen David reads: שם כי יהוה כי שדי שדי אדני אלהם אילי יראיל אבי יי. The message on the other figure is: שם כי יהוה אכי שדי אילי כילי אבי יְיָ.

66. Nahum N. Glatzer, "The Synagogue of the Negro Jews in New York," trans., *Almanach des Schocken Verlags*, Berlin 1938/9, 121–129, in Black Jews vertical file, Blaustein Library of the American Jewish Congress, New York City, 3.

67. Alfred Werner, "King Solomon's Black Children," *Chicago Jewish Forum* 4 (Winter 1946): 89. Arnold Sherman gives a similar description in "The Black Jews of Harlem," *Chicago Jewish Forum* 15 (Spring 1957): 170.

68. *Smichah* is the Hebrew word for rabbinical ordination. David Pryce-Jones, "The Black Jews," August 1966, publication unknown, Black Jews vertical file, the Blaustein Library of the American Jewish Congress, New York City.

69. Patrick Polk, "Sacred Banners and the Divine Cavalry Charge," in Donald J. Cosentino, *Sacred Arts of Haitian Vodou* (Los Angeles: UCLA Fowler Museum, 1995), 325–347; Elizabeth McAlister, "A Sorcerer's Bottle: The Visual Art of Magic in Haiti," ibid., 305–321; also see discussion and photographs of bottles and flags throughout the volume.

70. On Garveyism's educational and religious aspects, see James, *Holding Aloft the Banner of Ethiopia*, 79; Burkett, *Garveyism as a Religious Movement*.

71. L. A. McKethan, "Another Great Moses," *Malach*, March 1966, 1, quoted in Waitzkin, "Black Judaism in New York," 19.

72. Gail Bederman, *Manliness & Civilization: A Cultural History of Gender & Race in the United States, 1880–1917* (Chicago: University of Chicago Press, 1995).

73. Lawrence W. Levine, *Black Culture and Black Consciousness: Afro-American Folk Thought from Slavery to Freedom* (New York: Oxford University Press, 1977), 33.

74. Glatzer, "The Synagogue of the Negro Jews in New York," 128.

75. Ibid.

76. Waitzkin, "Black Judaism in New York," 20; Sherman, "The Black Jews of Harlem," 172.

77. "Black Jews Celebrate Rosh Hashona with Hebraic World," *New York Amsterdam News*, September 19, 1936.

78. Glatzer, "The Synagogue of the Negro Jews in New York," 3.

79. "Jewish Followers to Mark Passover: U.N.I.A. and Christian Group Will Join in Tribute to King," publication unknown, March 25, 1931, Black Jews Vertical File, Schomburg Center.

80. On the religiosity of freemasonry in the Progressive Era, see Lynn Dumenil, *Freemasonry and American Culture* (Princeton: Princeton University Press, 1984).

81. See Elly M. Wynia, *The Church of God and Saints of Christ: The Rise of Black Jews* (New York: Garland, 1994); "Ford, Arnold Josiah—Rabbi," in *Who's Who in Colored America: A Biographical Dictionary of Notable Persons of Negro Descent in America*, ed. Joseph J. Boris (New York: Who's Who in Colored America Corpora-

tion, 1927); Vertella S. Valentine Gadsden (daughter of Samuel Valentine), interview by author, August 12, 1995, New York, New York, tape recording.

82. "Harlem Leader of Black Jews Says Race Deserted Its Faith: Rabbi Matthew Hopes to Reconvert Millions to Hebrew Religion," *Afro-American*, February 8, 1936, 18; Harry A. Williamson, "Bogus Masonic Organizations," Harry A. Williamson MS, Schomburg Center.

83. Glatzer, "The Synagogue of the Negro Jews in New York," 126.

84. "Harlem Leader of Black Jews Says Race Deserted Its Faith," *Afro-American*, February 8, 1936, 18.

85. Ottley, *New World A-Coming*, 148.

86. Rabbi W. A. Matthew, "The 51st Annual Conference of the Ethiopian Hebrew Congregations at 1 W. 123rd St.," June 30, 1968, Beth Ha-Tefilah/Ethiopian Hebrew Congregation Records, Schomburg Center. If this dating is correct, then Matthew actually started his church in 1917, although the membership log begins in 1919. See "Membership Record," Commandment Keepers Ethiopian Hebrew Congregation, 1, Box 1, Schomburg Center.

87. On white supremacy in America, see George M. Fredrickson, *The Black Image in the White Mind: The Debate on Afro-American Character and Destiny, 1817–1914* (Middletown: Wesleyan University Press, 1971).

88. "Harlem Leader of Black Jews Says Race Deserted Its Faith," *Afro-American*, February 8, 1936, 18.

89. Ibid.

90. Certificate in "Miscellaneous" folder of the W. A. Matthew Collection, Schomburg Center. Another intriguing possible link between the Church of God and Saints of Christ and the Commandment Keepers is the presence of one Alice Crowdy among the founding members of the Commandment Keepers. Federal Census records indicate that Alice Crowdy was born in Virginia to two Virginian parents, and that she had a son named William Crowdy.

91. Edgar T. Rouzeau, "Impressive Services Planned at Harlem Temple of Sect," September 8, 1934, Black Jews vertical clipping file, Schomburg Center.

92. "Black Jews Celebrate Rosh Hashona with Hebraic World," *New York Amsterdam News*, September 19, 1936.

93. "Israel in Harlem," *New Yorker*, October 1, 1938, 15.

94. Roi Ottley, "The Black Jews of Harlem," *Travel* (July 1942): 20.

95. Secretary Revivalist J. Reide, "Conference 1948" August 4–7, 1948, Commandment Keepers Ethiopian Hebrew Congregation Collection, Box 1, folder 1, Schomburg Center.

96. James H. Hogans, "Pews and Pulpits: Ethiopian Jews to Mark Advent of the New Year," *New York Age*, September 29, 1951, 10.

97. "Rabbi in Chicago to Start Hebrew School," *Chicago Defender* (National Edition), December 27, 1952, 2; Arnold Rosenzweig, "Hebrews Here Find Link to Ethiopian Past," *Chicago Defender* (National edition), February 2, 1963, 1.

98. See, for example, James Baldwin, "Negroes Are Anti-Semitic Because They Are Anti-White," *New York Times*, April 9, 1967; on millenarianism, see Martha F. Lee, *The Nation of Islam: An American Millenarian Movement* (Syracuse: Syracuse University Press, 1996).

99. It is also true, however, that the Black Power era also featured condemnations of Christianity, linking it to slavery and Black oppression, much like the criticism of the New Negro period. See discussion below. On Israelites and spiritualists in Detroit who taught the concept of the Black Christ before Cleage, see Hans A. Baer, *The Black Spiritual Movement: A Religious Response to Racism* (Knoxville: University of Tennessee Press, 1984), 82–83; James E. Landing, *Black Judaism: Story of an American Movement* (Durham, N.C.: Carolina Academic Press, 2002), 66–69, 372–373; Jacob S. Dorman, "Black Orientalism and Black Gods of the Metropolis," in Edward E. Curtis IV and Danielle Brune Sigler, eds., *The New Black Gods: Arthur Huff Fauset and the Study of African American Religions* (Bloomington: Indiana University Press, June 2009), 116–142. On Cleage, see Albert B. Cleage, Jr., *The Black Messiah* (New York: Andrews and McMeel, 1968); Angela D. Dillard, *Faith in the City: Preaching Radical Social Change in Detroit* (Ann Arbor: University of Michigan Press, 2007).

100. L. A. McKethan, "Another Great Moses," *Malach*, March 1966, 1, quoted in Waitzkin, "Black Judaism in New York," 19; Chief Rabbi Levi Ben Levy, "Bet Din 011793," January 17, 1993, Beth Elohim Ethiopian Hebrews Collection, folder "I.B.R.," Schomburg Center.

101. Maude McCleod, "'I Did Not Join the Hebrew Faith—I Returned'," interview with David Isay, *New York Times Magazine*, September 26, 1999, 116.

CONCULSION

1. Lawrence W. Levine, *Black Culture and Black Consciousness: Afro-American Folk Thought from Slavery to Freedom* (New York: Oxford University Press, 1977), 23, 43.

2. Melville J. Herskovits, "Social Pattern: A Methodological Study," *Social Forces* 4, no. 1 (September 1926): 61.

# BIBLIOGRAPHY

MANUSCRIPT SOURCES
*New York, New York*

**New York Public Library, Rare Books and Manuscripts Division**
Committee of Fourteen Collection
Herbert G. Gutman Papers
National Civic Federation Papers
People's Institute Collection
Recreation File
Welfare Department Subject File


*New York Public Library, The Schomburg Center for Research in Black Culture*

**Manuscript Collections**
B'nai Adath Kol Beth Yisrael Ethiopian Hebrew Congregation Papers
Claude Barnett Papers
Bermuda Benevolent Association Papers
Beth Elohim Ethiopian Hebrew Congregation Papers
Beth Ha-Tefilah Ethiopian Hebrew Congregation Papers
British Virgin Islands Benevolent Association Papers
Egbert E. Brown Papers
Club Cubano Records
Commandment Keepers Ethiopian Hebrew Congregation Papers
Aaron Douglas Papers
DuPree African American Holiness Pentecostal Collection
Ethiopian Hebrews Congregation Papers
James Reese Europe Papers
G. E. Haynes Papers
Knights of Pythias Papers

Kohol Beth B'nai Yisrael Ethiopian Hebrew Congregation Papers
David Levering Lewis Papers
M. W. King Solomon Grand Lodge Papers
Wentworth A. Matthew Papers
Moorish Science Temple Papers
Morris Jumel Oral History Transcripts
Arthur A. Schomburg Papers
Sheet Music Collection
Stewart Pentecostal Papers
Symphony of the New World Papers
Temple Beth Ab Shalom Ethiopian Hebrew Congregation Papers
Rochelle Thompson Baby Grand Café Papers,
U.N.I.A. Central Division Records
W.P.A. Writers Collection
Frederick Wells Papers
Harry A. Williamson Masonic Papers

*Photo Collections*
Ceremonies
Mosaic Templars
Mystics
Parades & Processions
Riots
Street Scenes
Women


*New York University, Tamiment Library of Labor History*

Harold Cruse Papers
Soloman/Kaufman Research Files on African-Americans and Communism
Rand School of Social Sciences Papers
Socialist Party, New York Papers
Immigrant Labor History Collection


*New York City Municipal Archives, Department of Old Records*

Certificates of Incorporation
Mayor LaGuardia Papers
Mayor Walker Papers


*Union School of Religion Archives*

Sunday School Collection

*American Jewish Congress, Blaustein Library*

Black Jews Vertical File

*Chicago, Illinois*

*The University of Illinois at Chicago*

James Landing Papers

*Bethesda, Maryland*

*The National Archives and Records Administration of the United States*

State Department Series on Ethiopia 884.55
Department of Justice FBI Files

*Durham, North Carolina*

*Duke University Rare Books, Special Collections, and Archives Library*

Nell Irvin Painter Papers

*Tel Aviv, Israel*

*Sourasky Central Library, Tel Aviv University*

Jacques Faitlovitch Collection

INTERVIEWS

Block, Rabbi Irving J. Interview by author, August 11, 1995, New York, New York. Tape recording.

Brooks, Rabbi Eliezer. Interview by author, August 14, 22, 1996, Bronx, New York, Tape recording.

Caldwell, Rabbi Curtis. Telephone interview by author, May 7, 2007.

DuPree, Sherry Sherrod. Telephone interview by author, April 1998.

Ford, Abiyi. Interview by author, May 10, 11, 1999, Washington, D.C. Notes.

Ford, Yoseph. Interview by author, May 11, 1999, Washington, D.C. Notes.

Gadsden, Vertella S. Valentine. Interview by author, August 12, 1995. New York, New York. Tape recording.

Gladstone, Yaakov. Interview by author, April 28, 1996, New York, New York. Tape recording of telephone call.

Horton, Hermann Mordechai. Interview by author, April 24, 1996, New York, New York. Tape recording.

Paris, Hailu Moshe. Interview by author. May 1999. Harlem, New York. Notes.

Straw, Arlene Ford. Interview by author. May 18, 1999, Coney Island, New York. Notes.

Trainin, Rabbi Isaac N. Interview by author, August 31, 1995, New York, New York. Tape recording.

Williams, Martha Leah Poinsett. Interview by author, April 25, 1996, Brooklyn, New York. Notes.


NEWSPAPERS

*African Times* (New York)
*American Examiner*
*Baltimore Afro-American*
*Chicago Defender*
*Daily Gleaner* (Kingston, Jamaica)
*Hadassah Magazine*
*Jewish Chronicle* (New York)
*JTA Daily News Bulletin*
*National Jewish Post* (New York)
*Negro World* (New York)
*New York Age*
*New York Amsterdam News*
*New York Herald Tribune*
*New York Newsday*
*New York Post*
*New York Times*
*New York Sun*
*Philadelphia Tribune*


BOOKS, ARTICLES, THESES, AND DISSERTATIONS

Abdel-Malek, Anouar. "Orientalism in Crisis." *Diogenes* 11, no. 44 (December 1963): 103–140.

Adas, Michael. *Machines as the Measure of Men: Science, Technology, and Ideologies of Western Dominance*. Ithaca: Cornell University Press, 1989.

Adeleke, Tunde. *UnAfrican Americans: Nineteenth Century Black Nationalists and the Civilizing Mission*. Lexington: University of Kentucky Press, 1998.

Adkin, Clare Jr., *Brother Benjamin: A History of the Israelite House of David*. Berrien Springs, Mich.: Andrews University Press, 1990.

Albanese, Catherine L. "Black Center: African-American Religion and Nationhood." In *America, Religions and Religion*, 2nd ed., 191–216. Belmont, Calif.: Wadsworth, 1992.

———. *A Republic of Mind and Spirit: A Cultural History of American Metaphysical Religion*. New Haven: Yale University Press, 2007.

Allen, Ernest Jr. "Religious Heterodoxy and Nationalist Tradition: The Continuing Evolution of the Nation of Islam." *Black Scholar* 26, no. 3–4 (Fall–Winter 1996): 2–34.

Alpert, Rebecca. *Out of Left Field: Jews and Black Baseball.* New York: Oxford University Press, 2011.

Anderson, Allen. *An Introduction to Pentecostalism: Global Charismatic Christianity.* Cambridge: Cambridge University Press, 2004.

Anderson, Benedict. *Imagined Communities: Reflections on the Origin and Spread of Nationalism.* London: Verso, 1983.

Anderson, Jeffrey E. *Conjure in African American Society.* Baton Rouge: Louisiana State University Press, 2005.

Anderson, Jervis. *This Was Harlem 1900–1950.* New York: Farrar, Straus, Giroux, 1981.

Anderson, Nicole, and Scott London. "South Africa's Newest 'Jews': The Moemedi Pentecostal Church and the Construction of Jewish Identity." *Nova Religio: The Journal of Alternative and Emergent Religions* 13, no. 1 (August 2009): 92–105.

Anderson, Robert Maples. *Vision of the Disinherited.* New York: Oxford University Press, 1979.

Andrews, Thomas F. "Freedmen in Indian Territory: A Post-Civil War Dilemma." *Journal of the West* 4, no. 3 (July 1965): 367–376.

Aptheker, Herbert. *Anti-Racism in U.S. History: The First Two Hundred Years.* New York: Greenwood, 1992.

Arnesen, Eric, ed. *Black Protest and the Great Migration: A Brief History with Documents.* New York: Bedford/St. Martin's, 2002.

———. "Up from Exclusion: Black and White Workers, Race, and the State of Labor History." *Reviews in American History* 26, no. 1 (1998): 146–174.

Baer, Hans A. "Black Spiritual Israelites in a Small Southern City." *Southern Quarterly* 23, no. 3 (Spring 1985): 103–124.

———. *The Black Spiritual Movement: A Religious Response to Racism.* Knoxville: University of Tennessee Press, 1984.

Baer, Hans A., and Merrill Singer. *African-American Religion in the Twentieth Century: Varieties of Protest and Accommodation.* Knoxville: University of Tennessee Press, 1992.

Bakhtin, Mikhail M. *The Dialogic Imagination: Four Essays.* Edited by Michael Holquist, translated by Caryl Emerson and Michael Holquist. Austin: University of Texas Press, 1981.

———. *Rabelais and His World.* Translated by Helene Iswolsky. [1968] Bloomington: Indiana University Press, 1984.

Baraka, Amiri. *Blues People: Negro Music in White America.* New York: W. Morrow, 1963.

Barkan, Elazar. *The Retreat of Scientific Racism: Changing Concepts of Race in Britain and the United States between the World Wars.* New York: Cambridge University Press, 1992.

Barkun, Michael. *Religion and the Racist Right: The Origins of the Christian Identity Movement.* Chapel Hill: University of North Carolina Press, 1997.

Barnai, Jacob. "From Sabbateanism to Modernization: Ottoman Jewry on the Eve of the Ottoman Reforms and the Haskala Sephardi and Middle Eastern Jewries." In *History and Culture in the Modern Era,* edited by Harvey Goldberg, 73–80. Bloomington: Indiana University Press, 1996.

———. "Messianism and Leadership: The Sabbatean Movement and the Leadership of the Jewish Communities in the Ottoman Empire." In *Ottoman and Turkish Jewry: Community and Leadership,* edited by Aron Rodrigue, 1967–1982. Bloomington: Indiana University Press, 1992.

Baron, Ava. "Gender and Labor History: Learning from the Past, Looking to the Future." Introduction to *Work Engendered: Toward a New History of American Labor,* 1–46. Ithaca: Cornell University Press, 1991.

Barrett, Leonard E., Sr. *The Rastafarians.* Boston: Beacon, 1997.

Bartleman, Frank. *Azusa Street.* [1925] Reprinted with a foreword by Vinson Synan. Plainfield, N.J.: Logos International, 1980.

Bay, Mia. *The White Image in the Black Mind: African-American Ideas about White People, 1830–1925.* New York: Oxford University Press, 2000.

Bayoumi, Moustafa. "East of the Sun (West of the Moon): Islam, the Ahmadis, and African America." *Journal of Asian American Studies* 4, no. 3 (2001): 251–263.

Bederman, Gail. *Manliness & Civilization: A Cultural History of Gender and Race in the United States, 1880–1917.* Chicago: University of Chicago Press, 1995.

Bednarowski, Mary Farrell. "Spiritualism in Wisconsin in the Nineteenth Century." *Wisconsin Magazine of History* 59, no. 1 (Autumn 1975): 2–19.

Ben Ammi. *God and the Law of Relativity: New World Concepts of Love, Family, Salvation, Male/Female Relationships, and More.* Washington, D.C.: Communicators Press, 1991.

———. *God, the Black Man and Truth.* Washington, D.C.: Communicators Press, 1982.

———. *The Messiah and the End of This World.* Washington, D.C.: Communicators Press, 1991.

Ben-Jochannan, Yosef. *Black Man of the Nile and His Family.* 2nd ed. Baltimore: Black Classic Press, 1989.

Ben Yehuda, Shaleak. *Black Hebrew Israelites from America to the Promised Land: The Great International Religious Conspiracy against the Children of the Prophets.* New York: Vantage Press, 1975.

Ben Shaleak, Eliyahu, Raviyah Ben Israel, et al. *100 Amazing Facts on the African Presence in the Bible.* Nashville, Tenn.: Winston-Derek, 1992.

Bender, Thomas, ed. *The Antislavery Debate: Capitalism and Abolitionism as a Problem in Historical Interpretation.* Berkeley: University of California Press, 1992.

Bennett, Tony, Lawrence Grossberg, and Meaghan Morris, eds. *New Keywords: A Revised Vocabulary of Culture and Society.* Rev. ed. Malden, Mass.: Blackwell, 2005.

Bercovitch, Sacvan. *The Puritan Origins of the American Self.* New Haven: Yale University Press, 1975.

Beresniak, Daniel. *Juifs et francs-maçons.* Paris: Bibliophane, 1989.

Berger, Graenum. *Black Jews in America: A Documentary with Commentary.* New York: Commission on Synagogue Relations, Federation of Jewish Philanthropies of New York, 1978.

———. *Graenum: An Autobiography by Graenum Berger.* Pelham, N.Y.: John Washburn Bleeker Hampton, 1987.

Berger, Peter L. *Facing up to Modernity.* New York: Basic Books, 1977.

Berlin, Ira. "Herbert Gutman and the American Working Class." In *Power and Culture: Essays on the American Working Class / Herbert Gutman*, edited by Ira Berlin. New York, Pantheon, 1987.

———. *Many Thousands Gone: The First Two Centuries of Slavery in North America.* Cambridge: Harvard University Press, 1998.

———. "Time, Space, and the Evolution of Afro-American Society on British Mainland North America." *American Historical Review* 85 (February 1980): 44–78.

Bernstein, Iver. *The New York City Draft Riots: Their Significance for American Society and Politics in the Age of the Civil War.* New York: Oxford University Press, 1990.

Bernstein, Michael A. "Why the Great Depression Was Great: Toward a New Understanding of the Interwar Economic Crisis in the United States." In *The Rise and Fall of the New Deal Order, 1930–1980,* edited by Steve Fraser and Gary Gerstle, 32–54. Princeton: Princeton University Press, 1989.

Berry, Faith. *Langston Hughes: Before and Beyond Harlem.* Westport, Conn.: L. Hill, 1983.

Berson, Lenora E. *The Negroes and the Jews.* New York: Random House, 1971.

Besson, Jean. *Martha Brae's Two Histories: European Expansion and Caribbean Culture-Building in Jamaica.* Chapel Hill: University of North Carolina Press, 2002.

Best, Wallace D. *Passionately Human, No Less Divine: Religion and Culture in Black Chicago, 1915–1952.* Princeton: Princeton University Press, 2005.

Biondi, Martha. *To Stand and Fight: The Struggle for Civil Rights in Postwar New York City.* Cambridge: Harvard University Press, 2003.

Billington, Monroe Lee, and Roger D. Hardaway, eds. *African Americans on the Western Frontier.* Niwot: University Press of Colorado, 1998.

Blassingame, John W. *The Slave Community: Plantation Life in the Antebellum South.* New York: Oxford University Press, 1972.

Bleich, J. David. "Black Jews: A Halakhic Perspective." *Tradition: A Journal of Orthodox Thought* 15, no. 1–2 (Spring/Summer 1975): 48–79.

Bloch, Ruth, *Visionary Republic: Millennial Themes in American Thought, 1657–1800.* New York: Cambridge University Press, 1985.

Bloom, Harold. *The American Religion: The Emergence of the Post-Christian Nation.* New York: Simon & Schuster, 1992.

Blum, Edward J. *Reforging the White Republic: Race, Religion, and American Nationalism, 1865–1898.* Baton Rouge: Louisiana State University Press, 2005.

——. *W.E.B. Du Bois, American Prophet.* Philadelphia: University of Pennsylvania Press, 2007.

Blyden, Edward Wilmot. *Christianity, Islam, and the Negro Race.* [1888] Baltimore: Black Classic Press, 1994.

——. *The Jewish Question.* Liverpool: Lionel Hart, 1898.

Borchert, James. *Alley Life in Washington: Family, Community, Religion and Folklife in the City, 1850–1970.* Urbana: University of Illinois Press, 1980.

Boris, Joseph J., ed. *Who's Who in Colored America: A Biographical Dictionary of Notable Persons of Negro Descent in America.* New York: Who's Who in Colored America Corporation, 1927.

Bracey, John, and August Meir. *Strangers and Neighbors: Relations between Blacks and Jews in the United States.* Amherst: University of Massachusetts Press, 2000.

Bracey, John, and August Meir. "Towards a Research Agenda on Blacks and Jews in United States History." *Journal of American Ethnic History* 12, no. 3 (1993): 60–67.

Brag, Avtar, and Annie E. Coombes, eds. *Hybridity and Its Discontents: Politics, Science, Culture.* London: Routledge, 2000.

Braude, Ann D. *Radical Spirits: Spiritualism and Women's Rights in Nineteenth-Century America.* 2nd ed. Bloomington: Indiana University Press, 2001.

Brinkley, Alan. "The New Deal and the Idea of the State." In *The Rise and Fall of the New Deal Order, 1930–1980*, edited by Steve Fraser and Gary Gerstle, 85–121. Princeton: Princeton University Press, 1989.

Brodkin, Karen. *How Jews Became White Folks and What That Says about Race in America.* New Brunswick: Rutgers University Press, 1998.

Brotz, Howard. *The Black Jews of Harlem: Negro Nationalism and the Dilemmas of Negro Leadership.* New York: Free Press of Glencoe, 1964.

——. "The Negro-Jewish Community and the Contemporary Race Crisis." *Jewish Social Studies* 27, no. 1 (January 1965): 10–17.

——. "Negro 'Jews' in the United States." *Phylon* 13, no. 4 (December 1952): 324–337.

Brown, David H. "Conjure/Doctors: An Exploration of a Black Discourse in America, Antebellum to 1940," *Folklore Forum* 23, nos. 1–2 (1990): 3–46.

Brown, Elsa Barkley. "Negotiating and Transforming the Public Sphere: African American Political Life in the Transition from Slavery to Freedom." *Public Culture* 15 (1994): 107–146.

Brown, Jayna. *Babylon Girls: Black Women Performers and the Shaping of the Modern.* Durham: Duke University Press, 2008.

Brown, Karen McCarthy. *Mama Lola: A Vodou Priestess in Brooklyn.* Berkeley: University of California Press, 1991.

Bruce, Henry Clay. *The New Man: Twenty-nine Years a Slave, Twenty-nine Years a Free Man*. New York: Negro Universities Press, 1969.

Bruder, Edith. *The Black Jews of Africa: History, Religion, Identity*. New York: Oxford University Press, 2008.

Brune, Danielle E. "Sweet Daddy Grace: The Life and Times of a Modern Day Prophet." Ph.D. dissertation, Department of American Studies, University of Texas, Austin, 2002.

Bucalstein, Harry. "'Black Jews' in Brooklyn." *Religious Digest* (Grand Rapids, Mich.), January 1945, 83–85.

Bullock, Steven C. *Revolutionary Brotherhood: Freemasonry and the Transformation of the American Social Order, 1730–1840*. Chapel Hill: University of North Carolina Press, 1998.

Burkett, Randall K. *Garveyism as a Religious Movement: The Institutionalization of a Black Civil Religion*. Metuchen, N.J.: Scarecrow Press, 1978.

Butler, Jon. *Awash in a Sea of Faith: Christianizing the American People*. Cambridge: Harvard University Press, 1990.

———. "Born-Again History?" Unpublished paper, March 1994.

———. "Enthusiasm Described and Decried: The Great Awakening as Interpretive Fiction." *Journal of American History* 69, no. 2 (September 1982): 305–325.

Campbell, Alexander. *The Christian System: In Reference to the Union of Christians, and a Restoration of Primitive Christianity, as Plead in the Current Reformation*. Cincinnati: Standard Publishing, 1839.

Campbell, James T. *Songs of Zion: The African Methodist Episcopal Church in the United States and South Africa*. New York: Oxford University Press, 1995.

Candy, Catherine. "The Inscrutable Irish-Indian Feminist Management of Anglo-American Hegemony, 1917–1947." *Journal of Colonialism and Colonial History* 2, no. 1 (2001). http://muse.jhu.edu/ (accessed May 30, 2009).

Carby, Hazel V. *Race Men*. Cambridge: Harvard University Press, 1998.

———. *Reconstructing Womanhood: The Emergence of the Afro-American Woman Novelist*. Oxford: Oxford University Press, 1987.

Carney, George O. "Oklahoma's All-Black Towns." In *African Americans of the Western Frontier*, edited by Monroe Lee Billington and Roger D. Hardaway, 147–159. Niwot: University Press of Colorado, 1998.

Carpenter, William. *The Israelites Found in the Anglo-Saxons. The Ten Tribes Supposed to Have Been Lost, Traced from the Land of Their Captivity to Their Occupation of the Isles of the Sea: with An Exhibition of Those Traits of Character and National Characteristics Assigned to Israel in the Books of the Hebrew Prophets*. London: George Kenning, 1874.

Castel, Albert. "Civil War Kansas and the Negro." *Journal of Negro History* 51, no. 2 (April 1966): 125–138.

Chakrabarty, Dipesh *Provincializing Europe: Postcolonial Thought and Historical Difference*. Princeton: Princeton University Press, 2000.

Chatterjee, Partha. "Communities and the Nation." In *The Nation and Its Fragments: Colonial and Postcolonial Histories*, 220–239. Princeton: Princeton University Press, 1993.

———. "Whose Imagined Community?" In *The Nation and Its Fragments: Colonial and Postcolonial Histories*, 3–13. Princeton: Princeton University Press, 1993.

Chevannes, Barry. *Rastafari and Other African-Caribbean Worldviews*. London: Macmillan, 1995.

———. *Rastafari: Roots and Ideology*. Syracuse: Syracuse University Press, 1994.

———. *Social Origins of the Rastafari Movement*. Mona, Jamaica: Institute of Social and Economic Research, 1978.

Chidester, David. *Authentic Fakes: Religion and American Popular Culture*. Berkeley: University of California Press, 2005.

Chireau, Yvonne P. *Black Magic: Religion and the African American Conjuring Tradition*. Berkeley: University of California Press, 2003.

———, and Nathaniel Deutsch, eds. *Black Zion: African American Religious Encounters with Judaism*. New York: Oxford University Press, 2000.

Christian, William. *Poor Pilgrim's Work, In the Name of the Father, Son and Holy Ghost on Christian Friendship Works No. 3, First Man and Woman: Fallen Angels, or Gentiles in the Land of Nod; Adam and Eve are the Starting Point of the Black People: And Other Important Things*. Texarkana, Ark.: Joe Ehrlich's Print, 1896.

Clark, Anna. *The Struggle for the Breeches: Gender and the Making of the British Working Class*. Berkeley: University of California Press, 1995.

Clark, Elmer T. *The Small Sects in America*. New York: Abingdon-Cokebury, 1937; rev. ed. Nashville, Tenn.: Abingdon, 1949.

Clark, Kenneth Bancroft. *Dark Ghetto: Dilemmas of Social Power*. New York: Harper and Row, 1965.

Clarke, John Henrik, ed. *Marcus Garvey and the Vision of Africa*. New York: Vintage, 1974.

Clarke, Kamari Maxine. *Mapping Yorùbá Networks: Power and Agency in the Making of Transnational Communities*. Durham: Duke University Press, 2004.

Clawson, Mary Ann. *Constructing Brotherhood: Class, Gender, and Fraternalism*. Princeton: Princeton University Press, 1989.

Cleage, Albert B., Jr. *The Black Messiah*. New York: Andrews and McMeel, 1968.

Clemmons, Ithiel C., and Adrienne M. Israel. *Bishop C. H. Mason and the Roots of the Church of God in Christ*. Centennial ed. Bakersfield, Cal.: Pneuma Life, 1996.

Clifford, James. *The Predicament of Culture: Twentieth-Century Ethnography, Literature, and Art*. Cambridge: Harvard University Press, 1988.

Cohen, Lizabeth. *Making a New Deal: Industrial Workers in Chicago, 1919–1939*. New York: Cambridge University Press, 1990.

Cohen, Robert, ed. *The Jewish Nation in Surinam: Historical Essays*. Amsterdam: S. Emmering, 1982.

———. *Jews in Another Environment: Surinam in the Second Half of the Eighteenth Century*. Leiden: E. J. Brill, 1991.

Coleman, Robert. "A Black Jew Speaks." *Jewish Observer* 7, no. 1 (November 1970): 12.

Comaroff, Jean. *Body of Power, Spirit of Resistance: The Culture and History of a South African People.* Chicago: University of Chicago Press, 1985.

Comaroff, Jean, and John Comaroff. *Modernity and Its Malcontents: Ritual and Power in Postcolonial Africa*, edited by Comaroff and Comaroff, xv–xxii. Chicago: University of Chicago Press, 1993.

Comaroff, Jean, and John Comaroff. *Of Revelation and Revolution: Christianity, Colonialism, and Consciousness in South Africa*, vol. 1. Chicago: University of Chicago Press, 1991.

Coon, Carlton S. *Measuring Ethiopia and Flight into Arabia.* London: Jonathan Cape, 1936.

Corbould, Clare. *Becoming African Americans: Black Public Life in Harlem, 1919–1939.* Cambridge: Harvard University Press, 2009.

Cordley, Richard. *Pioneer Days in Kansas.* New York: Pilgrim Press, 1903.

Cosentino, Donald J., ed. *The Sacred Arts of Haitian Vodou.* Los Angeles: UCLA Fowler Museum, 1995.

Coulter, Charles E. *Take up the Black Man's Burden: Kansas City's African American Communities 1865–1939.* Columbia: University of Missouri Press, 2006.

Creel, Margaret Washington. *A Peculiar People: Slave Religion and Community-Culture among the Gullahs.* New York: New York University Press, 1988.

Crockett, Norman L. *The Black Towns.* Lawrence: Regents Press of Kansas, 1979.

Crowdy, Prophet William Saunders. *Prophet William Saunders Crowdy's Great Prophetic Sermon, Epistles of Warning and Consolation, Induction Sermon with Revelation, Slite History of His Beginning and End.* Philadelphia, Charles B. H. McNeill, n.d.

———. *The Bible Gospel Told; The Revelation of God Revealed; Set Forth by Bishop W.S. Crowdy of the Church of God and Saints of Christ; The World Evangelist; My Teacher is the Father, Son, and Holy Ghost.* Philadelphia: The Church of God Publication House, 1902.

Cunningham, Roger D. "Welcoming 'Pa' on the Kaw: Kansas's 'Colored' Militia and the 1864 Price Raid." *Kansas History* 25 (Winter 2000/2001): 87–101.

Curtis, Edward E. IV. *Black Muslim Religion in the Nation of Islam, 1960–1975.* Chapel Hill: University of North Carolina Press, 2006.

———. *Islam in Black America: Identity, Liberation, and Difference in African-American Islamic Thought.* Albany: State University of New York Press, 2002.

Curtis, Edward E. IV, and Danielle Brune Sigler. *The New Black Gods: Arthur Huff Fauset and the Study of African American Religions.* Bloomington: Indiana University Press, 2009.

Daniels, David D. III. "Charles Harrison Mason: The Interracial Impulse of Early Pentecostalism." In *Portraits of a Generation: Early Pentecostal Leaders*, edited by James R. Goff, Jr., and Grant Wacker, 255–270. Fayetteville: University of Arkansas Press, 2002.

———. "Pentecostalism." In *Encyclopedia of African American Religions*, ed. Larry G. Murphy, H. Gordon Melton, and Gary L. Ward, 585–595. New York: Garland, 1993.

Dann, Martin. "From Sodom to the Promised Land: E. P. McCabe and the Movement for Oklahoma Colonization." *Kansas Historical Quarterly* 40 (1974): 370–378.

Darnton, Robert. "The Symbolic Element in History." *Journal of Modern History* 58, no. 1 (March 1986): 218–234.

Davis, David Brion. *The Problem of Slavery in the Age of Revolution, 1770–1823*. Ithaca: Cornell University Press, 1975.

———. *Slavery and Human Progress*. New York: Oxford University Press, 1984.

Davis, Natalie Zemon. *The Gift in Sixteenth-Century France*. Madison: University of Wisconsin Press, 2000.

Debo, Angie. *And Still the Waters Run: The Betrayal of the Five Civilized Tribes*. Princeton: Princeton University Press, 1980.

de Certeau, Michel. *The Practice of Everyday Life*. Translated by Steven Rendall. Berkeley: University of California Press, 1984.

De Laurence, Lauron, William, comp. *The Book of Magical Art, Hindu Magic and Indian Occultism*. [1904] Chicago: De Laurence, 1915.

———, comp. *The Sixth and Seventh Books of Moses*. Chicago: De Laurence, 1910.

Department of Commerce. *Abstract of the Fourteenth Census of the United States*. Washington, D.C.: Department of Commerce, 1920.

Deleuze, Gilles and Félix Guattari. *A Thousand Plateaus: Capitalism and Schizophrenia*. Translation and foreword by Brian Massumi. Minneapolis: University of Minnesota Press, 1987.

Deren, Maya. *Divine Horsemen: The Living Gods of Haiti*. New York: Thames and Hudson, 1953.

Derrida, Jacques. *Of Grammatology*. Translated by Gayatri Chakravorty Spivak. Baltimore: Johns Hopkins University Press, 1998.

Deutsch, Nathaniel, "'The Asiatic Black Man': An African American Orientalism?" *Journal of African American Studies* 4, no. 3 (2001): 193–208.

Dillard, Angela D. *Faith in the City: Preaching Radical Social Change in Detroit*. Ann Arbor: University of Michigan Press, 2007.

Dillon, Elizabeth. *The Gender of Freedom: Fictions of Liberalism and the Literary Public Sphere*. Palo Alto: Stanford University Press, 2004.

Dinnerstein, Leonard, Roger L. Nichols, and David M. Reimers. *Natives and Strangers: Blacks, Indians, and Immigrants in America*. 2nd ed. New York: Oxford University Press, 1990.

Dobrin, Arthur. "A History of the Negro Jews in America." Unpublished paper, City College of NY, 1965, microfilm, Schomburg Center for the Study of Black Culture, New York Public Library, Astor, Lenox and Tilden Foundations.

Dorman, Jacob S. "Back to Harlem: Abstract and Everyday Labor during the 'Harlem Renaissance'." In *The Harlem Renaissance Revisited: Politics, Arts, and Letters*, edited by Jeffrey O. G. Ogbar, 74–90. Baltimore: Johns Hopkins University Press, 2010.

———. "Black Israelites aka Black Jews aka Black Hebrews: Black Israelism, Black Judaism, Judaic Christianity." In *Introduction to New and Alternative Religions in the*

*United States*, edited by Eugene V. Gallagher and W. Michael Ashcraft, 59–84. Westport, Conn.: Praeger, 2006.

———. "The Black Israelites of Harlem and the Professors of Oriental and African Mystic Science in the 1920's." Ph.D. dissertation, Department of History, University of California, Los Angeles, 2004.

———. "Black Orientalism and Black Gods of the Metropolis." In *The New Black Gods: Arthur Huff Fauset and the Study of African American Religions*, edited by Edward E. Curtis IV and Danielle Brune Sigler, 116–142. Bloomington: Indiana University Press, 2009.

———. "Hatzaad Harishon: Integration, Black Power and Black Jews in New York, 1964–1972." Honors thesis, Stanford University, 1996.

———. "'I Saw You Disappear with My Own Eyes:' Hidden Transcripts of New York Black Israelite Bricolage." *Nova Religio: The Journal of Alternative and Emergent Religions* 11, no. 1 (August 2007): 61–83.

———. "'Lifted out of the Commonplace Grandeur of Modern Times': Reappraising Edward Wilmot Blyden's Views of Islam and Afrocentrism in Light of His Scholarly Black Christian Orientalism." *Souls: A Critical Journal of Black Politics, Culture, and Society* 12, no 4 (October 2010): 398–418.

———. "Skin Bleach and Civilization: The Racial Formation of Blackness in 1920s Harlem." *Journal of Pan African Studies* Special Issue: Skin Bleaching and Global White Supremacy 4 no. 4 (June 2011): 46–79.

Douglas, Mary. *Purity and Danger: An Analysis of Concepts of Pollution and Taboo.* [1966] New York: Routledge, 2001.

Douglass, Lisa, and Raymond Thomas Smith. *The Power of Sentiment: Love, Hierarchy, and the Jamaican Family Elite*. Boulder, Colo.: Westview, 1992.

Drescher, Seymour. "The Role of Jews in the Transatlantic Slave Trade." *Immigrants and Minorities* 12, no. 2 (1993): 113–125.

Droge, A. J. "Retrofitting/Retiring 'Syncretism.'" In *Syncretism/Anti-Syncretism: The Politics of Religious Synthesis*, edited by Charles Stewart and Rosalind Shaw, 375–388. London: Routledge, 1994.

Droogers, André, and Sidney M. Greenfield, "Recovering and Reconstructing Syncretism." In *Reinventing Religions: Syncretism and Transformation in Africa and the Americas*, edited by Sidney M. Greenfield and André Droogers, 21–42. New York: Rowman & Littlefield, 2001.

Du Bois, W.E.B., ed. *The Negro Church: Report of a Social Study Made under the Direction of Atlanta University; Together with the Proceedings of the Eighth Conference for the Study of the Negro Problems, Held at Atlanta University, May 26th, 1903.* Atlanta: Atlanta University Press, 1903.

———. *The Souls of Black Folk*. [1892] New York: Penguin, 1903.

Duara, Prasenjit. "The Discourse of Civilization and Pan-Asianism." *Journal of World History* 12, no. 1 (2001): 99–130.

Dumenil, Lynn. *Freemasonry and American Culture*. Princeton: Princeton University Press, 1984.

——. *The Modern Temper: American Culture and Society in the 1920s*. New York: Hill and Wang, 1995.

Dunbar, Barrington. "Factors in the Cultural Background of the American Southern Negro and the British West Indian Negro that Condition Their Adjustments in Harlem." Master's thesis. Department of Political Science, Columbia University, 1935.

DuPree, Sherry Sherrod. *African-American Holiness Pentecostal Movement: An Annotated Bibliography*. New York: Garland, 1996.

——, ed. *Biographical Dictionary of African-American Holiness-Pentecostals, 1880–1990*. Washington, D.C.: Middle Atlantic Regional Press, 1989.

Durkheim, Emile. *The Elementary Forms of Religious Life*. [1912] New York: Free Press, 1995.

Dvorak, Katherine L. "After Apocalypse, Moses." In *Masters & Slaves in the House of the Lord: Race and Religion in the American South 1740–1870*, edited by John B. Boles, 173–191. Lexington: University Press of Kentucky, 1988.

Edmonds, Ennis Barrington. *Rastafari: From Outcasts to Culture Bearers*. New York: Oxford University Press, 2003.

Edsforth, Ronald. *Made in the U.S.A.: Mass Culture and the Americanization of Working-Class Ethnics in the Coolidge Era. Essays on the History of the Twenties*. Hanover, N.H.: University Press of New England, 1998.

Edwards, Holly, ed. *Noble Dreams, Wicked Pleasures: Orientalism in America, 1870–1930*. Princeton: Princeton University Press, 2000.

Ehrman, Albert. "The Commandment Keepers: A Negro Jewish Cult in America Today." *Judaism: A Quarterly Journal* 8 (Summer 1959): 266–270.

Eisenberg, Bernard. "Kelly Miller and the Problems of the Negro Leader, 1918–1939." Master's thesis, Department of Political Science, Columbia University, 1958.

Elias, Norbert. *The Norbert Elias Reader*. Edited by Johan Goudsblom and Stephen Mennell. Oxford: Blackwell, 1998.

Elkins, W. F. "William Lauron de Laurence and Jamaican Folk Religion." *Folklore* 97, no. 2 (1986): 215–218.

Emmanuel, Isaac Samuel, and Suzanne A. Emmanuel. *History of the Jews of the Netherland Antilles*. Cincinnati: American Jewish Archives, 1970.

Essien-Udom, Essien Udosen. *Black Nationalism: A Search for an Identity in America*. Chicago: University of Chicago Press, 1971.

Etherington, Norman. "The Historical Sociology of Independent Churches in South East Africa." *Journal of Religion in Africa* 10, no. 2 (1979): 113–115, 120.

Evans, Eifon. *The Welsh Revival of 1904*. Bridgend: Evangelical Press of Wales, 1969.

Evans, Eli N. *Judah P. Benjamin: The Jewish Confederate*. New York: Free Press, 1988.

Fabian, Johannes. *Time and the Other: How Anthropology Makes Its Object*. New York: Columbia University Press, 1983.

Farber, Eli. *Jews, Slaves, and the Slave Trade: Setting the Record Straight*. New York: New York University Press, 1998.

Fauset, Arthur Huff. *Black Gods of the Metropolis: Negro Religious Cults of the Urban North*. [1944] Philadelphia: University of Pennsylvania Press, 2002.

Fels, Tony. "Religious Assimilation in a Fraternal Organization: Jews and Freemasonry in Gilded-Age San Francisco." *American Jewish History* 74, no. 4 (1985): 369–403.

Ferguson, Charles W. *Fifty Million Brothers: A Panorama of American Lodges and Clubs*. New York: Farrar & Rinehart, 1937.

Ferguson, Jeffrey B. *The Sage of Sugar Hill: George S. Schuyler and the Harlem Renaissance*. New Haven: Yale University Press, 2005.

Feurlicht, Roberta Strauss. *The Fate of the Jews: A People Torn between Israeli Power and Jewish Ethics*. New York: Times Books, 1983.

Fields, Barbara J. "Ideology and Race in American History." In *Region, Race and Reconstruction: Essays in Honor of C. Vann Woodward*, edited by J. Morgan Kousser and James M. McPherson, 143–177. New York: Oxford University Press, 1982.

Findlay, Eileen J. Suárez. *Imposing Decency: The Politics of Sexuality and Race in Puerto Rico, 1870–1920*. Durham: Duke University Press, 1999.

Fink, Leon. "The New Labor History and the Powers of Historical Pessimism: Consensus, Hegemony, and the Case of the Knights of Labor." *Journal of American History* 75, no. 1 (June 1988): 115–136.

Foner, Eric. *Free Soil, Free Labor, Free Men: The Ideology of the Republican Party before the Civil War*. New York: Oxford University Press, 1970.

———. *Reconstruction: America's Unfinished Revolution*. New York: Harper and Row, 1988.

———. *The Story of American Freedom*. New York: W.W. Norton, 1998.

Foreign Missions Conference of North America. *Foreign Missions Conference of North America: Being the Report of the Twenty-Fifth Conference of Foreign Mission Boards in the United States and Canada*. Garden City, N.Y.: Foreign Missions Conference, 1918.

Foster, Henry Blaine. *Rise and Progress of Wesleyan-Methodism in Jamaica*. London: Wesleyan Conference Office, 1881.

Foucault, Michel. *The Foucault Reader*. Edited by Paul Rabinow. New York: Pantheon, 1984.

———. *History of Sexuality, Volume 1: An Introduction*. New York: Pantheon, 1978.

Fox, Richard G., and Barbara J. King, eds. *Anthropology beyond Culture*. Oxford: Berg, 2002.

Frank, Gelya. "Jews, Multiculturalism, and Boasian Anthropology." *American Anthropologist* 99, no. 4 (December 1997): 731–745.

Franklin, Jimmie Lewis. *Journey toward Hope: A History of Blacks in Oklahoma*. Norman: University of Oklahoma Press, 1982.

Franklin, John Hope. "Afro-American History: State of the Art." *Journal of American History* 75 (June 1988): 162–173.

———. *From Slavery to Freedom: A History of Negro Americans*, New York: World Publishing, 1961.

Fredrickson, George M. *The Black Image in the White Mind: The Debate on Afro-American Character and Destiny, 1817–1914.* Middletown: Wesleyan University Press, 1971.

——. "The Role of Race in the Planter Ideology of South Carolina" In *The Arrogance of Race: Historical Perspectives on Slavery, Racism, and Social Equality,* 15–25. Middletown: Wesleyan University Press, 1988.

Freud, Sigmund. *Moses and Monotheism.* New York: Vintage, 1939.

Freuder, Samuel. *A Missionary's Return to Judaism: The Truth about the Christian Missions to the Jews.* New York: Sinai Publishing, 1915.

Frey, Sylvia R., and Betty Wood. *Come Shouting to Zion: African American Protestantism in the American South and British Caribbean to 1830.* Chapel Hill: University of North Carolina Press, 1998.

Friedman, Saul S. *Jews and the American Slave Trade.* New Brunswick, N.J.: Transaction, 1998.

Fulop, Timothy E. "The Future Golden Day of the Race: Millennialism and Black Americans in the Nadir, 1877–1901." *Harvard Theological Review* 84 (1991): 75–99.

Fuller, Hoyt W. "An Interview: The Original Hebrew Israelite Nation." *Black World,* May 1975, 62–85.

Gaines, Kevin. *Uplifting the Race: Black Leadership, Politics, and Culture in the Twentieth Century.* Chapel Hill: University of North Carolina Press, 1996.

Gardell, Mattias. *In the Name of Elijah Muhammad: Louis Farrakhan and the Nation of Islam.* Durham: Duke University Press, 1996.

Garvey, Marcus. *Philosophy and Opinions of Marcus Garvey.* Edited by Amy Jacques Garvey. New York: Arno Press, 1968.

Gates, Henry Louis. *The Signifying Monkey: A Theory of Afro-American Literary Criticism.* New York: Oxford University Press, 1988.

Gatewood, Willard B., Jr. *Black Americans and the White Man's Burden, 1893–1903.* Urbana: University of Illinois Press, 1986.

Gay, Ruth. *Unfinished People: Eastern European Jews Encounter America.* New York: W. W. Norton, 2001.

Geertz, Clifford. *The Interpretation of Cultures: Selected Essays by Clifford Geertz.* [1973] New York: Basic Books, 2000.

——. *The Religions of Java.* Glencoe, Ill.: Free Press, 1960.

Genovese, Eugene D. *Roll, Jordan, Roll: The World the Slaves Made.* New York: Pantheon, 1972.

——. *The World the Slaveholders Made.* Middletown Connecticut: Wesleyan University Press, 1969.

Gerber, Israel J. *The Heritage Seekers: American Blacks in Search of Jewish Identity.* Middle Village, N.Y.: Jonathan David, 1977.

Gianakos, Perry E. "The Black Muslims: An American Millennialistic Response to Racism and Cultural Deracination." *Centennial Review* 23, no. 4 (1979): 430–451.

Gilfoyle, Timothy J. "White Cities, Linguistic Turns, and Disneylands: The New Paradigms of Urban History." *Reviews in American History* 26, no. 1 (1998): 175–204.

Gilliard, Edward M. "The Housing Problem in Harlem." Master's thesis, Department of Political Science, Columbia University, 1926.

Gilmore, Glenda E. *Gender and Jim Crow: Women and the Politics of White Supremacy in North Carolina.* Chapel Hill: University of North Carolina Press, 1996.

Gilroy, Paul. *The Black Atlantic: Modernity and Double Consciousness.* Cambridge: Harvard University Press, 1993.

Ginzburg, Carlo. "Blacks, Jews, and Animals: Voltaire and the Eighteenth-Century Origins of Multiculturalism." Paper delivered at UCLA European History Colloquium, Spring 1999.

———. *The Cheese and the Worms: The Cosmos of a Sixteenth-Century Miller.* Translated by John and Anne Tedeschi. [1976] Baltimore: John Hopkins University Press, 1992.

———. "Latitude, Slaves, and the Bible: An Experiment in Microhistory." Paper delivered at UCLA European History Colloquium, June 5, 2000.

Girard, René. *Violence and the Sacred.* Translated by Patrick Gregory. [1972] Baltimore, Johns Hopkins University Press, 1977.

Glatzer, Nahum N. "The Synagogue of the Negro Jews in New York." Translated into German in *Almanach des Schocken Verlags,* Berlin (1938/9): 121–129. Black Jews vertical file, Blaustein Library of the American Jewish Congress.

Glaude, Eddie S., Jr. *Exodus! Religion, Race, and Nation in Early Nineteenth-Century Black America.* Chicago: University of Chicago Press, 2000.

Glazer, Nathan, and Daniel P. Moynihan. *Beyond the Melting Pot: The Negroes, Puerto Ricans, Jews, Italians, and Irish of New York City.* Cambridge: MIT Press, 1963.

Godbey, Allen H. *The Lost Tribes a Myth: Suggestions towards Rewriting Hebrew History.* Durham: Duke University Press, 1930.

Goff, James R., Jr. *Fields White unto Harvest: Charles F. Parham and the Missionary Origins of Pentecostalism.* Fayetteville: University of Arkansas Press, 1988.

Goff, James R., Jr., and Grant Wacker, eds. *Portraits of a Generation: Early Pentecostal Leaders.* Fayetteville: University of Arkansas Press, 2002.

Goffman, Erving. *The Presentation of Self in Everyday Life.* New York: Anchor Books, Doubleday, 1959.

Goings, Kenneth W., and Raymond A. Mohl, eds. *The New African American Urban History.* Thousand Oaks, Cal.: Sage, 1996.

Gold, Roberta S. "The Black Jews of Harlem: Representation, Identity, and Race, 1920–1939." *American Quarterly* 55, no. 2 (June 2003): 179–225.

Goldberg, B. Z. "A Negro Bris." *B'Nai B'Rith Magazine* (New York) 41, no. 11 (August 1927): 465–466.

———. Untitled. In *Negro and Jew: An Encounter in America,* ed. Shlomo Katz, 52–59. New York: Macmillan, 1967.

Goldschmidt, Henry, and Elizabeth A. McAlister, eds. *Race, Nation, and Religion in the Americas.* New York: Oxford University Press, 2004.

Goldstein, Eric L. *The Price of Whiteness: Jews, Race, and American Identity*. Princeton: Princeton University Press, 2006.

Gomez, Michael A. *Black Crescent: The Experience and Legacy of African Muslims in the Americas*. New York: Cambridge University Press, 2005.

———. *Exchanging Our Country Marks: The Transformation of African Identities in the Colonial and Antebellum South*. Chapel Hill: University of North Carolina Press, 1998.

———. *Reversing Sail: A History of the African Diaspora*. New York: Cambridge University Press, 2005.

Gorn, Elliot J. "Black Spirits: The Ghostlore of Afro-American Slaves." *American Quarterly* 36, no. 4 (Autumn 1984): 549–565.

Gottdiener, M. *The Social Production of Urban Space*. 2nd ed. Austin: University of Texas Press, 1994.

Gramsci, Antonio. *The Antonio Gramsci Reader: Selected Writings 1916–1935*. Edited by David Forgacs. New York: New York University Press, 2000.

Grant, Colin. *Negro with a Hat: The Rise and Fall of Marcus Garvey*. New York: Oxford University Press, 2008.

Greenberg, Cheryl Lynn. *Or Does It Explode? Black Harlem in the Great Depression*. New York: Oxford University Press, 1991.

———. *Troubling the Waters: Black-Jewish Relations in the American Century*. Princeton: Princeton University Press, 2006.

Greenblatt, Stephen. *Marvelous Possessions: The Wonder of the New World*. Chicago: University of Chicago Press, 1991.

Greenfield, Sidney M. "Recasting Syncretism...Again: Theories and Concepts in Anthropology and Afro-American Studies in Light of Changing Social Agendas." In *New Trends and Developments in African Religions*, edited by Peter B. Clarke, 1–15. Westport, Conn.: Greenwood, 1998.

Gregory, James N. "The Southern Diaspora and the Urban Dispossessed: Demonstrating the Census Public Use Microdata Samples." *Journal of American History* 82, no. 1 (June 1995): 111–134.

Griffith, R. Marie, and Barbara Dianne Savage. *Women and Religion in the African Diaspora: Knowledge, Power, and Performance*. Baltimore: Johns Hopkins University Press, 2006.

Grinde, Donald, and Quintard Taylor. "Red vs. Black: Conflict and Accommodation in the Post Civil War Indian Territory, 1865–1907." *American Indian Quarterly* 8, no. 3 (Summer 1984): 211–229.

Grossman, James R. *Land of Hope: Chicago, Black Southerners, and the Great Migration*. Chicago: University of Chicago Press, 1991.

Guglielmo, Thomas A. *White on Arrival: Italians, Race, Color, and Power in Chicago, 1890–1945*. New York: Oxford University Press, 2003.

Guha, Ranajit. "The Prose of Counter-Insurgency." In *Selected Subaltern Studies*, edited by Ranajit Guha and Gayatri Chakravorty Spivak, 45–88. Delhi: Oxford University Press, 1988.

Gump, James O. "A Spirit of Resistance: Sioux, Shosa, and Maori Responses to Western Dominance, 1840–1920." *Pacific Historical Review* 66, no. 1 (1997): 21–52.

Gunner, Frances. "A Study of Employment Problems of Negro Women in Brooklyn." Master's thesis, Department of Political Science, Columbia University, 1923.

Gupta, Akhil, and James Ferguson. "Beyond Culture: Space, Identity and the Politics of Difference." In *Culture, Power, Place: Explorations in Critical Anthropology*, edited by Gupta and Ferguson, 33–51. Durham: Duke University Press, 1997.

Gurock, Jeffrey S. *When Harlem Was Jewish, 1870–1930*. New York: Columbia University Press, 1979.

Gutman, Herbert G. *The Black Family in Slavery and Freedom, 1750–1925*. New York: Pantheon, 1976.

———. *Work, Culture, and Society in Industrializing America: Essays in American Working-Class and Social History*. New York: Knopf, 1976.

Habermas, Jürgen. *The Structural Transformation of the Public Sphere: An Inquiry into a Category of Bourgeois Society*. Translated by Thomas Burger and Frederick Lawrence. Cambridge: MIT Press, 1999.

Habtu, Hailu. "The Fallacy of the Triple Heritage Thesis: A Critique." *Issue: A Journal of Africanist Opinion* 13 (1984): 26–29.

Hackett, David G. "The Prince Hall Masons and the African American Church: The Labors of Grand Master and Bishop James Walker Hood, 1831–1918." *Church History* 69, no. 4 (December 2000): 770–802.

HaGadol, Prince Gavriel, and Odeyah B. Israel. *The Impregnable People: An Exodus of African Americans Back to Africa*. Washington, D.C.: Communicators Press, 1993.

Haley, Alex. *The Autobiography of Malcolm X*. New York: Ballantine Books, 1964.

Hall, David D. *Worlds of Wonder, Days of Judgment: Popular Religious Belief in Early New England*. New York: Knopf, 1989.

Hall, Neville A. T. *Slave Society in the Danish West Indies: St. Thomas, St. John, and St. Croix*. Mona, Jamaica: University of the West Indies Press, 1992.

Hall, Stuart. "Cultural Studies and Its Theoretical Legacies." In *Cultural Studies*, edited by Lawrence Grossberg et al., 277–294. London: Routledge, 1992.

Hamilton, Kenneth Marvin. "The Origin and Early Developments of Langston, Oklahoma." *Journal of Negro History* 62 (1977): 270–282.

Hanegraaff, Wouter J. "Beyond the Yates Paradigm: The Study of Western Esotericism between Counterculture and New Complexity," *Aries* 1, no. 1 (2001): 5–37.

Harding, Vincent. "Religion and Resistance among Antebellum Negroes, 1800–1806." In *The Making of Black America*, vol. 1, edited by August Meir and Elliot Rudwick, 179–197. New York: Athenaeum, 1969.

Hardy, Clarence E. "From Exodus to Exile: Black Pentecostals, Migrating Pilgrims, and Imagined Internationalism." *American Quarterly* 58 no. 3 (September 2007): 737–757.

Harvey, Paul. "'The Color of Skin Was Almost Forgotten': Biracialism in the Twentieth-Century Southern Religious Experience." In *Warm Ashes: Issues in Southern History at the Dawn of the Twenty-First Century*, edited by Winfred B. Moore, Jr.,

Kyle S. Sinisi, and David H. White, Jr., 159–180. Columbia: University of South Carolina Press, 2003.

Hayes, Kevin J. *Folklore and Book Culture*. Knoxville: University of Tennessee Press, 1997.

Haynes, Elizabeth Ross. "Negroes in Domestic Service in the United States." Master's thesis, Department of Political Science, Columbia University, 1923.

Haynes, George E. *The Negro at Work in New York City: A Study in Economic Progress*. [1912] New York: Arno, 1968.

——. "Report: Impressions from a Preliminary Study of Negroes of Harlem, 1921." Unpublished report for the National Urban League. George Edmund Haynes Papers, Box 1, folder 1921 Report. Schomburg Center for Research in Black Culture, New York Public Library, Astor, Lenox and Tilden Foundations.

Haywood, Harry. "The Nation of Islam: An Estimate." *Soulbook* 6 (Winter–Spring 1967): 137–144.

Hebdige, Dick. *Subculture: The Meaning of Style*. London: Methuen, 1979.

Heijbroek, J. F. "Ford, Arnold Josiah." In *American National Biography*, edited by John A. Garraty and Mark C. Carnes, 217–218. New York: Oxford University Press, 1999.

——. "Matthew, Wentworth Arthur." In *American National Biography*, edited by John A. Garraty and Mark C. Carnes, 275–276. New York: Oxford University Press, 1999.

Hellwig, David J. "Black Images of Jews: From Reconstruction to Depression." *Societas* 8, no. 3 (1978): 205–223.

Hemenway, Robert E. *Zora Neale Hurston: A Literary Biography*. Urbana, Ill.: Illini Books, 1980.

Hempton, David. *Methodism: Empire of the Spirit*. New Haven: Yale University Press, 2006.

Herskovits, Melville J. "Age Changes in Pigmentation." Schomburg Center Vertical File. N.p., n.d. New York Public Library, New York.

——. *The American Negro: A Study in Racial Crossing*. Bloomington: University of Indiana Press, 1928.

——. "Correlation of Length and Breadth of Head." Schomburg Center Vertical File. N.p., n.d. New York Public Library, New York.

——. "A Further Discussion of the Variability of Family Strains in the Negro-White Population of New York City." *Journal of the American Statistical Association* 20 (September 1925): 380–389.

——. "The Influence of Environment on a Racial Growth Curve." Schomburg Center Vertical File. N.p., n.d. New York Public Library, New York.

——. "Introduction." In *Acculturation in the Americas*. Edited by Sol Tax, 48–63. *Proceedings and Selected Papers of the XXIX International Congress of Americanists*, vol. 2. Chicago, University of Chicago Press, 1952.

——. *The Myth of the Negro Past*. [1941, 1958] Boston: Beacon, 1990.

———. "The Negro and the Intelligence Tests." Schomburg Center Vertical File. N.p., n.d. New York Public Library, New York.

———. "The Negro in the New World: The Statement of a Problem." *American Anthropologist* 32 (1930): 145–156.

———. *The New World Negro: Selected Papers in Afroamerican Studies*. Edited by Frances S. Herskovits. Bloomington: Indiana University Press, 1966.

———. "On the Negro-White Population of N.Y.C." Schomburg Center Vertical File. N.p., n.d. New York Public Library, New York.

———. "On the Relation between Negro-White Mixture." Schomburg Center Vertical File. N.p., n.d. New York Public Library, New York.

———. "The Physical Form and Growth." Schomburg Center Vertical File. N.p., n.d. New York Public Library, New York.

———. "Preliminary Observations." Schomburg Center Vertical File. N.p., n.d. New York Public Library, New York.

———. "Race Relations in the U.S., 1928." Schomburg Center Vertical File. N.p., n.d.

———. "Social Pattern: A Methodological Study." *Social Forces* 4, no. 1 (September 1926): 57–69.

———. "Social Pattern." Schomburg Center Vertical File. N.p., n.d. New York Public Library, New York.

———. "Social Selection and the Formation of Human Types." *Human Biology: A Record of Research* 1, no. 2 (May 1929): 250–261.

———. "Social Selection in a Mixed Population." Schomburg Center Vertical File. N.p., n.d. New York Public Library, New York.

———. "Some Effects of Social Selection on the American Negro." *Publications of the American Sociological Society* 32 (1926): 77–82.

———. "Some Physical Characteristics of the American Negro Population." Paper presented before the National Academy of Sciences, Philadelphia, November 18, 1926, printed in *Social Forces* VI, no. 1 (September 1927): 93–98.

———. "Variability and Racial Mixture." Schomburg Center Vertical File. N.p., n.d. New York Public Library, New York.

Higginbotham, Evelyn Brooks. *Righteous Discontent: The Women's Movement in the Black Baptist Church, 1880–1920*. Cambridge: Harvard University Press, 1993.

Higham, John. *Send These to Me: Immigrants in Urban America*. [1975] Baltimore: John Hopkins University Press, 1984.

———. *Strangers in the Land: Patterns of American Nativism 1860–1925*. [2nd ed. 1955] New Brunswick: Rutgers University Press, 1988.

Hill, Herbert. "The Problem of Race in American Labor History." *Reviews in American History* 24, no. 1 (1996): 189–208.

Hill, Robert A. "Dread History: Leonard Howell and Millenarian Visions in Early Rastafari Religion in Jamaica." *Epoché: Journal of the History of Religions at UCLA* 9 (1981): 30–71.

——— . "King Menelik's Nephew: Prince Thomas Mackarooroo, aka Prince Ludwig Menelik of Abyssinia." *Small Axe* 12, no. 2 (June 2008): 15–44.

——— , ed. *The Marcus Garvey and Universal Negro Improvement Association Papers* 10 vols. Berkeley: University of California Press, 1983–2006.

——— . "Racial and Radical: Cyril V. Briggs, THE CRUSADER Magazine, and the African Blood Brotherhood, 1918–1922." Introduction to *The Crusader: September 1918–August 1919*, vol. 1, ed. Robert A. Hill, v–lxvi. New York: Garland, 1987.

Hine, Darlene Clark. "Lifting the Veil, Shattering the Silence: Black Women's History in Slavery and Freedom." In *The State of Afro-American History, Past, Present, and Future*, edited by Hine, 223–249. Baton Rouge: Louisiana State University Press, 1986.

——— , ed. *The State of Afro-American History: Past, Present, and Future*. Introduction by Thomas C. Holt. Baton Rouge: Louisiana State University Press, 1986.

Hine, Edward. *Forty-Seven Identifications of the British Nation with the Lost Ten Tribes of Israel*. London: S. W. Partridge, n.d.

Hirsch, Arnold R. *Making the Second Ghetto: Race and Housing in Chicago, 1940–1960*. Chicago: University of Chicago Press, 1983.

Hiss, William Charles. "Shiloh: Frank W. Sandford and the Kingdom: 1898–1948." Ph.D. dissertation, Department of Church History. Tufts University, 1978.

The Historical Committee of the Church of God and Saints of Christ. *The Re-Establishing Years (1847–1908). History of the Church of God and Saints of Christ*, vol. 1. Suffolk, Va.: Church of God and Saints of Christ, 1992.

Hobart, George H. *The Negro Churches of Manhattan (New York City)*. New York: Greater New York Federation of Churches, 1930.

Hobsbawm, Eric. *The Age of Empire 1875–1914*. New York: Pantheon, 1987.

Hobsbawm, Eric, and Terence Ranger, eds. *The Invention of Tradition*. Cambridge: Cambridge University Press: 1993.

Hodes, Martha, ed. *Sex, Love, Race: Crossing Boundaries in North American History*. New York: New York University Press, 1999.

——— . *White Women, Black Men: Illicit Sex in the Nineteenth-Century South*. New Haven: Yale University Press, 1999.

Hoerder, Dirk. "How the Intimate Lives of Subaltern Men, Women, and Children Confound the Nation's Master Narratives." *Journal of American History*, "Round Table, Empires and Intimacies: Lessons from (Post) Colonial Studies" 88, no. 3 (December 2001): 874–881.

Hoganson, Kristin L. *Fighting for American Manhood: How Gender Politics Provoked the Spanish-American and Philippine-American Wars*. New Haven: Yale University Press, 1998.

Hogg, Donald William. "Jamaican Religions: A Study in Variations." Ph.D. dissertation, Department of Anthropology, Yale University, 1964.

Hollenweger, Walter J. *Pentecostalism: Origins and Development Worldwide*. Peabody, Mass.: Hendrickson, 1997.

Holt, Thomas C. "An Empire over the Mind: Emancipation, Race, and Ideology in the British West Indies and the American South." In *Region, Race, and Reconstruction: Essays in Honor of C. Vann Woodward*, edited by J. Morgan Kousser and James M. McPherson, 283–313. New York: Oxford University Press, 1982.

———. "Marking: Race, Race-Making, and the Writing of History." *American Historical Review* 100, no. 1 (February 1995): 1–20.

Hopper, Ernest Jasper. "A Northern Negro Group." Master's thesis, Department of Political Science, Columbia University, 1912.

Huggins, Nathan Irvin. *Harlem Renaissance*. New York: Oxford University Press, 1971.

Hughes, Langston. *The Big Sea: An Autobiography*. [1940] New York: Hill and Wang, 1963.

Hunt, Lynn, ed. *The New Cultural History: Essays*. Berkeley: University of California Press, 1989.

Hunt, Lynn, and Victoria E. Bonnell, eds. *Beyond the Cultural Turn: New Directions in the Study of Society and Culture*. Berkeley: University of California Press, 1999.

Hurston, Zora Neale. *Moses: Man of the Mountain*. [1939] Urbana: University of Illinois Press, 1984.

———. *Mules and Men*. [1935] New York: Perennial Library, 1990.

Hutnyk, John. "Clifford Geertz as a Cultural System: A Review Article." *Social Analysis* 26 (1989): 91–107.

Ingram, William L. "God and Race: British Israelism and Christian Identity." In *America's Alternative Religions*, ed. Timothy Miller, 119–126. Albany: State University of New York Press, 1995.

Isaac, Rhys. *The Transformation of Virginia, 1740–1790*. New York: W. W. Norton, 1982.

Jackson, John L., Jr. *Real Black: Adventures in Racial Sincerity*. Chicago: University of Chicago Press, 2005.

Jackson Lears, T. J. "The Concept of Cultural Hegemony: Problems and Possibilities." *American Historical Review* 90, no. 3 (June 1985): 567–593.

———. *No Place of Grace: Antimodernism and the Transformation of American Culture, 1880–1920*. Chicago: University of Chicago Press, 1981.

Jackson, Kenneth T. "The Capital of Capitalism: The New York Metropolitan Region, 1890–1940." In *Metropolis 1890–1940*, edited by Anthony Sutcliffe, 319–354. London: Mansell, 1984.

Jackson, Sherman. *Islam and the Black American: Looking toward the Third Resurrection*. New York: Oxford University Press, 2005.

Jackson, Walter. "Melville Herskovits and the Search for Afro-American Culture." In *Malinowski, Rivers, Benedict and Others: Essays on Culture and Personality*, edited by George W. Stocking, Jr., 95–126. Madison: University of Wisconsin Press, 1986.

Jacob, Margaret C. *Living the Enlightenment: Freemasonry and Politics in Eighteenth-Century Europe*. New York: Oxford University Press, 1991.

——.*The Origins of Freemasonry: Facts and Fictions.* Philadelphia: University of Pennsylvania Press, 2006.

Jacobs, Claude F., and Andrew J. Kaslow. *The Spiritual Churches of New Orleans: Origins, Beliefs, and Rituals of an African-American Religion.* Knoxville: University of Tennessee Press, 1991.

Jacobson, Matthew Frye. *Barbarian Virtues: The United States Encounters Foreign Peoples at Home and Abroad 1876–1917.* New York: Hill and Wang, 2000.

——. *Roots Too: White Ethnic Revival in Post-Civil Rights America.* Cambridge: Harvard University Press, 2006.

——.*Whiteness of a Different Color: European Immigrants and the Alchemy of Race.* Cambridge, Mass.: Harvard University Press: 1998.

Jacoby, Russel. "New Intellectual History?" *American Historical Review* 97, no. 2 (April 1992): 405–424.

James, Winston. *Holding Aloft the Banner of Ethiopia: Caribbean Radicalism in Early Twentieth-Century America.* London: Verso, 1998.

Janken, Kenneth Robert. *White: The Biography of Walter White, Mr. NAACP.* New York: New Press, 2003.

Jenkins, Philip. *Mystics and Messiahs: Cults and New Religions in American History.* New York: Oxford University Press, 2000.

Jentz, John. "A Note on Genovese's Account of the Slaves' Religion." *Civil War History* 23, no. 2 (1977): 161–169.

Johnson, James Weldon. *Black Manhattan.* New York: Knopf, 1930.

Johnson, Sylvester A. *The Myth of Ham in Nineteenth-Century American Christianity: Race, Heathens, and the People of God.* New York: Palgrave Macmillan, 2004.

——. "The Rise of Black Ethnics: The Ethnic Turn in African-American Religions, 1916–1945." *Religion in American Culture: A Journal of Interpretation* 20, no. 2 (Summer 2010): 125–163.

Johnstone, Robert Zachariah, "The Negro in New York—His Social Attainments and Prospects." Master's thesis, Department of Political Science, Columbia University, 1911.

Jones, Elias Fanayaye. "Black Hebrews: The Quest for Authentic Identity." *Journal of Religious Thought* 44, no. 2 (1988): 35–49.

Jordan, Winthrop D. *White over Black: American Attitudes toward the Negro, 1550–1812.* New York: W. W. Norton, 1968.

Joyner, Charles. *Down by the Riverside: A South Carolina Slave Community.* Urbana: University of Illinois Press, 1984.

Kaganoff, Nathan M., and Melvin Urofsky, eds. *Turn to the South: Essays on Southern Jewry.* Charlottesville: University Press of Virginia, 1979.

Kantrowitz, Stephen. '"Intended for the Better Government of Man': The Political History of African American Freemasonry in the Era of Emancipation." *Journal of American History* 96, no. 4 (March 2010): 1001–1026.

Kaplan, Amy. "Left Alone with America: The Absence of Empire in the Study of American Culture." In *Cultures of United States Imperialism*, edited by Amy Kaplan and Donald E. Pease, 3–21. Durham: Duke University Press, 1993.

Kaplan, Amy, and Donald E. Pease, eds. *Cultures of United States Imperialism*. Durham: Duke University Press, 1993.

Kaplan, Benjamin. "Judah Philip Benjamin." In *Jews in the South*, edited by Leonard Dinnerstein and Mary Dale Palsson, 75–88. Baton Rouge: Louisiana State University Press, 1973.

Kaplan, Steven. "A Brief History of the Beta Israel." In *The Jews of Ethiopia: A People in Transition*, 11–29. New York: Jewish Museum, 1986.

Kaplan, Steven, Tudor Parfitt, and Emanuela Trevisan Semi, eds. *Between Africa and Zion: Proceedings of the First International Congress of the Society for the Study of Ethiopian Jewry*. Jerusalem: Ben Zvi Institute, 1995.

Katz, Dovid. "A Late Twentieth Century Case of *Katoves*." In *History of Yiddish Studies: Papers from the Third Annual Oxford Winter Symposium in Yiddish Language and Literature*, ed. Dov-Ber Kerler, 141–164. Philadelphia: Harwood Academic Publishers, 1991.

Katz, Jacob. *Jews and Freemasons in Europe 1723–1939*. Translated by Leonard Oschry. Cambridge: Harvard University Press, 1970.

Katz, Shlomo, ed. *Negro and Jew: An Encounter in America. A Symposium Compiled by Midstream Magazine*. New York: Macmillan, 1967.

Kaufman, Jonathan. *Broken Alliance: The Turbulent Times between Blacks and Jews in America*. New York: Charles Scribner's Sons, 1988.

Kaufman, Menahem. *An Ambiguous Partnership: Zionists and Non-Zionists in America, 1939–1948*. Detroit: Wayne State University Press, 1991.

Kaye/Kantrowitz, Melanie. *The Colors of Jews: Racial Politics and Radical Diasporism*. Bloomington: Indiana University Press, 2007.

Kelley, Robin D. G. *Hammer and Hoe: Alabama Communists during the Great Depression*. Chapel Hill: University of North Carolina Press, 1990.

———. "Notes on Deconstructing 'The Folk.'" *American Historical Review* 97, no. 5 (December 1992): 1400–1408.

———. *Race Rebels: Culture, Politics, and the Black Working Class*. New York: Free Press, 1994.

———. *Yo' Mama's Disfunktional!: Fighting the Culture Wars in Urban America*. Boston: Beacon, 1997.

———. *Freedom Dreams: The Black Radical Imagination*. Boston: Beacon, 2002.

———. "People in Me." *ColorLines Magazine* 1, no. 3 (Winter 1999): 5–7.

Kessler, David Francis. *The Falashas: The Forgotten Jews of Ethiopia*. 3rd rev. ed. [1982] London: Routledge, 1996.

Keyes, Cheryl Lynette. *Rap Music and Street Consciousness*. Urbana: University of Illinois Press, 2002.

King, Kenneth J. "Some Notes on Arnold J. Ford and New World Black Attitudes to Ethiopia." In *Black Apostles: Afro-American Clergy Confront the Twentieth Century*, edited by Randall K. Burkett and Richard Newman, 49–55. Boston: G. K. Hall, 1978.

Kirshenblatt-Gimblett, Barbara. "Making a Place in the World: Jews and the Holy Land at World's Fairs." In *Encounters with the 'Holy Land': Place, Past, and Future in American Jewish Culture*, edited by Jeffrey Shandler and Beth Wenger, 60–82. Philadelphia: National Museum of American Jewish History, 1997.

Kissick, Robert G. *The Irish Prince and the Hebrew Prophet: A Masonic Tale of the Captive Jews and the Ark of the Covenant.* New York: Masonic Publishing, 1896.

Klein, Kerwin Lee. "Reclaiming the F word, or Being and Becoming Postwestern (frontier history)." *Pacific Historical Review* 65, no. 2 (May 1996): 179–215.

Knight, Franklin W. *The Caribbean: The Genesis of a Fragmented Nationalism.* 2nd ed. New York: Oxford University Press, 1990.

Kobre, Sidney. "Rabbi Ford." *Reflex* 4, no. 1 (January 1929): 25–29.

Kolchin, Peter. "Reevaluating the Antebellum Slave Community: A Comparative Perspective." *Journal of American History* 70 (December 1983): 579–601.

Könighofer, Martina. *The New Ship of Zion: Dynamic Diaspora Dimensions of the African Hebrew Israelites of Jerusalem.* Piscataway, NJ: Transaction Publishers, 2008.

Kolsky, Thomas A. *Jews against Zionism: The American Council for Judaism, 1942–1948.* Philadelphia: Temple University Press, 1992.

Korn, Bertram Wallace. *American Jewry and the Civil War.* Philadephia: Jewish Publication Society of America, 1951.

——— . *Jews and Negro Slavery in the Old South, 1789–1865.* Elkins Park, Pa.: Reform Congregation Keneseth Israel, 1961.

——— . "Jews and Negro Slavery in the Old South, 1789–1865." In *Jews in the South*, edited by Leonard Dinnerstein and Mary Dale Palsson, 89–134 Baton Rouge: Louisiana State University Press, 1973.

Kramer, Paul A. "Empires, Exceptions, and Anglo-Saxons: Race and Rule between the British and United States Empires, 1880–1910." *Journal of American History* 88, no. 4 (March 2002): 1315–1353.

Kulikoff, Allan. "The Transition to Capitalism in Rural America." *William and Mary Quarterly* 3rd series 46, no. 1 (January 1989): 120–144.

Kusmer, Kenneth L. "The Black Urban Experience in American History (with Comments by Lawrence W. Levine and James Oliver Horton)." In *The State of Afro-American History, Past, Present, and Future*, edited by Darlene Clark Hine, 92–135. Baton Rouge: Louisiana State University Press, 1986.

LaCapra, Dominick. "Intellectual History and Its Ways." *American Historical Review* 97, no. 2 (April 1992): 425–439.

LaFeber, Walter. *The Cambridge History of American Foreign Relations, Volume II: The American Search for Opportunity, 1865–1913.* New York: Cambridge University Press, 1993.

———. *New American Empire: An Interpretation of American Expansion, 1860–1898*. New York: Cornell University Press, 1963.

Lal, Vinay. "Walking with the Subalterns, Riding with the Academy: The Curious Ascendancy of Indian History." *Studies in History* (New Delhi) 17, no. 1 (2001): 102–133.

Landes, Ruth. "Negro Jews in Harlem." *Jewish Journal of Sociology* 9, no. 2 (1967): 175–189.

Landing, James E. *Black Judaism: Story of an American Movement*. Durham, N.C.: Carolina Academic Press, 2002.

Lange, Dierk. "Hausa History in the Context of the Ancient Near Eastern World." In *Ancient Kingdoms of West Africa: Africa-Centered and Canaanite-Israelite Perspectives: A Collection of Published and Unpublished Studies in English and French*, 215–305. Dettelbach: J. H. Röll, 2004.

Leach, William. *Land of Desire: Merchants, Power, and the Rise of a New American Culture*. New York: Vintage, 1993.

Lee, Hélène. *The First Rasta: Leonard Howell and the Rise of Rastafarianism*. Translated by Lily Davis and Hélène Lee, edited by Stephen Davis. Chicago: Lawrence Hill Books, 2003.

Lee, Martha F. *The Nation of Islam: An American Millenarian Movement*. Syracuse: Syracuse University Press, 1996.

Legum, Colin. *Pan-Africanism: A Short Political Guide, Revised Edition*. New York: Praeger, 1965.

Lerner, Gerda. *The Creation of Patriarchy*. New York: Oxford University Press, 1986.

Leslau, Wolf. *Falasha Anthology*. New Haven: Yale University Press, 1951.

Lesourd, Howard Marick. "A Harlem Neighborhood." Master's thesis, Department of Political Science, Columbia University, 1913.

Lester, Julius. *Lovesong: Becoming a Jew*. New York: Little, Brown, 1988.

Lévi-Strauss, Claude. *The Savage Mind*. Chicago: University of Chicago Press, 1966.

Levine, Lawrence W. *Black Culture and Black Consciousness: Afro-American Folk Thought from Slavery to Freedom*. Oxford: Oxford University Press, 1977.

———. "The Folklore of Industrial Society: Popular Culture and Its Audiences." *American Historical Review* 97, no. 5 (December 1992): 1369–1399.

———. *Highbrow/Lowbrow: The Emergence of Cultural Hierarchy in America*. Cambridge: Harvard University Press, 1988.

———. *The Opening of the American Mind: Canons, Culture, and History*. Boston: Beacon, 1996.

———. *The Unpredictable Past*. New York: Oxford University Press, 1993.

Levy, Sholomo B. "Ford, Arnold Josiah." In *Harlem Renaissance Lives: From the African American National Biography*, edited by Henry Louis Gates and Evelyn Brooks Higginbotham, 205–207. New York: Oxford University Press, 2009.

Lewis, David Levering. *When Harlem Was in Vogue*. 2nd ed. [1979] New York: Penguin, 1997.

Lewis, Martin W., and Karen E. Wigen. *The Myth of Continents: A Critique of Metageography*. Berkeley: University of California Press, 1997.

Lincoln, Bruce. *Holy Terrors: Thinking about Religion after September 11*. Chicago: University of Chicago Press, 2006.

———. "Retiring Syncretism." In *Syncretism/Anti-Syncretism: The Politics of Religious Synthesis*, edited by Charles Stewart and Rosalind Shaw, 453–460. London: Routledge, 1994.

Lincoln, C. Eric, *The Black Church in the African-American Experience*. Durham: Duke University Press, 1990.

———. *The Black Muslims in America*. Rev. ed. Westport, Conn.: Greenwood, 1973.

Linton, Ralph. "The Vanishing American Negro." *American Mercury* 64, no. 278 (February 1947): 133–139.

Lippy, Charles H. "Slave Christianity." In *Modern Christianity to 1900*, edited by Amanda Porterfield, 291–316. Minneapolis: Fortress Press, 2007.

Lipsitz, George. *The Possessive Investment in Whiteness: How White People Profit from Identity Politics*. Philadelphia: Temple University Press, 1998.

———. *Time Passages: Collective Memory and American Popular Culture*. Minneapolis: University of Minnesota Press, 1990.

Littlefield, Daniel F. *The Cherokee Freedmen: From Emancipation to American Citizenship*. Westport, Conn.: Greenwood, 1978.

Littlefield, Daniel F., and Lonnie E. Underhill. "Black Dreams and 'Free' Homes: The Oklahoma Territory, 1891–1894." *Phylon* 34 (1973): 342–357.

Litwack, Leon F. *Been in the Storm So Long: The Aftermath of Slavery*. New York: Knopf, 1979.

Lock, Graham. *Blutopia: Visions of the Future and Revisions of the Past in the work of Sun Ra, Duke Ellington, and Anthony Braxton*. Durham: Duke University Press, 1999.

Locke, Alaine, ed. *The New Negro*. [1925] New York: Maxwell Macmillan International, 1992.

Locke, Benjamin H. "The Community Life of a Harlem Group of Negroes." Master's thesis, Department of Political Science, Columbia University, 1913.

Long, Carolyn Morrow. *Spiritual Merchants: Religion, Magic, and Commerce*. Knoxville: University of Tennessee Press, 2001.

Long, Charles H. *Significations: Signs, Symbols, and Images in the Interpretation of Religion*. Philadelphia: Fortress, 1986.

Long, Kathryn T. "Palmer, Phoebe Worrall." In *Historical Dictionary of the Holiness Movement*, ed. William C. Kostlevy, 196–198. Lanham, Md.: Scarecrow Press, 2001.

Lott, Eric. *Love and Theft: Blackface Minstrelsy and the American Working Class*. New York: Oxford University Press, 1993.

Lounds, Morris. *Israel's Black Hebrews: Black Americans in Search of Identity*. Washington, D.C.: University Press of America, 1981.

Lovejoy, Owen R. *The Negro Children of New York*. New York: Children's Aid Society, 1932.

Ludtke, Alf, ed. *The History of Everyday Life: Reconstructing Historical Experiences and Ways of Life*. Translated by William Templer. [1989] Princeton: Princeton University Press, 1995.

Luker, Ralph. *The Social Gospel in Black and White: American Racial Reform, 1885–1912*. Chapel Hill: University of North Carolina Press, 1991.

Mackesy, Piers. *British Victory in Egypt, 1801: The End of Napoleon's Conquest*. London: Routledge, 1995.

Macleod, Dianne Sachko. "Cross-Cultural Cross-Dressing: Class, Gender and Modernist Sexual Identity." In *Orientalism Transposed: The Impact of the Colonies on British Culture*, edited by Julie F. Codell and Dianne Sachko Macleod, 63–85. Brookfield, Vt.: Ashgate, 1998.

MacRobert, Iain. *The Black Roots and White Racism of Early Pentecostalism in the USA*. Basingstoke: Macmillan, 1988.

Maesen, William A. "Watchtower Influences on Black Muslim Eschatology: An Exploratory Story." *Scientific Study of Religion* 9, no. 4 (Winter 1970): 321–325.

Majors, M. A. "Black Jews Black Irishmen Black Dutchmen." *Chicago Defender*, July 19, 1913, 2.

Makalani, Minkah. *In the Cause of Freedom: Radical Black Internationalism from Harlem to London, 1917–1939*. Chapel Hill: University of North Carolina Press, 2011.

Malcion, Jose V. *How the Hebrews Became Jews*. New York: U. B. Productions, 1978.

Malone, Ann Patton. *Sweet Chariot: Slave Family and Household Structure in Nineteenth-Century Louisiana*. Chapel Hill: University of North Carolina Press, 1992.

Manning, Patrick. *Slavery and African Life: Occidental, Oriental, and African Slave Trades*. Cambridge: Cambridge University Press, 1990.

Mansingh, Ajai. "Rasta-Indian Connection." *Daily Gleaner* (Kingston), August 8, 1982 and July 18, 1982.

Mansingh, Ajai, and Laxmi Mansingh. "Hindu Influences on Rastafarianism." In *Caribbean Quarterly Monographs: Rastafari*, edited by Rex Nettleford, 96–115. Kingston: Caribbean Quarterly, 1984.

Marcus, Jacob Rader. *The Colonial American Jew, 1492–1776*. 3 volumes. Detroit: Wayne State University Press, 1970.

Markowitz, Fran. "Israel as Africa, Africa as Israel: 'Divine Geography' in the Personal Narratives and Community Identity of the Black Hebrew Israelites." *Anthropological Quarterly* 69, no. 4 (October 1996): 193–205.

Marr, Timothy. *The Cultural Roots of American Islamicism*. Cambridge: Cambridge University Press, 2006.

Matory, J. Lorand. *Black Atlantic Religion: Tradition, Transnationalism, and Maternity in the Afro-Brazilian Candomblé*. Princeton: Princeton University Press, 2005.

Mays, Benjamin E. *The Negro's Church*. [1969] New York: Russell & Russell, 1933.

Mazrui, Ali A. "The Semitic Impact on Black Africa: Arab and Jewish Cultural Influences." *Issue: A Journal of Africanist Opinion* 13 (1984): 2–8.

McAlister, Elizabeth. "A Sorcerer's Bottle: The Visual Art of Magic in Haiti." In *The Sacred Arts of Haitian Vodou,* edited by Donald J. Cosentino, 305–321. Los Angeles: UCLA Fowler Museum, 1995.

McBride, James. *The Color of Water: A Black Man's Tribute to His White Mother.* New York: Penguin Putnam, 1996.

McCalman, Ian. *Radical Underworld: Prophets, Revolutionaries and Pornographers in London, 1795–1840.* New York: Cambridge University Press, 1988.

McCarthy, Charles F. "'Sui Generis': A History of Harlem Hospital." Master's thesis, Department of Political Science, Columbia University, 1969.

McCloud, Sean. "Putting Some Class into Religious Studies: Resurrecting an Important Concept." *Journal of the American Academy of Religion* 75, no. 4 (2007): 840–862.

McGuinn, Henry Jared. "A Study of Commercial Recreation as It Affects Negro Life in Seventeen Cities." Master's thesis, Department of Political Science, Columbia University, 1927.

McKay, George. *Senseless Acts of Beauty: Cultures of Resistance.* London: Verso, 1996.

Melnick, Ralph. "Billy Simons: The Black Jew of Charleston." *American Jewish Archives* 32, no. 1 (1980): 3–8.

Melton, J. Gordon. *Encyclopedia of Protestantism.* New York: Facts on File, 2005.

Menke, John G. *Mulattoes and Race Mixture: American Attitudes and Images, 1865–1918.* Ann Arbor: UMI Research Press, 1979.

Michelson, S. "The Black Jews & Their Synagogues in New York." Group XVI, Negro Group, The Black Jews of Abyssinia and Harlem, WPA Writers Program New York City, Negroes of New York 1939. Microfilm, Schomburg Center for Research in Black Culture, New York Public Library, Astor Lenox and Tilden Foundations.

Miller, Ivor. *Voice of the Leopard: African Secret Societies in Cuba.* Jackson: University of Mississippi Press, 2009.

Mills, Frank L., S. B. Jones-Hendrickson, and Bertram Eugene. *Christmas Sports in St. Kitts–Nevis: Our Neglected Cultural Tradition.* No place, no publisher, 1984.

Mintz, Steven Wilfred. *Sweetness and Power: The Place of Sugar in Modern History.* New York: Viking, 1985.

Mintz, Steven Wilfred, and Richard Price. *The Birth of African-American Culture: An Anthropological Perspective.* Boston: Beacon, 1992.

More, Hannah. *The Works of Hannah More: First Complete American Edition,* volume 1. New York: Harper and Brothers, 1843.

Moore, Barrington Jr. *Moral Purity and Persecution in History.* Princeton: Princeton University Press, 2000.

Moore, R. Laurence. "Black Culture and Black Churches—The Quest for an Autonomous Identity." In *Religious Outsiders and the Making of Americans,* 173–200. New York: Oxford University Press, 1986.

Morand, Paul. *New-York.* Paris: E. Flammarion, 1930.

Morgan, Edmund. *American Slavery, American Freedom: The Ordeal of Colonial Virginia.* New York: W. W. Norton, 1975.

Morris, Robert. *Freemasonry in the Holy Land, a Narrative of Masonic Explorations Made in 1868, in the Land of King Solomon and the Two Hirams.* La Grange, Ky.: published for the author, 1879.

Muhammad, Elijah. *Message to the Blackman.* Philadelphia: Hakim's Publications, 1965.

Mumford, Kevin J. *Interzones: Black/White Sex Districts in Chicago and New York in the Early Twentieth Century.* New York: Columbia University Press, 1997.

Muraskin, William A. *Middle-Class Blacks in a White Society: Prince Hall Freemasonry in America.* Berkeley: University of California Press, 1973.

Murphy, Joseph M. *Working the Spirit: Ceremonies of the African Diaspora.* Boston: Beacon, 1994.

Murphy, Joseph M., and Mei-Mei Sanford. *Ósun across the Waters: A Yoruba Goddess in Africa and the Americas.* Bloomington: Indiana University Press, 2001.

Murrell, Nathaniel Samuel, William David Spencer, et al. *Chanting down Babylon: The Rastafari Reader.* Philadelphia: Temple University Press, 1998.

Nadell, Pamela Susan, Jonathan D. Sarna, and Lance Jonathan Sussman. *New Essays in American Jewish History: Commemorating the Sixtieth Anniversary of the Founding of the American Jewish Archives.* Cincinnati: American Jewish Archives of Hebrew Union College-Jewish Institute of Religion, 2010.

Nance, Susan. "Crossing Over: A Cultural History of American Engagement with the Muslim World, 1830–1940." Ph.D. dissertation, University of California, Berkeley, 2003.

———. *How the Arabian Nights Inspired the American Dream, 1790–1935.* Chapel Hill: University of North Carolina Press, 2009.

Nash, Gary B. *Red, White and Black: The Peoples of Early North America.* Englewood Cliffs, N.J.: Prentice Hall, 1974.

———. *The Urban Crucible: The Northern Seaports and the Origins of the American Revolution.* Cambridge: Harvard University Press, 1979.

Nelson, Charles William. "Social Activities of the Negro in Chelsea District, New York City." Master's thesis, Department of Political Science, Columbia University, 1922.

Nelson, G. A. "Rastafarians and Ethiopianism." In *Imagining Home: Class, Culture and Nationalism in the African Diaspora,* ed. Sidney Lemelle and Robin D. G. Kelley, 66–84. New York: Verso, 1994.

Nelson, Shirley, and Rudy Nelson. "Frank Sandford: Tongues of Fire in Shiloh, Maine." In *Portraits of a Generation: Early Pentecostal Leaders,* edited by James R. Goff, Jr. and Grant Wacker, 51–69. Fayetteville: University of Arkansas Press, 2002.

Nichols, David G. *Conjuring the Folk: Forms of Modernity in African America.* Ann Arbor: University of Michigan Press, 2000.

Nye, David E. *American Technological Sublime.* Cambridge: MIT Press, 1994.

O'Connor, Kathleen Malone. "Alternative to 'Religion' in an African American Islamic Community: The Five Percent Nation of Gods and Earths." In *Introduction to New and Alternative Religions in America*, edited by Eugene V. Gallagher and W. Michael Ashcraft, 23–58. Westport, Conn.: Greenwood, 2006.

Oded, Arye. "The Bayudaya of Uganda: A Portrait of an African Jewish Community." *Journal of Religion in Africa* 6, no. 3 (1974): 167–186.

Okihiro, Gary. *Cane Fires: The Anti-Japanese Movement in Hawaii 1865–1945*. Philadelphia: Temple University Press, 1991.

Omi, Michael, and Howard Winant. *Racial Formation in the United States: From the 1960s to the 1980s*. New York: Routledge, 1986.

Oppenheim, Samuel. "The Jews and Masonry in the United States before 1810." *Publications of the American Jewish Historical Society* 19 (1910): 1–94.

Oren, Michael B. *Power, Faith and Fantasy: America in the Middle East, 1776 to the Present*. New York: W. W. Norton: 2007.

Orsi, Robert Anthony. *Between Heaven and Earth: The Religious Worlds People Make and the Scholars Who Study Them*. Princeton: Princeton University Press, 2005.

———. "Everyday Miracles: The Study of Lived Religion." In *Lived Religion in America: Toward a History of Practice*, edited by David D. Hall, 3–21. Princeton: Princeton University Press, 1997.

———. *The Madonna of 115th Street: Faith and Community in Italian Harlem, 1880–1950*. New Haven: Yale University Press, 1985.

Ortiz, Ramon. *Cuban Counterpoint, Tobacco and Sugar*. Translated by Harriet De Onís, introduction by Bronislaw Malinowski; prologue by Herminio Portell Vilà, with a new introduction by Fernando Coronil. Durham: Duke University Press, 1995.

Ortner, Sherry B. "Resistance and the Problem of Ethnographic Refusal in Comparative Studies." *Society and History* 37, no. 1 (January 1995): 173–193.

Osofsky, Gilbert. *Harlem: The Making of a Ghetto: Negro New York 1890–1930*. New York: Harper Torchbooks, 1963.

Otlley, Roi. "The Black Jews of Harlem." *Travel*, (July 1942): 18–21, 32.

———. *New World A-Coming*. New York: Houghton Mifflin, 1943.

Painter, Nell Irvin. *Exodusters: Black Migration to Kansas after Reconstruction*. New York: Knopf, 1977.

———. "Millenarian Aspects of the Exodus to Kansas of 1879." Nell Irvin Painter Papers, Box 94, Duke University Rare Books, Special Collections, and Archives Library, Durham.

———. *Standing at Armageddon: The United States: 1877–1919*. New York: W. W. Norton, 1987.

Palmié, Stephan. *Wizards and Scientists: Explorations in Afro-Cuban Modernity and Tradition*. Durham: Duke University Press, 2002.

Parfitt, Tudor. *Journey to the Vanished City: The Search for a Lost Tribe of Israel*. London: Hodder & Stoughton, 1992.

———. *The Lost Ark of the Covenant: Solving the 2,500 Year Old Mystery of the Fabled Biblical Ark*. New York: HarperOne, 2008.

————. *The Lost Tribes of Israel: The History of a Myth*. London: Weidenfield & Nicolson, 2002.

Parfitt, Tudor, and Emanuela Trevisan Semi, eds. *Jews of Ethiopia: The Birth of an Elite*. London: Routledge, 2005.

Parfitt, Tudor, and Emanuela Trevisan Semi, eds. *Judaising Movements: Studies in the Margins of Judaism*. London: RoutledgeCurzon, 2002.

Parham, Charles F. *The Everlasting Gospel*. Baxter Springs, Kan.: Apostolic Faith Bible College, 1911. Reprinted in *The Sermons of Charles F. Parham, "The Higher Christian Life" Sources for the Study of the Holiness, Pentecostal, and Keswick Movements*, edited by Donald W. Dayton. New York: Garland, 1985.

————. *A Voice Crying in the Wilderness*. Baxter Springs, Kan.: R. L. Parham, 1944. Reprinted in *The Sermons of Charles F. Parham, "The Higher Christian Life" Sources for the Study of the Holiness, Pentecostal, and Keswick Movements*, edited by Donald W. Dayton. New York: Garland, 1985.

Parham, Sarah E., ed. *The Life of Charles F. Parham: Founder of the Apostolic Faith Movement*. [1930] New York: Garland, 1985.

Parrish, Charles H., Jr. "Social Organization among the Negroes of a New Jersey Town." Master's thesis, Department of Political Science, Columbia University, 1921.

Patterson, Zella J. Black. *Churches of Langston*. Oklahoma City: Western Heritage Books, 1982.

Paul, Seymour. "A Group of Virginia Negroes in New York City." Master's thesis, Department of Political Science, Columbia University, 1912.

Payne-Jackson, Arvilla, and Mervyn C. Alleyne. *Jamaican Folk Medicine: A Source of Healing*. Mona, Jamaica: University of West Indies Press, 2004.

Payne, Wardell J., ed. *Directory of African American Religious Bodies: A Compendium by the Howard University School of Divinity*. Washington, D.C.: Howard University Press, 1991.

Peavler, David J. "Creating the Color Line and Confronting Jim Crow: Civil Rights in Middle America: 1850–1900." Ph.D. dissertation, Department of History, University of Kansas, 2008.

Peck, Abraham J. "That Other 'Peculiar Institution': Jews and Judaism in the Nineteenth Century South." *Modern Judaism* 7 (1987): 99–114.

Pederson, Susan. "National Bodies, Unspeakable Acts: The Sexual Politics of Colonial Policy-Making." *Journal of Modern History* 63, no. 4 (December 1991): 647–680.

Peet, Rev. Stephen D. ed. "The Scope of Our Journal" (unsigned editorial). *Oriental and Biblical Journal* (Chicago) 1, no. 1 (January 1880): 22–23.

Pegrum, Rev. Robert. "Mannaseh's Identification." *The Banner of Israel: A Weekly Journal, Advocating the Identity of the British Nation with the Lost Ten Tribes of Israel* (London) 5 (July 20, 1881): 298–299.

Phillips, Harold Cooke. "The Social Significance of Negro Churches in Harlem." Master's thesis, Department of Political Science, Columbia University, 1922.

Phillips, William M., Jr. *An Unillustrious Alliance: The African American and Jewish American Communities*. New York: Greenwood, 1991.

Pinn, Anthony B. *Terror and Triumph: The Nature of Black Religion*. Minneapolis: Fortress Press, 2003.

Piterberg, Gabriel. "Domestic Orientalism: The Representation of Oriental Jews in Zionist/Israeli Historiography." *British Journal of Middle Eastern Studies* 23, no. 2 (November 1996): 125–145.

Pitts, Walter F., Jr. *Old Ship of Zion: The Afro-Baptist Ritual in the African Diaspora*. New York: Oxford University Press, 1993.

Plummer, Brenda Gail. *Rising Wind: Black Americans and U.S. Foreign Affairs, 1935–1960*. Chapel Hill: North Carolina University Press, 1996.

Polk, Patrick A. "Other Books, Other Powers: The 6th and 7th Books of Moses in Afro-Atlantic Folk Belief." *Southern Folklore* 56, no. 2 (1999): 115–133.

——— . "Sacred Banners and the Divine Cavalry Charge." In *Sacred Arts of Haitian Vodou*, edited by Donald J. Cosentino, 325–347. Los Angeles: UCLA Fowler Museum, 1995.

Prakash, Gyan. "Subaltern Studies as Postcolonial Criticism." *American Historical Review* 99, no. 5 (December 1994): 1475–1490.

Prashad, Vijay. "Afro-Dalits of the Earth, Unite!" *African Studies Review* Special Issue on the Diaspora 43, no. 1 (April 2000): 189–201.

——— . *Everybody Was Kung Fu Fighting: Afro-Asian Connections and the Myth of Cultural Purity*. Boston: Beacon, 2001.

——— . *The Karma of Brown Folk*. Minneapolis: University of Minnesota Press, 2000.

Pretorius, Henne, and Lizo Jafta. "'A Branch Springs Out': African Initiated Churches." In *Christianity in South Africa: A Political, Social, and Cultural History*, edited by Richard Elphick and Rodney Davenport, 211–226. Berkeley: University of California Press, 1997.

Proctor, Samuel, and Louis Schmier, eds. *Jews of the South: Selected Essays from the Southern Jewish Historical Society*. Macon: Mercer University Press, 1984.

Punter, Percival. "Interests of Negro Boys." Master's thesis, Department of Political Science, Columbia University, 1935.

Purnell, Benjamin Franklin, and Mary Purnell. *The Seven Books of Wisdom*. Benton Harbor, Mich.: Israelite House of David, c. 1914.

Quirin, James. *The Evolution of the Ethiopian Jews: A History of the Beta Israel (Falasha) to 1920*. Philadelphia: University of Pennsylvania Press, 1992.

Rabinowitz, Howard N. "Nativism, Bigotry and Anti-Semitism in the South." *American Jewish History* 77, no. 3 (1988): 427–451.

Raboteau, Albert J. *A Fire in the Bones: Reflections on African-American Religious History*. Boston: Beacon, 1995.

——— . "Rethinking American Religious History: A Progress Report on 'Afro-American Religious History: A Documentary History Project'." *Council of Societies for the Study of Religion Bulletin* 20, no. 3 (1991): 57–61.

———. *Slave Religion: The "Invisible Institution" in the Antebellum South*. New York: Oxford University Press, 1978.

Raboteau, Albert J., and David W. Wills. *Canaan Land: A Religious History of African Americans*. New York: Oxford University Press, 2001.

Rapoport, Louis. *Redemption Song: The Story of Operation Moses*. New York: Harcourt Brace Jovanovich, 1986.

Reed, Christopher Robert. *All the World Is Here!: The Black Presence at White City*. Bloomington: Indiana University Press, 2000.

Renda, Mary A. *Taking Haiti: Military Occupation and the Culture of U.S. Imperialism, 1915–1940*. Chapel Hill: University of North Carolina Press, 2001.

Roach, Joseph. *Cities of the Dead: Circum-Atlantic Performance*. New York: Columbia University Press, 1996.

Robbins, Jerrold. "The Americans in Ethiopia." *American Mercury* 29 (May 1933): 69.

Robbins, Keith. *England, Ireland, Scotland, Wales: The Christian Church 1900–2000*. Oxford: Oxford University Press, 2008.

Roberts, Mary Louise. *Civilization without Sexes: Reconstructing Gender in Postwar France, 1917–1927*. Chicago: University of Chicago Press, 1994.

Rodgers, Daniel. "Exceptionalism." In *Imagined Histories: American Historians Interpret the Past*, edited by Anthony Molho and Gordon S. Wood, 21–40. Princeton: Princeton University Press, 1998.

Rodney, Walter. *A History of the Guyanese Working People, 1881–1905*. Baltimore: Johns Hopkins University Press, 1981.

Roediger, David R. *The Wages of Whiteness: Race and the Making of the American Working Class*. London: Verso, 1991.

Rogers, Shepherd Robert Athlyi. *The Holy Piby: The Blackman's Bible*. Edited by Ras Sekou Sankara Tafari. [1924] Kingston: Headstart, 2000.

Rolinson, Mary G. *Grassroots Garveyism: The Universal Negro Improvement Association in the Rural South, 1920–1927*. Chapel Hill: University of North Carolina Press, 2007.

Rose, Arnold. *The Negro's Morale: Group Identity and Protest*. Minneapolis: University of Minnesota Press, 1949.

Rose, Craig. *England in the 1690s: Revolution, Religion, and War*. Oxford: Blackwell, 1999.

Rosenberg, Emily S. *Spreading the American Dream: American Economic and Cultural Expansion, 1890–1945*. New York: Hill and Wang, 1982.

Rosenberg, Rosalind. *Divided Lives: American Women in the Twentieth Century*. New York: Hill and Wang, 1992.

Rosenzweig, Roy. *Eight Hours for What We Will: Workers & Leisure in an Industrial City, 1870–1920*. New York: Cambridge University Press, 1983.

Roth, Cecil. *A History of the Jews in England*. Oxford: Clarendon Press, 1949.

Ryan, Mary P. *Civic Wars: Democracy and Public Life in the American City during the Nineteenth Century*. Berkeley: University of California Press, 1997.

Rydell, Robert W. "A Cultural Frankenstein? The Chicago World's Columbian Exposition of 1893." In *Grand Illusions: Chicago's World's Fair of 1893*, edited by Claudia Lamm Wood, Patricia Bereck Weikersheimer, and Rosemary Adams, 143–170. Chicago: Chicago Historical Society, 1993.

Said, Edward W. "Michael Walzer's *Exodus and Revolution*: A Canaanite Reading." *Grand Street* 5, no. 2 (Winter 1986): 86–106.

———. *Orientalism*. New York: Vintage, 1978.

Salzman, Jack, and Cornel West, eds. *Struggles in the Promised Land: Toward a History of Black-Jewish Relations in the United States*. New York: Oxford University Press, 1997.

Samarin, William J. *Tongues of Men and Angels: The Religious Language of Pentecostalism*. New York: Macmillan, 1972.

Sand, Shlomo. *The Invention of the Jewish People*. Translated by Yael Lotan. London: Verso, 2009.

Sanders, Cheryl J. *Saints in Exile: The Holiness-Pentecostal Experience in African American Religion and Culture*. New York: Oxford University Press, 1996.

Sanders, Rufus G. W. *William Joseph Seymour: 1870–1922*. Sandusky, Ohio: Xulon Press for Alexandria Press, 2003.

Santamaria, Ulysses. "Black Jews: The Religious Challenge or Politics versus Religion." *Archives Europeennes de Sociologie* (Paris) 28, no. 2 (1987): 217–240.

Sassen, Saskia. *The Global City: New York, London, Tokyo*. Princeton: Princeton University Press, 1991.

Savage, Barbara Dianne. *Your Spirits Walk beside Us: The Politics of Black Religion*. Cambridge: Belknap Press of Harvard University Press, 2008.

Saville, Julie. *The Work of Reconstruction: From Slave to Wage Labor in South Carolina, 1860–1870*. New York: Cambridge University Press, 1996.

Schechter, Patricia A. *Ida B. Wells-Barnett and American Reform, 1880–1930*. Chapel Hill: University of North Carolina Press, 2001.

Scheible, Johann, and Joseph Ennemoser. *The Sixth and Seventh Books of Moses: or, Moses' magical spirit-art, known as the wonderful arts of the old wise Hebrews, taken from the Mosaic books of the Cabala and the Talmud, for the good of mankind. Translated from the German, word for word, according to old writings*. New York, 1880.

Scheiner, Seth M. *Negro Mecca: A History of the Negro in New York City, 1865–1920*. New York: New York University Press, 1965.

Schmier, Louis. "For Him the Schwartzers Couldn't Do Enough: A Jewish Peddler and His Black Customers Look at Each Other." *American Jewish History* 73, no. 1 (1983): 39–55.

Schoenfeld, Julia. "The Amusements of the Working Girls in New York City: The Social and Moral Aspects." Master's thesis, Department of Political Science, Columbia University, 1911.

Scholem, Gershom. *Kabbalah*. New York: New American Library, 1978.

———. *Sabbatai Sevi: The Mystical Messiah, 1626–1676*. Translated by R. J. Zwi Werblowsky. Princeton: Princeton University Press, 1973.

Schorsch, Jonathan. *Jews and Blacks in the Early Modern World.* New York: Cambridge University Press, 2004.

Schwartz, Jordan A. *The New Dealers: Power Politics in the Age of Roosevelt.* New York: Knopf, 1993.

Scobey, David. "Commercial Culture, Urban Modernism, and the Intellectual Flaneur," a review of *In Pursuit of Gotham: Commerce and Culture in New York,* by William R. Taylor (1992). *American Quarterly* 47, no. 2 (June 1995): 330–342.

Scott, James C. *Domination and the Arts of Resistance: Hidden Transcripts.* New Haven: Yale University Press, 1990.

———. *Weapons of the Weak: Everyday Forms of Peasant Resistance.* New Haven: Yale University Press, 1985.

Scott, Joan. "Gender: A Useful Category of Historical Analysis." *American Historical Review* 91, no. 5 (December 1986): 1053–1075.

Scott, William R. "Rabbi Arnold Ford's Back-to-Ethiopia Movement: A Study of Black Emigration, 1930–1935." *Pan-African Journal* 8, no. 3 (Summer 1975): 191–202.

———. *Sons of Sheba's Race: African-Americans and the Italo-Ethiopian War, 1935–1941.* Bloomington: Indiana University Press, 1993.

Sellers, Charles. *The Market Revolution: Jacksonian America, 1815–1846.* New York: Oxford University Press, 1991.

Sellers, Cleveland, and Robert Terrell. *The River of No Return—The Autobiography of a Black Militant and the Life and Death of SNCC.* New York: William Morrow, 1973.

Sengupta, Gunja. "Elites, Subalterns, and American Identities: A Case Study of African-American Benevolence." *American Historical Review* 109, no. 4 (October 2004): 1104–1139.

Sernett, Milton. *Bound for the Promised Land: African American Religion and the Great Migration.* Durham: Duke University Press, 1997.

Sevitch, Benjamin. "When Black Gods Preached on Earth." In *Black Religious Leadership from the Slave Community to the Million Man March,* edited by Felton O. Best, 73–90. Lewiston, N.Y.: Edwin Mellon, 1998.

Shack, William A. "Ethiopia and Afro-Americans: Some Historical Notes, 1920–1970." *Phylon* 35, no. 2 (1974): 142–155.

Shankman, Arnold. "Friend or Foe? Southern Blacks View the Jew 1880–1935." In *Turn to the South: Essays on Southern Jewry,* edited by Nathan M. Kaganoff and Melvin Urofsky, 105–123. Charlottesville: University Press of Virginia, 1979.

Shapiro, Deanne. "Factors in the Development of Black Judaism." In *The Black Experience in Religion,* edited by C. Eric Lincoln, 254–272. Garden City, N.Y.: Anchor/Doubleday, 1974.

Shepperson, George. "Ethiopianism and African Nationalism," *Phylon* 14, no. 1 (1953): 9–18.

Sheridan, Richard. "From Slavery in Missouri to Freedom in Kansas: The Influx of Black Fugitives and Contrabands into Kansas, 1854–1864." *Kansas History* 12, no. 1 (Spring 1989): 28–47.

Shouk, Ahmed I. Abu, J. O. Hunwick, and R. S. O'Fahey. "A Sudanese Missionary to the United States: Satti Majid, 'Shaykh al-Islam in North America', and His Encounter with Noble Drew Ali, Prophet of the Moorish Science Temple Movement." *Sudanese Africa* 8 (1997): 137–191.

Silverman, Jason H. "Ashley Wilkes Revisited: The Immigrant as Slaveholder in the Old South." *Journal of Confederate History* 7 (1991): 123–135.

Singer, Merrill. "Now I Know What the Songs Mean!" *Southern Quarterly* 23, no. 3 (Spring 1985): 125–140.

Skocpol, Theda, Ariane Liazos, and Marshall Ganz. *What a Mighty Power We Can Be: African American Fraternal Groups and the Struggle for Racial Equality.* Princeton: Princeton University Press, 2006.

Slkar, Martin J. *The United States as a Developing Country: Studies in US History in the Progressive Era and the 1920s.* New York: Cambridge University Press, 1992.

Smith, Jane I. *Islam in America.* New York: Columbia University Press, 1999.

Smith, Timothy L. "Slavery and Theology: The Emergence of Black Christian Consciousness in Nineteenth Century America." *Church History* 41, no. 4 (1972): 497–512.

Smith-Rosenberg, Carroll. *Disorderly Conduct: Visions of Gender in Victorian America.* New York: Oxford University Press, 1985.

Smythe, Hugh H., and Martin S. Price. "The American Jew and Negro Slavery." *Midwest Journal* 7 (1956): 315–319.

Sokolow, Jayme A. "Revolution and Reform: The Antebellum Jewish Abolitionists." *Journal of Ethnic Studies* 9, no. 1 (1981): 27–41.

Spencer, John H. *Ethiopia at Bay: A Personal Account of the Haile Selassie Years.* Hollywood, Cal.: Tsehai Publishers, 2006.

Stallybrass, Peter, and Allon White. *The Politics and Poetics of Transgression.* Ithaca: Cornell University Press, 1986.

Stancil, Phyllis A. "Trends of Opinion among Negroes in the United States." Master's thesis, Department of Political Science, Columbia University, 1932.

Stansell, Christine. *American Moderns: Bohemian New York and the Creation of a New Century.* New York: Metropolitan, 2000.

———. *City of Women: Sex and Class in New York 1789–1860.* Urbana: University of Illinois Press, 1987.

———. "Women, Children, and the Uses of the Streets: Class and Gender." *Feminist Studies* 8 (Summer 1982): 308–335.

Stein, Judith. *The World of Marcus Garvey: Race and Class in Modern Society.* Baton Rouge: Louisiana State University Press, 1986.

Stein, Renee. "Housing Conditions in New York City 1917–1922." Master's thesis, Department of Political Science, Columbia University, 1949.

Stern, Malcolm H. "Portuguese Sephardim in the Americas." *American Jewish Archives* 24, no. 1 (Spring/Summer 1992): 141–178.

Stevenson, Brenda E. *Life in Black and White: Family and Community in the Slave South*. New York: Oxford University Press, 1996.

Stevenson, David. *The Origins of Freemasonry: Scotland's Century 1590–1710* New York: Cambridge University Press, 1988.

Stocking, George W., Jr. *Victorian Anthropology*. New York: Free Press; London: Collier Macmillan, 1987.

Stoler, Ann Laura. "Tense and Tender Ties: The Politics of Comparison in North American History and (Post) Colonial History." *Journal of American History* 88, no. 3 (December 2001): 829–865.

Stone, Josephine. "Amusements for Young Women in New York City." Master's thesis, Department of Political Science, Columbia University, 1909.

Stone, Sarah M. "Song Composition, Transmission, and Performance Practice in an Urban Black Denomination—The Church of God and Saints of Christ." Ph.D. dissertation, Kent State University, School of Music, 1985.

Storatz, Denise. "The New York *Age*: 1880–1960." Master's thesis, Department of Political Science, Columbia University, 1969.

Stout, Harry S. "Religion, Communications, and the Ideological Origins of the American Revolution." *William and Mary Quarterly* 3rd series 34, no. 4 (October 1977): 519–541.

Stovall, Tyler. *Paris Noir: African Americans in the City of Light*. Boston: Houghton Mifflin, 1996.

Strege, Merle D. "Church of God (Anderson, Indiana)." In *Historical Dictionary of the Holiness Movement*, ed. William C. Kostlevy, 51–52. Lanham, Md: Scarecrow Press, 2001.

Stuckey, Sterling. *Slave Culture: Nationalist Theory and the Foundations of Black America*. New York: Oxford University Press, 1987.

Summers, Martin. *Manliness and Its Discontents: The Black Middle Class and the Transformation of Masculinity, 1900–1930*. Chapel Hill: University of North Carolina Press, 2004.

Sundiata, Ibrahim K. *Brothers and Strangers: Black Zion, Black Slavery, 1914–1940*. Durham: Duke University Press, 2003.

Sundquist, Eric J. "Red, White, Black and Blue: The Color of American Modernism." *Transition* 70 (1996): 94–115.

Synan, Vinson. *The Holiness Pentecostal Tradition: Charismatic Movements in the Twentieth Century*. Grand Rapids, Mich.: William B. Eerdmans, 1997.

Szved, John. *Space Is the Place: The Lives and Times of Sun Ra*. New York: Pantheon, 1997.

Takaki, Ronald. *A Different Mirror: A History of Multicultural America*. Boston: Little, Brown, 1993.

Taylor, Quintard. *In Search of the Racial Frontier: African Americans in the American West 1528–1990*. New York: W. W. Norton, 1998.

Tchen, John Kuo Wei. *New York before Chinatown: Orientalism and the Shaping of American Culture 1776–1882*. Baltimore: Johns Hopkins University Press, 1999.

Teall, Kaye M., ed. *Black History in Oklahoma: A Resource Book*. Oklahoma City: Oklahoma City Public Schools, 1971.

Tedlow, Richard S. "Judah P. Benjamin." In *Turn to the South: Essays on Southern Jewry*, edited by Nathan M. Kaganoff and Melvin Urofsky, 44–54. Charlottesville: Published for the American Jewish Historical Society by the University Press of Virginia, 1979.

Thomas, Gordon, and Max Morgan Witts. *Voyage of the Damned*. New York: Stein and Day, 1974.

Thomas, Keith. *Religion and the Decline of Magic*. New York: Oxford University Press, 1971.

Thompson, Edward P. *The Making of the English Working Class,* New York: Pantheon, 1963.

———. *Customs in Common: Studies in Traditional Popular Culture*. New York: New Press, 1993.

Thornton, John. *Africa and Africans in the Making of the Atlantic World, 1400–1680*. New York: Cambridge University Press, 1992.

Thurman, Wallace. *Negro Life in New York's Harlem: A Lively Picture of a Popular and Interesting Section*. Girard, Kan.: Haldeman-Julius, 1925.

Toews, John E. "Intellectual History after the Linguistic Turn: The Autonomy of Meaning and the Irreducibility of Experience." *American Historical Review* 92, no. 4 (October 1987): 879–907.

Tong, Alan. "Interpretive Anthropology and Thick Description: Geertz and the Critics." *Eastern Anthropologist* 50, no. 3–4 (1997): 215–227.

Toomer, Jean. *Cane*. 1923. New York: Modern Library, 1994.

Touchstone, Blake. "Planters and Slave Religion in the Deep South." In *Masters & Slaves in the House of the Lord: Race and Religion in the American South 1740–1870*, edited by John B. Boles, 99–126. Lexington: University Press of Kentucky, 1988.

Trafton, Scott. *Egypt Land: Race and Nineteenth-Century American Egyptomania*. Durham: Duke University Press, 2004.

Trotter, Joe William, ed. *The Great Migration in Historical Perspective: New Dimensions of Race, Class, & Gender*. Bloomington: Indiana University Press, 1991.

Tuleja, Tad. *Usable Pasts: Traditions and Group Expressions in North America*. Logan: Utah State University Press, 1997.

Turner, Victor, ed. *Celebration: Studies in Festivity and Ritual*. Washington, D.C.: Smithsonian Institution Press, 1982.

———. *The Forest of Symbols: Aspects of Ndembu Ritual*. Ithaca: Cornell University Press, 1967.

———. *The Ritual Process*. Chicago: Aldine, 1969.

Tweed, Thomas A. *Retelling U.S. Religious History*. Berkeley: University of California Press, 1997.

Van Deburg, William L. *New Day in Babylon: The Black Power Movement and American Culture, 1965–1975.* Chicago: University of Chicago Press, 1992.

Van der Meiden, G. W. "Governor Mauricius and the Political Rights of the Surinam Jews." In *The Jewish Nation in Surinam: Historical Essays,* edited by R. Cohen, 49–50. Amsterdam: S. Emmering, 1982.

Vickers, Brian. "Frances Yates and the Writing of History." *Journal of Modern History* 51, no. 2 (June 1979): 287–316.

Vincent, Theodore G. *Black Power and the Garvey Movement.* Berkeley: Ramparts Press, 1971.

———. *Keep Cool: The Black Activists Who Built the Jazz Age.* London, Conn.: Pluto Press, 1995.

Wacker, Grant. *Heaven Below: Early Pentecostals and American Culture.* Cambridge: Harvard University Press, 2001.

Waitzkin, Howard. "Black Judaism in New York." *Harvard Journal of Negro Affairs* 1, no. 3 (1967): 12–44.

Walker, Beersheba Crowdy. *Life and Works of William Saunders Crowdy.* Edited by Elfreth J. P. Walker. Philadelphia: Elfreth J. P. Walker, 1955.

Walker, Clarence E. *Deromanticizing Black History: Critical Essays and Reappraisals,* Knoxville: University of Tennessee Press, 1991.

Walker, Corey D. B. *A Noble Fight: African American Freemasonry and the Struggle for Democracy in America.* Urbana: University of Illinois Press, 2008.

Walker, David. *David Walker's Appeal to the Coloured Citizens of the World, but in particular, and very expressly, to those of The United States of America.* Introduction by Sean Wilentz. [1829] Rev. ed. New York: Hill and Wang, 1995.

Walker, Elfreth John Prince, ed. *The Armor Bearer: Bishop Groves as I Knew Him.* Philadelphia: Elfreth John Prince Walker, 1925.

Walkes, Joseph A., Jr. *Black Square and Compass: 200 Years of Prince Hall Freemasonry.* New York: Writer's Press, 1979.

Walzer, Michael. *Exodus and Revolution.* New York: Basic Books, 1985.

Washington, Booker T. *A New Negro for a New Century; An Accurate and Up-to-Date Record of the Upward Struggles of the Negro Race.* [1901] Miami: Mnemosyne, 1969.

Washington, Joseph R., Jr. *Black Sects and Cults.* New York: Doubleday, 1972.

———. *Jews in Black Perspectives: a Dialogue,* edited with an introduction by Joseph R. Washington, Jr. Rutherford, NJ: Fairleigh Dickinson University Press; London; Cranbury, NJ: Associated University Presses, 1984.

Watkins-Owens, Irma. *Blood Relations: Caribbean Immigrants and the Harlem Community, 1900–1930.* Bloomington: Indiana University Press, 1996.

Watson, B. F. "Oklahoma Inquiries Answered." *Christian Recorder* (Philadelphia), April 9, 1891.

Watts, Jill. *God, Harlem U.S.A.: The Father Divine Story.* Berkeley: University of California Press, 1992.

Webb, James. *The Flight from Reason*. Vol. 1 of *The Age of the Irrational*. London: Macdonald, 1971.

Weber, Max. *The Protestant Ethic and the Spirit of Capitalism*. Translated by Talcott Parsons. London: Routledge, 2001.

Weibe, Robert. *The Search for Order 1877–1920*. New York: Hill and Wang, 1967.

Weintraub, Bernard. "The Brilliancy of Black." *Esquire* 67, no. 2 (January 1967): 130–135.

Weisbord, Robert G., and Richard Kazarian, Jr. *Israel in the Black American Perspective*. Westport, Conn.: Greenwood, 1985.

Weisbord, Robert G., and Arthur Stein. *Bittersweet Encounter: The Afro-American and the American Jew*. Westport, Conn.: Negro University Press, 1970.

Weisbrot, Robert. *Father Divine and the Struggle for Racial Equality*. Urbana: University of Illinois Press, 1983.

Weisenfeld, Judith. *African American Women and Christian Activism: New York's Black YWCA, 1905–1945*. Cambridge: Harvard University Press, 1997.

Weisenfeld, Judith, and Richard Newman. *Hollywood Be Thy Name: African American Religion in American Film, 1929–1949*. Berkeley: University of California Press, 2007.

Weisenfeld, Judith, and Richard Newman, eds. *This Far by Faith: Readings in African-American Women's Religious Biography*. New York: Routledge, 1996.

Weiss, Nancy J. *Farewell to the Party of Lincoln: Black Politics in the Age of FDR*. Princeton: Princeton University Press, 1983.

Weiss, Richard. *The American Myth of Success: From Horatio Alger to Norman Vincent Peale*. New York: Basic Books, 1969.

Werbner, Richard. "Afterword." In Rosalind Shaw and Charles Stewart, eds., *Syncretism/Antisyncretism: The Politics of Religious Synthesis*, 212–215. London: Routledge, 1994.

West, Michael O. "An Anticolonial International? Indians, India and Africans in British Central Africa." In *Antinomies of Modernity: Essays on Race, Orient, Nation*, edited by Vasant Kaiwar and Sucheta Mazumdar. Durham: Duke University Press, 2003: 146–179.

———. "Crossing Boundaries: Research Notes on South Asians and Africans in Africa, the Americas and Europe." *Comparative Studies in South Asia, Africa and the Middle East* 16, no. 2 (1996): 48–52.

Wexler, Laura. *Tender Violence: Domestic Visions in an Age of U.S. Imperialism*. Chapel Hill: University of North Carolina Press, 2000.

Wexler, Paul. *The Ashkenazic Jews: A Slavo-Turkic People in Search of a Jewish Identity*. Columbus, Ohio: Slavica Publishers, 1993.

———. *Jewish and Non-Jewish Creators of "Jewish" Languages: With Special Attention to Judaized Arabic, Chinese, German, Greek, Persian, Portuguese, Slavic (Modern Hebrew/Yiddish), Spanish, and Karaite, and Semitic Hebrew/Ladino: A Collection of Reprinted Articles from across Four Decades with a Reassessment*. Wiesbaden: Harrassowitz: 2006.

———. *The Non-Jewish Origins of the Sephardic Jews*. Albany: State University of New York Press, 1996.

White, Landeg. *Magomero: Portrait of an African Village*. New York: Cambridge University Press, 1987.

White, Richard. *"It's Your Misfortune and None of My Own": A History of the American West*. Norman: University of Oklahoma Press, 1991.

Wilder, Craig. *In the Company of Black Men: The African Influence on African American Culture in New York City*. New York: New York University Press, 2001.

Wilentz, Sean. *Chants Democratic: New York City and the Rise of the American Working Class, 1788–1850*. New York: Oxford University Press, 1984.

Williams, Eric. *Capitalism & Slavery*. Chapel Hill: University of North Carolina Press, 1944.

Williams, Joseph J. *Hebrewisms of West Africa: From the Nile to the Niger with the Jews*. [1930] New York: Biblo and Tannen, 1967.

Williams, Raymond. "Base and Superstructure in Marxist Cultural Theory." In *Problems in Materialism and Culture: Selected Essays*, 31–49. London: Verso, 1980.

———. *Keywords: A Vocabulary of Culture and Society*. [1976] Rev. ed. New York: Oxford University Press, 1983.

Wills, David W., and Richard Newman. *Black Apostles at Home and Abroad: Afro-Americans and the Christian Mission from the Revolution to Reconstruction*. Boston: G. K. Hall, 1982.

Wills, David W. *Aspects of Social Thought in the African Methodist Episcopal Church, 1884–1910*. Cambridge: Harvard University Press, 1975.

Wilmore, Gayraud S. *Black Religion and Black Radicalism*. Garden City, N.Y.: Doubleday, 1972.

Wilson, Peter Lamborn. *Sacred Drift: Essays on the Margins of Islam*. San Francisco: City Lights Books, 1993.

Windsor, Rudolph R. *From Babylon to Timbuktu: A History of the Ancient Black Races Including the Black People in America Today*. Philadephia: Windsor's Golden Series Publications, 1988.

Wirth, Louis. "Urbanism as a Way of Life." *American Journal of Sociology* 44, no. 1 (July 1938): 1–24.

Wolcott, Victoria W. *Remaking Respectability: African American Women in Interwar Detroit*. Chapel Hill: University of North Carolina Press, 2001.

Wolf, Edward. "Negro Jews: A Social Study." *Jewish Social Service Quarterly* 9 (June 1933): 314–319.

Woods, Randall B. "Integration, Exclusion, or Segregation? The 'Color Line' in Kansas, 1878–1900." *Western Historical Quarterly* 14, no. 2 (April 1983): 181–198.

Woodson, Carter G. *The History of the Negro Church*. Washington, D.C., Associated Publishers, 1921.

Woodward, C. Vann. *Origins of the New South, 1877–1913*. Baton Rouge: Louisiana State University Press, 1951.

———. *The Strange Career of Jim Crow*. New York: Oxford University Press, 1974.

Works Progress Administration, Federal Writer's Project. *New York City Guide*. New York: Random House, 1939.

Works Progress Administration. *Oklahoma: A Guide to the Sooner State: Compiled by Workers of the Writers' Program of the Work Progress Administration in the State of Oklahoma*. Norman: University of Oklahoma Press, 1941.

Wynia, Elly M. *The Church of God and Saints of Christ: The Rise of Black Jews*. New York: Garland, 1994.

Yates, Frances A. *Giordano Bruno and the Hermetic Tradition*. Chicago: University of Chicago Press, 1964.

———. *The Rosicrucian Enlightenment*. London: Routledge, 1972.

Yelvington, Kevin A. "The War in Ethiopia and Trinidad, 1935–1936." In *The Colonial Caribbean in Transition: Essays on Postemancipation Social and Cultural History*, edited by Bridget Brereton and Kevin A. Yelvington, 189–225. Gainesville: University Press of Florida, and Mona, Jamaica: University of the West Indies Press, 1999.

Yentis, David. "The Negro in Old Brooklyn: An Experiment in Sociological Reconstruction of the Life of a Racial Minority in a Northern City." Master's thesis, Department of Political Science, Columbia University, 1937.

Zane, Wallace W. *Journeys to the Spiritual Lands: The Natural History of a West Indian Religion*. New York: Oxford University Press, 1999.

# INDEX